COLLINS

ALAN MITCHELL'S TREES OF BRITAIN

Alan Mitchell's Trees of Britain is the companion guide to *Collins Field Guide Trees of Britain and Northern Europe* by Alan Mitchell (ISBN 0 00 219213 6)

COLLINS

ALAN MITCHELL'S TREES OF BRITAIN

HarperCollins*Publishers*

HarperCollins*Publishers* Ltd 1996

77–85 Fulham Palace Road

London W6 8JB

ISBN 0 00 219972 6

Cover photograph © Bruce Coleman Ltd, young Beech trees (*Fagus sylvatica*) by Geoff Dore

The copyright in the photographs belong to Alan Mitchell apart from: Jane Bown 6; Ecoscene 205; FLPA 346 (B. Borrell), 83 (H.D. Brandl), 322 (J. Hawking), 61, 241, 250 (David Hosking), 90, 132, 173, 187, 242, 273 (E. and D. Hosking), 192, 216 (Philip Perry), 204 (Michael Rose), 33, 129, 274 (Silvestris), 261 (R. Tidman), 77 (Tony Wharton), 53 (Roger Wilmshurst); John Glover 214; Bob Gibbons, Natural Image 10, 26, 96, 226; E.H. Herbert 281, 341; S & O Matthews 11; Keith Rushforth 57, 171; Wildlife Matters 50, 101, 103, 197, 213, 236, 248, 325.

Produced by HarperCollins Hong Kong

CONTENTS

ALAN MITCHELL (1922–1995)

Dendrologist

Alan was brought up in Essex and served with the Fleet Air Arm in the Far East during the war. He read forestry in Dublin at a combination of Trinity and Albert Agricultural College and was appointed as an assistant geneticist at the Forestry Commission's Alice Holt Research Station. He later crossed over to provenance studies and then, in 1970, was appointed dendrologist with responsibility for Bedgebury National Pinetum and Westonbirt Arboretum. These responsibilities allowed him to travel around Britain, collecting information on trees (and birds). This led to his involvement in the third International Conifer Conference in October 1970, with the results of Alan's lists forming the bulk (pages 123–293) of the 1972 report, *Conifers in the British Isles*. The Forestry Commission also published as Booklet 33 his *Conifers in the British Isles, A Descriptive Handbook* in 1972.

Alan enjoyed jazz music, particularly Louis Armstrong. He had strong left wing views, with no patience for bureaucracy. He suffered fools badly, but for those truly interested in trees (or any other pertinent subject) he was generous with his time and an excellent speaker, freely leading groups around arboreta or lecturing for the Field Studies Council or to WI's and other interest groups. The University of Surrey gave him an honorary MA and other awards included the Victoria Medal of Honour from the Royal Horticultural Society in 1970, which he valued highly and which is limited to 63 living recipients representing each year of Queen Victoria's reign. He is survived by his second wife Philippa and daughters Clio and Julia.

INTRODUCTION

The object of this work is to give a complete account of all the trees which grow naturally or are cultivated in Great Britain and which have attained, or seem likely to attain, a size which justifies their being looked on as timber trees.

Although these words were written in 1906 by Elwes and Henry in the introduction to their monumental work *The Trees of Great Britain and Ireland*, they are apt here. Alan Mitchell spent much of the past forty years seeking out and measuring the fine specimens listed by Elwes and Henry in their seven volumes, and measuring all other large trees encountered, in total some 80,000 trees. This work is being continued by TROBI, the Tree Register of the British Isles, which Alan co-founded with Vicki Schilling.

The outcome of this mission is distilled here, giving a history of the principal large growing trees encountered in the British Isles, together with a sample of the largest and best specimens and an indication of the botanical or horticultural features. In case that makes the book sound like a dull series of lists and heights, apart from the text being very readable, it is enlivened by anecdotes, and more provocatively, by personal opinions. Whilst some of the opinions expressed might be debated (as might some of the omissions from the species list), what tree-lover with more than the faintest glimmer of aesthetic sensitivity can fail to agree with Alan on the blight of purple foliaged beeches which disfigure our pleasant land?

KEITH RUSHFORTH

Estimating the age of a tree

The height and spread of a tree reach a maximum size then stop increasing and after a variable time start to decrease as senility sets in. Neither of these features can thus be measured to give an estimate of age except in young trees. But the circumference of the bole of any tree must increase in some measure during every year of its life. The age of the tree is thus some function of the circumference alone. The circumference (girth) is measured at five feet from the highest point of the surrounding ground.

It would seem that much calculation and many graphs would be needed to cope with the changes in the increase in girth with advancing age, different species and differing individual vigour. It so happens, though, that trees of the most diverse species very largely conform to the simplest possible rule. Only metrification robs us of the final touch – the mean growth in girth of most trees with a full crown is one inch a year. A tree eight feet in girth is usually about 100 years old. Grown in a wood, it will be 200 years old, and in an avenue, or slightly hemmed in, it will be

150 years old. This has been found to be true of hundreds of specimens of almost every species, coniferous or broad-leaved, of the large growing trees.

Such a rule needs some refining. The simplicity arises from the fact that early growth in almost any tree is rather faster than one inch of girth per year, then there is a period of about that rate followed by a long period of a slower rate. So, for much of its life, a tree's girth is near one inch for each year of its life. Evidently allowance should be made for young trees and for very old trees, and there are also species which are, when growing normally, much faster, and few much slower than the general rule allows.

Young oaks on a good site often grow one and a half to two inches a year for their first 60–80 years. From then on until they are about 20–22ft in girth they maintain the 'standard' rate. Thereafter they slow further, the decrease depending on the loss of leafing crown. They seldom survive with a slower rate than one inch in five to six years. The major exceptions are:

Normal growth two to three inches per year (rarely to six inches in Wellingtonia): Wellingtonia, Coast Redwood, Low's Fir, Grand Fir, Cedar of Lebanon, Monterey Cypress, Sitka Spruce, Douglas Fir, Western Red Cedar, Western Hemlock, Cricket-bat Willow, Black Italian and other hybrid poplars, Wingnuts, Nothofagus spp., Red and Chestnutleaf Oaks, Hungarian and Turkey Oaks, Tulip-tree, London Plane and most Eucalyptus spp.

Normal growth soon falling much below one inch per year: most small-growing trees, Scots Pine, Norway Spruce, Yew (see below), Horse-chestnut and Common Lime.

The Yew has a unique growth. Few Yew trees have achieved the standard inch for the first 100 years, but apart from few good data, it is apparent that most grow at about half this rate and gradually, over 400–500 years fall to one inch in five to fifteen years, whilst the crown is still at full vigour and increasing its spread annually. Without an earlier record of its girth, it is thus very difficult to estimate the age of a large Yew and few can be properly measured. A rough guide is 8ft: 200–250 years old; 16ft: 600 –800; 20ft: 800–1,000; 30ft: 1,500–2,000+.

Height

An instrument designed to measure tree height is called an hypsometer. Modern hypsometers are simple, robust and rather expensive. They are basically a well-damped pendulum which shows directly on a different scale for each of several suitable ranges (distances from the tree) the length of a tree below and above the level of the observer's eye.

Heights can be measured fairly accurately with simpler or even makeshift equipment. The simplest of all, but quite accurate if used with care, is a length of stick (grass or bracken or similar). A length is broken or cut to the exact distance from the eyeball to the farthest stretch of the grasping hand (this length is constant for any one observer). The stick is then held at this distance, by its middle and quite vertical. The tree is then aligned, using one eye and moving back and forth until the tip and base are exactly in line with the upper and lower end of the stick. A mark is scored on the ground at this point. The height of the tree is now the precise distance of this mark from the centre of the tree at its base. This can be measured by a tape or by pacing. (One should establish how many paces one takes on different kinds of ground to measure, say 100ft.)

A somewhat more sophisticated method requires a ruler and a second person. The ruler is notched at the one inch mark and is held vertically at a fixed distance from the eye (full stretch is the easiest constant distance), and the tree aligned so that it lies exactly between 0 and 12in. The second man stands by the tree and is guided ('up a little. No, down a bit.') until he has a narrow piece of white (paper, cloth, chocolate wrapper) exactly in the notch, centred on the one-inch line, to the satisfaction of the observer. He marks this point on the tree. The height of this point above the ground, in inches, is the height of the tree in feet. That is so because it is one twelfth of the total height. For trees over 80ft tall, the correct point for the marker cannot be reached, so a notch on the half-inch mark is used, and the resulting height of the marker in inches is half the height of the tree in feet. For use with metric scales, a 30cm ruler notched at 3cm would cause the mark to be one tenth of the height of the tree.

At all times when measuring heights it must be realised that only in spire-topped trees (usually young conifers) is the apparent top shoot as seen from, say 100ft, the true top. In most trees, especially broadly-domed or widely branched trees, shoots on the nearest branches appear to be well above the true top-centre. It is easy to make a Cedar of Lebanon 130ft tall by aiming at a tip that is really on a branch spreading far towards you, when the centre and highest point may be less than 100ft above the ground.

In estimating heights without experience, it is almost invariable that trees of 25–50ft true height are under-estimated. In general, a narrow, columnar or spire-like tree, like a Lombardy poplar, looks much taller than it really is, and broad and domed trees look less tall then they are. Really tall trees, of 170–200ft, seldom look anything like their true height, however, because the upper parts are much fore-shortened to an observer beneath, and they may be among other very tall trees that give the eye a wrong scale by which to judge. Only when on its own, towering out of normal woodland-height trees does the giant show plainly its great height.

CONIFEROUS TREES

LOVELY FIR

Abies amabilis

The foliage of this tree usually lives up to its name, but specimens run the gamut from beautiful and vigorous to stunted and downright ugly. While the reasons for this can sometimes be attributed to the climate of the garden in which they are growing, this is by no means always so, and one tends to blame the provenance. This is not very convincing as the tree has a limited natural range within a uniform climate and, from what I have seen of that, the trees are equally good over large parts of it.

The beauty seen by David Douglas in the tree, who discovered it near Grand Rapids in the Oregon Cascades in 1825, lies in both the form of the tree and foliage. In Mount Baker National Forest, Washington, roadside trees to 200ft tall are narrowly columnar, tapering to the tip, with small level branches. The trunks are clear for half their height or more and pale grey to white. The foliage is a contrasting black from a distance, but even from 150ft below, the silvery white undersides of the leaves can be seen. In the hand, the foliage has an attractive pattern as the leaves are long and radiate in layers pressed down on the shoot, the centre-line leaves pointing straight forward and the laterals fanning out. Each spray ends in a broad fan of leaves, all parallel-sided to an abruptly truncated tip. New growth, especially

Lovely Fir (*Abies amabilis*): close-up of needles

11

on young trees, is often blue-grey above, and all leaves are broadly banded beneath with silvery white bands. Crushed foliage has a strong scent of tangerines.

The Lovely Fir has had an unhappy start in cultivation. The seed that Douglas collected and sent in 1830 yielded only two known plants, neither of which flourished and both of which were felled by 1905. In the 1850s several seedlots from Lobb and Jeffrey turned out to be Grand Fir or Low's Fir. The true species was not found again in the wild until Sargent sent it in 1880 from Silver Mountain near the Fraser River and, a few days later, it was also found in Douglas's locality. During this time a few grafts were raised from the original trees and made very poor specimens. The next seed from the wild was sent in large quantities from the Cascades in Oregon by C.S. Pringle in 1882, and it is from this that all our oldest specimens derive. Many of these are free from the crippling effects of the adelgid that causes gouty swellings at the joints of the shoots. These older healthy trees are now restricted to cool and wet western and northern areas. Young trees in drier and warmer eastern parts often make a good start and are shapely for perhaps 50 years but succumb soon after. Trees have grown in Sussex to 75ft but now there is none known in the southeast more than 30ft tall.

Young trees growing well have a distinctive shape. The whorls of branches and foliage lie very flat and the leading shoot, alone among the silver firs, bears small lateral shoots from its mid-section, rising vertically. Older trees, healthy or not, often share a curious feature with the Red Fir – a plainly barrel-shaped stem. It still shows in those trees which are now becoming moribund.

The biggest bole can be found beside the main track through Taymouth Castle Gardens above Loch Tay at Kenmore. It is a curious phenomenon. Since it was first measured in 1956 it has been 65/13ft, a languid, barrel-shaped hulk, noted in 1975 as 'nearly dead'. In 1991 it was the same condition and size. A few low sprouts bear a little new foliage every year. After 35 years of no measurable growth, it is peculiarly difficult to devise a likely age for the tree. It is on a top class site for the growth of conifers from the pacific slopes. It stands close to and a little below several of the finest specimens of Noble, Red and Grand Fir, two Coast Redwoods and one of the biggest Giant Sequoias in Europe. The loch shore and the mile-long base of 1000ft Drummond Hill is never short of water. It faces north perennially in the humid conditions that give optimum growth in silver firs. The Noble Firs date from about 1872, but the Giant Sequoia is recorded as being planted in 1859 and the two Coast Redwoods almost certainly date from a little after 1851. The biggest Nikko Fir in Britain is also there and will not have been planted before 1880, so there has been planting in this remarkable area for some decades. It is likely that a plant from the 1882 Oregon seed would have been added.

From the growth of vigorous Lovely Firs it can be seen that on the best sites they can add a mean of two inches a year to their girth. One at Durris House added three inches a year over 17 years. The Taymouth tree is 156in round and was that size by 1957. We cannot know how long it had been static or how abruptly it slowed down, but assuming the fast growth of two inches a year, it would have taken 62 years to reach that size had it come to an abrupt stop. That puts its date at 1895, but it must be allowed some years to have tapered off its growth, so an 1882 origin is quite likely.

A tree in the lower edge of Leckmelm Garden near Ullapool was 132/8ft in 1986, if my guess as to its identity, with no foliage in full sight, was correct. A fine tree by the Golden Gate at Benmore, Argyll, which was 75/6ft in 1956, was 115/10ft in 1983. The biggest of several at Castlewellan, County Down, in 1983 was 110/11ft. In Charleville, by Powerscourt in County Wicklow, one among a group of Nordmann Firs is 115/9ft. Endsleigh Lodge in Devon has lost several big specimens over the years, but one in the Upper Georgia is 98/8ft. An old tree, now far past its best, on the hill at Ochtertyre near Crieff, is 52/9ft. In 1955 it was re-growing a broken top and was 40/8ft. In the trench where the pinetum at Ardross Castle in Easter Ross was planted in 1900, the survivor of two Lovely Firs is 72/9ft. The larger of two at Auchterarder House in 1977 was 58/10ft. At Crarae Garden, Argyll, one planted in 1927 above the garden entrance was 82/7ft in 1987. A promising young tree at Crathes Castle, Kindcardineshire, in a little group of mixed conifers of the same age in the woods is 55/6ft. Planted in 1962 in the David Douglas Memorial Garden on the North Inch in Perth, a Lovely Fir was 40/3ft in 1987. One in the Vivod Forest Garden above Llangollen, planted in 1954 at 1000ft altitude, was 60/4ft in 1988.

Of the 38 specimens noted before 1932, only four survive, one in Herefordshire at Hergest Croft, the Ardross tree, and two in Ireland. So except for those in cool damp places the general outlook for the tree is bleak.

BRISTLECONE FIR

Abies bracteata

Large genera of plants, with numerous species, tend to include one or two which differ from the rest in important ways. Among the 150 or so maples, only one has more than three leaflets; of over 120 species of pine, only one has needles consistently in fours. The silver firs, about 40 species in the genus *Abies*, have a prize maverick species in the Bristlecone Fir which stands apart from the others in four features. It is unique in the long slender processes which curve out one and a half inches from the tip of each cone bract; it has long acute-conic buds like a beech, unlike those of any other conifer; it has hard, acutely long-spined tips to its leaves where nearly all the others are leathery and broadly tipped or rarely acute, and it is the only one with quite glabrous cone-scales. It also has the heaviest timber, sheds its seed and cones as early as September and has a curious long-spired top to its crown.

It is restricted to a few north-facing lower slopes and bases of small canyons and

13

Bristlecone Fir (*Abies bracteata*):
Eastnor Castle, Herefordshire

ravines in the Santa Lucia Mountains, south of the Golden Gate in the Coast Range of California, at 2000–5000ft, from Bear Canyon to above Big Sur. It is not only hard to find, but I found it was unknown to locals, even at the Ranger Station at Big Sur. At my first attempt, I headed up the Nacimiento Valley scanning the hillsides, but soon the track was steep and rocky and the long bonnet of the Buick was obscuring the view of the road ahead. I was then among Coulter Pine and Madrone which was much too high. I returned to Big Sur and asked for guidance at the library. No one there had heard of the tree, and after pointing out to them that two good specimens bearing cones were in their garden, I gave up. On the next visit, I went straight to the Forest Ranger Station. The two women there tried to be helpful and found a book which mentioned the tree, and they thought this was real progress. We got no further. But at least two more people in Big Sur had now heard of it!

The Bristlecone, or Santa Lucia Fir, was discovered in March 1832 by Dr Thomas Coulter. Coulter, not know as a collector, had called in on Douglas at Monterey in November, 1831, to invite him on a trip to the south. At that time Douglas was obsessed with arranging a vast expedition across Siberia, and declined to go, but he went to see the trees that summer. From confused accounts in Douglas's letters, and by Elwes in 1907, he was credited with discovering it in March. William Lobb, collecting for Veitch's, introduced it in 1853 and Beardsley sent more seed in 1856. Veitch's raised many trees from Lobb's seed and sent plants out to numerous gardens.

In its native woods, this tree receives no rain from April to November, but the sea-fog winds extend to this area in west-facing basins. The valley-bottom soils remain moist and humidity high, so it would be expected to grow best in the cooler, western wetter parts of Britain. In fact, growth has been very variable with a scatter of very vigorous trees among a much larger number of dead and feeble trees of no great age.

The standard bearer for a long time was the tree beside a glade at Eastnor Castle in Herefordshire. It was planted in 1865 and within 43 years it was 77/9ft. It maintained this rate until 1961 when it was 115/15½ft, but was not much bigger when it died of honey-fungus around 1975. A second, younger tree in the woods beyond, was 111/11ft in 1981 but missing by 1985. A very fine pair on the university campus at Exeter stands on the terrace at Streatham Hall. One of them had two stems of equal size from the base, until the heroic decision to remove one, flush at the base, was taken and by 1983 the single stem was 85/12ft. The second tree was 124/12ft. Equally notable is a seedling which arose under nearby shrubs during wartime neglect in about 1940. By 1983 it was 50/3½ft.

One at Bodnant, Gwynedd, was planted in 1909 in the minor ravine at the eastern end. In 1989 it was 88/8½ft. A younger tree in Horsebridge Wood at Wakehurst Place, Sussex, survived the gales and is now 98/7ft. Some rapid growth is shown by one in a 1960s extension at Grayswood Hill, Surrey. In 1982 it was 30/4ft and by 1990 it was 57/7ft. A splendid front garden, roadside tree at Upper Hartfield in Sussex, was 70/6½ft in 1968 and 88/8½ft by 1984. As far north as Dundonnell House, Wester Ross, one 30 year old was 52/4ft in 1986, and a thriving young tree in the woods at Crathes Castle, Kincardineshire, was 42/4½ft before being blown down. But of the 46 trees recorded before 1931, only five are known to have survived.

GRECIAN FIR

Abies cephalonica

Everything about this tree is sturdy, spiky and hard. As a young plant, it puts out stout shoots which radiate straight, well-separated, stiff needles with two-pronged tips. Stout branches themselves tipped by three big brown buds and raised at 45 degrees soon build a regular broad conic-ovoid crown. All too many soon develop a low whorl of heavy, upcurved branches which level out at height in a Cedar of Lebanon manner to become large but ungainly trees. The minority that maintain a clear single bole for 30ft or so are nearly all younger and lesser trees.

The specimens with spreading crowns bear great numbers of cones, standing like rows of nine-pins and mixed with the central spikes remaining from the cones of the year before. This extra weight makes the top branches vulnerable to gales, but not to wet snow since it rarely comes before the cones have disintegrated.

Grecian Fir (*Abies cephalonica*):
original 1827 tree at Hampton Park,
Surrey

Growing as they often do, clear of the shelter of nearby trees, many of these crowns are shorn of lengths of thick branches.

Another failing is that the lateral shoots, including the terminal ones on the lower crown, open their buds early. In late spring frosts these are scorched. Luckily the buds higher in the crown open later and are rarely damaged. The vital central bud of the leading shoot opens later still and usually escapes, thus the tree grows on apace, but maybe with a restricted and bushy lower crown.

The tree is native only to Greece, from Macedonia to the Pelepponese, and was introduced in 1824 when General Napier sent seed. Trees from this seed were known in 1864 on half a dozen estates but today can be found only on one, a single tree at Hampton Park, Seale, Surrey, which in 1984, at 88/13ft, had outlived its use as an ornament and was expected not to be tolerated for long. It is frequent in big gardens in all parts, even in East Anglia, where silver firs are scarce, while the biggest and broadest are mostly in central Scotland and further north and west.

Until recently the variety *apollinis* was distinguished by its needles, being less fully radiating and more above the shoot than below, where they are pectinate. It is said to be the form growing on Mount Parnassus, but it is now generally accepted that there is an influence of *Abies alba* coming in from the north and that this form is part of the variation and should not be given a varietal name.

The finest Grecian Fir is in the valley at Melbury Park, Dorset, 98/15ft with a clear stem for 70ft, and highly impressive. It has hardly grown in height for the last 30 years, nor does its flat top look as if it will in future. In that time it has added 17in to its girth. Two more good boles are at Highclere Park, Berkshire, one in the Castle garden area 115/15ft with no low branches, the other by the adjoining Milford Lake House, 115/12ft. The Ravine at Bodnant, Gwynedd, has lost one very tall tree but still has another. This dates from 1876 and is 124/12ft with a fine stem. A much bigger trunk with some low branches but of moderate weight is 92/16ft at Ridgbourne House, Hergest Croft. Two similar and bigger are at Woodstock, County Kilkenny. That by the ha-ha is 118/18ft and that above the lawn is 105/18ft. A tree dating from 1852 at Merton House, Norfolk was 80/14ft in 1981.

Of the really branchy old trees impossible to tape at above three feet, the biggest is at Culcreuch, Fintry, Stirlingshire, an enormous tree 115/24ft at three feet. At Whittingehame House, East Lothian, a tree is 102/18ft at two feet while in the pinetum at Scone, Perthshire, probably planted in 1866 a spreading tree is 95/17ft measurable only at one foot. A good tree at Logie House, Perthshire, is 85/16ft and a branchy one is 75/15ft at two feet. A good tree by the drive to the Den at Dupplin Castle, Perthshire is 90/15ft.

Westonbirt Arboretum, Gloucestershire, has two old trees dating from 1855 or thererabouts, both with several heavy low branches. That on Holford Drive is 108/13ft and that by Mitchell Drive is 111/13ft and neither is in any way handsome. The fastest growth recorded is that of the tree in the 1900 Avenue at Hergest Croft which is 111/13ft, but the Melbury tree noted above must have made early growth at much the same speed, as it is unlikely to date from before 1840.

GRAND FIR

Abies grandis

The Grand Fir is one of the most widely successful of all our introduced conifers and had until 1990 given us our tallest tree, among the tallest in Europe. It has been planted commonly for a hundred years in big gardens and in woods in all parts, yet it is hardly known beyond the narrow circles of foresters and keen gardeners. Few trees have equalled, and fewer surpassed, its rapidity in achieving 100ft on most sites, or 150ft on good sites. Only the Douglas Fir is as numerous at this latter height.

The foliage is easily distinguished among all the silver firs as the leaves on lower shoots are uniquely flat-pectinate at right angles to the shoot, long, leathery and strongly scented of tangerines when bruised. The only complications are that shoots from the upper crown, (often scattered beneath by squirrels), or on branches broken out, have their leaves variably raised, often with some vertical along the centre, more like normal shoots of Caucasian Fir. Also some trees, raised from seed from the southern parts of the range, tend towards the closely related Low's Fir. Their leaves curl slightly up and inwards, but the shoot is olive-green brown in Grand Fir and coppery brown in Low's.

Some Grand Firs have grown splendidly to over 100ft on poor sandy soils in East Anglia and other low rainfall areas, but as with most silver firs and trees from the Pacific Slopes, it is in the high rainfall, high humidity and cool summers of the western and northern mountain areas that the best, fastest and biggest trees are found. There, trees can be of perfect shape, superbly regular whorls of short level branches making a narrow conic crown until over 50 years old and 130ft tall. A few self-sown trees of this sort over 80ft tall are by the drive to Balmoral Castle at 1000ft above sea level. A stand of a few acres on the Atholl Estates, Dunkeld Section, at Dalmarnoch on the west of the River Tay, planted in 1941, are all of this quality and when 45 years old some were 120ft tall and 8ft around. The best trees of all, at 200ft tall, are a little less shapely, and on more exposed sites it is common for the tops to have been blown out at 120–140ft. From there on there are four or five vertical stems with three-foot leaders 160ft up and going strong.

The Grand Fir ranges from near the northern end of Vancouver Island and the mainland nearby, along the coast to California, where the last stand is with a Sitka Spruce outpost at Caspar and a few single trees to the Albion River. On the eastern flanks of the Cascades are unmixed stands of smaller trees, and there is a big outlier in Montana and Idaho. David Douglas discovered the tree in 1825, probably in Washington, but did not introduce it until 1831, probably from California, but his last journey is poorly recorded as his notes were lost in the Fraser River. The biggest trees were on the eastern side of Vancouver Island and in the Olympic mountains. It was reported to reach 300ft, but today none above 264ft has been found.

The tallest tree in the British Isles, and probably nearly the tallest in Europe until 1990 when the top eight and a half feet died, is at Strone House, Cairndow, Argyll. It is the first tree ever known to attain and pass the 200ft mark in Britain, and is still among the most shapely. It also has a bole which is surpassed in girth by barely half a dozen, and in its smooth, cylindrical quality by none at all. It was planted in 1875 and when 100 years old it was 185/17ft. By 1989 it was 208/19ft and both the stem and crown taper evenly in the upper half, despite reported loss of the top few feet in the 1970s. It has no branch or snag for 30ft and then only light ones shaded out and drooping, soon to be shed.

Among the huge Giant Sequoias and Western Hemlocks along the East Drive into Murthly Castle, Perthshire, is a tree 170/23ft. Unlike the Strone tree it has multiple stems from an old breakage 80ft up and some big branches, but the lower trunk is cylindric among some light branches and staggeringly massive and impressive as the eye can follow its apparently untapering progress through them for at least 80ft. The crown is broad columnar until the top 30ft.

A tree at Balmacaan, Drumnadrochit, Inverness-shire, is a little bigger, but is so beset with vast branches from the base upwards that its 170/23ft has to have its girth measured at six feet up. It is of deplorable shape, therefore, and much broken in its upper crown. Two huge trees at Abercairney, Crieff, are better. One by the drive is 132/20ft and an 1861 tree in the pinetum is 170/19ft. Another, at Lochanhead Hotel on the Kirkcudbright–Dumfries border, has an untidy, open crown, standing in the open in a windy place, but is among the biggest at 140/22ft. It is not known how such an early specimen came to be planted on its own in this small garden. At the end of the old East Drive into Brahan Estate, prominent on the skyline ridge from Muir of Ord, Easter Ross, a Grand Fir has suffered much breakage but is 170/20ft with a fair trunk. It was planted in 1861. At Forglen House, Aberdeenshire, a tree near the drive is 150/19ft. The only Grand Fir seen with layered branches was blown down in 1987 at Sheffield Park, Sussex, when it was 135/17ft and the crosscut stump showed it to have been planted, despite its great size, in about 1909.

To return to the very tall and beautiful trees, the tallest tree in Wales was planted as late as 1888 at Leighton Park, Powys. It is 205/12ft and stands in a group with several others around 200ft tall and of superb shape. At Moniack Glen, Inverness-shire, on a bank above several Douglas Firs of 200ft is one Grand Fir 180/14ft with a grand bole. Diana's Grove at Blair Castle is also full of a mixture of conifers of towering heights. Of a dozen Grand Firs, the most imposing is a tremendous bole,

Grand Fir (*Abies grandis*):
Strone, Argyll

19

number 47, which is a tree 180/17ft and like a factory chimney, with number 26 nearby 185/16ft. They were planted in 1872.

Two tall Grand Firs can be seen towering from woods from a distance, prominent from public roads. The more exposed and striking is seen from a length of the A9 north of Auchterarder, half a mile to the east on a long flat plain. It is on Dupplin Castle Estate and is 170/15ft. The other is on Ardverikie Estate, 2.2 miles along the drive from the entrance bridge, the most prominent of many along the five-mile drive, all seen plainly across Loch Laggan from the A86 for miles. Its long, slender top extends well above the many similar trees strung along this drive. It is 175/13ft.

Among the best of the as yet second rank in size, more or less standard-kit Grand Firs in Scotland, which would be top class specimens in any other species and country, a good one is at Ardverikie again. This one is in the garden area behind the Lodge from the Loch and was planted in 1881. It is 155/18ft, with a superb, smoothly rounded stem. One by the drive to Dunkeld House Hotel has a multiple top but a great stem growing fast and is 150/18ft. A similar tree, planted in 1864 in the Policies at Glamis Castle, Angus, is 120/18ft. At Inveraray Castle, Argyll, the bigger of two in the castle garden is 145/18ft, and one by the drive to Conon House in Easter Ross is also 145/18ft. One by Balathie House, Perthshire, is 150/17ft, the same size as one at Drummuir, Banff. The westernmost tree in the extraordinary strip between the A827 and Loch Tay, Taymouth Castle gardens, was over 170ft tall before it shed its top 30ft in a gale, but has been re-growing fast and is now 160/18ft. Two planted by the drive at Castle Milk, Lockerbie, in 1886 are well visible from a short stretch of the A74 and they are much the same size. The larger is 170/17ft. By the entrance-drive to Blair Drummond, Perthshire, a rather rough-crowned tree is 170/16ft.

More classic in shape is one on the Lower Terrace at Murthly Castle, dating from 1852 and 165/16ft with light branches a long way up the stem. A similarly branched bole is on the tree at Cawdor Castle, Nairn, which is 150/16ft in the pinetum. Half a dozen classic smooth clear boles and long slender tops are in the Burial Ground along Orrin Drive at Fairburn Castle, Easter Ross, the biggest of which is 170/16ft. A good tree by the drive through Durris Estate, Deeside, is 140/17ft.

Mention must be made of an extraordinary tree for its situation, even if it may be there no longer. In 1977 there was a Grand Fir at Crowsley Park, Oxfordshire, in the chalklands behind Henley, and it was 130/18ft with a good stem. The only original Douglas tree known is at Curraghmore, Waterford, planted in 1835. In 1975 it was 118/18ft. In Skelgill Wood, Ambleside, two beautiful stems like pillars are 165/12ft and 150/13ft.

Among many records of exceptionally rapid growth there is one at Bodnant planted in 1903 now 115/16ft; one by the drive at Blair Castle planted in 1926 is 115/16ft; a splendid tree in the 1927 stand at Miners' Bridge, Betws-y-Coed is 154/10ft and one in Alan Bloom's garden at Bressingham, Norfolk, was 82/6ft when 25 years old.

There are no recognised surviving cultivars at all of Grand Fir. But at Powerscourt there are two extraordinarily attractive trees with dense, upswept acutely conic crowns of no recorded origin. One by the Japanese Garden is 85/6½ft and one below the Pepperpot Garden is 118/8ft. From across the great hollow of the terrace, this stands out like a supremely shapely Giant Sequoia.

NIKKO FIR

Abies homolepis (plate 1)

Several conifers from the central mountains of Honshu, Japan, grow very well in our areas of high, year-round rainfall, but in regions with dry, warm summers make poor growth and have a relatively short life. Veitch's Silver Fir, the Tigertail Spruce and, to some extent, the Hiba (*Thujopsis*) are prominent among these. Silver firs are in general trees that need constant humidity and it is remarkable that the Nikko Fir from the central mountains of Honshu is among the best of the genus for growth in dry sites, and moreover, in or near towns where it has at times been long-lived. The foliage is handsome and substantial, with stout white shoots marked by creases into plates, and broad leaves thickly banded beneath with silvery white; and the tree is sturdy, making a solid central axis to the tip.

Unfortunately, the natural range of Nikko Fir was outside the limited area available to the collectors in 1860 and James Gould Veitch could not discover it or send seed in 1861, as he did with so many Japanese conifers. It is not known who did discover and introduce it, but it was thought to have been in the trade by about 1870. Supplies must have been short for a long time after that, for numerous trees are grafts on Common Silver Firs, some of which are not more than seven feet round. One, in a field above Wansfell House, near Ambleside, has a huge basal boss of rootstock on which sits a tree 88/9½ft.

The oldest surviving tree was planted in 1880 at the east end of Loop Walk in Westonbirt Arboretum. It has grown steadily but not fast, and is now 102/9ft. The tallest is an undated tree, a graft on Common Silver Fir, in the old pinetum at Brahan House, Easter Ross, at 115/10½ft in 1989. Nearby, in the 1901 pinetum, the better of two was then 102/8½ft. The second tallest dates from only 1929 in the pinetum of that date in the wood above Burnside House, Angus, and in 1990 that was 111/8½ft while a graft by the drive below was 105/9½ft. At Ardross Castle, Easter Ross, a graft near the drive was 80/10ft in 1989 when a seedling planted in 1900 in the pinetum below was 70/7½ft.

It can be seen that the biggest and fastest growing Nikko Firs mentioned so far are in the regions of Scotland, known for their long days and cool, wet summers, perfect for the growth of conifers. The best tree of all continues that trend by being in Taymouth Castle Gardens at Kenmore in Perthshire, a place unsurpassed for giant conifers. This Nikko Fir was by far the biggest I had seen when I found it in 1957 and it was 92/10ft. Today close rivals are known, but at 108/12½ft it has the biggest trunk. Glamis Castle, Angus, also grows big Nikko Firs and in 1981 the biggest of three in the pinetum was 85/11ft. Endsleigh Lodge in Devon also grows some of the biggest conifers in Britain, and a Nikko Fir in the Upper Georgia is 85/12ft. Similarly, Caledon Castle in County Tyrone, had one 98/10ft in 1983, and Leighton Hall, Powys, with one now 82/11ft, and Powerscourt, County Wicklow, where one below the Pepperpot is now 95/9½ft.

Other large specimens include one 70/10ft at Castlewellan, County Down, in 1983 and one at Whittingehame House, East Lothian, 88/10ft in 1987. The resistance of the tree to industrial pollution is shown by one at Trentham Park, Staffordshire, 82/8ft in 1976 before cleaning the air and river there had proved effective. An early tree, planted in 1898 in the Avenue at Hergest Croft in Herefordshire, was 85/9ft in 1985.

CALIFORNIA RED FIR

Abies magnifica

The name 'Red Fir' is relevant only in the high altitude stands in the Sierra Nevada in California, where many trees have a rich, deep red bark. A hint of red is occasionally discernible on some older trees here but nearly all seem to be like those in Oregon and most of the Sierra where the bark is nearly black and coarsely ridged grey. The Latin epithet *magnifica* actually refers to the cone, which may be nine inches tall with a smooth purple barrel, not to either the fine blue-grey long-leafed foliage or to the sometimes majestic form of the tree in the wild.

The tallest I found was 230ft, among the Giant Sequoias on the Congress Trail. The best to photograph are a close line of three on the edge of a pull-out a few miles from Glacier Point, Yosemite. I parked to take pictures and was the only person there, preoccupied with composing a good picture with the nearest tree prominent at 175/20ft, with a long, smooth trunk. I was only 300ft along the road, and returned in a few minutes to find the lay-by crowded with cars and a party starting to botanise in the alpine meadow behind the trees. I joined them of course, a class or society from Sacramento, I think. A woman asked my interest and when I said I was there to see the trees she said 'Perhaps you can tell me how big the Sequoia on the left of the Tuolumne Grove is.' 'Sixty-two feet, four inches round and two hundred and twenty-five feet tall', I said, 'Yesterday.' She showed no hint of surprise and cannot have seen how odd it was to ask an English visitor for information of this tree many miles away, nor to have known that there are only about two Americans who measure the big trees in California.

John Jeffrey discovered this tree, in the Shasta Fir form, and sent a large

California Red Fir (*Abies magnifica*): Dunkeld House, Perthshire

parcel of seed from Shasta Mountain on October 10th 1852, labelled 'Picea nobilis'. William Lobb also sent seed from Summit in the Sierra Nevada in 1852, and Jeffrey sent more from there, this time labelled 'amabilis' in 1853. He is often said to have discovered the tree in 1851, but his travels before 1852 were all to the north of the tree's range.

In Britain, the tree is an erratic performer, except in Perthshire and Northumberland. Many have grown very well in England for decades but then die or are blown down. A very fine tree planted in about 1910 in Borde Hill, Sussex, was 95/9ft and the most shapely in England, until it was blown down in 1980. Only one of the 15 cited in Elwes and Henry around 1907 is known today. They grow a remarkably symmetrical crown with short, very level branches, and rapidly make a big trunk, which often looks to be barrel-shaped. Even in Perthshire where most are in full vigour, what had been the tallest, in the deep shelter of Diana's Grove at Blair Castle, 124ft in 1978, has died back about ten feet recently. That was planted in 1872 and is the oldest known. The second oldest was planted by the drive near the Castle at Balmoral in 1877. It is 102/12ft but is a rough tree, now unhealthy and the owners are unlikely to tolerate it much longer.

The prime specimen is the third oldest, and again at Blair Castle, in St Bride's Churchyard above Diana's Grove. It is splendidly placed in the centre, symmetrical with a Noble Fir of the same age, a wonderful pair for comparisons. Planted in 1878 it was 68/10ft in 1931 and is now 130/16ft and flourishing. An excellent tree on the lawn at Dunkeld House, Perthshire, is now 132/12½ft, exceeded in height only by two in Taymouth Castle Gardens. One of these towards the eastern end is 140/12½ft but the good trunk holds a rough crown which has begun to die back. The more westerly tree also has a splendid trunk and maintains a reasonable crown, with a live top, now 144/11ft.

Further north, there are big trees at Balivil, Inverness-shire, 88/10ft in 1982; at Fairburn Castle, Easter Ross in the Old Garden, 98/7ft and in the same county, the larger of a pair in the pinetum at Ardross Castle. Planted in 1900, this, despite being a graft on Common Silver Fir, is 92/12½ft.

In England, Northumberland has the best trees. One by Dunkeld Drive at Cragside is now 121/12ft. (One in the rock-garden below the house has long been labelled 'Abies magnifica' but is a normal Noble Fir.) At Beaufront Castle, Hexham, Northumberland, a good tree was 82/9ft in 1982. In Ayrshire, a shapely young tree in the Happy Valley at Culzean Castle is 102/7ft. In the south of England, a tree by the drive at Adhurst St Mary, near Petersfield, Hampshire, in 1985 was 88/7ft. One surviving from the group planted in 1925 at the National Pinetum, Bedgebury, Kent, is 75/7½ft. Rapid early growth is also shown by one planted at 1000ft in Vivod Forest Garden, Clwyd, in 1954, 60/6½ft in 1988; and similar growth by one also planted in 1954 in the Ten Acres at The Hillier Arboretum, Hampshire, which was 50/6½ft in 1991. This one is of the Shasta Fir form, with scales protruding from the cones, but this occurs sporadically throughout the natural range of the species and is no longer separated by botanists. The foliage of the two forms is identical.

CAUCASIAN FIR

Abies nordmanniana

The silver fir of the eastern shores of the Black Sea was known by Pallas before 1800 in small populations on the western spurs of the Caucasus Mountains. It was regarded as the most easterly extension of the range of European Silver Fir, *Abies alba*. In 1837, the Finnish Professor Nordmann at Odessa, using foliage from Imeretia in the western Caucasus, recognised this as a separate species and it was named after him in 1839 by Steven.

Humboldt acquired seed from the Caucasus in 1848, but Lawson of Edinburgh introduced the tree to Britain in 1847. A tree in the Kuban Valley was known to be

213/15ft and others were over 370 years old. Today the largest reported is 225/20½ft, the tallest conifer outside the American Pacific region.

The Pacific Coast conifers sent by David Douglas before 1832 were showing great promise by 1850, but his silver firs were in very short supply until Jeffrey and Lobb's imports of 1851 and later. The sudden upsurge in the planting of pineta then in full flood depended for its big silver firs largely on *Abies alba* but this was falling out of favour as young trees were being crippled by infestations of the aphis, *Adelges nusslinii*. The early plantings of Caucasian Fir also suffered but many escaped or recovered and became more healthy, vigorous trees, a valued addition to the stocks for pineta. A remarkable and peculiarly timely event then assured wide use of the tree. The Oregon Association was founded at a meeting in November 1849 by George Patton and J. H. Balfour to facilitate and fund the collection of more seed of the Douglas species, and to find new species. The Association had employed John Jeffrey with great success, and by 1859 it considered its task complete. It disbanded on May 30, 1859, four days after its last act of accepting the offer of £50 worth of seed of Caucasian Fir from Mingrelia in the Caucasus. This huge quantity of seed was distributed among the nurseries with whom the Association dealt, and very soon this species was a standard component of the sets of conifers sent to new pineta. Today there are specimens in almost every pinetum, partly due to this last minute extension of its proper area by the Oregon Association.

Although recorded as the dominant tree on the limestones of its native woods, the Caucasian Fir is far from noted for its growth on calcareous soils in Britain. It will attain over 100/10ft on or just above limestones, but rarely succeeds on chalk. The best furnished and biggest, finest specimens are in the northern and western areas which experience cool humid summers and high rainfall, suitable for almost all large conifers.

The only dated tree which must have been from the Lawson 1847 seed, is one at Pencarrow, Cornwall, dated 1848. This was 92/12ft in 1988. A smaller tree in the same garden is dated 1845, but this must be an error. A tree 88/9½ft is at Fota Island, Cork, dated 1852, and this could be from the same seedlot. An 1860 tree at Scone Palace, Perth, at 118/12ft, is a year or two too early to be from the Oregon Association and could be from an unrecorded import of the 1850s. A good tree at Cortachy Castle, Angus, now 130/14½ft, is the next oldest, dated 1872.

Two of the most outstanding specimens on all counts are the widely parted pair along the slope above Loch Tay at Taymouth Castle Garden. Now 124/14½ft and 130/15½ft they are luxuriantly foliaged to the ground, but not heavily branched, and have broad but shapely crowns. They were not recorded until 1955 when they were 12½ft and 13ft round, showing good growth. The tallest tree is a slender crowned, young looking 152/11½ft below the iron bridge at Cragside, Northumberland. Others about the same height are in the ravine at Bodnant, Gwynedd, 150/13½ft; near the top of the avenue at Benmore, Argyll, 150/11ft, and by the east drive to Meikleour House, Perthshire, 150/12ft. The biggest bole is at the bottom of the bank in the New Plantation

Caucasian Fir (*Abies
nordmanniana*): Hillier
Arboretum, Hampshire

at Endsleigh Lodge, Devon, now 105/17ft. A good clean trunk is by the entrance
to the Arisaig Hotel, near Mallaig, Inverness, at 102/15ft. In the same county, by
the River Nairn at Wester Elchies, a big tree is 135/13½ft. At Dunans, Glendaruel,
Argyll, a splendid tree on the lawn is 142/11½ft. At Charleville, near Enniskerry,
County Wicklow, a tree is 141/12ft. A tree with a sort of pedestal base, planted in 1876
by the pinetum at Ardross Castle, Inverness, is 98/15ft and one in the pinetum itself,
dating from 1900 is 82/10ft. More rapid growth is shown at Innes House, Morayshire,
where one planted in 1932 was 88/8ft after 59 years.

SPANISH FIR

Abies pinsapo

The Spanish or Hedgehog Fir has two features of general interest and two of horticultural merit, but so often it is a tree of no charm and negligible growth. The botanical name *pinsapo* is a contraction of *pinus saponis*, the conifer of soap. In its very small native locale the shoots are macerated to yield a soapy detergent. It is a relict species growing only on limestone or serpentine slopes which face due north in the shade of precipices and peaks of ranges running east to west in the Sierra Nevada, southern Spain. There are four main groves a few miles long, and a few smaller ones, scattered in the district around Ronda, long menaced by fire and goats. It was discovered in 1836 and introduced in 1839.

Horticulturally, its value is as the most resistant of the silver firs to both chalky soils and to hot, dry sites. The former is to be expected in view of its native sites, but the latter is not, and conflicts with its inability to colonise anywhere which receives more than the absolute minimum of sun in the coolest, highest areas. It is therefore one of only three silver firs, with the Grecian and Algerian, to succeed on the chalks and limestones of East Anglia. Despite this, the biggest and best trees are, as in so many conifers, in the cool and wet of the far west and north today, a fact which was not evident to Elwes in 1909.

As a young tree, Spanish Fir is highly attractive, with a regularly conic, open crown of whorled branches and grey-green or bright blue-grey, neat foliage. Unfortunately it matures badly. A few retain their good shape but the crown becomes crowded with dead twigs, and growth declines seriously. Upper branches fan out and colourful new growth is minimal. Some trees, presumably with bushy inclinations when young, break into numerous very heavy, sinuous trunks from low down and become monstrously misshapen. The growth of big trunks can become so slow that in any other tree it would be fatal. One at Pampisford, Cambridge, added four inches in 22 years then added one inch in the next 38 years before it died in 1968, after taking 60 years to add five inches. Two healthy trees at Murthly Castle, Perthshire, added five inches each in 30 years. The increase in girth of two trees, over a ten year period, was not detectable with a tape. Mortality is high, such that only one survives now of the 16 specimens noted in 1909 and six of the 42 noted in 1931.

The tallest Spanish Fir is also one of the few of the big trees to maintain a single stem through to the tip, and a slender, evenly small-branched crown. By the Rhinefield Ornamental Drive in the New Forest, it is 115/7ft and probably dates from 1859. Three specimens are known with trunks 12ft round, and they could not be much wider apart geographically. The larger, by an inch or so, is at Lydhurst, Warninglid, Sussex. It is 80ft tall, with some heavy branches, but not badly out of shape. The second is at Rosehaugh on the Black Isle in Inverness-shire and 75ft tall with a highly impressive clean bole for eight feet, but a ragged top. The third, at

Spanish Fir (*Abies pinsapo*): Forres,
Morayshire

Clonmannon, County Wicklow, is 80/12½ft with 18ft clear bole. The next two biggest
trees are in adjacent estates in County Wicklow. The taller and better shaped is at
Charleville, by a woodland path to the wall-garden. It has a good trunk and is 108/11ft.
The Powerscourt tree is in the meadow with the two big Jeffrey Pines between the
Gardens and the Dargle Valley. It was planted in 1867 and is 80/11ft and soon divides
into three trunks which persist to the top.

A superior tree is in the Pleasure Walk at Longleat, Wiltshire. It is 72/10ft 8in
with a well-cleaned long bole. An excellent tree in Forres town, Morayshire, is
splendidly sited for public viewing. It it right beside the main road to Elgin in the
front border of the garden at the Park Hotel. It was planted in about 1875 and is the
only specimen seen to be a graft. The union is at ground level and not enough bark
shows to confirm whether the rootstock is the expected *Abies alba*. It is a very fine
tree, 75/9ft 8in with a smoothly cylindric bole, clear of snags or branches, and a
single stem through regular and quite big slightly drooping branches to a broad-
based obtuse but well-defined tip.

A fine bole bearing an upper crown of poor shape stands in a thin line of trees
and shrubs bordering a cut-off from the main Perth-Dundee road, the A92, in what

was part of Seggieden Estate. The tree is 80/10ft. In the pinetum at Cawdor Castle, Nairn, a good tree is 60/10ft. A big, ugly tree at Pitt House, Chudleigh in Devon, has many low trunks curving to the vertical. It is 95ft tall and, threading the tape among the branches, 11ft round.

NOBLE FIR

Abies procera

The Noble Fir is native to the Cascade Mountains and a few peaks in the Coast Range in Washington and Oregon. It was discovered and introduced by David Douglas in 1830.

An original tree could be found at Dropmore, Buckinghamshire, until it died in 1968. A number of specimens of unknown origin date from 1843 and 1844. Many fine trees owe their origin to seed sent in 1850 by William Lobb, but some of the finest date from 1872 and later unknown seedlots. Several very big trees are grafts, at the base, on *Abies alba* roots, probably dating some of them to before 1850, when plants were very scarce and the original Douglas trees were propagated in this way. Some others, though, are plainly var. *glauca* which can be multiplied only by grafting to be sure of the true blue-white foliage. Botanists are less willing to admit var. *glauca* than are nurserymen, because the best forms are only the extreme of wide variation in the wild.

Noble Firs tend to bear cones rather early in life. They are much clustered along the topmost shoots and each almost the size of a pint mug, leading to frequent breakages and a misshapen top. It is therefore a great credit to a tree to be over 100ft tall and retain a proper spire top. The two tallest are half as tall again and still growing from a narrowly conic apex and rank among the finest of all. With the silvery grey trunk extending right through the crown seeming, as in beech, to be untapering to a great height, these are imposing trees. One of these is on a bank among tall beech by the drive down to Ardkinglas House, Argyll. It is 165/11ft and was planted, probably in 1875, as it is just above the bridge by the pinetum of what is now Strone House. Its growth has been helped by the annual rainfall of about 90in and its shape by the surrounding beech.

The similar tree is in Diana's Grove, on the banks of the Banvie burn at Blair Castle, Blair Atholl, Perthshire. It is even more impressive as it has a clear trunk for over 30ft and is 165/13ft in a line of trunks of more Noble and Grand Firs, many of which are 165/180ft tall and make clear views of the tops difficult. It is No.11 in the Grove and may, like most of the trees there, date from 1872 or around 1880. Two much bigger Noble Firs at Blair Castle also rank among the best. One is in St Bride's Churchyard, above Diana's Grove. It dates from 1872 and is paired with a California Red Fir, the biggest known here, giving a splendid chance to compare

Noble Fir (*Abies procera*): Balmoral, Grampian

the two species side by side. By 1931, the Noble Fir was 88/11½ft and now, a superb tree, it has a massive, clean bole 18½ft round and is 120ft tall. The other is rougher but has a full crown with branches sweeping the ground but the interior is now cleaned of basal branching. It was planted either in 1872 or 1878 and was 75/8½ft in 1931. It has now grown to be 92/18ft, standing near the car park by the drive east of the Banvie, rugged and failed at the top but a venerable tree of rapid growth.

The most impressive bole of Noble Fir is in Stagshaw Wood, across the road from Kirkennan House south of Dalbeattie, in Kirkcudbrightshire. It towers from a wood of beech and oak with some tall Douglas Firs, a cylindric, branchless smooth silvery bole beside a small clearing, with no branch or snag for 60ft. Planted in 1875, it has grown rapidly in the last 60 years. It was 111/7½ft in 1931 and 132/10½ft in 1954. Already hugely imposing, it was more so in 1970 at 135/12½ft and yet more in 1985 when it was 140/14½ft.

Taymouth Castle Gardens, along the north bank of the eastern end of Loch Tay, has a dozen big Noble Firs even after losing several in gales since 1950. Their blue crowns are prominent in the view across the loch. A count of the rings in one blown tree gave a planting date of 1872 and this is probably when all the biggest were planted. Two today are outstanding specimens. One between the magnificent 165ft

Giant Sequoia and the road above is 153/18½ft and the other, near the western end by the path, is 132/19ft.

Three more massive and clean, smooth boles are in the northeast of Scotland. The furthest north is by the drive to Ardross Castle, near Alness, Easter Ross. It is one of the oldest, being given the pre-Lobb date of 1849, and one of the best. It is 111/16ft and was 75/10ft in 1931. This is a close twin of the undated one on the bank near Cawdor Castle in Nairn, at 144/16ft. One in the Glen at Durris House, Kincardineshire, near the Diagonal Path, has lower branches and a broader crown and is thus a little less impressive, but it is in fact somewhat bigger. It is 147/16½ft and sufficiently sheltered in this narrow trench to go further, although a Western Hemlock beside it was blown down some years ago.

Still in this corner of Scotland, a huge tree at Fairburn Castle, Muir of Ord, Easter Ross, is bigger than the last three but less shapely and has branches quite low on the trunk. It stands opposite the Castle, prominent on the corner where the drive divides. In 1970 it was 105/16ft and has added well to its girth to be 111/18½ft by 1987. Argyll has numerous contenders for mention and the chosen one is at Uig, the wood opposite the main gate to Benmore, near Dunoon. Standing back from the road in a line of big trees edging the wood, it is extraordinarily imposing. It is one of the tallest of all at 165ft and its clear bole was 16½ft round in 1983.

Cumbria has few outsize conifers, and the Noble Fir in Skelgill Wood, a National Trust property near Ambleside, must be included for its quality rather than its present size. On a slope among even taller Grand Firs it was at least 144/10½ft in 1983. The bole was clean and almost cylindric for some 40ft.

HIMALAYAN FIR

Abies spectabilis

The foliage of the Himalayan Fir is so beautiful and bold that it is a pity that the tree itself is so ungainly and unreliable. The branching is sparse and level and the interior of the crown bare and open, so even the best furnished trees look rather gaunt and show the untidily flaking dull grey bark. A few trees in England have lived for a hundred years or more and achieved a good size, but all have died, except one in Northumberland, for conifers an outpost of the far north and west. All the rest of the big and old trees are now in those regions from North Wales to Kincardineshire and in Ireland. It ranges from Afghanistan to Nepal along the Himalayas from where it was first successfully introduced in 1822.

The cones are of the blue, barrel-shaped kind of this Asiatic group of silver firs and unusual in being borne often low in the crown and remaining in one piece through the winter. The very stout pale brown to orange shoot has narrow longitudinal grooves filled with a dense growth of rusty brown hairs. The leaves are in two well-parted ranks, densely set, the outer rows to two inches long. They are slightly decurved towards their hard, acutely notched tips and very broadly banded beneath with flashing silvery white.

The best bole, clear of branches for some ten feet, is on the tallest tree at Fasque House, Kincardineshire. This tree rises from shrubs edging the lawn and is 95/12ft. A bigger bole, now over 13ft round, is on a tree at Gosford Castle, County Armagh. It has big, long branches spreading from four and eight feet up and an irregular crown 72ft high. Another, 13½ft round bole, is at Kilmacurragh, County Wicklow, on an 88ft tree with many low branches. A quite shapely big tree at 92/10ft is in the little pinetum at Torloisk House in the west of Mull where it is very well sheltered. A similar tree is in the pinetum in a dell towards the sea at Howick in Northumberland. It was probably planted in 1851 and was 87/10ft in 1978 and growing very slowly, since it was 74/9ft in 1931 and 50/8ft in 1909.

At Keir House, Dunblane, Perthshire, two trees were planted in 1850. One was 56/5ft in 1909 but has died back recently to 60/9ft. The other is a good, typical tree, 70/9ft. A short avenue was planted in 1856 at Castle Kennedy, Wigtownshire. It has suffered losses from recent gales and only two now remain, the larger of which is 92/9ft. At Inveraray Castle in Argyll, there are two trees dating from 1876 in the Limekiln Wood which have been growing very slowly in the last 60 years. The better tree is 92/9ft.

There is a splendid tall tree in North Wales, in the wood just above the village at Portmeirion. It has no big low branches, has 20ft clear, and is 95/10ft, one of the very best. Cumbria has a good tree, on the rocks around Aira Force in Patterdale, 85/9ft. At Bicton in Devon, in the collection planted in 1918 mainly from various seedlots sent from China by Ernest Wilson, one of the trees surviving the gales is 82/6ft. A younger tree showing more rapid growth is at Benmore, Argyll. In the 1937 plantings by the drive to the Golden Gates, it was 82/6ft 3in in 1983, having increased four feet exactly in girth in 27 years.

The variety *brevifolia* is probably a form from the western Himalayas. It has foliage half the size and greenish white bands beneath. Fine white streaks above make it look dark blue-green. Only four big trees are known. The outstanding specimen is near the extreme western end of the grove of giant conifers at Taymouth Castle by Loch Tay. It is a slender tree 115/10ft. It was 75/8ft in 1931 so has grown slowly. This is more evident still in the tree in the pinetum at Dupplin Castle, Perthshire. For this was 92/7ft in 1931 and is now 98/8ft. A tree at Birkhill in Fifeshire is 88/8ft and one of some size is by the gate into Crathes Castle, Kincardineshire, at 60/7ft.

VEITCH'S SILVER FIR

Abies veitchii

This tree shows as much as any of the mainland Japanese conifers the need for cool wet summers and year round high rainfall. In eastern England many have died between the ages of 55 and 85 years and none is now known to be over 60 years old. Even in the far western and northern regions where older trees survive and some of them are flourishing, a proportion show short bunched shoots around the top, the symptoms of approaching death. A few have died.

John Gould Veitch, the nurseryman-collector, discovered this tree on the slopes of Fuji in 1860. For some reason it was not among the great number that he introduced in 1861, but was first sent, by Mayr, in 1879. As a seedling it is one of the most vigorous and upstanding of the silver firs, and after a few years it may grow leading shoots two to two and half feet long. Except in high rainfall, growth declines early. The foliage is splendid, with dark red resinous buds and long leaves often blue-tinted in the first year. They are laid forward covering the shoot and banded beneath with bright silvery white. The crown is neat, narrowly conic, with lower branches sweeping down in an elegant curve. The upper crown is a narrow spire. The other main feature, highly characteristic of the species, is much less meritorious. The trunk starts almost from the beginning to grow rounded fluting. As this becomes more marked, deep pockets develop under the branch-insertions. In some old trees this has become slightly grotesque, but it is a useful, unfailing

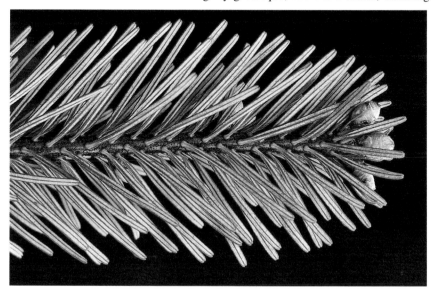

Veitch's Silver Fir (*Abies veitchii*): close-up of needles and cones

spot feature to separate the species from *A. mariesii, amabilis* or *nordmanniana* in which some foliage can be similar to Veitch's.

Only two trees outside of Scotland merit a mention for size and likelihood of surviving long enough to justify it. Both are in cool, moist sites. At Stourhead, Wiltshire, one was planted in 1924 in a group of conifers between two lakes on a slope facing east and sheltered by tall beeches. It is 70/5ft. The tree in the garden at Hergest Croft, Herefordshire, is the only one which is a graft, on a base of *A. alba*. It is also of good size, 82/7ft in 1980.

The biggest by far is one of the four big specimens at Dochfour near the northern end of the west bank of Loch Ness, in the pinetum. Although it has a triple top for most of the way up it has a good stem and crown. It is 78/10ft, and one a little taller is 80/7ft. At Balivil, Inverness-shire, there is one 65/8ft which has remarkably blue foliage. Pitcarmick in Strathardle, Perthshire, tends to have groups of each species in the pinetum planted in 1925. There are nine big Veitch's, the best of which is 70/8ft. On the hill at Ochtertyre near Crieff, a tree which must have been among the first planted, was 30/2ft in 1908. Now it is 85/8ft and despite showing some die-back at the top, has plenty of healthy foliage.

A sturdy, rather broad specimen at Dunkeld, by the fence between the Cathedral grounds and the Cathedral Grove, appears in a photograph taken in 1908 featuring the two Cathedral larches when the larger had died after lightning strike and was about to be felled. The picture is in the passage at Blair Castle which is panelled with the wood of the larch. The Veitch's Fir is a splendidly shapely tree about 30ft tall. It then grew increasingly slowly to be 60/7ft in 1955 and only 75/8ft in 1994. It is still in good shape but the shoots are crowded and the top is becoming obtuse with the slow growth. Crarae Gardens in Argyll has several big trees. One near the house was planted in 1914 and is 80/7ft; one by the burn, undated but likely to be of the same vintage, is 88/7ft. At Benmore Younger Botanic Garden in the same county, a tree near the Golden Gate probably less than 50 years old in 1983 was 88/5ft and promises to become a champion. Dawyck in Peebles has several by the drive and more on Policy Bank. The biggest at 88/7ft in 1982 is on this bank, where most of the planting dates from between 1910 and 1920. It too shows promise, like one nearby at 84/7ft.

MONKEY-PUZZLE : CHILE PINE

Aracaria araucana

Archibald Menzies trained as a gardener at Castle Menzies near Aberfeldy and had the greatest good fortune open to a botanist in the late eighteenth century to catch the eye of Sir Joseph Banks. For 50 years Banks largely organised and financed expeditions and the natural sciences. But thereafter Menzies's luck deserted him

Monkey-puzzle (*Aracaria araucana*): Forres, Morayshire

disastrously. Banks's only known weaknesses were not his fault, but he was neither allowed the naval ships of his choice nor the commanders. From 1791–5 Banks sent Menzies on what should have been the most momentous plant exploration of the Americas. But the ship had to be *The Discovery*, a Whitby collier with cramped accommodation. The captain was George Vancouver who did not agree with Banks using a member of his crew to help with drying specimens, herbarium work and collecting plants in Wardian cases and caring for them during the voyage. Relations between Vancouver and Menzies became so strained that the help of the seaman was removed and Menzies was partly confined to a locker-like cabin. His plants all died and only dried foliages could be used for descriptions at Kew.

The expedition rounded the Cape and crossed the Pacific, coasting north from the Puget Sound to reach Nootka in Alaska in 1792. Returning south by the coast of Chile, the leaders were entertained to dinner by the Spanish Viceroy in Valparaiso. Here Menzies saw strange nuts for dessert and was curious because they could not tell him what they were. Menzies put five in his pocket and sowed them in pots back on board. He arrived at Kew to present Banks with the plants, who planted two at his Thames-side home, Spring Grove. They became known as Joseph Banks's Pine. It was after 1850 that a lawyer visiting Pencarrow saw one of the early trees there and remarked that 'it would puzzle a monkey to climb that', and started the vogue for calling it the 'Monkey-puzzler'. The 'r' was later discarded.

The tree had been discovered well before Menzies had the seed. The Spanish traveller, Dendariarena, looking for naval timbers had noted it in 1780. But an engraving of two unmistakeable Araucasias flanking a statue in a garden at Kleve in North Germany was made in about 1650. These are believed to have been derived from an expedition to the Araukuru in Valdivia in 1642. The trees are in the garden of John Maurits, and show six whorls of branches.

This bizarre tree can merge with a mixed group of conifers but its use in large numbers is very restricted. A clump can make a feature isolated on a knoll and stands very well at the base of a cliff or rocky bluff, but otherwise it is best used in the formation of lines or avenues. These are not universally admired, but the uniformity of the cylindric trunk is excellent for that purpose. The breadth of the crown is highly varied from narrowly cylindric to much broader than it is tall. A fork is nearly unknown but several trees have a bracket-like outgrowth holding a minor narrow crown. Basal sprouts are frequent and may be strong and numerous, seeming to be seedlings.

Only one tree which bears flowers of both sexes is known today. This is in Mrs Trost's garden at Woodhouse Eaves in Leicestershire and yields fertile seed. Until 1987 the 98ft tree in Nymans garden, blown in that year, had been noted as bearing both sexes but since 1955 it had been male only. The avenue to Bicton House in Devon was raised from seed sent by William Lobb in 1843. Few were missing by 1959 when 13 bore male flowers, 14 bore female flowers and 6 showed no sex. The mean heights and girths were within one foot in height and one inch in girth. The largest and the biggest on record today is 92/13ft. The largest elsewhere are: an 1836 tree by the drive to Hafodunas, Clwyd, 80/11ft 3in; a male tree at Weir's Lodge, Powerscourt Waterfall in County Wicklow, planted in 1867 and 72/12½ft in 1989; the 1837 tree at Holker, Cumbria, 88/11½ft in 1992, having been re-erected after being blown flat around 1900; a very sturdy boled female at Craigievar Castle, Deeside, 75/12ft 3in in 1993; a fine broad tree at Mourne Park, County Down, 62/12½ft; a female tree, 85/12ft, at Fairall Mains, Kinnaird Castle, Angus, and a superb female below the road from Nannau Hall near Dolgellau, 82/12½ft in 1991.

INCENSE CEDAR

Calocedrus decurrens

The true Cedars, *Cedrus*, are Old World trees and there are only four species. The New World 'cedars' have no botanical connection at all with them. The early settlers found strange conifers new to them, and with their hard, aromatic timber were most easily sold as 'cedar'. They were a mix of junipers, cypresses and their near relatives, including this Incense Cedar which is very similar to the Thujas. It has

Incense Cedar (*Calocedrus decurrens*): Holme Lacey, Herefordshire

strongly, but not particularly pleasantly, aromatic foliage, scented like a turpentine-based shoe polish.

The peculiarity of this tree is the reaction shown by the shape of the crown to wholly obscure factors in different regions. In the wild, from mid-Oregon to the Mexican border, it is a conic tree with level branches, very like Western Red Cedar, until at great age and size it loses the lower two-thirds of the crown and becomes columnar. In the Sierra Nevada young plants are broad with sparse, open crowns, and in the south Coast Range it can remain as a broad, open bush. Only near San Diego are there some narrow, upright small trees.

Planted in England, it has grown tightly fastigiate. In the Midlands and east, it remains that way to a pencil-slim 100ft. In the west the branches, little more than lateral shoots, become lax and the crown is broad-columnar. In Ireland and Scotland the trunk divides into either two or three, or there are heavy near-vertical branches. The crown is broad-conic. This is also the form of a big planted tree in Tacoma, 500 miles north of the range. In the eastern USA, they are narrow and columnar but not fastigiate, and the same is seen in Geneva and southern France. This does not correlate with latitude, temperature, rainfall or humidity, and has not been satisfactorily explained.

This tree was discovered in 1846 by Fremont and introduced by Jeffrey in 1853 from the Klamath Mountains. A few trees from Jeffrey's original 1853 seed are known and many from Lobb's seed of the next few years, but only very few could be called big trees. Despite the narrow crown, the tree is vulnerable to windthrow and, in regions where it grows large branches or a forked stem, to the loss of large parts of the crown. The gale of January 1990 took the top 40ft or so out of the hitherto tallest specimen of all, a shapely tree in the shelter of Georgia, Endsleigh, at 130/14ft.

The two biggest trees are 150ft apart on the open flat at Doune House, Dunblane, Perthshire. Being in the north, both have some heavy, steeply rising branches but the bigger has ten feet of trunk before it divides into four stems. It is 124/19ft and none equals it for size. The other is 105/17ft with a longer single stem. A near rival is even further north, at Achnagarry House, a few miles west of the southern end of Loch Ness. This one, in the garden, is 105/16ft, a little branchy but narrow, while two by Dark Mile, not far away, are remarkably shapely for Scotland, the larger at 98/12ft.

Eastnor Castle, Ledbury, has 16 big specimens. That towards the village school is reputed to be an original tree and was one of the biggest in the country in 1906. It still is at 105/18ft but a low fork prevents a girth measure above three feet so it cannot be classed above the second tree at Doune. Towards the stables is a line of five superb trees to 108/11ft. The bigger of two by the upper road to the Castle is 111/12ft.

Westonbirt Arboretum has at least 46 specimens, 42 of which are quite big. Much the oldest is by Mitchell Drive, 110/12ft, but more famous is the very photogenic group of 11 very slender trees planted at six-foot spacing in 1910. The mean size is about 90/6ft and the biggest is 105/7½ft. A very shapely big tree at Adhurst St Mary, Petersfield, is 121/11ft. A far from shapely, typical northern tree at St Bride's Church, Blair Castle, is big, at 98/15ft, but the girth is swollen by low branching.

An original tree, planted in 1854 in Fota Garden, County Cork, is 88/13ft, the girth swollen by the beginning of a forked bole. A good tree sheltered in the woodland garden at Mount Usher, County Wicklow, is 115/12ft. A tree quite broad but not too heavily branched in the wall-garden at Charleville in the same county is 98/14ft. At Kinfauns Castle, outside Perth, a tree of 105/16ft owes some of the girth to an incipient fork. A very splendid tree in a wet hollow at Heckfield, Hampshire, is 85/14ft with a clear single bole.

BLUE ATLAS CEDAR

Cedrus atlantica var. *glauca*

This is the most numerous and widespread of the large size conifers in parks and gardens, especially in suburban areas. It owes this partly to its strong blue-white colour, the greatest selling attraction in young conifers, and partly to its pleasing shape. It also grows well in trying conditions. It withstands town air and soils, drought and considerable exposure, chalky soil and the hardest frosts. Like nearly all conifers it grows fastest to the biggest sizes in good soils with a high rainfall, but it is vigorous almost everywhere. Only the deplorable practice of buying tall, leggy plants, needing staking for years, ensures a period of struggle to become established and slow growth. When they emerge from this, growth is inconveniently fast for many of the sites chosen. It is common to see what was once a nice little lawn with rosebeds, shaded out and dominated by what was at first a small tree planted as a centrepiece. A lawn must, of course, remain an open glade kept strictly free of a central tree.

The species had been introduced four years prior to Lord Somers finding this very blue form in a valley in Algeria in 1845. He planted one at his home, Eastnor Castle in Herefordshire, by an interior gate. Today, at 100/15ft, it has a good straight

Blue Atlas Cedar (*Cedrus atlantica* var. *glauca*): Bodnant, Gwynedd

trunk persisting high through the crown and a spreading, flat top. There are many in England, and a few in Wales, Scotland and Ireland of about this size, but crowns damaged by wet snow disfigure some. The selection here can be thinned down by covering the best, so far unshorn, specimens.

In a field sloping up to the A49 at Brockhampton Park in Herefordshire a tree was 126/14ft in 1978 and a splendid specimen. A broader tree, probably dating from 1851 at Bowood, Wiltshire, in the pinetum, is 120/17ft. An 1850 tree in Fota Garden, County Cork, is 105/12ft. At Bodnant in Gwynedd, the much pictured tree trained over the ornamental water was planted in 1876. It has many branches spreading level from low on the trunk and is 72/15ft. Another of the same date, in the ravine, has a long clear trunk and small upper branches, and at 120/13ft is among the very best specimens. Sezincote in Gloucestershire and Emo Court in County Leix both have trees 85/15ft with good boles. Another of the same size in 1975 is at Lynhales, Herefordshire. At Adhurst St Mary in Hampshire a very good tree by the rose garden is 105/14ft. Wansfell House south of Ambleside has several big trees hanging over the main road, and the biggest is at the north gate, 85/15ft. Batsford Park near Moreton-in-the-Marsh has a score of big, well-coloured specimens, the biggest two being below the Drive. One is 80/14ft and the other, below the House, is 67/14ft.

The biggest in Scotland are by the Dunkeld Drive entrance to Murthly Castle, close to and below the A9 to Perth. Two near the southern end of this avenue are 124/17ft and 98/16ft, the former being the biggest in Britain, taking height and girth together. The Gardens at Dupplin Castle, south of Perth, have a good tree, at 115/12ft.

The rapidity of growth in some trees is shown by a fine big tree at Powis, on the bank opposite the Castle. It dates from 1892 and when three years short of its hundredth birthday it was 80/13ft. On the private lawn at Wilton House, one of the dated trees, planted in 1901 which was 50/5ft when 30 years old, was 85/12ft when 86 years old. One of a group of the silvery foliaged form, 'Argentea', planted in 1909 at West Dean House near Chichester, was 82/12ft when 72 years old. A shapely, sturdy tree by the drive into Peamore near Exeter dates from 1923 and when 60 years old it was 70/11ft.

DEODAR

Cedrus deodara

The Deodar is the only cedar whose natural range is not in the Mediterranean region, as it grows only in northern Afghanistan, Kashmir, Pakistan, northwest India and western Nepal on the middle slopes of some of the highest mountain ranges in the world. It is therefore used to a much more intense wet season and cooler summer

Deodar (*Cedrus deodara*): an ornament of value, but only for a short time

than the others. This shows very little in its growth in the British Isles where there are big trees in all parts and only a slight tendency for the biggest to be in the cool, damp west and north. It differs from the other three in minor details: longer and bigger leaves, cones and male flowers, usually zoned on branches of different sex. More noticeably it grows a single, straight trunk persisting through the crown to a slender spire top. Where it does divide in mid or lower crown, each stem still persists to a spire, and the failure of the main stem seems always to be the result of damage from an ice-storm or a gale. Another feature is the pendulous or arched outer shoots and leading shoot, most noticeable in immature trees. The bowed leading shoot allows the tree to grow through overhead branches on its way from being an understorey tree to becoming a dominant. This method of growth is shared by only two other common conifers: the Lawson Cypress and Western Hemlock.

Young trees often have quite silvery-grey long-pendulous foliage and are very attractive. Much of these features are lost before too long. They then grow fast into a densely crowned rather twiggy dark tree of no distinction until they begin to acquire the dignity that comes with great size and good shape. In small plantings, therefore, the Deodar is an ornament of value but for a limited period only, and a replacement every ten years or so is needed.

There is a little evidence that the first Deodars came in 1822, but it is generally accepted that it was introduced by the Hon. Melville in 1831. Many trees were raised from this seed, which was distributed through the Horticultural Society, and many estates have specimens, although gales have removed some. Many more date from 1840–1850 and by late Victorian times it was popular as a constituent of screens around properties on the outskirts of towns. As these gardens were engulfed in the spreading towns, many found themselves in semi-urban parks, although many still surround the old estates, and it is a very common tree around towns. It adapts to town air very well, so some are quite big trees.

Dropmore in Buckinghamshire has several original trees planted in 1834 but none is particularly big, whereas one planted in 1840 by the lake is among the biggest anywhere. It has a fine bole and a good crown and is 102/17ft. The most impressive trees bigger than this are of unknown age. At Eastnor Castle a broad avenue and each side above the grain store grows an unrivalled group of Deodars. One is 124/17ft, another 124/16ft and at the top of the avenue one is 120/16ft. The biggest bole is at Conan House, Easter Ross, in the wall-garden. In 1908 it was only 43/9ft 9in, although outsize for that time. Now it is 90/19ft with a good clean lower trunk. The best all round is at Ballindean on the Perth-Angus border near Dundee. In a field above the garden it stands on its own, a classic shape, 98/16ft.

A splendid tree in Stratford Park outside Stroud in Gloucestershire is 108/16ft. The best bole among known originals is on the 1832 tree at Walcot Park in Shropshire, smooth and round, it was 105/13ft in 1975.

At Emo Court, County Leix, a tree by the statue 'Summer' below the house is 88/16ft and a good tree, although there are branches on the lower trunk. A fine tree with a clean bole stands near the front of Orchardleigh House near Frome, Somerset. It has grown well over the last thirteen years and is now 118/15ft. At Dalvey House in Morayshire an exceptionally good tree is 80/15ft, and a similarly good one at Whitfield House in Herefordshire is 120/15ft. One of the most impressively smooth boles is at Leonardslee, Sussex, near the top of the long bank of fine trees running northwest from the old house. It is 112/15ft without a branch for over 30ft. At Lynhales, in Herefordshire, a tree of this quality was 95/14ft in 1975, and near Hereford, at Holme Lacey, another is 80/15ft.

CEDAR OF LEBANON

Cedrus libani (plate 1)

A Georgian mansion ought to have, in addition to the Southern Magnolia on the wall, a Cedar of Lebanon on the lawn. Or a pair, or three or four, for the grander mansions. They may be passed off by the proud owner as contemporary with the house, and their appearance may seem to support that, but in many cases they were planted after 1800 and very few pre-date 1770. Only a handful of plantings from before 1740 survive today because the very severe frosts in that year, not experienced again until 1962, killed all the young trees and nearly all the numerous plantings of the years after 1680. No deaths nor damage were reported in 1962, and this is not only because of the maturity of the trees, because it was the same among the young trees, but may reflect some selection for hardiness by the latter day use of seeds from cultivated trees in Britain, or more likely, on the Continent.

This 1740 carnage should torpedo the more romantic and more remote origin of the trees where one is asked to believe that Queen Elizabeth I was involved in the planting. And, in any case, she died 35 years before the first seed arrived. There is another more interesting influence that the frost had. The writer Miles Hadfield pointed out that this meant that Lancelot 'Capability' Brown (Benny Green's 'Culpability' Brown) probably knew only cedars 10–15 years old when he was drawing up his earlier plans, and at that age this tree is a slender conic tree. In 1755 none of the conifers from western North America was known, and the Italian Cypress was not, at that time, regarded as hardy. So where Brown wanted a neatly conic or columnar conifer, and we would plant a Lawson or Leyland Cypress, Thuja or Incense Cedar, he had to use Cedar of Lebanon. The great spreading crown subsequently grown will not have been in his mind.

This tree does grow very fast, as dated trees on the lawn at Wilton and elsewhere show, and when the total volume of timber in one of the big-branched and multi-stemmed lawn specimens is calculated, it has been found to be comparable with the best Grand Firs and Coast Redwoods and perhaps with the Giant Sequoia. The timber, although aromatic and of the highest quality for furniture, is not normally on the market in this country because of the erratic supply and the very branchy form of most of the blown trees, causing damage in falling and difficulty in extracting usable lengths.

The mention of seed origins, above, suggested that some came from the Continent. This is because the peculiar flowering habits of this and the other cedars, unique to them among conifers, makes viable seed unlikely in most years in Britain. A few gardens have raised their own progenies but there are few years in which this has been successful. For no reason that one can think of, the true cedars all flower in autumn. The Atlas flowers in September and is the most likely to give good seed, but the Deodar and Cedar of Lebanon do so in mid or late October. Given warm, dry weather they release huge quantities of pollen in visible clouds. By mid October, in sunny weather, there is inevitably a heavy dew. Pollen is hygroscopic, and will not dry readily. It needs longer drying than it is likely to get at that time, before the afternoon dew starts to condense.

Cedars of Lebanon span the range between the near-perfect single stems without a heavy branch, as in a good larch, to massive, overgrown bushes with numerous stems and big branches from ground-level. The majority are nearer the second, and this includes all those specimens with girths over 30ft. The tallest is a remarkably larch-like tree at Leaton Knolls, Shropshire, among beech trees on a bank. This is 140/12ft. The biggest trunk and all-round finest tree is as nearly of this form as could be expected of a cedar of its size. It is near the cricket ground at Goodwood House, in Sussex. It is 132/29ft, clear of any branch for ten feet, then with moderately big branches up the stem, some of which were damaged in recent gales. It has a history unusual in both its precision and its interest. It is one of 1500 planted by the Duke of Richmond and Gordon in 1761 and it is said that he obtained this big order from his fishmonger. Which has one wondering if he went to his nurseryman for his kippers. About 20 of these early trees survive and several are nearly as big, but none is of the same quality nor height.

There is little doubt that the first seeds were brought to England in 1638–9 by Dr Edward Pocock, well pre-dating the trees at Enfield and Chelsea, the earliest quoted by many writers. Pocock was a scholar of Arabic at Oxford and Chaplain to the Turkey Company at Aleppo in 1629. He is known to have made several journeys to Syria until 1639. His brother was chaplain to the Earl of Pembroke at Wilton, and the tradition is that Edward gave his brother cones he collected on his last visit. Two of the trees raised were planted on the lawn at Wilton and one kept in the orangery for giving back to Edward. Two trees cut in 1874 had, according to careful counting, 236 rings, showing almost suspiciously exact dating to 1638. Edward was awarded the living at Childrey when he retired, and planted his tree in the Rectory lawn, in 1646. It stands today 52/26ft, flat-topped with some very low, level branches but a good straight trunk. It may not be the only surviving original tree, for one at Adare Manor, County Limerick, against the house and forking low, is thought to have been planted in 1645. It is 60/31ft at two feet, but nothing seems to be known of its history.

Another tree, which survived the 1740 winter when it was very young, is the best of several at Peper Harow near Godalming in Surrey. It was planted in 1735 and is 105/26ft with ten feet clear of branches and a long single stem. It suffered breakage to some of the big upper branches in October 1987 but is still a splendid specimen. Even bigger and just as good is an undated tree below the Cascade at Blenheim Palace, Oxfordshire. It is 95/28ft with a very good bole. No big cedar bole starts out from the ground so smoothly cylindric, like a Norman pillar, as the tree by the lake at Claremont Garden near Esher. It is 105/23ft and without branch or blemish for 50ft. At Stanway Park in Gloucestershire, a magnificent tree on the hill is 115/28ft with ten feet clear; at Stowe Park, Buckinghamshire, by the Temple of Charity and Virtue, 20ft clear on a tree 95/26½ft makes an imposing specimen, as is the tree on the lawn among the 1767 planting at Highclere Castle, Berkshire, which is 72/23ft with 36ft clear. Two smaller trees making up in length of clear bole what they lack in size, are at Belvedere, Windsor, 120/18ft clear for 42ft and at Woburn Abbey, 95/19ft with 45ft clear. One in the Evergreens is 85/23ft clear for 15ft. The tree at Rousham, Oxfordshire, is also of note for its height. Standing on a bank, it is 138/19ft with 18ft clear. At Albury Park, Surrey, a cedar on the hill rears up in a small clearing, 115/17ft with a smooth clear bole for 30ft. A fine tree by the house at Snalsgrove House near Newbury is 125/21ft, clear and round for 20ft.

Among the big bushes, the best is that at Pains Hill, Cobham, Surrey, at the Bath House. It is about 130/33ft at three feet, with an enormous, spreading crown. A curious tree at Addington Palace, Surrey, is reputed to be among the oldest. It is only 52/25ft at one to two feet, among the branches, but grows out only on one side to the absurd distance of over 240ft. At Gray House, outside Dundee, a spreading tree is 92/35ft at two feet. At Gathmyl, near Newtown, Powys, one 95/24ft breaks into four fairly equal stems at about five feet. A 1739 tree on the public lawn at Wilton is 70/29ft at three feet.

Examples of rapid early growth can be found on the Wilton lawns, although second and third visits show that date plaques tend to wander among the trees and some care is needed in making comparisons. It seems safe to credit a 1903 tree with 75/15ft by 1987; a 1908 tree with 50/13ft and one from 1909 with 85/12ft. A tree on the bank at Powis Castle, however, beside a plaque dated 1909 and now 60/20ft, does raise an eyebrow, even in that area of rapid growth.

LAWSON CYPRESS

Chamaecyparis lawsoniana

The tree which is responsible for so much monotonous funereal gloom in suburban parks and gardens is nonetheless one unsurpassed in no less than three important aspects. In cultivation it is a great deal more variable than any other conifer, despite being singularly uniform in its native stands. It has yielded cultivars of an extraordinary range of patterns of foliage, textures, and every colour which is available to a conifer. It is, with its cultivars, the prime tree in garden layouts for shelter, winter colour, backbone and winter form, for eye-catchers and other colour-features, for cover for birds nesting and roosting. It can also be shaped into topiary. It is bone hardy and grows happily on most soils. It is the ideal, general purpose and ornamental tree, with forms available to suit any space. Garden planning in Britain is primarily the study of Lawson Cypresses. Other plants are just infilling.

Its timber is the highest quality of any conifer. It is strong, hard, durable, aromatic, easy to work, takes a high finish, and is resistant to salt water and to acids. Within ten years of the discovery of the tree there were a dozen ports built along the Siskiyou Mountain coastland from Crescent City to Port Orford, for shipping coffin-planks, much prized by the wealthy in China and Japan. Sir Thomas Sopwith would have no other timber for the interior of his luxury and racing yachts. Inferior grades were used for floors, sleepers and fence-posts while supplies lasted, but later

Lawson Cypress (*Chamaecyparis lawsoniana*): Bonskeid, Perthshire

it was valued particularly for separator plates in batteries, for duckboards, Venetian blind slats, and for matchsticks.

Lawson Cypress was probably discovered and introduced by John Jeffrey in 1853 when he was in the Siskiyous and in the next year in the Trinity Mountains. However his journals were not sent and were published only in 1952. He customarily sent only small packets of seed, some of which did not arrive. The credit is therefore given to Andrew Murray who collected seed in the Trinity Mountains by the Upper Sacramento River in 1854. He sold most of it to Lawson's Nurseries at Bangholm, Edinburgh, and it rapidly became a component of the standard stocking of northwestern American and Japanese conifers sold for the foundation of hundreds of Victorian pineta planted after 1860.

Anthony Waterer at Knaphill either bought some seed direct from Murray or from Lawson. In 1854 he raised the first of what soon became an avalanche of cultivars, the deplorable 'Erecta Viridis', which disfigures nearly every churchyard in the land. It begins life as a tightly erect, acutely pointed, bright green tree of some promise. It soon contrives to become forked and to lose shape, then wet snow continues the work, bending the branches irretrievably and making a gappy, untidy crown showing much dead interior. Lawson himself produced the tall, pendulous 'Intertexta' with hard, remote foliage in 1869, and the Dutch nurseries had joined in by 1880. By 1950 there were over 200 varied forms, including dwarfs, of which none had arisen in the tree's homeland. It is a little odd to see 'Fletcheri' common in Vancouver and to know that it arose in Chertsey, Surrey, and 'Lutea' in San Francisco, aware that its home was Tooting, London.

The tree seeds copiously from an early age. Seedlings spring up in or near the shade of damp woodlands, and grow a foot or two a year. Nurseries raise them by the million and always these show a range of colours from dark green to pale, rather blue-green. Hedges show this well. Mercifully only good, plainly distinctive new forms are selected for propagation and given a name, or the flood would be quite unmanageable. Most of those that have been selected are strikingly blue or gold and many, like 'Lane', 'Hillieri' and 'Stewartii' carry the names of their nursery of origin, or like 'Pembury Blue' and 'Milford Blue Jacket' the name of the locality of the nursery.

The Lawson Cypress is markedly slower than the Western Red Cedar in building a big trunk and much more prone to crown breakage and to windthrow. Hence, although introduced at the same time and planted abundantly in the same regions and gardens, no Lawson is as big or tall as a good many red cedars. The biggest Lawson by a fair margin is at Powerscourt, beside the Dargle Drive. It is 102/16ft, and planted probably in 1867. It is still growing very fast, having added 24in to its girth in the last 14 years. The tallest is a slender-crowned, splendidly shapely tree at Ardkinglas, Argyll, in the grounds of Strone House. It was planted in 1875 and is 135/8ft. The oldest seems to be an 1858 tree at Belsay Castle, Northumberland, for there have been big losses amongst the early recorded trees. This one is 72/11ft. The second largest in girth is a rather rough tree on a terrace at Kinnettles Castle, Angus, at 82/15ft. By Dark Mile on Achnagarry Estate, Inverness-shire, a good tree is 118/15ft. One that is growing fast in the wall-garden at Fairburn, Easter Ross, is 85/14ft and branchy.

A good big bole for clear length is in the Rhinefield Ornamental Drive in the New Forest. Planted in 1859 it is 125/15ft, clear for 15ft, but dividing. Another there is 115/13½ft. An 1866 tree at Kinfauns Castle, Perth, has a fine bole, 85/12ft. Balmacaan at Drumnadrochit, Loch Ness, has two outstanding specimens by the drive. One is 132/14ft and among the best, and the other is 115/13ft. Another exceptionally big and fine tree is at Doune House, Dunblane. This is 121/14ft and although there are small branches on the trunk, it runs up to 56ft before it forks. The greatest length of clear bole seen is the 36ft on a tree 95/8ft along the walk to the lake at Tullynally Castle, County Westmeath.

A tree planted in 1881 by the drive to Ardross Castle, Easter Ross, is 82/13ft with a good bole. One at Portmeirion, above the village, is similar at 100/13ft. A big bole but poor crown is in the Dell at Dalvey House, Moray, on a tree 111/13ft, and at Stradbally House, County Leix is a tree 72/13ft. An outstandingly good tree at Culdees House, Perthshire, is 118/11ft and in the same county, one on the lawn at Bonskeid House is 105/13ft.

In the far west, most notably in Ireland, low branches tend to root as a ring of layers. The worst case may be one at Woodstock, County Kilkenny which is 85/10ft with 25 such rooted layers.

NOOTKA CYPRESS

Chamaecyparis nootkatensis

It must be admitted that this is a gloomy tree. Its foliage is a dull dark green and hangs in a depressed looking way. It never looks as if conditions are to its liking or that it will tolerate them much longer. It sheds interior foliage after a few years use leaving its crown thin and open in the inside and adding to the general impression of it being ill at ease. Yet, this is illusory, because few trees are as free from disease, as frost-hardy, generally tough and untroubled by the vagaries of soil. It is the longest lived tree in British Columbia, in the middle of its range, exceeding 2000 years and grows slowly to a great size. One prominent above the road into Cypress Park near Vancouver is 130/30ft.

In cultivation, it can grow quite vigorously for some 50 years, but after that its progress is slow. Despite its unexciting foliage, it can make an eye-catching planting if placed in small, well-spaced groups. Westonbirt has many of these, now 70–80ft tall and their effect depends on the extreme uniformity of shape. They are perfect cones, like dunces' hats, and hardly a tree anywhere is different, except for a few slightly less acute because the stem forks. In Ireland a much broader shape is normal, and low branches often bend to the soil, root and sweep up again, in a circle around the main stem. A good group has the pleasing quality of a clutch of cooling-towers at a power station.

The cone, which is navy blue in the summer on the Weeping form, but less so in this type, is unique in the genus *Chamaecyparis* in taking two years to ripen and in having a prominent beak on each scale. The prominent beak is inherited in the hybrid Leyland Cypresses along with the hardiness. Although the foliage sprays are weeping, the branches or main shoots are strongly ascending. In its native Cascades Mountains it appears even more dolorous than it does in Britain.

This tree was discovered by Archibald Menzies in 1794 around Nootka Sound on Vancouver Island, and given its botanical name by D. Don in 1826. David Douglas must have encountered it many times but did not introduce it. Perhaps his seeds went down in one of his two canoe disasters. It was first sent by John Jeffrey from Vancouver Island on one of his two visits in late 1851. It is a sea-level and glacier-foot tree along almost all the Pacific Coast of Alaska and British Columbia and its islands. In Washington State it follows the mountains inland and at increasing altitude south in the Oregon Cascades. It only just enters California in the Klamath Mountains. It is a tree typical of the Alaskan flora, which extends here south to the Klamath and Siskiyou Mountains.

In the British Isles it is grown in all parts in the larger gardens, most frequently in the western half of England and in Wales and in mid-Scotland and Ireland, less often in the far north, although there are some big trees there. Plants seem to have been scarce until after 1870, for few trees are known to be older than that. It is a difficult species from which to choose favourite specimens, because it grows rather slowly, most of the large trees are of similar age, and it is extraordinarily uniform in shape, and little affected by soil and site. With such uniform crowns and branching, the size of the bole varies very little, and there is little to choose for beauty of shape.

The tallest tree is, I think, one below the Rustic Bridge in Cragside, Northumberland, which I made 108/7ft in 1992. At least four trees are 102ft tall, two of them at Westonbirt, one by Main Drive, the other, planted in 1870, by Loop Walk. The third is by the pinetum at Blair Drummond in Perthshire, 102/9ft and the fourth is above the farm buildings in Eastnor Castle in Herefordshire, 102/7ft. All are, needless to say, of impeccable shape. Eastnor has a bigger, broader one by the paddock on the northwestern edge, 88/10ft. At Powerscourt in County Wicklow,

Nootka Cypress (*Chamaecyparis nootkatensis*): Westonbirt, Gloucestershire

one planted in the Dargle Glen in 1885 is 98/10ft. The pinetum at Dupplin Castle, Perthshire, has seven big specimens, the best in 1985 being 98/8ft and 95/10ft.

The oldest dated tree is at Oxenfoord Castle, Midlothian, planted in 1856 and 72/10ft in 1985; and one at Dawyck, planted in the Rhododendron Walk in 1859 was 80/10ft in 1982. The biggest trunk is in a little wood below Nannau House near Dolgellau, well hidden across the road, near the immense Monkey-puzzle, and is 70/11ft with a single trunk for eight feet. Only a few forking trunks are bigger, and none of those qualifies here. Other notable trees are all much the same: 71/10ft at Armadale Castle, Isle of Skye; Dunans House, Argyll, 85/10ft; Doune House, Perthshire, 72/10ft and Stourhead, Wiltshire, 92/10ft for example.

SAWARA CYPRESS

Chamaecyparis pisifera

This is something of a Cinderella among garden trees. The type tree is uncommon, little known and passed over as a feeble Lawson Cypress when it is seen. The main cultivars, which are common and distinctive, have no popular names and their botanical names deter all but the dedicated plantsmen. So there are none mentioned in popular books, and many people starting their interest in trees by walks in the local park armed with one of those books must soon be faced with some good puzzles.

The species grows only in Japan which has a very long history in selecting garden forms, such as cherries, tree-peonies, chrysanthemums and maples. The Sawara Cypress was among them. Partially juvenile and fully juvenile forms were raised and propagated by cuttings, except for a few that, juvenile as they were, yielded cones and seed. A limited range of coloured forms, mostly gold-tinged or fully gold also arose.

Sawara Cypress (*Chamaecyparis pisifera*): close-up of leaves

Japan was however a closed country until 1854 and although the only European visitors allowed from the Dutch East Indies Company were largely restricted to the few acres of the mud island, Deshida, their medical officers Kaempfer, Thunberg and Siebold will have seen or had specimen foliage brought to them. Only one was brought out of Japan before 1881 except the two boatloads amazingly spirited away by the daring Siebold in 1829 and 1830.

One form of the Sawara Cypress, the Moss Cypress, 'Squarrosa', was in the shipment from which Siebold established a botanic garden at Buitenzorg (later Batavia, now Jakarta) on Java. It was sent to Europe and Britain in 1843, but the parent tree and the other forms had to wait until the big imports of 1861. Soon after that, the Sawara Cypress and four cultivars were in the stock sets of conifers from North America, the Himalayas and Japan that were sent out by the big nurseries like Veitch's to all the landowners wishing to start a pinetum. The type tree probably aroused the least interest of these and remains the least commonly seen.

A feature of the type is the pale mid brown, soft-looking bark, with shallow ridges running straight and parallel well into the crown, and the frequency at which the stem forks at six feet. The foliage is hard and fine, composed of tiny long-pointed scale-leaves dark green above with small but bright blue-white centres on the undersurface. When crushed it emits a strong, rather acrid, resinous scent. Mature trees are densely crowded with cones a few inches back from the tips of the spray. Each cone is the size, shape and, until it ripens, the colour of a small garden-pea, slightly wrinkled. Hence the adjective 'pisifera' – pea-bearing.

Notable trees of this seldom notable or noticeable tree are well spread over the country. Near Ullapool one in Leckmelm Garden is 50/9ft. South of that, at Strone Garden, Argyll one is 75/7ft. West, in Ireland, at Woodstock, County Kilkenny, an extraordinary tree 80/5ft, spreads its 51 other stems growing up from layered branches, across a great area. In the southwest of England, Devon has three of note, two of them in Killerton. These are not many yards apart and have very fine stems. They are broken to 35/8½ft and 66/9ft. The other is at Endsleigh Lodge at 85/7ft. A tree at Lythe Hill Park near Haslemere, Surrey, has a very superior stem, without a branch for 15ft, and is 75/7ft. Not far across the Sussex border, an early specimen, planted in 1870 in Cowdray Park, Midhurst, is 92/9ft.

THREAD-BRANCH (SAWARA) CYPRESS 'Filifera'

This depressed looking, dull tree, one of the 1861 incomers, is in many gardens, without adding much to their charm. It dangles exceedingly dull matt dark green strings of foliage, as its name in America 'String Cypress' suggests. It is more prone than its siblings to layer its branches in a circle, even when not in Ireland. Parts of the crown sometimes revert to the type foliage. Only the interest of two original specimens raised in 1861 by Veitch from his first import, allow an entry in these pages. One was 60/8ft at Golden Grove, Carmarthen, in 1982. The other is at Lower

Coombe Royal at Kingsbridge, Devon, 80/8ft in 1988. Both gardens have 1861 specimens of other forms of Sawara. Another big and possibly original tree is at Minterne in Dorset, 82/8ft with a forking stem. Longleat in Wiltshire and Trelissick in Cornwall also have trees of this size.

PLUME (SAWARA) CYPRESS 'Plumosa'

This and its golden form (below) are the most frequent of these Sawara Cypresses, and are a great stand-by in little town parks with poor soil, small beds and polluted air. They are the coniferous equivalents of the Spotted Laurel, *Aucuba*, in their resistance to the fumes of Jeyes Fluid, to judge from their use around toilets. They are of inestimable value to small birds in parks and gardens in providing year-round cover of the right density for nesting and roosting. The green form at Golden Grove, from Veitch's 1861 import was planted in 1863 and was 62/9ft in 1982. One the same size is on the terrace at Buxted Park Hotel in Sussex and has seven feet of trunk before it forks. It survived the gales into 1991. The only one bigger is at Hafodunas, Clwyd, which is 56/10ft but taller trees are an 1870 planting at Cowdray Park, 77/8ft and one below the old house at Leonardslee, Sussex, which is 75/6ft.

GOLDEN PLUMOSE (SAWARA) CYPRESS 'Plumosa Aurea'

Exactly like the green form in origin and date, this tends to fade to the same colour. Some specimens need a good ray of sunshine for a decision to be made. A partially reverted tree with type foliage in the upper crown is 56/8ft at Whiteways, near Exeter. A big one in the Pepperpot Garden at Powerscourt, County Wicklow, is 72/8ft and at Kilmacurra in the same county, one is 66/8ft. The tallest is at Strone House, Argyll, 82/6ft.

MOSS (SAWARA) CYPRESS 'Squarrosa'

The Americans use this name for the very distinctive form common in this country but bigger in the USA. Its crown is a bright fluffy blue and very dense. The trunk usually forks at six feet but the best specimens are single to the tip. The bark is red-brown, often quite bright chestnut, a distinct difference from that of the other forms. This is the tree that Siebold took to Java and which came to Britain in 1843, eighteen years before all the other forms. Nonetheless, the 1863 trees at Lower Coombe Royal and at Golden Grove are the earliest plantings identified. The former is 75/10ft and the latter 54/8ft. The Pepperpot Garden at Powerscourt has three fine specimens in an open group, the best two are 82/8ft and 75/9ft. One planted in the ravine at Bodnant in 1890 is 66/8ft and one at Blairhoyle, Menteith, Perthshire, is 72/8ft. At Endsleigh Lodge in Devon one by the Coach Drive is 52/9ft and the best trunk is at Kitlands, Leith Hill, Surrey, where a tree at 56/8ft is unbranched for 35ft.

JAPANESE RED CEDAR

Cryptomeria japonica

The Japanese Red Cedar is not a true cedar, but one of the far-flung representatives of the old Redwood family. Originally of the old continent, Gondwanaland, it drifted north with the break up of that land-mass. It is the Asiatic equivalent of the Giant Sequoia and is far more like it than any other of the redwoods. It is, in a somewhat reduced form, also the Asiatic version in the great height, girth and age that it can achieve, reputed to be 280ft tall and 70ft round, but none is recorded over 400 years old.

The history of the tree in cultivation is complicated by there being three forms. The typical Japanese form was noted in 1692 by Kaempfer, but not introduced until 1879 by Maries. The Chinese form, var. *fortunei*, was discovered in 1701 by James Cunningham and introduced from Chusan Island in 1842 by Captain Sir Everard Hume. Fortune sent it in quantity in 1844 from Chekiang. The distinctive Japanese variant, 'Lobbii', had been grown for some years at Buitenzorg (Jakarta) Botanic Garden when it was brought to Britain by William Lobb in 1853. So the oldest trees in Britain are all var. *fortunei*, known by its open foliage of long, slender, drooping shoots, or 'Lobbi' with its densely tufted crown of short, rising shoots.

Like the other conifers from Japan, especially those from the interior mountains, *Cryptomeria* revels in a high, year-round rainfall. It shows this by its best growth and specimens being confined to the far west and the cool, moist north of Britain, notably in Cornwall, Ireland, North Wales and Perthshire. Unlike most of the others, it can make a rapid start and go on to being a moderately big tree in the drier eastern regions. At Bedgebury Pinetum in Kent, for example, a group of three on the highest ground, planted in 1925, were 75/8ft in 1980 and their smooth, orange-red trunks like columns were an inspiring sight. A great spotted woodpecker, finding the timber very soft, severely upset the superintendent, Mr Westall, by drilling out a neat but prominent nest-hole in the best of them. In 1990 one of the trees was blown down, but the biggest, with its hole, is 82/8ft, but now growing much more slowly.

Japanese Cedar (*Cryptomeria japonica*): leaves and cones in May

Fota Garden near Cork has the best set of big trees and one of them nearly ended my visit there in 1966. Tony Hanan, then in the Irish Forestry Service, and I had been told of some of the idiosyncrasies of the delightful owner, the tiny and formidable Mrs Dorothy 'Dotty' Bell. Before taking visitors round she would make them pass an examination, all unaware that it was one, to see if it would be a waste of her time. Having satisfied herself that it was worthwhile, she took them on her fixed route, the visitor abiding by the strict rules. We apparently were passed as fit and were being shown the best trees in the correct sequence when Tony had a lapse of memory as we were headed towards an *Oxydendrum*. He cried out, 'What a superb stem of *Cryptomeria* over there.' Mrs Bell stopped short, faced him and said 'Young man. You do not see that tree from here. You see it when I show it to you'. It was one of the two best of the seven dating from 1847–52, an 1847 tree, now 115/15ft. The other is an 1852 tree, 105/15ft. Both have long, clean columnar trunks.

Pencarrow, Cornwall, has an 1845 tree and one from 1848, very *fortunei*, and both 80/11ft. A magnificent tree above the gate at Monk Coniston, Cumbria, is 108/18ft but less obviously the Chinese form. It has grown so much since 1957 when it was 14ft round that it could be the Japanese form from after 1879. One at The Gliffaes near Brecon is as big, 72/18ft but with a much shorter good bole and very heavy branching. This is plainly a Chinese tree. An even bigger one, at 88/19ft, is at Kilmory Castle, Argyll, but the bole is composed of four trunks which diverge well above five feet. One at Seaford, County Down, is 95/15ft measured across a branch-scar. A very rough veteran in Taymouth Castle Gardens by Loch Tay is 95/14ft, and a better one is 108/12ft. One at the top of the bank of the old pinetum at Tregothnan, Truro, is a little battered and 95/17ft. A line of ten very broad, heavily branched Chinese form trees by the Dolphin Pool at Powerscourt was planted in 1860. The best trees are now 88ft tall and 72/13ft. A handsome tree in the ravine at Bodnant dates from 1877 and is 105/12ft.

The tallest *Cryptomeria* is a tree of the form 'Lobbii' and so is the second biggest trunk. This is unexpected because not many old specimens have been found, and the original William Lobb tree of 1853 planting, by the lake at Dropmore, is a puny, although shapely 92/7ft. The tall tree is in the bank of enormous trees known as 'Georgia' at Endsleigh Lodge. It has a persistent straight stem to the top or near it, and is 135/10ft, and will date from near 1860. The outsize trunk is at Bocconoc in Cornwall, in the pinetum. It was excelled in girth by only one *Cryptomeria* of any form in 1928, when it was 82/13ft and has maintained quite rapid growth to date, to be 90/18ft with a great, branchy crown. One of the other of the few big trees is at Woodstock, County Kilkenny, which was planted in 1857 and is 92/13ft. A similar, but undated tree, is at Tregrehan, 102/13ft.

At Westonbirt Arboretum, the woodland on the inside of Circular Drive not far from the entrance, is dominated by the tufty but slender spires of seven tall 'Lobbii' which make a unique view from the Drive. All the trees are close to 95/8ft, and two more nearly as big, stand by Loop Walk a few hundred yards to the northeast. These are original cuttings from Veitch's Nursery of Lobb's 1853 import.

CHINESE FIR

Cunninghamia lanceolata (plate 2)

This tree appears to be a newly decorated Monkey-puzzle, polished up and re-painted, with bright green, glossy leaves marked below with silver bands, and orange-brown interior dead foliage, together with a bark of bright chestnut red. And the last feature is a clue, for it is an aberrant redwood. Nearly all the redwood family are aberrant, because they are the scattered remnants of a once worldwide group and any linking species that there once were are no longer there. The one feature common to the survivors is the fibrous, ridged red bark, clearly separating them from the Monkey-puzzle with their close, hard, dark grey bark fissured into squarish blocks.

The two *Cunninghamia*, the Formosan one hardly differing from the one on mainland China, have a few peculiarities of their own. They coppice easily and their stems show remarkably little taper between the rather sparse whorls of branches, but drop their diameter at each whorl. They seem to be a series of cylinders standing in a column, each one a little smaller than the one on which it stands. Their flowering is often decidedly wayward as some trees break the cardinal rule of the separation of the sexes in the Coniferae. They have terminal female cones closely surrounded at the base by rings of male flowers. The cone is like the other redwoods incommensurate with the grandeur of the tree, and, like most, in being fragile and not ornamental.

Although coming from Taiwan and south China where summers are warm and wet and winters are mild, the indications are that these trees are hardier than was at first thought. In 1925, W. Dallimore divided the 20 trees he had for planting at Bedgebury Pinetum, notorious for its summer frosts and hard winters, into two groups. He planted some at the top of the highest of the ridges with very good air-drainage as an insurance against complete loss of those planted in better soil and some sheltered in a valley down near the lake, where air-drainage is poor. All the trees in both groups survived and grew well, but most of them in each group were grazed down by rabbits on their first night out, and had to use their power of coppicing to become the 65ft trees they are now.

The most venerable specimen is in Claremont garden at Esher which was planted in 1819. It is almost certainly an original tree from the seed collected by William Kerr at Canton in 1804 and grown in a pot under glass for years. The next recorded import was sent in 1844 by Robert Fortune. The Claremont tree, on the edge of a shrubbery near the lake, has grown very little in the last 20 years and is now 70/7ft with a broad, low crown, but healthy. The only other pre-Fortune tree known is less robust and seems likely soon to follow its mate which was in such poor shape that it was cut down in 1906, and showing 63 annual rings. If that was precisely correct, the tree will have been planted, or at least raised, by 1843. The survivor, on the edge of the Chapel Garden at Killerton, was gaunt and narrow-crowned, 92/8ft in 1992.

The fine tree at Pencarrow, Bodmin, is currently the biggest in Great Britain and is almost certainly from Fortune's seed, planted out in 1850. It is 88/9ft, and was 40/4ft 8in in 1905. Ireland has the only one bigger, at Mount Usher. One of a pair planted side by side in about 1880, it is 88/9ft 7in and has grown markedly faster than the Pencarrow tree, for it was 35/2ft 3in in 1903. Another in County Wicklow has, however, grown much more slowly. At Kilmacurragh, it was 25/1ft in 1903 and is now only 52/6ft 8in. Two other big ones in England are one at Glendurgan 65/8ft, and the other at Tregrehan, 65/9ft, both in Cornwall. The best clear bole is at Oakley Park, Ludlow, which was 70/6ft in 1978.

It seems that high summer rainfall is more important than high summer temperature. There are no trees of note in East Anglia or in the northeast. Two big trees show a compromise between heat and high rainfall. In Sussex there is a remarkably broad-crowned tree at Holmbush near Horsham, dying back a little at the top, but 52/8ft, and at Tottenham House in Savernake Forest, a forked tree is 52/9 + 6ft.

ARIZONA BLUE CYPRESS

Cupressus arizonica var. *glabra*

This beautiful tree has so many features that make it ideal for small and medium-sized gardens that the wonder is that there are any without it. For a start, it is bright dove-grey blue, a colour that sells young conifers as well as any. Then, while exceedingly robust, it grows only to a moderate size and is never rampant. It is also strikingly shapely at all ages (yet to be seen here), beginning as a slim conic-columnar erect-branched tree and growing to be only a little broader, swelling out to a tall ovoid with a regular and smooth outline. At its biggest it is still a trim egg shape. Then it has highly decorative bark, very rare among conifers. It is smooth and dark red until it begins to flake to leave cream patches which mature to red-brown before flaking again. By now the background bark is purplish red-brown and the pale mottling stands out until eventually there is much grey on spiralling ridges. From June onwards the blue-grey foliage is closely freckled with pale yellow male flowers, which remain until the next April before shedding pollen.

But that is not all. This paragon of a tree is also imperturbably hardy, never seen to scorch in the most severe winters. It is unaccountably rare in Scotland, but a fine tree at Drum Castle inland from Aberdeen shows that it is not the cold that causes

Arizona Blue Cypress *(Cupressus arizonica* var. *glabra)*: ideal for small and medium-sized gardens

this. More likely it is the lack of sunshine and heat in the west. Above all, this tree is utterly indifferent to the niceties of soil types, from clay to light sand and it thrives equally in ferociously acid peaty sand, in chalky soil and on pure limestone.

It is to its credit that it can grow at all in British summers, for its native stands are by streams in the mountains of Arizona where summers are long, hot and dry. Like the other cypresses from the southwestern USA, its shape there differs from the upswept ovoid or columnar seen here. The native trees, seen in Oak Creek Canyon, south of Phoenix, and those planted in hedges in Merced, California, have long, very level, rather slender lower branches curved up near their tips, and an upper crown of an abrupt, slender spire of very short, level shoots. This makes a broad based cone tapering sharply towards the top.

The type tree was introduced in 1888 but is rare. It has dull grey, spirally ridged bark like a willow, and usually nearly green foliage, with very few white resin spots. The form *glabra* was distinguished in 1907. A superior form with thicker shoots, bluer, and heavily sprinkled with white spots, was selected at Hillier's Nursery in 1928. Its branch-tips turn upwards in turrets, and, named 'Pyramidalis', it is steadily replacing straight *glabra* in plantings today.

Since all Arizona Blue Cypresses are uniformly excellent, the only criterion for mention can be that of size. The biggest in girth is tree 3209 at Birr Castle, in the Extension, behind the Water Garden. Planted in 1927 it is 75/7ft. The tallest is at Wisley RHS Gardens, on the south edge of the path into the pinetum. It is a slightly loose, open-crowned tree, 85/5ft. A better tree, of classic shape and pretty bark, is in the northern half of the pinetum, at 66/6ft. Two trees at Powerscourt, below the Dolphin Pool, are 56/6ft and 62/5ft. A classic shaped tree at Leighton Hall, Welshpool, is

60/6ft and has the distinction of being the parent of x *Cupressocyparis notabilis*, the Alice Holt Cypress, picked from it in 1956.

At Westonbirt House a fine tree in the lower garden is 72/6ft. One planted in 1927 at Bodnant is 75/4ft, and a slender, tall tree in The Dell, Victoria Park, Bath, is 72/6ft. In the same city, one by a gate into Henrietta Park is 70/4ft. A broader tree is prominent in Cheltenham by a crossroads, and in the College grounds. It is 56/7ft, similar to that in the Botanic Garden part of Roath Park in Cardiff, which is 46/6ft. In Scotland, the tree in the Royal Botanic Garden, Edinburgh, is 56/4ft.

'Pyramidalis' has not been around long enough to have reached these sizes, but its denser crown seems to build up the bole more quickly. At Mount Usher, down among the tall Eucalypts, there is one 56/6ft, and the one mentioned above at Drum Castle, Aberdeenshire, is 40/6ft at four feet. An excellent tree in the Pepperpot Garden at Powerscourt is 66/5ft and one in the City of Westminster Cemetery in Acton, 44/5ft, shows that the tree can shrug off urban air, too, as does the tree, 50/5ft, in Bute Park in Cardiff.

MONTEREY CYPRESS

Cupressus macrocarpa

The two trees which dominate coastal landscapes in Devon, Cornwall and many parts of the far west, are not the native species that they would seem to be but are emphatically exotic. They are two of the select group of 'Monterey trees' which on their return migration from Mexico after the Ice Ages went by an extreme western route along the coast and were trapped on the Monterey peninsula by the erosion of the coast to the north. An inland diversion had become too dry and hot for them, and as the climate they were aiming to follow moved north some 700 miles to the Puget and Vancouver Island areas, they had to brave it around Monterey. They do not like it there and the native stands of Monterey Pine and Monterey Cypress are stunted and small, while both trees grow with startling vigour anywhere around the Irish Sea, and in fifty years are bigger, and much more shapely than any native trees twice their age.

The Monterey Cypress is the more extreme case. It has two tiny native stands: one of a few hundred acres on low conglomerate cliffs at Point Lobos, the other across Carmel Bay by Cypress Point with Crocker's Grove and extending for some miles south in private gardens. A few young trees spreading the colony to the carpark at Point Lobos are the most bizarre shapes. Their crowns are about six snaky, rope-like stems closely wreathed in dense foliage, rising and twisting out. The old trees are wind-battered, contorted 30ft bushes with pale grey bark on thick, twisting trunks. Sixty miles north, in San Francisco, planted trees are like our Cedar of Lebanon with upright branches spreading layers of flat-topped crown. Another

600 miles north, on Vancouver Island, the trees are narrowly conic with spire tops. That is the shape grown in eastern England, where young trees rise rapidly as strictly erect-branched narrow columns with conic tops. In Ireland and western Britain generally they send out long branches somewhat raised and are soon immense, broad, branchy trees, some with a single stem persisting high in the crown.

The introduction of this tree was unusual. An envelope of cones was found on a desk at Kew in 1838, with no explanation. The seeds sown yielded many plants and although Douglas had seen Monterey Cypress in 1832 and it had been described by D. Don, the cones and plants could not be positively assigned to that species. They were named *Cupressus lambertiana* after the conifer specialist at Kew. Many plants must have been sent out under that name, mainly to Devon and Cornwall, for old trees on many estates there were long labelled or recorded under it. The first documented introduction was in 1846 from Theodore Hartweg. In 1851 William Lobb sent more.

The tree is invaluable as an outer defence against sea winds along western coasts. In broad belts, its spreading and very imperfect shape matter little, and its occasional vulnerability to gales and loss of big branches in wet snow are unimportant. It is surprisingly common by the east coast of England, where it makes a slender tree, and also in village and town gardens far inland. The Monterey Cypress was popular for garden hedges before Leyland Cypress took over, since its habit of losing lower

Monterey Cypress (*Cupressus macrocarpa*): Bideford, Devon

59

foliage and its being scorched by sustained freezing easterly winds, are failings signally absent in the Leyland.

Where this tree grows best, it extends big branches from near, sometimes at, and occasionally below ground-level, and all along the trunk. The existence of clear smooth lower lengths depends on very early pruning or the tree emerging from surrounding shrubs. Several of the biggest have been pruned relatively late in life and their boles are crowded with the big swellings at the origins of the stubs. They can be measured easily, if without great precision, and are better to look at as trees than the vast overgrown bushes. Before it was blown down in 1990, the biggest yet found was near Bideford, Devon, and 132/32ft. An immense size for less than 150 years growth, but extremely rough with numerous branches rising strongly from low on the trunk.

The great tree at Montacute House, Somerset, has a much less heavily snagged bole from judicious pruning some 30 years ago and is quite respectable now at 120/25ft with a shapely nearly ovoid crown. The only one bigger and measurable at five feet is at Johnstown Castle, Wexford, and has not been pruned at all, but is easily taped among the branches, avoiding them all. It has a broad but fairly regular crown held on rising branches and is 132/26ft. Next to it stands an unrepentant bush, 118/31ft measurable only at three feet with difficulty.

The outright champion bush is at Powerscourt near the dam. It was planted as recently as 1898 and is 95/39ft if the tape be taken round the outside of the basal branches, at ground-level. There is space, however, to take it, still at ground level, inside a number of these branches and that gives a reading of 31ft. On the same estate, in the Dargle Glen, two trees have seven feet of fine clear bole, from growing among dense cherry-laurel. One, 105/25ft, is slightly marred by incipient forking from ground-level, the other is a grand tree at 111/22ft. A similar tree with a smooth, cylindric basal seven feet at Drum Manor, County Tyrone, is 108/21ft.

Among those trees pruned early enough to have smoothed over the scars, an unusually urban one in Fisher Street, Paignton is clear for nine feet and 92/20ft. A superb tree at Adare Manor, County Limerick, is clear for 16ft, and is 70/23ft. In Northern Ireland, in County Down, there are two most impressive clear boles; at Finebrogue, 85/21ft, and on the lawn at Ballywalter, 105/22ft. At Birr Castle, County Offaly, the tree in the River Garden has 15ft clear and is 102/19ft. At Torloisk, on Mull, the tree in the little arboretum has a clear bole for seven feet and is 115/20ft. At Melbury, in Dorset, on Chapel Bank a tree with a less clean trunk is 130/20ft.

At Strete Ralegh House, near Exeter, one tree on the lawn is 118/24ft measurable on a good bole, among low branches, while next to it is one of the bush kind 118/33ft at one foot. Others of this form are a huge tree at Bodorgan on Anglesey, 120/23ft at six feet; one in Kilmacurragh, County Wicklow, hemmed in but broad and 105/27ft at three feet; one near the house at Tregrehan, Cornwall, 105/26ft, and a real bush at Emo Court, Leix, 115/31ft at ground level.

MEDITERRANEAN CYPRESS

Cupressus sempervirens

The name 'Mediterranean Cypress' is preferable to 'Italian Cypress' as the populations believed to be truly wild range from Greece and the Greek Islands, through Crete and Cyprus to the Levant, Asia Minor, Iran and the Elburz Mountains, but not westward to Italy. It was introduced to Tuscany at an early date, and is planted also to the east of its range through India. The woods, believed to be wild, are of broad trees with widely spread branches, but most of the extended range is of the more familiar strictly erect, narrowly spire-like form, which breeds true. Interestingly, but arguably, the type on which the name is founded was of this form which Linnaeus described and named in 1753 from a tree in Tuscany, as *Cupressus sempervirens*. It then became necessary to distinguish the wild type as var. *horizontalis*, from Miller in 1768. Current taxonomy, however, insists that it is *C. sempervirens* var. *sempervirens*.

The Mediterranean Cypress was introduced some time in the Middle Ages well before its first mention by Turner in 1548. It was widely planted by then and was an important element in garden design when Gerard wrote his *Herbal* in 1597. It was valued for its ability to take close clipping as topiary in formal designs and as

Mediterranean Cypress (*Cupressus sempervirens*): introduced in the Middle Ages

a hedge, and also for variously shaped columns at corners and ends of hedges. It was strongly advocated by John Evelyn in 1670, who said it was thriving in gardens everywhere. It was the only known conifer of columnar growth before those from western North America were introduced after 1850 so it could have had 300 years of unrivalled popularity were it not for the climate. There had been no mention of its growth in the north but evidently it was well suited to much of England, until Evelyn noted that the severe winter of 1683–4 was damaging nearly all the trees and killing many. That must have deterred planters for a long time, and Evelyn changed his recommendation to the Yew. Lancelot Brown was not interested in planting parterres or topiary gardens, but had there been a hardy conifer of columnar growth known to him he might well have made clumps on knolls of this cypress. In 1770 it was probably still unsafe to plant it, and Brown used Cedar of Lebanon.

Today there seems to be no restriction to southern parts. The very severe winter of 1962 had no visible effect on the trees around Edinburgh; a healthy tree at Tulloch, Easter Ross, is 42/3ft and one at Innes House, Morayshire, is 33/2ft. A fine, if rather bushy tree, at Biel, East Lothian, is 56/9½ft at two feet. One near the house at Howick, Northumberland, is 46/5½ft. The oldest was planted in 1814 at Fota Garden near Cork and was 82/8½ft in 1984. One dating from 1875 at Orton Hall, Huntingdon, was 46/10ft at two feet in 1983. Singleton Abbey, near Swansea has several good, tall trees to 75/7½ft.

Lord Selborne collected cones from trees at Scutari in Greece in 1884 and sent them to Blackmoor, Hampshire, where his father kept them 11 years before sowing them. He raised many plants which, in the fashion then, were planted against the pilasters of the house, where one was 72/3½ft in 1982. A tree in the open at Mamhead House near Exeter is 50/6ft. One of several along the Statue Walk at Kilruddery House in County Wicklow is 56/6ft. At Tan-y-Bwlch in Gwynedd a tree by the steps is 52/9ft at two feet. Although all of these are of the type, columnar form, none is a notable, slender, tapering spire. A fine pair of that kind, 70ft tall at Nymans, and a few more in Sussex, were lost in the gales of 1987 and 1990, and the best now are in Ireland. A small line was planted in 1912 at Powerscourt in County Wicklow in front of the Pepperpot tower. The best is exceedingly slender and is 77ft tall. Another is by the Upper Walk in Birr Demesne, County Offaly, at 62/2ft. A splendid pair at the gate to Bristol Zoo in Avon, owe their dense and perfect symmetry to being regularly clipped. A selected cultivar, 'Green Pencil' in the Scree Garden at the Hillier Arboretum, Hampshire, is 42/2ft. In Surrey, seedlings from cones brought from Italy grow rapidly into slender columns, adding nearly three feet annually for several years. North Somerset has frequent sizable trees in roadside gardens.

LEYLAND CYPRESS

x *Cupressocyparis leylandii*

It can be said that garden design in Britain is largely a matter of where the Lawson Cypress cultivars are placed. They give the form, background and colour features. But for the big features, shelter and screens, Leyland Cypress forms have become the essential plants. Their ability to outgrow almost any plant on almost any soil in almost any situation makes them invaluable in the making of a new garden, defining the area, giving vital shelter and occasional single specimens or groups with extraordinary rapidity. Moreover, they are the favourite roost and nesting site for many garden birds, and can make instant hedges of great density.

In short, the arrival of the Leyland Cypress is a horticultural event on a par with the invention of the spade. The story of its origins is unavoidably complex and includes several intriguing mysteries. It may be taken as beginning in 1926 when an American botanist stayed the night at Leighton Hall near Welshpool on his way to a botanical meeting in Chester. On his evening stroll, he saw a cypress which puzzled him, as he knew the diverse species of the southwestern States, and it was not one of those or any other he had seen. He took shoots to the meeting and showed them to William Dallimore, the Kew specialist on conifers, who was there. Dallimore wrote to Leighton Hall for details and was told that this tree was raised in 1911 from Monterey Cypress seeds and that six other peculiar cypresses had been raised in 1888 and had been taken to the other home of the Leyland-Naylor family at Haggerston Castle in Northumberland in 1892. Dallimore was sent shoots from two of these, which had been raised from a Nootka Cypress.

He was fortunate that the two samples of the six Nootka offspring included what we know as tree '5', for this one alone is almost exactly like the Leighton tree, from a Monterey Cypress, which was the one he had been brought. Where the other five at Haggerston have fine ultimate divisions of foliage, well parted and spraying out at all angles, tree '5' and the Leighton tree (now 'Leighton Green') have broad ultimate divisions closely set and arranged in sprays flat each side of the shoot, like the frond of a fern and like the Nootka Cypress. They also bear numerous cones and male flowers where the others very rarely bear any.

From this somewhat lucky chance, Dallimore was confronted with two apparently identical foliages, one from a Nootka seedling and one from a Monterey seedling. Therefore the trees were hybrid progenies, the cross between these species. The description and drawings were made and the hybrid Leyland Cypress was established, and named after C. J. Leyland (born Naylor) who picked the 1888 seed. At Leighton Hall it was seen that the Nootka Cypress in the garden had a Monterey Cypress nearby and the Monterey Cypress that yielded the 1911 seed, the tree by the Henhouse, had several Nootka Cypresses nearby. Oddly, though, the drawing made has the foliage of the other Haggerston tree that Dallimore received, but there are many cones on it, which must surely have belonged to one of the other two.

So that establishes the first two origins, reciprocal crosses, in 1888 and 1911. Both arose at Leighton Hall, and nowhere else had been known to have yielded another until 1940, 52 years later, which is odd. But Castlewellan grows two cuttings made in 1949 deriving ultimately from a tree at Rostrevor, which, I am told by the grandson of one who knew it, was 'a huge tree when it was blown down' in or before 1914. I had taken the cuttings to be 'Leighton Green' which is the common clone in Ireland generally, but was told that I was wrong. I see it now, and can identify small plants as 'Rostrevor', distinct from 'Leighton Green'. That means that, despite very rapid growth in County Down, this was of independent origin at least 30 years before 1914, possibly more. 'Rostrevor' is thus almost certainly the first clone to arise. And that leads to the first mystery – both parent trees must have been flowering there, or elsewhere, by 1880 and probably before. But few if any gardens in Ireland had either species before 1850 and flowers are rare on Monterey Cypresses in their first 30 years.

The first cuttings from the Haggerston trees were three from one. They were planted in Kyloe Woods nearby in 1897. From there, several estates received trees before the hybrid was named. At Bicton, I unearthed a cast-iron label saying 'Cupressus ignotus' under the 1916 tree on the dam. In 1966 there were four trees at Headfort, County Meath, which from their size and the history of the mass planting in a few days there, date from 1915. Two remained by 1980. The Duke of Argyll probably received one at about that time, judging by the size of the tree at Inveraray Castle, by Frews Bridge, it was 105/11ft in 1982 but was blown down in 1985.

The first general distribution started in 1927 when Dallimore sent cuttings he had rooted from his specimen shoots to several important gardens. At Bedgebury, Wakehurst Place, the Royal Botanic Garden, Edinburgh and Wisley both 'Leighton Green' and a Haggerston clone were received, but at Kew there were only Haggerston trees. Since these were not distinguished until 1961, this was a matter of luck. The pair at Wisley were instructive before they were blown down in 1987. On the same poor, very sandy, acid soil, the Haggerston tree when 54 years old was 98/7ft 10in, when the 'Leighton Green' tree was 92/9ft 3in and went on to be 10ft 6in round when it was 60 years old.

The second 1911 tree at Leighton Hall was planted up in Park Wood and came into cultivation only when it was blown down in 1954 when it was 90/6ft. Cuttings were taken and the foliage was found to be finely divided, very irregularly bunched, like its maternal parent, Monterey Cypress, but pale and dark blue-grey. It was therefore named 'Naylor's Blue'. It has been sent since 1960 to several gardens but it remains quite rare.

In sum, there were nine clones known before 1940, one from Rostrevor and eight arising at Leighton Hall, six of them sent to Haggerston Castle and two planted at

Leyland Cypress (x *Cupressocyparis leylandii*): planted in 1927

Leighton. There are today six big Leylands in the gardens at Leighton and in 1961 I was able to show that these were one cutting each from the Haggerston trees, and confirmed with Mr Naylor that they had been sent as a birthday present in 1927, from Haggerston.

Another remains a complete mystery. In 1985, I saw a very big Leyland Cypress in the garden of the old vicarage at Clun in Shropshire. Having found it was 85/9ft 3in I pulled down some foliage. The tree had seemed a standard sort of 'Haggerston 2' but it is not. It has fine, hard, rather distant foliage, distinct in being dark blue-grey. It is now 'Clun Vicarage' of unknown origin, presumably arising around 1930 at the latest. The mystery was deepened when I was shown the foliage of two quite young trees felled at Kew as victims of Coryneum fungus. They were assuredly 'Clun Vicarage'. So is a 35ft tree at Leonardslee, which, unnoticed by Robin Loder, grows where, he says, no one would have planted it with his father's knowledge, on the bank of an old bonfire pit in the garden.

Until 1940 none other seems, at present, to have arisen. In 1940 seed of western American trees could not be had from imports, so Mons. Barthelemy, a Belgian nurseryman at Stapehill, Dorset, collected cones from a Monterey Cypress in a front garden, a mile from his nursery. Two of the seedlings were not Monterey Cypress and were planted in the nursery as stock plants. Shoots from the more shapely one were grafted on to Monterey Cypress seedlings and sold, mainly along the south coast. Barthelemy could find no Nootka Cypresses in Stapehill, and neither could I, but the trees are Leyland Cypresses. The one sold, 'Stapehill 20', is very distinct. It has a moth-eaten look in the hand, for every minor spray has its inner shoots cut short as if eaten, and from afar the tree is at once recognisable by its thin, bright outer foliage and the inner foliage turning brown and then being shed. So the crown is open but twiggy. The foliage is otherwise of the 'Leighton Green' flat spray kind, but each scale projects to give it a knobbly, rough look and feel. The original tree, planted in 1941, was 52/5ft in 1984. Despite appearances, it can grow fast and one at Stowe School, by the shop, of unknown date, was 66/7ft in 1986.

The other tree, 'Stapehill 21', has better foliage, at first sight exactly 'Leighton Green', but it has more than faint signs of the moth, and of the roughness. The original was 52/6ft in 1984 and this greater vigour is shown in trials where it is either equal to or marginally ahead of 'Leighton Green'. At Alice Holt, in the trial plot planted in 1967, it was 50/5½ft when 25 years old. No older trees are known from this clone.

Three more clones arose in 1962 in Northern Ireland, and carry on the strange tradition of the province producing golden conifers. The snows of 1962–3 broke a branch from the big Golden Monterey Cypress at Castlewellan, County Down. The next tree is a slightly golden Nootka Cypress, 'Lutea', and Mr McKeown extracted seeds from the numerous cones. Two golden Leylands were raised. One, 'McKeownii', is not very gold and has poor growth, so that went no further. The other is the 'Castlewellan Gold' that is rife in suburbia. It was planted in the arboretum somewhat hidden and shaded, because it was to be registered under the Plants Variety Rights Act. But this did not deter raiders, and much of its early foliage went over the wall by night and turned up as 'Galway Gold', 'Mellow Yellow' and other names. It took a while to recover and is now 42/4ft and growing very fast.

In 1962 also, Mr Robinson, head gardener at Bangor Castle, County Down, noticed a little golden seedling that was revealed by clearance of a rhododendron jungle. He marked it with a stick and later put it in a cat-food tin and had it on his kitchen window-sill. Then he planted it on the little lawn outside and by 1982 it was 36/3ft and a splendid gold. It has foliage of the flat, frond kind like 'Leighton Green' and so is distinct from 'Castlewellan Gold', and is usually more consistently gold than the more gold-tipped green of that tree. Again, the male parent is a mystery as there is a Golden Monterey Cypress at Bangor, but no Nootka Cypress. 'Robinson's Gold' is in the trade, but only very recent plantings are seen.

And that is the total of independent origins known. Many cultivars have been raised from sported shoots of the commonly planted two. 'Silver Dust' was raised from 'Leighton Green' in the United States and has been planted here since 1977. It is, of course, a flat-sprayed tree, and has fairly large patches of off-white at random. On similar lines in colours is 'Harlequin' but that is a sport, found by the late Earl of Bradford in his Weston Park nursery in Staffordshire, from a hedge of 'Haggerston 2'. It has much bolder patches of bright white. Whole shoots arise without chlorophyll so they grow less than the green shoots and some fail, giving the plant a tendency to fork or to grow very strong lateral branches. The best golden Leyland is 'Golconda' which was a sport on a nursery hedge of the common Haggerston clone at Wyboston in Bedfordshire and has been grown since 1977 but only very lately beyond a few gardens.

Since the big trees are all of one of two clones, there is little to choose among the specimens beyond exceptional size or speed of growth. The only exceptions are the six clones of original 1888 origin at Haggerston Castle. The prominent one in the castle yard is 72/8ft but on West Lawn, one is 95/ft and the odd one out for foliage, clone '5' is 92/9ft and laden with cones.

The biggest is the original 'Leighton Green' planted in 1912 in the arboretum above the Leighton park house and now owned by the Royal Forestry Society. Having lost its top at least once it has re-grown to 111/12ft. In 1933, Hillier's Nurseries started to sell Leyland and their stock plant was evidently 'Leighton Green'. Trees of this date are the one in Sand Earth, Westonbirt, now 94/9ft and probably the clump by the drive to Westonbirt House, with one tree 92/8ft; the tree in Bethlehem Wood at Wakehurst Place, 88/9ft; the tree at Powerscourt County Wicklow in Pepperpot Valley now 80/10ft, and the one remaining after the 1987 gale in the 1935 planting in Gore's Wood, Borde Hill, Sussex, now 102/8ft. A cutting from one of these was planted at Heaseland, Haywards Heath, in 1965 and was 62/6ft when only 25 years old. One in the picnic area at Birr Castle, County Offaly, planted in 1960 was 75/6ft by 1989.

The tallest 'Haggerston 2' is one of the pre-Dallimore trees, received by Lord Clinton at Bicton, Devon, and planted in 1916. Planted in the shelterbelt for the Wilson collection, it is now 118/10ft but has not added to its height measurably for ten years. The other 1916 tree there is on the dam and is 115/9ft and has grown about ten feet in the last eight years. At Headfort, the larger of the two 1915 trees left by 1980 was 103/9ft. At Leighton Hall the very columnar tree planted beside the Hall in 1927 was 102/11ft in 1991 and is possibly Clone '1'. The best of the three in the triangle at Kew, planted in 1929 was 100/7ft in 1989. Of several trees of about this age at Wakehurst Place, one above the main pinetum is 111/7ft. A survivor in a short avenue planted at Bedgebury in 1935 is 85/9ft. At Alice Holt, one planted in 1958 by Station Ride by the Danish tree-breeding pioneer, Dr Syrach Larsen, is 70/6ft in 31 years. In the 1963 Pinetum at Anglesea Abbey, Cambridge, the specimen is 72/6ft, even in that low rainfall. And similarly in Essex, at Cracknells, one planted in 1975 was 40/3ft when 10 years old.

At Kyloe Wood, two of the 1892 triangle survive and are 111/10ft and 98/9½ft, while one near Bogle Cottage, probably planted in 1906, is 115/9ft. Another notable specimen of a Haggerston clone is at Sotterley Hall, Suffolk, planted in 1936 and 85/7½ft in 1985. Some big young specimens of 'Leighton Green' are: Thorp Perrow,

Yorkshire, planted 1940 and 85/8ft in 1991; Stowe Park garden, 95/7ft; Cefn Onn, Cardiff, near the gate, 80/7ft.

The best 'Naylor's Blue' are: RHS Gardens, Wisley, 66/4ft; A3 border, planted 1972, 52/4ft; Alice Holt Genetics Nursery, planted 1954, 75/5½ft in 1989 and Wakehurst Place, Golf Ground Extension, planted 1962, 65/5½ft in 1993.

MAIDENHAIR TREE: GINKGO

Ginkgo biloba (plate 2)

For oddity and eccentricity, the Ginkgo leaves all other starters at the post. It has not only many more peculiarities than any other tree, but each one is either unique or extraordinary. They embrace its basic botany and structure, its geological history, horticultural history, growth, variation in shape, and tolerance of some very harsh conditions.

As a good beginning, the Ginkgo is not a conifer, nor of course is it a broad-leaf. It is a gymnosperm all right, but entirely on its own, the only survivor of an order which dominated the Jurassic tree world. Its pollen does not grow a pollen-tube down the style, it produces motile sperms which swim to the ovary. The Ginkgo pre-dates the development of a system of veins with branching and a network; its broad, flat leaves are served by a fan of single veins, one or two splitting once, but none connecting with another vein.

Wild Ginkgos may still be found in the preserved woods around monasteries in south and southwest China, from Chekiang to Yunnan. But this is not universally agreed because they have been planted as far north as Korea for perhaps a thousand years . They were taken to Japan before that, and planted by temples. It was in Japan that Ginkgo was first seen by a westerner. Engelbert Kaempfer, a German physician, spent his two years with the Dutch East India Company incarcerated on Deshida Island from 1690. He saw it on one of the obligatory annual escorted expeditions from the little man-made mud island to Tokyo via Osaka to pay respects to the Emperor and the Mikado. His descriptions of plants was published in 1712. In about 1730 a ship left Nagasaki with Ginkgo seeds for Holland and by 1734 a tree was in the botanic garden at Utrecht, where it still is today.

The first tree in Britain was raised in 1754 in James Gordon's Mile End nursery from seed received with the Pagoda-tree and Chinese Thuja. It was sold to the Duke of Argyll for his garden at Whitton Place, Hounslow. When the Duke died in 1761 it was still possible to move his trees of Ginkgo and Pagoda-tree down river a few miles to Kew where the Botanic Garden was being established on 11 acres in the north-east part of the Palace Garden. Fearful about its hardiness, they planted it against the wall of a boiler-house. That was pulled down in 1861 and the tree has been free-standing ever since. Its early years may account for its bad shape as it divides at just above three feet where it is 14ft 4in round. It is 80ft tall.

The splendid good health of this 230 year old tree is part of the story of the species. It has no relatives at all, and it is some 30 million years since Ginkgos were growing in the London Basin. There is therefore no insect or other pest that recognises it as food, or will move across to it as a plant related to its normal host. Above ground there is nothing to trouble it. Below ground, however and alas, there is a fungus or two, including honey-fungus, that either has not itself changed in the interval, or is prepared to tackle anything. However, all the big old trees mentioned look to be in fine health.

A peculiarity in growth is that the terminal bud, even on a vigorous young tree, is very liable to open out a few leaves and not an inch of new shoot. It may be three years before normal extension is resumed. Lateral buds may grow rosettes and make spurs or send out long shoots. Progress upwards is erratic and unpredictable. The shape of the tree is much more of a gamble. Some trees grow into straight, regularly tapered poles with very few branches, often quite level and short. Others have become very big bushes and a few are the shape of a good oak tree. Some never seem to get started properly and become erect bundles of sticks. There is a marked tendency for the shapely slender-crowned trees to be female and the branchy ones, like the Kew original, to be male.

There are, however, two more peculiarities. First, in Britain, females often flower and fruit when less than 50 years old but males bearing catkins are nearly always about 150 years or more in age. It is not known if all females flower when young and if that were so, all big non-flowering trees would be male whatever their shape. If it is not so, some of them may be female. Second, in Pennsylvania, and particularly in Philadelphia, where Ginkgos line suburban streets, they say that only male trees can be used as these are tall and narrow, while females are low-branched and sprawling. To confirm this, they have one female tree, in the Morris Arboretum, which is exactly that. They do use the very strictly narrow 'Sentry Ginkgo' which is a male clone, but the general roadside trees are not 'Sentry' but seedlings, presumably selected by shape in the nursery lines, for there is no way known of sexing a ginkgo before it flowers. A female there in the street would block the traffic, yet in Britain females would be preferred. In New York to the north, Charleston to the south, and St Louis to the west big trees of both sexes stand side by side and are indistinguishable by crown shape.

Ginkgos in North America relish the long, hot summers and grow very much faster than they do in Britain. Many of the biggest have big low branches which reach out straight at a rising angle to a great distance, but some are rather upswept and goblet-shaped. In drier, hotter parts in the prairie states, round to southern California, they are sparsely branched and can be of bizarre shapes. They are the downtown tree par excellence almost everywhere and tolerate the canyons between skyscrapers, the heat and dust, and restricted and paved-over root-runs better than any other tree (except the Honeylocust, *Gleditsia*). In Britain the big trees are confined to the south of England and Wales, although there are some tall trees in North Wales. In Scotland, none is of any size and the four in the garden at Novar, Easter Ross, are erect, twiggy little trees less than 30ft tall. Ireland has two trees of very moderate size, a bushy 60/8ft at Kilmacurra and 80/7ft at Ashbourne House, County Cork.

The biggest bole is on a tree 75/15ft at Maesllwch, Powys, which is thought to have been planted, like the Whitfield House tree not far away in Herefordshire, in 1780. The latter is 65/14ft. Both are broad in the crown. The bigger of two fine trees at Blaize Castle near Bristol had, in 1903, a reputation for having come on the same ship from Japan as the trees at Kew and at the Bishop's Palace at Wells, but there is no evidence that the Kew tree came from Japan, rather than China. The tree is a good one, 80/13ft. In a private garden which was part of Claremont in Esher, a tree a little damaged by the 1987 gale is 88/14ft. At Peckover House, Wisbech, another damaged tree is 60/13ft. Cobham Hall School in Kent has two big trees side by side, both of the 'bushy oak-tree' form, 65/12ft and 62/10ft. A similar tree by the running track at Stowe School is 82/11ft. A very different form of tree, tall, with a long trunk, is 92/12ft at Carclew in Cornwall.

Three more oak-like trees with fine stout trunks are: 60/12ft at Ham Golf Course near Worthing; 80/12ft at Engelfield House, Berkshire, and 70/12ft at Antony House, Cornwall. Another is beside Corsham House in Wiltshire, 82/9ft. Beside Farnham Castle in Surrey, a tree 85/10ft forks some way up and its close stems, clothed only in short little branches, makes the tree resemble a tuning-fork. A tree in Candie Park on Guernsey is 70/10ft and one in the Pleasure Walk at Longleat House is 82/10ft.

Most of the tall specimens have a single stem persisting to the top, and sparse, raised lower and middle branches of fair length but only a few minor shoots from the long spire. They cast almost no shade and so can be the central point in a bed of annuals, as is the typical one in the Jephson Gardens, Leamington Spa. This is 87/6ft. Two like it are in a flower bed by the gate to the Botanic Garden at Bath, where the superior one is 85/6ft. One with rather bigger, strongly raised middle branches is beside a path and flower-beds in the Terrace Garden at Richmond, 90/9ft. The tallest is near the gate into Sezincote Garden in Gloucestershire and 98/6ft.

Some trees have adopted this sort of shape perhaps because they are to some extent shaded, being in a wooded valley. One of the eight trees at Abbotsbury, Dorset, is so placed and is 95/5ft. One at Tregrehan, Cornwall, is 95/7ft. By the Cascade bridge at Bodnant, Gwynedd, one is 85/6ft and one, more in the open, by the gate to the garden below Powis Castle is 88/6ft. More shaded again is one of a small group at Portmeirion, 85/6ft.

EUROPEAN LARCH

Larix decidua

The common European Larch is among the most valuable and decorative of all the trees we grow. Its early flush of brilliant green may have upset Wordsworth, but everyone else is content to admire it, with the bright pink 'larch roses' strung along the shoots which hang elegantly from upcurved branches, and the soft gold of its foliage late in autumn. Larches attract a variety of birds, crossbills feed on the seeds available to them from August while their staple diet of Scots Pine seeds is not yet ready; tits feed in summer on caterpillars and aphids and in the winter on aphid eggs; redpolls, siskins and bullfinches nest in plantation trees, and buzzards and ravens in the spreading tops of big old trees. The light, deciduous foliage allows the persistence or development of the pre-vernal herb layer so prized under oakwoods: bluebell, bugle, sanicle, wood-sorrel, and grasses, and their associated butterflies and other insects.

It is an exceedingly tough, light-demanding pioneer and mountain dweller, able to grow to over 110ft at nearly 2000ft in the Upper Dee Valley and parts of Morayshire and Banff. Plantations can be thrown or snapped in the most severe gales but resist normal winds well, while big, rugged old open-grown trees withstand anything. On well-drained soils of quite low fertility, young trees commonly grow shoots three feet long. Added to these merits, it yields top quality timber, as hard and strong as Douglas Fir, often with no knots, or very small ones for good straight lengths. It is the most prized conifer for boatskin wood, the aim of many forest estates in Scotland. Its great strength in big timbers made it the tree for the heavy beams needed in trawlers. It is a poor fuel, but who wants to burn a timber like that? It is highly durable in the ground or the air and is the traditional wood for fencing stobs on farms.

Although Parkinson in 1629 knew of a few trees 'grown by lovers of rarity', he had not seen it flower or cone. It seldom takes more than eight to ten years to flower, so the first trees will have arrived in around 1620. But it was the early larches in Scotland that attracted stories and legends the most. Although three trees are known to have been planted at Lee House in Lanark in 1683, brought from Venice by Lockhart of Lee, and a dozen in 1725 at Dawyck, Kailzie and Stobo, all near Peebles, it is the plantings of the Dukes of Atholl at Dunkeld and Blair Castle that dominate the field. The first larches at Dunkeld were two planted in 1727. Their early progress was very rapid. Warren Hastings noted them in 1787, but they were then lost and forgotten. The stage was taken by the Menzies larches. John Menzies of Culdars, now Meggernie Castle, in Glenlyon, brought from London in 1737 a hamper of larches for the second Duke of Atholl. He left a few at some of his resting places on the way, beginning with two at Wallington Hall, Northumberland, then six at Monzie Castle, Crieff, five at Dunkeld House, a dozen at Blair Castle, then had a few for himself. Stories arose of a plant here and a couple there inveigled or stolen from Menzies' hamper at many estates on the journey, at Dungarthill, Delvine and Dalguise, all near Dunkeld, and with big larches of reputed 1738 planting; Gask House, Keir Castle and Kippendavie, also in Perthshire, with Lude and Urrard Houses near Blair. It did not stop there, for larches of similar form and age further off route at Birkhill, Fifeshire and Kinloch House, Angus were assigned the hamper origin, and, much further north, two trees each at Gordon Castle, Moray and Belladrum Estate near Inverness.

Most of these larches are still standing and some have a big low branch curving sharply up about ten feet from the trunk. They are broad crowned and rugged, yet majestic trees, quite close copies of the remaining tree at Dunkeld Cathedral. The bigger of the two at Kinloch House is a splendid specimen and, in my view, the most likely of these off-route trees to be a Menzies tree.

The Dunkeld story became confused soon after 1800. The Duke had one cut down in 1789, apparently to demonstrate his authority over his forester who refused to do such a thing. Two more were cut for their timber in 1801, to make the gunboat 'Woolwich' and show the Admiralty the value of larch for shipbuilding. So only two remained. By 1812 these had been wrongly identified as the lost trees of 1727

European Larch (*Larix decidua*): The Whittern, Herefordshire

72

and then they were taken to be the origin of all the larches planted in the eighteenth century on Atholl Estates, and were dubbed the 'Parent Larches'. From bad to worse, they were said to be the first larches in Scotland, then the first in Britain. In 1832, the third duke published an authoritative account which set things right, but was known to few writers. From this report it is seen that as early as 1750 quantities of larch were bought from London nurseries, and that Menzies brought his hamper from London also, despite a score of accounts attributing his source to 'The Tyrol'. Unfortunately the Duke did not confirm the strong assumption that the magnificent trees on Kennel Bank, across the drive, were the first progeny of the 1738 Menzies Cathedral group, and planted in 1750.

Of the pre-Menzies 1737 trees, the best specimens today are 1725 trees at Dawyck, by the Dynamo House, 100/14ft and at Kailzie, 100/13ft, with a less good one at Stobo, 85/12ft. A tree by the entrance to Blair Drummond, Perthshire, 85/13ft is from a 1736 planting.

The known 1737 Menzies trees include the remaining 'Parent Larch' at Dunkeld Cathedral, now 105/18ft, its larger companion having been struck by lightning in 1899 and felled in 1906. At Monzie Castle, the best is the tree that has always been the biggest larch reported in any list and now probably the biggest in the world, for only one in the Italian Tyrol is about as big. The Monzie tree is 102/19ft with a smooth, clear bole for 20ft. At Blair Castle, the tree by Gunroom Bridge is 85/15ft with a dense, broad crown. At Blair Bridge one, leaning from a rocky perch, was blown down in 1989 and the better of the remaining pair is a superb, tall tree, 140/14ft dividing into several trunks about 40ft up. At Wallington Hall, the survivor of the pair was 105/14ft in 1958.

The best of the probable or possible Menzies trees are the very fine tree at Kinloch House, 105/16ft, and the more rugged tree by the drive at Gordon Castle, Fochabers, which is 100/18ft. A big spreading tree, forking at eight feet, at Birkhill, Fife, is 120/15ft and the better of two tall trees at Urrard House is 111/13ft. At Gask House, and at Keir Castle in Perthshire, there are broad, stocky trees, 95/14ft and 62/15ft respectively, and a good tree near the A85 outside Dundee, at Miln, is 70/15ft. Two fine trees with long straight trunks at Lude House, Blair Atholl, reputed to be of Menzies origin and planted in 1737, are 135/14½ft and 135/13½ft.

Two plantings of second generation Menzies trees include some outstanding trees. None more than Tree 6 in the 1750 Kennel Bank group referred to above. This is regarded as the finest quality long stem of conifer in Europe. From a faint curve near the base it rises 90ft smoothly rounded with little taper to its first branch. Then it spreads a level-branched crown above the beeches among which it grows. It is 132/11ft. Tree 3 nearby is similar, 130/11ft but of lesser quality and Tree 11 above is a rough tree, 130/14ft.

In 1780, 12 trees were planted at Ardvorlich on the south bank of Loch Earn. They were raised from Atholl trees but it is not known if the origin was the Cathedral group or whether they came from Blair Castle. All 12 are still there, six each side of the public road in an informal avenue. The third tree from the east on the south side is 130/16ft and the fifth is 140/13ft.

The pick of the monstrous or misshapen trees are the three biggest of the eight known 'pedestal' larches, and the layered larch at Kelburn Castle, Ayrshire. This last is 52/14ft and has several enormous branches curving down to root about 20ft from the bole and spreading far. The biggest pedestal larches seem to date from around 1740. A huge boss of twisted roots rises six or eight feet before abruptly narrowing to a perfectly normal but very big stem. The king of them all is at The Whittern in Herefordshire in which a tree 70/18ft surmounts at six feet a mass of spiralled roots 34ft round at five feet. A similar tree in a field near Pothill Farm, Auchterarder is 52/18ft six feet up on a boss 26ft round at five feet. One by Dunkeld House is 82/16ft at six feet up on a boss about 25ft round. At Nonsuch House, Bromham, Wiltshire, a pedestal larch 66/16ft on a small boss is beside a normal tree 80/17ft.

The tallest larch found so far is a beautiful tree in the deep glen at Glenlee Park, Newton Stewart, 150/10ft with 60ft clear and smooth. Very similar in size but not quite of the quality is a tree on Parkhatch Estate south of Godalming. It was planted in 1855 and is 148/10ft. A small group planted in 1769 at Linley Hall, Shropshire, is of good form with clean boles and one is a big tree at 135/12ft. At Crarae Garden, Argyll, a tree planted in 1800 by the burn, now 105/11ft, has 30ft of prime, smooth trunk.

A few outsize trunks remain for mention. The second biggest of all is at Foulis Castle, Easter Ross, 66/18ft, tapering sharply in the broad crown. At Innes House, Morayshire, a good tree is 65/17ft and by the drive at Yester House, Haddington, a broad low tree is 60/17ft. In Ireland the biggest are at Emo Court, Leix, 102/16ft dividing into four trunks at 15ft and looking very sick in 1992, and a spreading tree at Kilruddery Park, County Wicklow, 62/16ft. At Bonskeid near Tummel Bridge a tree just above the road is 111/16ft.

HYBRID LARCH

Larix x *eurolepis* (plate 3)

When the Duke of Atholl planted out his new Japanese Larches in 1887 at Dunkeld House he put one, together with two European Larches, in a hollow, isolated from other larches by beechwoods. This may have been to see if a hybrid could be raised. Seedlings in the Ladywell nursery at Dunkeld were selected in 1904 from the progeny of the 11 Japanese Larches in the crescent by the drive, and probably also of this tree. They stood out as taller and with pale shoots. Several were planted around the Atholl estates in 1905, at Ladywell, Inver and Blair Castle. When a wood at Bargrenach by the A9 at the top of the Atholl Estates was felled in 1955 it was found to contain many hybrid trees among the Japanese Larches. This wood had been planted in 1897, so the hybrid had arisen unnoticed in that year.

When it was seen that the Japanese Larch was a vigorous tree on soils too poor for the good growth of the European, and that it rarely suffered from canker, the idea of growing a hybrid between the two became attractive. The superior crown and timber quality of the European could be combined with the robust growth and health of the Japanese, and, moreover, there should be some hybrid vigour, heterosis.

Heterosis is exhibited only by the first generation cross, that is by trees whose parents are different species, the F_1, and is negligible or nil in the plants raised from a stand of hybrids, as these give offspring which are F_2 or second generation hybrid. Many first cross stands have been used in Scotland as sources of seed and some which yield good plants. This is because the parent stand often has a mixture of pure Japanese or European Larch due to difficulties in selecting only the true hybrids in a nursery. Hence some of the progeny from such a mixed stand will be backcrosses to one parent or the other and these are likely to be good trees.

First generation hybrid seed has been collected from a stand of the two species near the gate at Glamis Castle and a few other places, but, as in the Dunkeld drive trees, the proportion of hybrid trees is unpredictable and may be low. There was a need therefore for a more reliable source. Syrach Larsen at Hørsholm in Denmark pioneered grafted seed-orchards before 1940. In Britain, the Earl of Dundee was the first when in the 1950s he made plantings at Birkhill of alternate Japanese Larch and of European Larch selected from seedlings from the Great Wood at Cawdor.

The next stage in Britain was the creation of grafted seed-orchards by John Matthews of the Forestry Commission. In these, grafts made from the most vigorous and healthy trees with the straightest and least tapering stems that extensive countrywide surveys could find, were planted in various patterns to increase the chances of inter-pollination. By 1960 there were a dozen of these, using all the most promising trees known. Controlled pollinations gave progenies of known father and mother for trials, from which the performance of each tree was assessed for value as a good breeding tree, but this fascinating project was wound down when Sitka Spruce replaced almost all species and hybrid larch became of minor interest. The first cross progenies were a remarkable sight at the end of their season in their rows. Every plant in each lot was the union of the same two parents, a state of affairs almost never occurring in open-pollinated seedlots. They also had the uniformity that hyrbids should always show. Here then were lines of hundreds of two-year-old plants, all closely around three feet tall and all of the same shape and branching.

The first recorded original trees, by Gunroom Bridge at Blair Castle, are now 88/7ft and 80/10ft, the latter with long, level branches from about ten feet up on a massive clean bole. Similarly, the tree at Munches, Kircudbrightshire, of unknown origin is 92/10ft. The best in the line to Bishop's Walk, Dunkeld, are 98/8ft at the cathedral end and 132/7ft behind the Giant Sequoia. Near the bottom south corner of the pinetum at Strone House, Argyll, is another as tall at 132/8ft. At Dawyck near Peebles, two dating from 1910 are 85/8ft and 82/8ft and by the drive at Bonhard House, Perthshire, one is 75/9ft. A group of three in the Bog Garden at Coverwood, near Peaslake, Surrey was planted in 1910 and the best tree is 92/6ft. A broad tree among the oaks at Edinburgh Royal Botanic Gardens probably dates from 1912 and is 66/8ft. A 1916 tree in the Policies at Glamis Castle is 98/8ft.

The line along the Bishop's Walk, running west from the old Cathedral larch at Dunkeld, is an interesting mixture of very good hybrid and Japanese Larches. Boring a few stems showed that the first trees, at the eastern end were planted in 1900. It seems very probably that these were early progenies of the Japanese trees in the Avenue across the field, and that they were added to over the next few years.

JAPANESE LARCH

Larix kaempferi

Compared with the European the Japanese Larch is the broad-beamed rumbustious and colourful brother among his slim, elegant and rather quiet sisters. Slender, light-branched conic trees can be found, but they never have the airy grace of the gently up-curved branches dangling lines of slender hanging shoots of the European. The norm is broad, with strong level branches when open grown, with the interior crown more crowded because the annual extension shoots, leader and branches, bear many lateral shoots, while European Larch have none except in the uncommon very vigorous eastern provenances from the Tatra Mountains and Poland which have a few. The shoots of the Japanese tree are stouter and orange-brown or dark purple with a blue bloom, where the Europeans are pale straw, pink or almost white. The leaves of the Japanese are more densely held, broader, never the bright fresh green of the other, but darker more blue-green and the undersides quite glaucous. The bark is dark red-brown, becoming flaked.

The Japanese Larch had a bad start in Britain. One of the few trees said to be from Veitch's original seed, received in 1861, is at Tortworth Court, Gloucestershire, and it has always been a singularly unimpressive one. By 1904 it was only 44/4ft and in 1931 it was only 48/5ft. Forty years after that it was 66/6ft. Another, suspected of being of that origin, at Brook House, Sussex, was even smaller, and a third, planted at Kew in 1868, was only 64/4ft in 1971. This was bad luck, for later plantings in better sites showed by 1900 that early growth was commonly exceedingly vigorous and sturdy.

It was a few Scottish landowners who brought trees back from the Yokohama nurseries to Abercairney, Dunkeld and Munches in 1883–5, that changed the picture. Their trees made great progress and are now the biggest and finest, all surviving and many rating a mention below. By 1900 many estates in Scotland and a few in England were making plantations, most of which have by now been harvested.

The Japanese Larch is highly resistant, but not immune to, the larch canker that caused much damage in the many nineteenth century plantations of European Larch. So it became popular once these early plantings had shown what it could do. Then it was found to make better growth and a heavier crop than European Larch on peats at higher altitude, and replaced that species except on the better soils and lower slopes. It has a very heavy leaf fall which suppresses some undergrowth, and is resistant to fire. Together these features gave it a vogue as an edging to fire-rides in woods, and as a tree able to grow up among thickets of rhododendron and suppress that.

Seedlings are often a little shorter than those of European Larch, but they are sturdier and have a much more dense root-system so they were adopted as rootstocks for grafting the trees for seed-orchards. These must be in pots, and the thick stems are easier to put a graft on.

The two finest trees are both from the Duke of Atholl's 1885 seed, planted in 1887. One is in Diana's Grove, that wonderland of giant trees by Blair Castle. This is 132/10ft with a highly impressive bole, clear and with little taper for 30ft. At Dunkeld House, fourteen were planted, eleven in a shallow crescent by the drive, two along the edge of the wood to the east, and one, with two Europeans, in a hollow towards the house. It is the most easterly, nearest Dunkeld town, which is the biggest. It is 98/11ft and a shapely broad conic crown with long, level, but not excessively big branches from low on the bole on the open side. It is less impressive as a stem than the Blair tree, but it can be seen as a whole from a long stretch of the drive, whereas Diana's tree is much hidden among conifers 150–180ft tall. This avenue tree is strange, in that its shoots are pale, pinkish and slender where the Crescent trees have singularly dark purplish-red and stout shoot, and it has, alone among the Japanese Larch, flowers of uniform pale pink. It has, therefore, features more like the Hybrid Larch, but there is no possibility of it being one, because there

Japanese Larch (*Larix kaempferi*): close-up of female flowers on branch

77

were no earlier Japanese Larch on the estate before these came. It is also surprisingly unimpressive as a parent when crossed with European Larch, compared with the smaller trees nearby.

The Crescent is notable for the long, level low branches reaching out to the drive. The biggest tree among the 11 is the second from the House end, at 98/9ft with strong branches. It yields the biggest hybrid progeny, but those from Tree 11, the second smallest tree, are taller and more slender in their early years.

Since the European Larch on Kennel Bank, beside and behind the Crescent of Japanese Larch, are believed to be the first progeny of the trees by the Cathedral across the field, it would make a pleasing symmetry to have the first progeny of the Crescent trees along the fence near the Cathedral. And that is what I believe this long line of mixed Japanese and hybrid larch to be, started in 1900 and continued to the Bishop's Walk until about 1910. The first trees, nearest the Cathedral, are fine Japanese, and the biggest was bored in 1955 and showed 55 rings. It is now 130/9ft with a narrow crown and one of the very best.

Colonel Drummond Moray's 1883 seed yielded at least two big trees still standing at Abercairney, near Crieff. Much the larger is 88/10ft. At Munches in Kirkcudbrightshire, the two from 1885 seed are 92ft and 98/8ft in Waggon Wood, beside a much bigger Hybrid Larch of unknown origin.

The only tree in Scotland known to pre-date these, is a graft planted in 1876 in the Limekiln Wood above Inveraray Castle. By 1931 this tree, whose origin is not recorded, was 74/7ft and in 1982 it was 80/9ft, the union near the ground. An 1894 tree in the Policies at Glamis Castle is 78/8ft. One by the public road near Tummel Bridge, on Bonskeid Estate, is 95/9ft. An outstandingly good tree by the gate to Glen Estate near Peebles was planted in 1906 and has grown vigorously to be 98/10ft now. A very tall little stand below Bracelands in the Forest of Dean has trees to 124/7ft. A broad, branchy and surely early tree at Blairadam, near Kinross, is 62/9ft. Four big trees near the Castle garden at Drumlanrig were planted in 1906 and one of these is 80/9ft. In the Pleasure Grounds at Abbeyleix a good tree is 88/9ft. A number were planted in 1901 in the pinetum at Brahan House, Easter Ross, and five remain of excellent form. The best are now 121/8ft and 118/8ft.

DAWN REDWOOD

Metasequoia glyptostroboides

Were a fossil collector or student to find an ammonite crawling up the garden path, his or her feelings would be similar to those of the botanists in 1948 handling their first foliage of the Dawn Redwood. It belongs to an epoch long since past. It was a well known fossil of the Liassic Period and up to the Pliocene, but until a few years before, there had been no suspicion that any had escaped extinction many millions of years ago. The fossils are found across the northern hemisphere, including Spitzbergen and Greenland, dating from when the continents were further south, low in the sea and close together sharing a common flora.

Three living Dawn Redwoods were discovered in late autumn 1941 by T. Kan, a forester from Peking National Central University. They were in a hamlet, Modaoqui, in eastern Szechuan near the Hupeh border, where it curves round the area in which Henry and Wilson found their Davidias. Kan could not collect specimen foliage as the tree was bare, so the next year he asked the local schoolmaster to send some. He did, but they were lost. The schoolmaster, Lung-hsin-Yang was now interested and wanted to find out what the tree was. In 1944 he showed it to T. Wang of the Research Bureau surveying the area. Wang collected a few shoots and cones which eventually were received by Professor Cheng in Peking. In 1946 he sent one of his students, C. J. Hsueh, in February and May to collect better specimens and sent some of these for a second opinion, to Dr H. H. Hu, the leading dendrologist, and to the Arnold Arboretum.

It so happened that as the first trees were being discovered in 1941, Shigeru Miki in Japan was publishing his work founding the new genus *Metasequoia* to accommodate some Pliocene fossils which had been classified under *Taxodium* and *Sequoia*, but unlike those had opposite leaves and shoots. Dr Hu knew this paper and saw that the new tree was a *Metasequoia*. He and Professor Cheng published the name in mid 1948, so the tree was without a name for the first seven years after being discovered. Cheng sent a specimen to Dr Merrill at the Arnold Arboretum, who saw that it was a new species and asked for seed, sending a small contribution towards the cost. Inflation in China increased the value of this four thousand-fold and a big expedition was sent to Szechuan from Peking in autumn 1947. They found a thousand more trees in a neighbouring valley, and sent quantities of seed to arrive at the Arnold in January and March, 1948. This was made into more than 600 packets and sent to most of the botanic gardens and interested individuals in the world. Enough were kept to raise a hundred trees for experiment at the Bailey Arboretum, Long Island, and elsewhere. Luckily, germination was excellent and early growth extremely fast; also it was found that it was easily raised from cuttings. So the tree was spread rapidly although no more seed could be acquired from China for the next 30 years.

Taking the cue from the resemblance to Swamp Cypress, gardeners planted the first trees by watersides where they could, and in damp hollows. The biggest today in Britain are in many gardens like the University Botanic Garden at Cambridge; at Kew by the Lily Pool; at Sheffield Park, Sussex; Emmanuel College, Cambridge, and at Bodnant. Many others as big are less obviously supplied with water, mostly on lawns on clay or in fertile woodland sands. The biggest are somewhat grouped into three regions; East Anglia, across the south of England and in North Wales. Given that those in the low rainfall region of East Anglia are beside water, this seems to reflect an uneasy balance between hot summers and cool, damp summers

Dawn Redwood (*Metasequoia glyptostroboides*): Alice Holt Lodge Research Station, Hampshire

with high rainfall. The need for summer warmth may be the reason for there being few big trees in Devon or Cornwall, and fewer north of Liverpool to York. There are good but slower growing and hence smaller trees in Scotland northward to Morayshire and Sutherland The cool, high rainfall or humidity areas of Argyll and Perthshire which grow unequalled specimens of so many conifers, make very mediocre, slow Metasequoias.

Too much heat is also evidently a deterrent to good growth, although never a problem in Britain. In North America quite big trees are growing from Niagara Falls, Ontario, to New England and the biggest of all in New Jersey, on Long Island and south through Delaware and Philadelphia areas to Virginia. In the even hotter summers further south, despite high rainfall and humidity, there are few specimens and no big trees at all. Long Island, New York, seems to be an ideal place. The grove in the Bailey Arboretum is not beside water but on a lawn in a slight hollow. When I first found them, in 1975, the biggest bole was ten feet round and 26 years planted, nearly twice the size of any then in Britain. By 1982 it was 13ft round, an extraordinary rate of growth and by 1993 it was 16ft round. All around Philadelphia, 90–95ft narrow cones stand out of gardens, and because they have months of 90°F they are bearing in March foot-long curtains of orange-brown three-branched catkins. No male flower had been seen in Britain until 1992.

The first wave of planting, in 1949–51, was of original seedlings all genetically different. Subsequent plantings, until 1980, were all cuttings from these and some groups may therefore be of single clones. There are differences in the density of branches on the bole, the breadth of the crown, and the depth of flutes and hollows on the bole. In general it seems that the trees growing most freely have much less deeply indented boles than those which suffer exposure around their tops. Two examples are the Rock Garden tree at Leonardslee, 52/7ft 7in in 1988 and the tree at Trewidden, west Cornwall, 26/6ft 9in in 1979, with an extraordinarily convoluted bole. In contrast, some trees have fairly smoothly rounded boles, notably a 1952 cutting from the nearby 1949 tree at Snowdenham House, Bramley, Surrey. It has outgrown its parent, which has a mildly fluted bole and was 80/7ft 6in in 1987, while the cutting was then 75/8ft 2in. The biggest bole of all in Britain, 85/10ft 8in in 1991, is smoothly rounded, although the girth is somewhat inflated by the stem forking eight feet up. This is in Central Park, Bournemouth, a sheltered broad stream-bed, probably planted in 1950. The tall original at the top of the Savill Garden in Windsor Great Park, 93/6ft in 1990 and a shapely tree visible across Jesus Green, in Jesus College, Cambridge, 77/5ft 6in in 1990, have notably good stems.

It has been suggested that early cleaning up of the bole will make for a smoother bole, and it should do. But the few well cleaned up boles seen have preserved their initial flutes and pockets so these may be more inherent than modifiable by treatment. Although there can be no enormous or outstanding specimens yet, Dawn Redwood deserves inclusion to record its history and note a few of the best of the original trees.

The first tree planted in Cambridge is the one by the lake and nearest the Trumpington Road gate at the University Botanic Garden. The Director at the time, John Gilmour, told me, with some glee, that he arranged a dinner for the Superintendents of College and other gardens, to discuss the siting of the seedlings they all had, at the end of 1948. While they were safely gathered round the table he sent his gardener out to plant his tree a day ahead of the rest. It was for years the biggest in girth, a shapely tree, 75/9½ft in 1992. (The year of measurement becomes crucial in trees adding three and four inches every year.) The Clare College Garden tree overtook it after 1985 and was 60/9ft 4in in 1989, in a shrubbery, about 300ft from the Cam (Granta) but over a high water-table. It added 37in to its girth, between 1969 and 1981, and a further 30in between 1981 and 1989. The tree by the pool at Emmanuel College was 77/9ft 4in in 1990 having grown recently almost exactly at the same rate as the Clare tree, adding 29in from 1981 to 1990. The tree in Oxford University Botanic Garden, also planted in 1949, was slower at first, being only three foot, three inches round in 1970. From 1983 to 1989 it added 17in to become 66/8ft 4in.

A 1949 tree from Kew, planted in a front garden in Riverside Drive, Esher (but not near the river) has grown faster than that after a slower start, and after having had a large root severed as it seemed to threaten the house. In 1991 it was 68/9ft 1in after being only 28/1ft 9in in 1965 and 60/6ft 11in in 1981. At Wisley

RHS Gardens, the best of the 1949 trees is the one by the pool, 60/7ft 9in in 1988 and one of the pair in the Woodland Garden, 85/6ft 4in in 1988. In the shade of pines on Battleston Hill two very sparsely branched trees were over 75/4ft in 1983.

Of the 1950 planting at Leonardslee, the best trees are one on the long bank, by Upper Path, 85/7ft 4in, and two in The Dell, 85/8ft and 102/6ft in 1991. A line of three fine 1950 trees on the dam in Cefn Onn Park near Cardiff has one 82/6ft 5in and one 72/7ft 4in in 1990. At Ladham House, Kent, a 1950 tree in a damp hollow was 46/3ft 9in when 17 years old and 70/7ft 3in in 1984. At Headfort, County Meath, a 1950 tree was 42/5ft in 1980 but 56/7ft 4in by 1990. One planted in 1950 in a clay soil on a rather exposed lawn at Alice Holt Lodge Research Station in Hampshire was 38/3ft 4in when 20 years old and 48/5ft when 26, after which growth in height has almost ceased, but in girth it has accelerated and was 8ft 4in round by 1988.

The larger of two 1951 trees at Sheffield Park, Sussex, is on the bank of the bottom lake. It was 40/3ft 7in in 1974 and 66ft/8ft in 1988. Good trees certainly from the 1948 seed but of which the precise date of planting is not known are numerous. At Bodnant one in the main Dell was 75/7ft 5in in 1990, when the biggest in the upper Dell, with its roots in the stream by the stepping-stones, was 72/8ft 7in. Also in North Wales, but nowhere near open water, a fine tree in the wall-garden at Penrhyn Castle is growing apace. It was 16ft tall in 1959, 42/4ft 6in in 1974, 58/7ft 6in in 1986 and 70/8ft 8in in 1989. At Cockington Court, Torbay, a shapely tree was 72/7ft in 1984 and then its tip was blown out (the only wind damage seen in this species to date), and with a renewed top it was 72/8ft 2in in 1991. At Nymans, Sussex, one original tree is in the Magnolia Garden, sheltered by the gardener's house and 80/7ft 8in in 1990. The other is in the top end of the 1897 pinetum belt which was mostly blown down in 1987. Unharmed, the *Metasequoia* was 70/7ft 3in in 1990. At Antony House, Cornwall, the bigger of two by the path to the gardener's house was 50/5ft 7in in 1978 and had grown to 66/8ft by 1988.

At present it can be seen that the original trees are well out of their phase of rapid height growth, although far from culminating yet, particularly in good side-shelter and humidity. They are still increasing their rate of growth in girth, which is remarkable at this age. Probably a study of early figures for Giant Sequoia could show that it, too, was still accelerating at this age, but there can be few other trees that maintain an increasing rate so long.

NORWAY SPRUCE

Picea abies

The Norway Spruce is too dull and inherently mediocre in every aspect to detain us long. I can think of only one faintly interesting fact about it, and that concerns only its native range. Nothing it has done in this country in all the time it has been here is worthy of remark, except that peculiar fact itself. It was among the first conifers to be brought to England, and of course it is not known by whom, from where, to where or in what year. All that is known is that William Turner, gardener to the Duke of Northumberland at Syon House, in writing what he knew about trees in 1548, knew it was in the country. No trees from early plantings are known today. Not one of the 14 specimens cited in 1912 has been found, and only nine of 60 recorded in 1931. It must be not only short-lived but unlucky as well, for many of those were quite young trees. The oldest dated tree surviving as I write, goes back only to 1830. A few big ones, possibly still extant in Scotland, are suspected of dating to about 1770, but that is as far as they go.

The species ranges from a belt of introgression with the Siberian Spruce, *Picea obovata*, along the Ural Mountains, westward in a broad belt which divides each side of the Baltic Sea. One branch extends round the Karelian area to Norway and the other goes southwest to the Alpes Maritimes. This leaves a wide strip, the North European Plain, from the Tatra to the Baltic shore and everywhere to the west, except for a tiny outlier on the Harz Mountains, without any. This shows why the tree had no chance of reaching these Islands after the Ice Ages, and leads to the Interesting Fact. In Sweden the tree has spread right down to the southern tip, and across that region reafforestation has to be carried out with trees raised from seed from Central Europe, mainly Poland and Austria as these substantially outgrow the local native strain. And that is because the local strain has migrated round the far

Norway Spruce (*Picea abies*): close-up of cones

north of Finland to reach south Sweden and has thus been through a selection 'filter' which left only those most resistant to extreme cold. These are slow growing even though now in the mild far south.

One of the very few really big, good trees, and noted as such in 1905, was at Studley Royal, near Ripon until it died soon after 1952 at 156/14ft. Today there is a slender younger tree by the site of the old one, 132/8ft with a bole clear for ten feet. The inheritor of the title of best specimen today is at Lingholm Estate by Derwentwater. It stands in the middle of a broad path through beech and pine woods and can be seen well in all its majesty, at 141/15ft. The tallest is a slender tree by the burn at the entrance to Moniack Glen near Inverness, the home of 200ft Douglas Firs. This spruce will be of the same planting date, 1887, and is 170/8ft. There are several very tall spruce by the Cascade in Trebartha, Cornwall, one of which was 150/9ft in 1981. Another of the same size is at Cragside, Rothbury, in the Debden Valley.

The second biggest trunk is that of a tree planted in 1851 in a field above the gate to Ardross Castle, Alness, Easter Ross, which is 85/14ft. In the pinetum about 500ft below in a trench, one planted in 1900 shows, what is for this species, rapid growth and is 98/10ft. As good as any for shape is a tree in a clearing at Culdees House, Perthshire. Very symmetrical in crown and with a quality stem, it is 144/10ft. A very big, but not shapely tree at Abercairney, near Crieff, probably dates from 1867 and is 141/13ft. A more shapely tree of 1864 planting, by the drive at Glenlee Park, Newton Stewart, is 138/13ft. A tall tree by the gate to Ballindalloch Castle in Banffshire, has a splendid spire top with foliage hanging from the small branches and is 144/12ft. One with big branches, among many large specimens on the path from the garden to the Castle at Dupplin in Perthshire, is 132/13ft. A spruce likely to date back to about 1780 is beside the drive to Ardkinglas House in Argyll and is 135/12ft.

BREWER SPRUCE

Picea breweriana

This beautiful tree has not yet grown to an impressive size in Britain, but it will undoubtedly make large specimens in the not too distant future. Already those we have are prominent and striking trees. It is found in small scattered groves high in the Klamath and Siskiyou Mountains each side of the Oregon/California boundary from near the coast towards Mount Shasta. It was discovered at Black Butte, just west of Mount Shasta, in 1863 by Professor Brewer but not identified or named until refound near Waldo, Oregon, very near the California boundary, by Thomas Howell in 1884. The Shasta area has been searched fruitlessly many times since.

Until many other groves had been found, there was great concern for the survival

Brewer's Spruce (*Picea breweriana*): Westonbirt, Gloucestershire

of the species, because the small stands high on benches and top slopes were at risk from the burning of slash from the widespread felling on the lower slopes. On several occasions after 1904, R.F.S. Balfour of Dawyck joined Professor Brewer in expeditions to remove seedlings to safer places, and brought some home in 1906 and 1908. In 1911 he received at Dawyck a box made of Incense Cedar by a farmer with whom he had stayed, enclosing, unasked, many small seedlings. Plants from all of these parcels which were surplus to Balfour's needs at Dawyck were given to some of his wide circle of keen collectors of conifers, and are the chief source of the best trees today. The original Brewer Spruce, however, was a two-year seedling sent by Sargent at the Arnold Arboretum in 1897 and planted near the Pagoda at Kew. It had been lifted from the wild, and it stood until very recently, a gaunt object, no advertisement for the species at all. It was only 46/2ft in 1979.

Seedlings grow maddeningly slowly for some ten years before making good progress, and look sparse and unhappy the while. One well-known gardener would take me, every time I made a visit, to his seedling tree and say 'Now, do tell me I have been sold a pup and that this is a sickly Sitka Spruce'. On the last occasion he was 86 years old, so my emollient advice, to have patience for another five years, seemed no longer quite appropriate. A healthy one in my garden had achieved waist-height after 11 years, when I ignored my own advice and ejected it. Unfortunately, many gardeners are not prepared to wait and will accept the misshapen but weeping grafts that the trade offers instead. It should be obvious that attractive, long weeping shoots cannot be grown until there are branches far enough from the ground to allow them the room to hang unobstructed. Grafts at an apparently saleable age are only two or three feet tall and the weeping shoots trail on the ground and because of the congested branching from slow growth, they foul the branch beneath. And this shapeless tangle persists for a long time because spruce grafts, taken from lateral shoots, as these must be, tend to continue to grow as laterals, sideways rather than upwards, plagiotrophic rather than orthotrophic growth, and grow very slowly. Release, if it comes at all, will be delayed so long that a seedling would have grown into a good tree in the same time, and the graft will always have a crooked base.

The Balfour trees evidently inspired planters, and the poor specimen at Kew was luckily ignored. Only a shortage of plants retarded widespread planting after 1908 until about 1950. The tree is frequent in collections and large gardens, often in groups, everywhere. Although most of the older trees are in the south of England, those planted a little later in northern Scotland tend to be more luxuriant and vigorous. Once the tree is well established, growth in height will rarely exceed one foot a year, but growth in girth gradually becomes fast and the spindly seedlings begin to build up stout stems, as would be expected with such a mass of foliage.

The Dawyck trees have suffered several losses in gales, and the biggest in 1984 were of 1908 planting, though in the light of the slow early growth a few will have come from seed obtained in 1904. The tree in the spruce collection on Policy Bank was 62/6ft; one at the west end of the Bank was 50/5ft and one at Bell's Pool by the gate, was 48/5ft tall in 1982. A tree in St Clere Pinetum near Wrotham in Kent, at 700ft on the North Downs, was 50/5ft in 1984 and must have been a Balfour tree. Four were planted in 1910 in Sheffield Park, Sussex, and one, in the Conifer Walk, survived the 1987 gale and is now 60/5ft. An undated tree at Stobo, across the Tweed from Dawyck, was presumably a Balfour tree and is 56/5ft. One in Hergest Croft in Herefordshire was planted in 1913 by the reservoir and was 60/6ft in 1985 and five more were planted in 1916 in the gardens and Park Wood, the tree in the avenue being 65/5ft in 1985.

In the Policies at Glentanar near Ballater, one planted in 1922 is a superb specimen, but only marginally better than the one in the pinetum, planted in 1925 and 46/5ft in 1980. At Castlewellan, County Down, the tree planted in 1924 is now 52/7ft. At Headfort in County Meath, one dating from 1927 is now 56/6ft. An undated tree near the gate into Tong's Wood near Hawkhurst in Kent was 60/5ft in 1984. Mount Usher in County Wicklow has a tree planted in 1928 which is 52/6ft and one of the same date in Pitcarmick in Strathardle, Perthshire was 60/5ft in 1986. Westonbirt has groups planted in 1923 in the Arboretum, thinly crowned and lanky, but a single tree in Silk Wood, on Byham's Ride is a sturdy and handsome tree dating from 1933 and now 46/5ft. Bedgebury National Pinetum had eight fine trees along the Spruce Bank planted in 1926 and 1932. Only two were left after the 1987 gale, both from the 1932 planting, and now 46/4ft and 36/4ft. A well-grown specimen in the pinetum at Wisley may date from the first plantings there in 1927 or may be younger. It is now 60/4ft. At Kyloe Wood, Northumberland, a line of six at the front of a rocky outcrop had trees to 52/5½ft in 1991.

SERBIAN SPRUCE

Picea omorika

This remarkable tree has features of great interest to gardeners, designers of landscapes, botanists and foresters. To begin with the basics, it is a botanical anomaly of the greatest magnitude. It is a flat-leafed spruce and all the other spruces of that sort are native round the Pacific shores, with a tongue through China to the Himalayas. The spruces of western and northern Asia, Europe and eastern North America have leaves with quadrangular, mostly rhombic cross-sections. The Serbian Spruce is the only one of these earlier Tertiary species to have survived the Ice Ages in this part of the world. It is found only as a scatter of about 50 little groups totalling 150 acres on the Tara Mountains in the lower valley of the Drina River in Former Yugoslavia.

Those mountains are of limestone, so the tree is at home, as very few spruces are, on limey and chalky soil. It is also very at home on the most acid, sandy and peaty soil. In short, like many of our best trees, it takes no interest in pH and very little in soil. Although it flowers at the same time as the Sitka and most other spruces – in early May – its foliage buds do not extend until two or three weeks later. So it has not been seen to be cut back by late frosts which catch so many spruces.

It is the shape of the tree which makes these features so important in horticulture. It varies quite widely but only within the limits of a narrow, tall tree, striking wherever it is. The extreme form is a neat slim column, densely clad with very short, slightly depressed branches, a slender pillar to a conic apex. The leaves are longer than in other forms and stand nearly erect. Then there are gradations in conic crowns, from slightly tapered columns to medium conic. The broader forms have regular branches downswept then upcurved near their tips, and with an open crown.

Being so narrow, the Serbian Spruce can grow at a greater density than other spruces with more timber to the acre even than the Sitka Spruce. Its indifference to soils allows it to do this where Sitka would not be planted, including the frost-hollows, because of its late flushing. It should therefore be a great asset in forestry. But it is not grown except on a minute scale for several reasons. The seed is hard to obtain in quantity and yields plants variable in growth. The stands are unstable

Serbian Spruce (*Picea omorika*): Dropmore, Buckinghamshire

in wind, and prone to sporadic deaths from honey-fungus. In arboreta it is distressingly common to find the Serbian Spruces browning and on their way to dying. Several trees raised from the original 1889 seed were planted at Kew near the Pagoda and in the pinetum but only two survive. A triangle of three at Dropmore, Buckingham-shire, is quite possibly of the same origin, and was a fine sight in 1958, but by 1982 two had blown down and the last one was dying back. One of a pair planted soon after 1890 at Tregrehan was 95ft tall in 1979 but neither stood in 1981. All of which makes it a short-term exercise listing the biggest trees today, but a few have shown a robust will to survive recent stresses from gales, drought and disease.

Outstanding are three of the tallest and among the oldest and biggest on the Jubilee Terrace at Murthly Castle. The Jubilee in question was the Diamond Jubilee of 1897 and now the trees are all just under seven feet round and are 108ft, 92ft and 85ft tall, slender with gently tapered spires to the top. The pride of the single trees and of the pencil-slim dense columns is the one in the Conifer Walk at Sheffield Park, Sussex. Planted in 1910, this was 70ft tall in 1960, and now, after the 1987 gale ruffled its top a little, it is 88/6ft. A handsome, shapely tree planted in 1914 in Crarae Garden, Argyll is 80/5ft. The best of many at Westonbirt is very slender-conic among mixed conifers in a glade on the north of Willesley Drive. Planted in 1936, it is 88/5ft.

The first tree planted in the Savill Garden, Windsor Great Park was a Serbian Spruce below the present entrance, planted in 1933. It is a good, slender tree now 95/5ft. An excellent tree in the National Botanic Garden at Glasnevin, repaired its broken top well and is 88/3ft. Early breakage was not surmounted so well by one in the New Piece at Endsleigh Lodge, Devon, and it is one of the few anywhere with three stems from six feet up. It must have the biggest crown for it is 80/7ft and decidedly broad. Among the many groups of conifers dating from about 1928 at Pitcarmick, Strathardle, the three Serbian Spruces have one at 85/3ft.

CAUCASIAN SPRUCE: ORIENTAL SPRUCE

Picea orientalis

The former of these names is the better one, but it is less seen than the latter. 'Oriental' is a very vague term when used in western Europe and could be applied to a dozen spruce species in India, China and Japan. 'Caucasian' Spruce in contrast is precise and is the only spruce growing in that region.

Introduced in 1838 and sent in quantity in 1850, this tree became a component of the standard kit for a pinetum sent out by the big nurseries in mid-Victorian times. There is one or more in every pinetum today, and eight in Benmore and ten in the 1864 pinetum at Glamis Castle. The specimens of that period are of remarkably uniform size today, few being far either side of 90/8ft. Being a plant from the Caucasus they are exceptionally healthy and strong growing for many years, but the oldest may be near the end of the normal lifespan on the less fertile sites, for some are dying back at the top as they exceed 100ft.

Young trees make the best of all Christmas trees. They have well-spaced, superbly regular whorls of evenly sized branches, and a neat conic shape. The needles are the smallest of any spruce, less than half the length of those on the Norway Spruce, richer green and shining, and, important in slipping the decorations on, they lie closely along the shoot. The leading shoot is good but not out of proportion with the size of tree.

Usually seen in the interior of old pineta, Caucasian Spruce are not often blown down, unless the drainage has deteriorated. That they have good wind resistance is shown by several solitary tall trees in fields like one at Mickleham, Surrey, surviving on a slope fully exposed to the 1987 gale. The plot at Bedgebury Pinetum, a dense planting, was almost the only one left scarcely damaged at that time. Planted in 1949, it had made excellent progress with most trees around 58/3ft.

It is rare for a Caucasian Spruce to be misshapen, beyond a somewhat heavy branch, and few, if any species can better the record of 320 trees on the Register with only two not measurable at five feet. One had regular branches but so densely held low on the bole that access was impossible and a hands-and-knees crawl was needed to put a tape round it at ground level. The other had suffered early damage and divided into three stems at four feet up. There is, however, a strange aberration in a tree at Pencarrow, Bodmin, planted in 1847 and probably from the original seed. It is now 52/8ft but the height is not what it should be, for the stem bends out at 40ft and proceeds horizontally, with dense foliage wreathed along it. It was like this by 1927 when it was seven feet round. A few trees have a ring of layered branches round them. The biggest is at Doune House, Dunblane, its interior now well cleaned for access to the main trunk, which is 11ft round. The tree is 98ft tall.

The oldest known is unassailably the tree at Stanage Park, Powys, planted in 1840 when it must have been a one-year seedling. It was 111/11ft in 1978. Another original, but planted out in 1847 is a good tree in the pinetum at Highnam, now Churcham Pinetum, Gloucestershire, which is 102/10ft. The biggest in girth are both at Cortachy Castle, Angus, planted as late as 1873. They are 92/13ft and 107/12ft. The next is in the same county, at Brechin Castle, in the Lower Garden, 88/12ft. One at Bowood, Wiltshire, among trees of 1840 planting, is 120/10ft. At Monteviot Pinery in Roxburghshire a tree with big low branches is 74/12ft.

The best all-round specimens include the tallest, at Camperdown Park, Dundee, in the pinetum, rather exposed on a low ridge but 132/10ft with a regular crown,

Caucasian Spruce (*Picea orientalis*): a tree rarely misshapen

and one at Kilgraston School, Perthshire, a superbly shapely tree at 105/11ft in the woodland. Benmore has several grand trees, one of them 120/10ft, and in the Kitchen Garden at Rossie Priory near Dundee, one is 98/11ft.

It is seen that the biggest trees are in the cool, wet west and north, particularly in Angus and Perthshire, and one old tree in the English Midlands has grown less rapidly. Planted at Althorpe, Northamptonshire, in 1851 it is 92/8ft. Young trees show this to a smaller extent. A promising young tree planted at Anglesea Abbey, Cambridge, in 1963 was 52/3ft in 1991.

SITKA SPRUCE

Picea sitchensis

The Sitka Spruce has everything that the Norway Spruce so signally lacks. In the place of an obscure arrival with no knowable time, place nor origin, it has the impeccable history of the classic Pacific Northwest trees – discovered by Archibald Menzies in 1792, introduced by David Douglas in 1832 and his original trees grown on several known estates. Further, it has an extraordinary natural range; a unique uniformity of botanical features over its 1500 miles; it can be very much taller and bigger than any other spruce in the world, and is one of only three conifers exceeding 300ft. In Britain it is the tree planted in greater numbers than all others combined; it outgrows and outyields every other tree on vast tracts of poor, degraded wet mountain sites, and is one of only three species of tree so far to exceed 200ft here.

Far from the dull anonymity of the Norway Spruce, it has so much presence and such attractive foliage that with these other features it achieves glamour. And yet, it is popularly denigrated, even vilified, and the undiscerning public is blind to its virtues, and is encouraged to be so by legions of misguided conservationist, 'green', 'natives only' and anti-forestry bodies. Sitka plantations are dismissed as sterile blocks of alien conifers blanketing the beautiful moors in ugly rows of uniform dark green. They are better described as clothing the bare scars of a near-desert arising from centuries of gross mismanagement in high rainfall areas, the first stages in creating the most productive woods in the cool temperate world. The thicket stage attracts back to this desert huge populations of warblers, chats and voles and the short-eared owls and hen-harriers which prey on them. The maturing crops bring goldcrests, bullfinches and sparrowhawks. It was the Sitka Spruce plantations, with some of Norway, in the Forest of Ae in Dumfriesshire which provided the output of sparrowhawks which repopulated England where this bird had been nearly exterminated by crop-sprays.

In May the buds along the shoots and at their tips swell into big globes, brilliant green as the dense clusters of leaves extend into shaving-brushes and then hang before stiffening and straightening. As they are among and outside the older foliage which is deep blue-green with silvered undersides, they present a beauty unusual in conifers. Later, as they become blue-green, some of this attraction is lost, but anyone who appreciates trees at all will admire the sturdy, powerful shoots and the palpable vigour of the tree, particularly good to see on the poor, wet upland soils in exposure.

When the Forestry Commission was founded in 1919 it was given some Crown Woodlands in various parts, but it had to expand on to the cheapest land available in the market, run-down sheepwalk, blanket bog and high fells. The first Commissioners, under Lord Lovat, looked at trees in the Highlands to pick the best species for those sites and shrewdly picked the Sitka for vigour, health and persistence of stem in exposure, from its performance in policies. Even at that time, when the best trees were half as old and half the size that they are now, they projected from the general canopy unharmed. This is not surprising when leading and top shoots are seen on a felled tree. They are as thick as a thumb and very soon rigid.

The remarkable range from almost 60°N near Anchorage, Alaska, to nearly 39°N at Caspar, California, without morphological change, allows a pretty demonstration of the effect of day length. In a single planting, renewed occasionally, at the Alice Holt Research Station, Hampshire at 51°N, seedlings raised from various sources along the range are planted, two short rows per origin, in the order of their latitude of origin. Within two years it begins to show a wedge profile, rising regularly from the most northerly Alaskan origin, through those from the Panhandle-Skeena River, Vancouver Island-Puget areas to Oregon and northern California, descending a little at the two most southerly origins.

Trees from all the origins respond at the same time to the temperature rise to the point which initiates growth, but in Alaska that is later than in Hampshire, and the day is then much longer. It grows more slowly in days shorter than it is accustomed to, and the longest day on June 20th is still two hours short of requirements. Then the day length begins to decrease and before the tree has got into its stride, day length is down to that which, in Alaska, stops further growth. So this tree shows slow growth over a short season. In contrast, a tree from Oregon at 40°N for example, starts at the same time, and already the days are longer than its norm at home, so it can make more growth. At the period around the longest day it is enjoying longer growing hours than it can ever have known. Even some weeks into the shorter days afterwards, it is still a long day for this tree and it is about October before days short enough to inhibit growth arrive. So it has an extended season of enhanced growth throughout. The wedge tails off at the southern end only because the southernmost origins are liable to damage from our late spring or early autumn frosts in some years. The day length effect overrides any slight decrease in growth from our cooler summers, but that, in a spruce, is unlikely to be very marked.

More detailed series of plots show another effect, not so readily explicable nor so evident. That is that the best growth at any one latitude is shown by the origins from nearest the ocean and on the islands. Queen Charlotte Island and Vancouver Island Sitka is superior to that from the mainland at similar latitudes. This is a little odd because almost no Sitka grows out of sight of tidal water – hence the alternative name 'Tideland Spruce' – and the coasts of British Columbia and Alaska are the most fretted in the world, pierced by innumerable tongues of ocean. Only on Mount Rainier in Washington does one rely on a crystal clear day to see salt water. So the altitude is the main variable, but the tested sources were all very little above sea-level.

Early accounts tend to state that there were Sitka over 300ft but give no examples and no modern claims suggest that any were now known above about 280ft. But in 1989 an unlogged primeval wood including a 315ft tree was found in the Carmanah Valley at the southern end of Vancouver Island. Of course, this being in Canada, it was in a logging schedule, and as soon as it was known about, the schedule was advanced to have it and the whole wood pulled down quickly before too much fuss was made. For the first time ever, the conservation movement won the case and the area is now a nature reserve, and this 315ft tree and others nearly as big around it are preserved.

Selection of specimens to mention here has to be stringent and with a few exceptions the cut-off will be 150/20ft. Many trees were known to be from Douglas's seed of 1832 but storms and wartime felling removed them at Dawyck, Keillour Castle and other places, so now authentic specimens are known only in Ireland, at Abbeyleix and Curraghmore. At Curraghmore, County Waterford, the single tree is an 1835 planting and was 163/21ft in 1974. At the same time, another was 167/18ft in a group of similar size by a little bridge below, and these are almost sure to be of the same age. In the Pleasure Ground at Abbeyleix, the Sitka planted in 1837 is 121/17ft. Two more trees of no known origin or date, look very much as if they are unrecorded Douglas trees. The biggest of all the Sitkas is that at Castlehill, Devon, one of the most remarkable trees in Europe. Its lowest branches had rooted in a circle some 15ft out from the trunk, their tips curving to the vertical. They are now substantial 80ft trees, and their lowest branches sweep out to continue the process. The periphery was marked by a white post at intervals of some 20 years, at two points, and in 1970 the lines could be traced among the tangle of dead shoots for four or five posts. Recently the whole of the dead interior thicket has been cleared to allow access, and a view of the massive trunk, with its lowest branches cleaned, seen through the surrounding lesser trunks. The primary stem carries a broad-conic, good crown towering to 150ft from the centre of the group, and is 27ft round.

The other possible Douglas seed Sitka is the only close rival to the Castlehill tree. It stands on a long brae in Strathardle, the only big tree except for a giant Sequoia nearby, prominent from a length of the Kirkmichael to Pitlochry road half a mile away. These two are the only real trees in the garden of Woodside Cottage, and in 1987 were the same girth to the inch, both 26ft. The Sitka has a clean bole for 20ft and of even, slow, taper above the small root-swell, so at that girth it is immensely impressive. The crown is a regular cone with its lower branches rising from the trunk and arching over in big curves, giving it a big spread but tapering to its top at 141ft.

Most of the many huge Sitkas that were planted in and soon after 1852 will have come from William Lobb's seed of 1850 and some, probably from John Jeffrey's of the same date. The most striking planting is at Scone Palace, Perth, where the pinetum was started in 1852. In 1866 the pinetum was extended through the older planting which is now at the top end, to include avenues of Western Hemlock and Noble Fir to end in one of Giant Sequoia. The big feature of the old pinetum is the rectangle of four 1852 Sitkas. They are remarkably uniform in size and shape, and the sharp taper of the basal six feet of all the boles makes measuring them an imprecise operation and comparisons among them vary from year to year. They are all around 150ft tall with girths ranging only between 21ft and 23ft.

A superb tree, presumably of similar age, stands by the road through Drumtochty Glen in Kincardineshire, on a bank. This has less basal taper than the trees at Scone and has been cleaned to some 20ft and is otherwise just like them but taller. It is 160/23ft. Another just below the Drumnadrochit drive into Balmacaan is 156/22ft, and one at Castle Leod is 165/19ft. Fairburn Castle, Easter Ross, has one with heavy low branches, but not unshapely, on the lawn, with the third biggest girth, 25ft, and 150ft tall. The next biggest are one at Kilravock Castle, Nairn, planted in 1856 and now 138/24ft, and one at Caledon Castle, County Tyrone, also 138/23ft. A superb tree at Killinchassie near Aberfeldy with quite light branches is 144/ 23ft.

Two other very big trees have a surround of layered branches. At Forglen House, Aberdeenshire, a tree by the drive is 150/23ft, and at the Monteviot Pinery near Jedburgh, a tree on a bank is 124/20ft. The similar tree at Aira Force, Ullswater, has been fully cleaned up and is 120/20ft. Two of the biggest trees known to be younger than the Lobb trees are in Giant's Grove, below the tearoom at Powerscourt, County Wicklow. They were planted in 1867 and their long, slender tops project far from the tall trees around. One has died back 30ft but the other seems to be in good order and is 175/23ft. A widely spaced group in a wood towards the sea from Skibo Castle shows very rapid growth. The largest in 1980 was 156/20ft and in 1955 it was only 16ft round. By the entrance to Ardneisaig Hotel near Oban a fine tree is 130/21ft and one at Monk Coniston, well cleaned up, is 132/20ft. Rapid early growth is shown by the tree in the 1901 pinetum at Brahan House, Easter Ross, which is 135/15ft while one in Ardross pinetum dating from 1900 is 153/18ft.

The list so far has not included any of the tallest trees, more than 20ft round, for none happens to be so big. 'Adam' of the 1851 pair at Culzean Castle, Ayrshire, is 165/17ft, while 'Eve' has died back to 138/17ft. A tree near the Sequoia Avenue at Benmore, 15ft round is also 165ft tall and so is one on the hill beside the House at Kilkerran, Ayrshire. At Cullen House, Banff, an 1861 tree is 170/18ft and a presumably younger tree by the upper road in Belladrum, very lightly branched, is

175/17ft. At Dunans, Argyll, the Sitka among the tall Douglas Fir by the track to the Chapel, is 190/17ft and growing fast. In 1954 it was 140/13ft.

At Randolph's Leap by the River Nairn, a tall Douglas Fir and Sitka Spruce stand on the rim, both well seen from the roadbridge and with spire tops. The Sitka is 195/18ft. Doune House, Rothiemurchus, however, has a whole wood of slender trees of about that height. It is thought to have been planted in about 1870, and now seems about to culminate in height, for the leading shoots have been small for several years. There are 16 of 165ft and above, six over 180ft, and four about 195ft tall, with girths of 12–14ft, but one near the farm road is just about 200/17ft.

An estate near Comrie, Perthshire, which does not relish the idea of crowds of treewatchers swarming in to see it (if only big trees had such a fervent following) has a taller one. Very carefully checked by three measurers from both sides, it is agreed to be 202/17ft. Its slender spire has a good leading shoot, and if it is not yet quite the tallest spruce of any kind in Europe because of those elusive German or Swiss Norway Spruces, it very soon will be.

MORINDA SPRUCE

Picea smithiana

This has the longest needles of all the spruces, the second biggest cones and is clear second only to the Sitka in height and girth. It has long-pendulous tertiary shoots, matched only by the Brewer Spruce, and it makes a big tree in Britain. But with all these qualities, it remains a tree of no great presence, little grace and no glamour. It is at its best when still young and growing fast as its crown is still shapely and well-clothed but it is of coarse texture and the weeping habit is not yet well developed. By the time it is, the tree is all too often becoming gaunt and growing slowly. With greater age, many are decidedly scraggy with slender top or tops (for forking high is frequent), and few exceed ten feet in girth.

One interesting feature is that although many trees have died from what appears to be old age, the two original seedlings are still growing and in good health. The first seed was sent by Dr Govan to Hopetoun House, near the Forth Bridges, in 1818. Two plants were raised and planted out in the kitchen garden below the House in 1824 and a graft was made on Norway Spruce rootstock and planted with them in 1827. Today the seedlings are 88/10ft and 72/9ft and have well-furnished crowns. The graft has an obvious union about two feet up and is 88/9ft, having always been a little smaller than the seedlings.

Taymouth Castle Gardens on the banks of Loch Tay has the finest specimens, probably because of its perpetual high humidity and damp soil with considerable shelter particularly from the north. One forks low and is 115/12 + 11ft, misshapen but well foliaged and huge, but the other is far superior, 115/15ft, the biggest trunk

Morinda Spruce (*Picea smithiana*): a tree of no great presence

since the death in 1956 of an 1842 tree at Bicton, Devon, which was over 18ft round. The biggest planting of old trees, but of unknown age, is at Emo Court, Leix, where there are 13 big trees, the biggest 88/13ft. On the hill at Albury Park, Surrey, a tree planted in 1861 has a swollen base and is 102/12ft and one off the drive to Penrhyn Castle, Gwynedd, is 98/12ft. At Smeaton House, East Lothian, a tree planted in 1840 is 85/10ft and an 1854 tree at Keir Castle, Dunblane, is 105/10ft. Two very splendid trees in the sheltered hollow at Cuffnells, Lyndhurst, are 124/11ft and 126/10ft. On the dam in Bicton Gardens, a handsome tree is 111/11ft. A rather broad tree at Kilmacurragh, County Wicklow, is 88/12ft and one on a mound made of tree stumps in 1843 at Dropmore, Buckinghamshire, is 88/11ft. A fine, tall tree at Craighall, Rattray, Perthshire, is 102/11ft and one at Birkhill, Fifeshire, is 118/11ft. A broad-crowned tree at Castlewellan is 71/14½ft.

AROLLA PINE

Pinus cembra

Two conifers grow high in the winter snows of the Alps, the European Larch and the Arolla or Swiss Stone Pine. Only the pine has the dense evergreen foliage, and sturdy low branches to stabilise the snow above avalanche areas. It is the only tree there with foliage tough enough to withstand abrasion from driving snow and to resist the growth of fungi under the snow-cover. It is therefore vital that the pinewoods be preserved above winter-resorts. The cutting of new pistes in the skiing areas has therefore increased the danger of avalanches.

Like the Macedonian Pine, the Arolla is highly adapted to severe conditions, but is unable to exploit to any great extent the luxury of deep, fertile soils in shelter. It grows at much the same sedate and steady speed wherever it is planted. It is always a shapely, narrowly columnar tree with a conic apex until it is mature, when some upper branches become big and fan out. As a neat tree of slow growth, uninterested in its soil, it is a useful tree in small gardens. It is seen in some front gardens in the coniferous areas of Surrey and more in Scotland.

The Arolla Pine is the only pine outside southwestern North America whose cones do not open on the tree but are shed whole. Rodents eat out the seeds when it is on the ground. That leaves the spindle of the cone like a corncob but, when freshly attacked, with shining white pockets where the big seeds were. These pretty

Arolla Pine (*Pinus cembra*):
Powis Castle, Powys

objects will be found only under big maturing or old trees, because the cones, dark blue in summer, are not borne until the trees are quite big.

The Arolla Pine was introduced in 1746 by the Duke of Argyll to Whitton Park, Hounslow, and the original tree was there in 1903 but was not recorded thereafter. Only one known to have been planted before 1800 was known in 1970. It is plainly a tree with a short life in cultivation here, for most of the biggest trees that I found before 1960, notably those at Taymouth Castle and Murthly Castle in Perthshire, have died since then and of the 52 recorded in 1931 only five probably survive today. The 1795 tree at Dropmore was 66/8ft and leaning in 1970 but was not seen in 1982.

The distribution of specimens is a fairly even scattering from south to north but a marked bias towards the east and away from the west in England and Scotland, with very few in Cornwall, Devon, Wales or Ireland. If this reflects a dislike of high rainfall, it is odd that there should be several in Cumbria and a big one in Wester Ross.

The best specimen is at Castle Milk in Dumfries-shire, tall and slender-columnar, 115/9ft. The oldest of known date is in the Orchard at Blairquhan, Ayrshire, planted in 1856 and 60/8ft in 1984. The biggest are almost certainly older than that and are one of the remaining two at Taymouth Castle Gardens in Perthshire, at 82/9ft; a broad-crowned tree at Airthrie Castle, Stirling University Campus, is 72/10ft and three in the Park at Powis Castle. These have the big branches high in the crown, which are a sure sign of age, and they bear numerous cones. One by Poches Gate is 60/9ft; another on Rabbit Bank is 62/9ft and one by the Gwen Morgan wood is 72/8ft. A fine tree in the Pinery at Monteviot, Roxburghshire is 85/9ft. At Achnagarry near Loch Ness, by the drive, one is 88/9ft. At Preston House, Midlothian, one is 70/9ft and in the far west, a tree at Leckmelm near Ullapool is 85/7ft.

In the English Midlands, a tree at the Swiss Garden, Old Warden in Bedfordshire is 66/8ft; one at Waddesdon House in Buckinghamshire is 60/8ft and one in the pinetum at Chatsworth House is 72/8ft. A slender and quite young tree at Newby Hall in Yorkshire is 102/4ft.

MEXICAN WHITE PINE

Pinus ayacahuite

Mexico is a secondary world centre for both oaks and pines, and further species are being discovered as the more remote areas are being explored by botanists. It is a vast country with a fringe of tropical plains and an interior of seemingly endless plateaux at 6000ft with mountain ridges to 12,000ft high. Most of the oaks and all the pines are found on these ranges and almost all of the few Mexican trees that we can grow are high altitude conifers, largely pines. It might seem that trees from the snowy lower slopes and high valleys with severe winters would be hardy enough in our mild climate, but that ignores the factor of the intense insolation they receive in those latitudes at those heights. Hartweg's Pine, a relative of Montezuma Pine is a good tree at 13,200ft on Popocatepetl and grows quite well in southern England and Ireland, but the striking Michoacan and Lumholz Pines from not far below, cannot survive a normal winter anywhere.

In 1982 I was in a party that was driven 1200 miles from Guadalajara to San Cristobel in two days, 600 miles and one food-stop in each day of 13 hours. Tiny Miguel swung the big General Motors six-wheel Challenger bus with rear-slung, 312hp two-stroke diesel, V8, up and down about a dozen passes to 12,000ft smoothly and effortlessly, held up very briefly by a fuel-stop and a fire in the engine. Every time we snaked up above 8000ft we were among mixed pines with Mexican White Pine prominent. There was not one mile of level road.

This pine was discovered by Ehrenberg in 1836 and introduced in 1840 by Hartweg to the Chiswick garden of the Horticultural Society. The form with generally larger cones, was discovered by Roezl in the Serra Madre, and introduced by him in 1857. It was until recently given varietal status as var. *veitchii*, common in the central part of the range, and frequent among our specimen trees, but it is now submerged in the type. The name 'ayacahuite' seems to be the vernacular name in (Mexican) Spanish and with all the syllables given equal stress it is a mellifluous one.

No trees are known with dates before 1900, but the tree in the pinetum at Bicton in Devon may perhaps be as old as 1880. It is 90/9ft after some die-back at the top in 1982 and has added less than two feet to its girth since 1957. The oldest of known date were planted in 1902 on the pine bank near the eastern end of Bodnant, Gwynedd, and are the biggest stems we have, 80/11ft and 82/11½ft, and very fine trees. One of them was 50/5½ft in 1931 but whichever one it was, it has made much slower progress since.

A 1911 tree at Glasnevin National Botanic Garden, Dublin, is only 50/4ft now, but it is var. *veitchii* which is expected to be slow. A tree planted in 1912 at Dropmore, Buckinghamshire, was 88/7ft in 1982. At Avondale, County Wicklow, trees now 70/5ft and 92/6ft probably date from before 1910. A good tree in Stratford Park, Stroud, in Gloucestershire, is 72/7ft and is a graft at base. At Thorp Perrow, Bedale, Yorkshire, a tree dating from around 1930 is 62/6ft. One in Priestfield Arboretum in Buckinghamshire planted in 1929 was 62/6ft in 1983. At Brocken-hurst Park near Beaulieu in the New Forest a tree planted in 1939 was 52/5ft½ in 1986 and a more vigorous one at Coleton Fishacre near Dartmouth, Devon, planted in 1939, was 66/5½ft in 1984.

A big tree in the north is 75/8ft at Brechin Castle, Angus, by the drive, and well north of that, one at Dallas Lodge, Morayshire, is 46/3½ft. One in the Royal Botanic Gardens, Edinburgh, is now 46/4ft, and surprisingly rapid growth was made by one at

Achamore House on Gigha Island in Argyll which, planted in 1962, was 40/4ft in 24 years. In the Hillier Arboretum Valley in Hampshire, which was not planted before 1954, a tree labelled 'var. *veitchii*' was 36/4ft by 1983 and confirmed this atypical vigour by growing to 46/5½ft by 1990.

SHORE PINE and LODGEPOLE PINE

Pinus contorta

Between 1945 and 1980 the two forms of this species were the second most abundant tree planted in the British Isles, being used in re-afforestation to raise the planting limit many hundreds of feet and to extend planting on to deep peats. Despite all these millions of trees on thousands of acres in Wales, Scotland and Ireland the public remains unaware of the tree altogether and few outside the forestry world or even among gardeners know of its existence. One reason for this is that neither form has ever been more than rare as a specimen in pineta, where other Pacific Slope conifers are the most important elements, and this itself must be partly due to the planters' lack of knowledge of the species.

The Shore Pine, var. *contorta*, owes its debut into forestry to A.C. Forbes of the Irish Forest Service who found that some rogue pines coming up from a batch of Douglas Fir seed imported in about 1920 made good, strong plants. It was soon found that the early growth of the coastal origins was so great that the highly exposed sites for which the species was so well suited, caused the young trees to be swept sideways before making fully vertical growth, giving the crop basal bow. To overcome this, there was a move to the use of seed of the inland form, Lodgepole Pine, var. *latifolia* which makes a slower start. So seed from Alberta and from the Kootenay Valley was used, but the trees proved prone to multiple forking and despite this, the short foliage was sparse and could not shade out the heather, which is the first requirement for establishment on peat.

A second approach was far more successful. Because of the day length effect (enlarged upon under Sitka Spruce), moving the seed-source northwards slows the growth. At first the choice was for Lulu Island, in the dockland of Vancouver, straddled by Route 99, the Canadian end of Interstate 5, on a viaduct. This was a disaster and the words Lulu Island strike terror among foresters. The latitude may be right, and the site could not be more coastal but the trees there are bushy, bear masses of cones and so are collected from easily and cheaply. The progenies are spindly, lack vigour and fruit prolifically from the year of planting out. By the time this was known, large expanses of moorland were planted and fifteen years later I heard one forester, with hundreds of acres in his charge, admitting that the only economic remedy would be to encourage careless smokers. The trouble is now thought to be not only that scrub trees are all that is left and an easy source, but the population may derive largely from cones of poor inland sources washed down the Fraser River in floods.

The successful strategy was to collect from the Skeena River area in the Alaskan Panhandle. The tree form there is excellent and the latitude far enough north to slow growth adequately. There may also be some natural crossing with the good inland form up river and parts are intermediate, coastal to inland. The Skeena River trees are also very hardy where some Oregon and Californian source trees can be damaged by unseasonable frosts.

Of the very few big specimens in arboreta, all but one are Shore Pine, and the outstanding tree among these has long been the one in the ravine at Bodnant. Planted in 1888, it is now 110/10ft. Only one is known to be older, which is strange, because David Douglas was familiar with the tree and was at one time said to have introduced it from California in 1832, but now John Jeffrey is credited with the first seeds of both forms, in 1851, and no specimen older than an 1876 planting is known. This is the great mophead on Broad Drive in Silk Wood, Westonbirt Arboretum. Its nearly globular, very dense crown reaches a height of 72ft on a thick stalk 9ft round.

Since the Bodnant tree took 101 years to be ten feet round, the larger of two very fine trees on the bank below Tannadyce House, Angus, could possibly be from Jeffrey's seed. This one is 92/12ft, and the other, with a long, tapered crown, is 98/8ft. Another pair is at Bowood, Wiltshire, 80/8ft and 78/8ft. Castle Milk, Dumfries, has several specimens. The two biggest are not far from the Castle, 80/8ft and 82/7ft while a young tree in a Coronation planting along the drive, dating from 1953 was already 82/6ft, when 31 years old. At Blairquhan, Ayrshire, a tree is 68/7ft.

Lodgepole Pine (*Pinus contorta*):
Bedgebury, Kent

In the pinetum at St Clere, Kent, in a slight clay hollow perched at over 700ft up on the crest of the chalk Downs, a tree which dates from the first plantings in 1905 is now 70/8½ft. One of several planted in 1913 in the top pinetum at Wakehurst Place, Sussex, survived the 1987 gale with a broken top and is now 62/7ft.

The inland form, Lodgepole Pine, var. *latifolia*, has tangibly broader thicker leaves and they spray out from the shoot where the Shore Pine leaves are more densely held and point forward closely around the shoot. They are also rich deep green where those of Lodgepole are dull, dark yellowish green. The most evident difference, in cultivation as well as in the Rocky Mountains, is in the bark. The Shore Pine bark breaks very early into squarish thick blocks divided by regular pale or reddish brown fissures, and are checkered. The inland form has unfissured, dark red-brown, purple-tinted, smooth bark soon starting to flake finely. The Shore Pine ranges from the Alaska Panhandle and islands in a belt around 50 miles broad south to Puget Sound when it extends south in a very thin belt along the coast of Washington and Oregon to end in a few estuaries in Northern California and a small population distinguished by some as Bolander's Pine on the Mendocino Plains. The inland form sweeps broadly from Yukon and Alberta and western Wyoming where it is the dominant tree throughout Yellowstone National Park, to Colorado. In the west, it extends down the Cascades in Washington and across the Columbia River where it becomes var. *murrayana* and along the Sierra Nevada. Tiny southern outliers include one at Bluff Lake in San Bernardino Mountains where one 407 years old in 1971 was 20ft round.

A tree of the inland Lodgepole Pine at Westonbirt Arboretum, is a graft, planted in 1875 in Pool Drive and now 88/8ft. The rootstock is not readily identifiable but will probably be Scots Pine. It would be pointless to have used another *contorta* for this when both forms of it seemed to have been equally scarce. Scots is the standard stock for two-needle pines like this.

The tallest Lodgepole Pine is at Culcreuch Castle, Fintry, Stirlingshire, 98/7ft and typically forked many times in the upper crown. One of four planted at Dropmore in 1913 was 84/6ft in 1982 and a very shapely tree at Pitcarmick, Strathardle, dating from about 1925 is 52/6ft, very like one in the pinetum on the slight ridge at Camperdown Park, Dundee, which is 70/5ft.

COULTER PINE

Pinus coulteri

Dr Thomas Coulter was a chubby, cheerful Irish botanist and a highly independent soul who breezed in on David Douglas. Douglas had not known of any other collector within a thousand miles and was delighted to have a botanist to talk to in a time of frustration and disappointment. He spent much of a year fruitlessly waiting

Coulter Pine (*Pinus coulteri*): the tree
has very rapid early growth, but a short
life-span

for a permit from Russia to allow him into Siberia, and for a Russia-bound ship to call at Monterey. These ships all avoided it because of hostility from the Spanish and bans on travel and visits to that part of California. Douglas was botanising only desultorily and striving to organise his grand finale, a walk across Siberia. A few days before Coulter's appearance he had received a permit from the Russian Baron Wrangel to start his expedition provided he could reach Sitka in Alaska, so he resumed his watch on ships arriving, every day. He put off until spring the intended arrival at the near-arctic Sitka and hoped for an early start as far as Fort Vancouver to await a ship there. His local botanising had been much restricted by the bans on travel and he had been working almost wholly on local annuals. It was his large supply of these to London that began the fashion of carpet-bedding but he was dispirited by the onset of winter cutting the flowers down.

Thomas Coulter had no such problems. He ignored all bans and drifted around as he wanted, unknown and untroubled. He asked Douglas if he would like to join him on a cactus-hunt to Colorado and the Gila River. Douglas was thrilled by the idea, but having just received his permit, he had to keep up his watch for a useful ship. A scare that the Paisanos around Los Angeles had regrouped after defeat by Governor Victoria and might march on Monterey, saw Douglas and Coulter together drafted into an informal defence force, and no one was allowed to leave until March 1832. This was too late for Douglas to go, so he reluctantly saw Coulter off. Coulter returned in July with a big haul of specimens and seed and then fades from the story. He had discovered a pine in the Santa Lucia Mountains nearby. It was Douglas who worked on the specimens, until he took the ship in August to Hawaii, and sent them to Kew. The pine was named *Pinus coulteri* and in effect was introduced by Douglas who never saw it growing, nor described or named it, as this was the work of D. Don in 1836. In the wild, from near Monterey both sides of the Salinas River and on the Coast Range in Santa Lucia Range and scattered mountains south to Baja California, it is a bushy short-boled tree 40–60ft tall (although 137/13ft is recorded, and a fine tree at the Capitol in Sacramento is 105/8ft).

The distribution of the original seed is not recorded and in a tree seen now to have very rapid early growth and usually only a short life-span, estimating the age of big specimens is fraught with difficulty. The second seedlot was sent by William Lobb in 1851, but Kew planted a few trees in 1840. The Coulter trees will have been planted by about 1835 and trees probably from this lot were planted from 1838 to 1841 at Bayfordbury, Hertfordshire and Bury Hill, Surrey, but none survives today nor any Lobb trees. In fact, by 1960 not a single tree with growth recorded before 1950 was alive and today the oldest known is a 1928 tree at Westonbirt. Until 1974 there were two very big trees of similar size in gardens not far apart in Herefordshire. It was fun to speculate that if they had grown much as the closely related Ponderosa Pines planted in 1827, they could very easily have been original 1832 Coulter trees. One at Titley Court was 98/13ft when it died in 1970, and the other, at Bankfield House, Leominster, 75/12½ft eight years before its death in 1974. Now the biggest is an amazing young tree with a hugely spreading low crown and broad-conic top, planted in 1956 by the Trial Ground at Wisley Gardens in Surrey. It is 62/8½ft and growing apace as it was only 36/5ft ten years ago. The tallest is an undated tree in the Royal Botanic Garden, Edinburgh, at 85/6½ft, growing slowly, as it was 60/4ft in 1955. A younger tree of very rapid growth is one in the valley at the Hillier Arboretum, Hampshire, planted in 1964 and now 46/7½ft. The 1928 tree in Sand Earth, Silk Wood at Westonbirt, is only 62/7ft.

WESTONBIRT PINE

Pinus x *holfordiana*

None of the numerous species of pines in the world seems to have crossed with any other in the wild. Many hybrids have, however, been raised in gardens and in research stations, especially at Placerville in California. Hybrids between two-needle species are rare and hard to raise and those between three-needle pines are not more numerous. It is the five-needle pines which provide the only hybrids seen in some gardens, and the oldest, biggest and best is the Westonbirt Pine.

This was not raised deliberately, but by chance, and it was not identified as a hybrid until 29 years after it arose. There was a splendid Mexican White Pine of Veitch's variety, *Pinus ayacahuite* var. *veitchii*, planted in 1875 at Westonbirt by the gate from Circular Drive into Down Covert. Its cones were more than one foot

Westonbirt Pine (*Pinus* x *holfordiana*): Wisley, Surrey

long and one borne in 1926 was 22in long. Sir George Holford was proud of this tree and when it started to bear seed, in 1904, he collected enough to raise dozens of plants. In 1906 he planted groups of half a dozen in bays beside rides in the Arboretum and in Silk Wood. Neither Sir George, who died in 1926, nor Bruce Jackson who was compiling the catalogue, *Trees of Westonbirt* (published in 1927) thought that they were anything but Mexican White Pines, but when some of them started to cone in 1932, Jackson saw that they were hybrids and that the male parent was a Bhutan Pine then growing nearby. Jackson described the hybrid in 1933 and named it *Pinus* x *holfordiana*.

The first generation trees are all very vigorous and inherit the down on the young shoot of the Mexican tree and the broader cone with non-reflexed scales as in the Bhutan Pine, except for the basal few whorls which are reflexed in both parents. The tree has the long, spreading branches of the Mexican and the orange-brown bark of the Bhutan Pine. One group, off the Willesly Drive, is of younger trees, possibly planted in 1937, and seems to be typical second generation hybrids, some of them very like one parent and some like the other. The original groups have suffered losses, some to honey-fungus and some to wind-throw, but currently at least one tree survives in all and four or five in most. As with the big trees at Wisley, they litter the ground with cones so big that they are irresistible to visitors and a menace to children as they are covered in very viscid resin.

To increase a first generation hybrid the only way to raise new individuals is to make the cross again. Making grafts of the original seedlings will multiply those but cannot add to the number of genotypes in existence, and raising plants by seed from the originals will give second generation hybrids. They usually show little hybrid vigour and much variation in features between the parental types. The first cross is not known to have arisen again, although Holford may have raised more. It will not arise again until trees of the two species are adjacent and flowering, or pollen of one is collected in one collection and dusted on developing cones of the other somewhere. The biggest trees date from 1929 at Borde Hill and, probably within a year or two of that year, at Wisley and Lythe Hill. None is visibly a graft and I suspect that Jackson raised them at Westonbirt, although why Lythe Hill received one and not some of dozens of more famous gardens whose owners were known to Jackson, is a puzzle.

At Westonbirt, the spacing within each group was not enough to allow the spread of crown that is shown by the bigger, younger trees, so they have slender, small-branched crowns. They were all planted in 1906. By Holford Avenue the two best are 118/7ft and 115/7ft. The solitary survivor of the Loop Walk group is now 102/7ft. The survivor of the two trees in Gores Wood, Borde Hill, planted in 1929 is now 80/11ft with many big, low branches. The other was smaller and was blown down in October 1987.

In the nearer half of the pinetum at Wisley, the tree near the fence in the northeast has even bigger, lower and more spreading branches and is 80/11ft. One nearer the main path is more restrained and is 77/8ft while the tree in the other half of the pinetum is intermediate in form and has a very large crown, 70/9ft. The tree by the mid-path on the bank at Lythe Hill, Haslemere, Surrey, is narrower and 95/9ft. In 1969 it was 60/8ft. One in Batsford Park in Gloucestershire is 80/5ft while a rare, dated recent tree at Cliveden in Buckinghamshire was planted in 1950 and is now 52/3ft.

JEFFREY PINE

Pinus jeffreyi

After the death of David Douglas in 1834, there was a halt to the exciting discoveries of the great conifers of the Pacific slopes and of imports of seed from them. It was not known that Steuart Fotheringham had brought seed in 1846 to make an extensive planting of Douglas Fir with a few Sitka Spruce, at Murthly Castle near Perth. By 1849, when the Douglas introductions were 17–20 years old and showing immense promise, especially in Scotland, the situation called for action. In that year,

Veitch's Nursery sent their experienced collector, William Lobb, to California, and a group of Scottish landowners, mostly from Perthshire, set up the Oregon Association to finance their own collector. The first meeting was on November 22 in 1849 to add ten more members and establish the full Society, which met on February 6, in 1850. On February 28, they selected John Jeffrey from the Royal Botanic Gardens, Edinburgh, and gave him a three year contract as their collector. He went in June to York Factory on the Hudson Bay and made immense journeys through Canada, the Cascades, Shasta region, the Siskiyou Mountains and the Sierra Nevada, discovering and introducing about 20 fine conifers. He never came back. His seed-packets became smaller and smaller, and the journals that his contract demanded did not arrive so the Association, who could contact him only with difficulty and then not at all, asked the Lawson collector, William Murray, whether they should renew the contract. He advised against it. By March 1854 they could not make contact with Jeffrey and dismissed him. Without the journals, which only turned up years later, the precise localities and dates of his discoveries could not be known and many credited to Lobb, were really Jeffrey's. His tenth and last box of seed was sent from San Francisco on October 7, 1853. Several tales were told about Jeffrey's fate in 1854, knifed in a road-gang brawl in Arizona or when robbed as a trader by Indians in Mexico, all with a violent end, except one. That one has him going native in California and last seen heading into the Sierras with a string of squaws. Very plausible, and pleasant, but a sad end for one of the greatest collectors of all time.

Jeffrey Pine ranges from near the coast in southwest Oregon, through Shasta and down the length of the Sierra Nevada and a few mountain tops into Mexico. It is to some extent a high-altitude replacement of Ponderosa Pine above 6000ft and on the bare white granites to over 9000ft. There are magnificent trees in Yosemite above the valley-bottom Ponderosa and even better, to 220/17ft, in King's Canyon. It is less shapely, narrow-conic than the Ponderosa, with stouter, more spreading branches.

Jeffrey found it on October 24, 1852, in Shasta Valley and sent a quantity of seed, and the foliage and cone from which the type specimen was described and named. No subsequent import is recorded and plants seem not to bear cones in their first 20 years, so early trees are rare. Several trees dated 1860 and a few years after are likely to come from Jeffrey's seed and grown some years before planting out. As a garden tree, it makes the most handsome young plant, broad-conic, with well-spaced branches, level before curving gently to upswept tips of strong blue-white shoots clothed in long, grey-blue needles slightly drooped, like a fountain around a stout leading shoot, soon growing two feet a year. It looks hugely vigorous, but the first years are so slow that it may be no more than 20ft tall in 15 years. It is very hardy and is among the best of the very few West Coast conifers to make good trees in up-state New York. In the smaller native stands at high altitude, old trees have bushy crowns thick with the big, pale brown cones held at all angles, but in

Britain coning is sparse and sets in late in the life of the still shapely, spire-topped trees.

The oldest and biggest known in 1989 is the great tree in the pinetum at Scone Palace, Perth, at 132/14ft. It is in the lines added to the 1852 pinetum in 1866 and is recorded as dating from 1860, so it was six years in the nursery, which is about the average time before planting out. It has rather lost the formal conic shape but still has a good top with a dominant leading shoot, and is growing well. In 1891 it was 50/7ft and in 1970, 120/12½ft. Powerscourt in County Wicklow has five trees planted in 1866. Three splendid trees are in the field sloping from the gardens to the Dargle Glen. Probably the best of these was recorded as 75/9½ft in 1931, and 115/12½ft in 1989, when the other two were 102/12½ft and, standing rather apart from that pair, 121/12½ft. One in the Glen at the picnic-site was then 115/9ft, and the last, below the Pepperpot tower, was 95/11ft. A tree planted in 1875 on the hill at Ochtertyre, Crieff, Perthshire, has grown from 102/7½ft in 1970 to 105/9ft in 1987. An undated tree left in a field when the pinetum at Castle Menzies was felled long ago is a beautiful, classic shape, 70/9ft. A less shapely tree among several on the hill at Eastnor Castle, Herefordshire, is 92/10½ft and another somewhat rugged tree in a field beside Barr's Lane, on Knaphill Nurseries near Woking, Surrey, 56/8½ft in 1961, was 70/10½ft in 1990. Hampton Estate at Seale in Surrey had three trees in 1984 which seem likely to date from before 1870. One was broken to 46/12ft and the other two were 100/11ft and

Jeffrey Pine (*Pinus jeffreyi*): Holdfast Lane, Haslemere, Surrey

82/11ft bearing cones near ground-level. An undated tree by the drive to Culcreuch in Stirlingshire was 98/11ft in 1984. The most outstanding specimen for both growth and classic shape is in a front garden beside Holdfast Lane below Haslemere in Surrey. Brought back as seed in 1935 from an unrecorded source in the United States by former owners, it was already 56/5ft in 1963 and now in 1990, it is 82/10ft with a splendid trunk and unblemished crown to a long leading shoot.

BISHOP PINE

Pinus muricata

The Bishop Pine is a tree of character with many features of interest. Its English name derives from its discovery by Thomas Coulter in 1830 on the low hills near the coast in southern California around the town of San Luis Obispo, the town of Bishop Saint Louis. It has two populations differing in growth and appearance, most notably in cultivation; it is a 'Monterey Relict' species, and very much a fire-climax tree.

The 'Monterey Relicts' are three cypresses and three pines which used the extreme western route in their return migration north from Mexico after the Ice Ages. The low hills and coast on this route eroded ahead of and around them and they became isolated, unable to escape north from small enclaves along the present coast and islands. The Soledad Pine, *P. torreyana* has ended up as about 6000 trees at La Jolla and a narrow half-mile belt on Santa Rosa Island. *Pinus radiata* has over 3000 acres on the Monterey Peninsula; a four-mile patch to the north near Swanton; a five-mile area 60 miles to the south around Cambria, and a variety, *binata,* on Guadalupe Island, 460 miles south of that. The Bishop Pine has seven main groups of tiny populations scattered along 450 miles of coast and islands, with a variant on Cedros Island 500 miles further south, off Mexico.

The trees in the south, around San Luis Obispo have low, upswept, domed broad crowns, clustered with unopened cones. A tiny stand near Carmel is encircled by *P. radiata* and the trees have less room but are of the same aspect. The needles are greyish yellow-green, often shading to dull yellow towards the base. Well to the north, in Pigmy Forest, Mendocino, and particularly at the mouth of the Noyo River at Fort Bragg, they are very much of the northern form, columnar-conic, tall trees with more open crowns less crowded with cones, and bearing blue-grey needles. The division does not coincide with the Golden Gate, as would be expected, but is about 60 miles to its north, for two small areas near Point Reyes around 20 miles north of the inlet are of the southern form.

The Bishop Pine was introduced in 1846 by Hartweg, from San Luis Obispo and so was the southern form. Deliberate introduction of the northern form was by seed from New Zealand in 1958. The Forest Service there were aware of the highly

Bishop Pine (*Pinus muricata*):
Eastnor Castle, Herefordshire

superior growth of this form and its hugely vigorous growth on the poorest soils. The Forestry Commission put plots on the most acid sands known in Britain, at Bedgebury National Pinetum in Kent, where a few years later some trees were adding six feet a year. Study of older trees in other parts then showed that the northern form had been growing unrecognised in several collections, notably at Muckross Abbey, County Kerry and, from 1915 seed, at Wakehurst Place, Sussex.

The biggest and oldest trees are of the southern form, and the oldest with a documented date was an 1850 tree at Bayfordbury in Hertfordshire. When 56 years old it was only 44/4ft so its seniority did not show in its size and when last seen in 1973 at 50/8ft, it was exceeded by many younger trees. The next oldest was planted in 1856 at Castle Kennedy in Wigtownshire. When 48 years old it was 36/5ft 8in and 22 years later it was 48/7ft 9in. When 111 years old it was 75/9ft and then crowded on some speed to be 82/11ft by 1984 when 128 years old. That puts it among the biggest. I counted the annual whorls of retained cones on a branch in the lower crown and the score was 66.

The biggest tree, very probably older than either of these two and surely from the original seed, is a remarkable specimen in front of Eberno House near Petworth.

In 1983 it was 95/13ft 9in and had added only seven inches in the previous 12 years, so it must have made impressive growth in earlier years. Another which may be as old is in the pinetum at Dupplin Castle in Perthshire. By 1930 it was 83/9ft and then slowed down to be 85/10ft 7in in 1957 and 92/11ft in 1983. It is well adorned with cones. A tree at The Cottage, Compton, Surrey, must be about as old. In 1974 it was 72/11ft 7in but has no early recorded history. The finest specimen, and the most happily positioned, is at Eastnor Castle, Herefordshire, in the focal point where the drive turns left to the moat-bridge. It has 30ft of clear, smooth trunk. In 1907 it was 41/6ft and by 1961 it had grown to 88/10ft 3in and in 1989 it was 98/11ft 4in.

At Grayswood Hill near Haslemere in Surrey, where most of the early plantings was done in 1881, a rugged old tree is today 85/11ft. At Blackmoor, Hampshire, a tree now 82/9ft 4in is grafted at the base, but I cannot determine the rootstock species.

Among trees of known date planted in this century, some have grown very fast. Two at Bodnant, Gwynedd on the pine bank near the top pool, planted in 1903 are now 98/11ft 3in and 82/11ft 2in. Two of at least six planted in 1917 in the main pinetum at Wakehurst Place survived the 1987 gale. They were, in 1988, 82/10ft 7in and 82/9ft 7in while two, probably of the same age, in the Sands pinetum nearby, were 82/9ft and 85/10ft 4in. One at Birr Castle, County Offaly, planted in the pinetum in 1927 was 85/8ft 4in in 1985. At Bedgebury, the best of three very broad, southern form trees of the first plantings there, in 1925, is 66/9ft 2in. At Forde Abbey, near Chard in Somerset, one in the pinetum planted in 1950 was 52/6ft 6in in 1988. In the plot of northern, blue form at Lyndford Arboretum in Norfolk, planted in 1960, one standing apart was 42/4ft 2in when 17 years old; 66/5ft 10in when 23, and 70/7ft 5in when 29 years old.

CORSICAN and CRIMEAN PINES

Pinus nigra var. *maritima* and var. *pallasiana*

The Black Pine complex spreads on mountains from the Pyrenees to Eastern Turkey in four recognisable forms, of which these two are the only ones to have provided us with imposing big specimens. They could be called, if one likes such terms, the Queen and King of the group: the Corsican at best, elegant with slender, level branches to a spire top and open, long, fine foliage and rather smooth bark; and the Crimean, robust with a cluster of top shoots, dense, dark, shorter foliage and dark, heavily ridged bark.

The CORSICAN PINE (*Pinus nigra* var. *maritima*) is said (by Aiton, the first Director of Kew) to have been grown here since 1759, but he seems to have been quoting from a list in the 1759 edition of Phillip Miller's Dictionary and the identity of the pine there is not exactly known. The first date for a tree at Kew known today, and the earliest in Britain, is 1814, and it is known that the tree was very rare until after 1820. The history of both these forms, even until 1931, is hard to unravel as some specimens recorded as Corsican are Crimean and some Crimean and Corsican trees were recorded as Austrian.

The Corsican Pine is a very splendid tree to 150ft tall on the granite mountains of Corsica and grows also in Calabria, Southern Italy, and in Sicily. Despite being largely a tree of the interior parts, it is found in Britain to be valuable for its resistance to strong, salty sea-winds and has been widely planted on or just behind dunes in Norfolk, South Wales and on Anglesey. It was also found to be the conifer most resistant to industrially polluted air and was planted in the South Pennines around Sheffield and elsewhere. Its ability to grow well on limestones was an asset here, and it will make a crop on chalk.

On acid heaths in southern England and on calcareous sands in Breckland, it outyields the traditional Scots Pine by some 50 per cent, so has long replaced that tree as a crop. But low summer temperatures limit similar use in Scotland and the northeast of England as it becomes prone to the fungus *Brunchorstia*. Similarly on thin peats at some altitude it is a success in southern England alone.

A good specimen of Corsican Pine is, like one of Scots Pine, much more impressive than its mere dimensions suggest. That is because the bole is so smoothly rounded and evenly tapered, with a long, clear length, which can be seen through

Corsican Pine (*Pinus nigra* var *maritima*):
Eastnor Castle, Herefordshire

the open crown almost to the top. Very like a proper, plain, old-fashioned factory chimney.

The best example of this is a tree near the back drive to Whitfield House, Herefordshire, which has no branch at all for 80ft and a narrow, conic crown above that to 135ft. It is a young tree, seven feet round. Another similar, but with slender branches still on the trunk above about 20ft, is the bottom tree in a little group on the rocky hill above the house at Kinlochhourn, Inverness-shire. Far north for this species and enjoying some 100in of rain a year, this is 111/8ft. As far north, in the same county but in the much drier east, at Beaufort Castle by the Gardener's Cottage, a bigger stem, 108/10ft, is of classic shape. Not far away, one planted at Teanassie, Aigas, in 1877, is 118/9ft and similar. At Albury Park, Surrey, a beautiful tree is 105/13ft and of the same form. It was 102/7ft in 1905. Another of this form but more slender and with a long, clean, very impressive bole is in the hollow of giant trees at Cuffnells, Lyndhurst, Hampshire, which was planted in 1855. This tree is 130/10ft.

Some specimens have excellent boles but heavy upper branches and less shapely crowns. Two good examples are in the wood off the road to Dynefawr castle, Dyfed, towards the ruins. One is 92/13ft with 30ft of clean trunk, and the other is 92/9ft with a full 45ft clear. A tree below the House at Coed Coch, Clwyd, is 130/13ft. The old tree at Kew, planted by the Main Gates in 1814, has a clean trunk, but its crown suffered a severe pruning when a light aircraft took the top out long ago. It never seems to have grown other than slowly, for it was 85/9ft in 1903, and is today 85/10ft. One of the two at Charing Cross in Leaton Knolls Estate, Shropshire, has a good bole but broad, heavily branched crown and is 118/13ft. A better shaped tree in The Dingle there is 132/11ft.

The tallest known at present is 150/13ft at Adhurst St Mary an outstanding specimen. Some of the oldest trees bear big branches low and four of the biggest owe their size in some measure to this. One in a field near Llanfachreth, north of Dolgellau is 108/18ft forking into two stems at seven feet, and the biggest of three in the garden at Holkham House, Norfolk, is 105/15ft. The rugged and venerable one at Dropmore has a plaque announcing its 1829 planting, a fact confirmed by many subsequent records of its size in Victorian times, noted by the Head Gardener, Frost, and by many later writers. It is 120/15ft taped, without spurious increase, among the few low branches. An inspired planting in 1929 on the hundredth birthday of the old tree of another Corsican Pine beside it, shows how it may have grown. In 1982 this young tree was 80/6ft.

The CRIMEAN PINE (*Pinus nigra* var. *pallasiana*) was sent in 1790 by the Russian botanist, Pallas, to Lee and Kennedy, nurserymen in Hammersmith. It was collected from a very small population near the south coast of the Crimean Peninsular. Another even smaller group is on the southern flanks of the Caucasus Mountains a few miles to the east. Both are outliers of the Black Pine the other side of the Black

Sea, which dominates the mountains in Asia Minor, the latter, var. *caramanica*, named from the town of Karmana, central in the west of the plateau.

In Britain, both forms are intermediate in foliage between the Corsican and the Austrian. The needles are neither slender, long, twisted and greyish as in Corsican, nor stout, curved and short as in Austrian, but they are so dark green that from a distance the tree is as black. The big feature of the Crimean is that the trunk divides at 30–50ft into a number of close vertical stems curving sharply up from their origin, and some forking again higher up. This makes it look as if the tree had been beheaded or suffered grievous injury. The multiple top will be a contributory reason for the more rapid growth in girth in the Crimean than in the Corsican Pine. This can be seen when the two are of the same age in one planting, and is also apparent in that the specimens selected for mention here tend to be bigger, but not often taller.

The divided stem with three to six close vertical stems from about 15ft, like organ-pipes, is more frequent or noticed than the single-stemmed *caramanica* in which numerous straight branches of moderate size arise from all the way up the trunk and lean slightly away from it. Those in the upper crown arch gently out dangling short-pendulous foliage. Many of the younger trees are like this in its early stages, as seen in the 1925 group at Bedgebury. The specimen by the drive behind the House at Dropmore planted in 1821 is 121/15ft at three feet, the branches preventing a girth measurement above that. A bigger, more squat and more branchy tree of this kind is at Bishopsthorpe, the residence of the Archbishop of York, in York. It is 70/17ft measurable at five feet among the branches.

Some big trees with organ-pipes include a fine tree in the Park at Westonbirt House, 102/15ft, and one at Kingston Lacey, Wimborne, is 111/17ft at three feet. Rather more strictly organ-pipe are good trees in the Cedar Avenue at Pampisford, Cambridge, 102/12ft; one in the middle of Nuneham Courtnay Arboretum, Oxfordshire, 124/13ft and one at Rossie Priory, Dundee, 124/14ft. This one was 87/10ft in 1931. One outside the garden at Ickworth, Suffolk, is a handsome tree at 115/14ft. The finest of all was, in 1980, one in a dell of big conifers in the northwestern corner of Beauport Park near Hastings which was then 121/17ft and had been 84/11ft in 1904. It has since been blown down. A good one is at Leighton Knolls, Shropshire, 123/14ft, and on the hill at Eastnor Castle, one is 121/12ft.

The most strictly organ-pipe trees are in woodlands, which have shaded out the lower branches and left a clean trunk below the division. A good example is the tree at Cuffnells, typically outgrowing the Corsican Pine of the same age beside it and not of the superb quality of that tree. It is 132/13ft. Similarly beside a Corsican of lesser stature but superior form, the tree by the Gardener's Cottage at Beaufort Castle, Inverness, is 135/14ft. At the head of Loch Ness, in Aldourie, one is 111/12ft. A broader one which is more like the Westonbirt tree is at Fota Garden, near Cork, 95/14ft, the only big specimen seen in Ireland.

MARITIME PINE

Pinus pinaster (plate 3)

The adjective 'pinaster' translates as 'like a pine' which refers to some similarities to *Pinus pinea*, the Stone Pine, a better known tree in southern Europe. An alternative English name for the tree is the 'Bournemouth Pine' and the wooded residential outskirts of this town certainly grow an unusual number of the tree, while Cluster Pine, more frequently in use, is a reference to the whorls of big cones that persist in the crown for many years. The cones are up to ten inches long, a good classic cone shape, and shiny rich brown for some years, so are prized for summer occupation of fireplaces, and painted in silver and lurid colours for table decorations at Christmas. As in the closely related Stone Pine, this retention of cones, with the seeds in them viable for many years, is a sign that in the past the species has evolved in a fire-climax ecology but today there are no large tracts in its range where this is important, although it operates in some small areas.

The natural range of the Maritime Pine covers much of Portugal; large areas in central and southern Spain; Corsica; the French Riviera and the northwest coast of Italy, spreading up the Arno Valley. Small populations in the Rif and Atlas Mountains in Morocco have been separated as 'Atlantica', treated as a cultivar as suspected of being selected from stands in Spain. The big forests of Les Landes, so often quoted in the past as producing 'naval stores' (turpentine mostly), are now thought to be a planted extension from the natural range, probably using seed from Corsica where the best natural stands grow. It has been grown in Britain since a little while after 1500.

There was an early fashion for planting belts of Maritime Pine on the inland edge of advancing sand-dunes, but few trees remain. Young trees grow with remarkable vigour on the poorest sands and occasional stands are seen in Dorset of singular appearance. The heavy early top-growth caused the trees to be swept downwind and they straightened up leaving a big curve in the stem, parallel throughout the stand. The foliage stands only a little shade, so the lower crowns are transparent giving a clear view through the whorls of slender branches widely spaced up the stems.

The finest specimen was blown down in 1977. It was in a group near the second lake in Sheffield Park in Sussex, planted in about 1800. It had grown to 85/15ft with the trunk clear for about 40ft. Two others in the group are still there and are 98/11ft and 98/9ft. Several other estates in that part of Sussex had trees over 100ft tall, but most were lost in the 1987 gale. A tree dating from 1811 was at Hewell Grange near Bromsgrove and was 95/10ft in 1963. In Dorset, a big tree at Carey House near Wareham is 82/13ft, forking at six feet. At Oxenden House, near Leighton Buzzard, a tree is 88/12ft. At Trelissick in Cornwall, there is one 72/10ft. In Herefordshire, a tree with a splendid bole, all dark purple, red and brown rectangular scales for 40ft, is 92/11ft at Holme Lacey and at The Hendre outside Monmouth a tree of very mediocre form is 105/9ft. At Penrhyn Castle, Gwynedd, a tree below the Castle, very bare in its lower parts, is 82/9ft.

In Scotland, the specimens are fewer but one in the far northwest at Torridon House, Wester Ross, is 82/11ft and Crarae Garden, Argyll, has one 70/7ft while the furthest northeast seems to be one planted in 1970 in the Cruickshank Botanic Garden at Aberdeen University which was 16/2ft in 1987. In the southwest, an old tree at Monreith House, Wigtown, is 72/10ft, and apparently 82/9ft in 1905. In Ireland, a fine tree in the woods at Curraghmore in County Waterford was 102/10ft in 1968 and one at The Belvedere in County Westmeath is now 70/12ft.

STONE PINE

Pinus pinea

Most of the people who know this tree at all, know it as the 'Umbrella Pine' that they see in Italy. This is an apt name for the mature tree has a regular, parachute-shaped crown, prominent in some Mediterranean landscapes. It can, however, cause confusion with a very different tree for which 'Umbrella Pine' is the only English name, the highly eccentric redwood relict of an ancient flora, found in Japan and grown in many western gardens, more formally called *Sciadopitys verticillata*. The Stone Pine in Britain is not well known and it seems that some folk with either a fleeting acquaintance with conifers, or in the earliest stages of learning them, can mistake Austrian, Corsican or even Scots Pines for Stone Pines. I know that stage lasted a few weeks when I was at school among a few beginning an interest in natural history. It was also evidently rife in some ornithological circles, for I read the results of a survey of rookeries in Sussex, in which a high percentage of the nests were said to be in Stone Pines. Since this amounted to several hundred nests, and I know the trees of Sussex rather well, this brought on splendid visions of every Sussex specimen with its crown adorned with at least 50 rooks' nests.

The Stone Pine shares many features with the closely related Maritime Pine, including a western Mediterranean range and substantial woody cones, but also peculiar juvenile growth which is found only in these two species, the Aleppo Pine, Canary Pine and in the Mexican Nut-pine group. The seedling tree is a bushy but strictly upright plant bearing only long, silvery blue, 'primordial leaves'. Other pines do this during their first year from seed and then change to green adult needles in bundles. But the Stone Pine seedling, and those in this group, grow for another two or three years in this form and are erect, leafy, silvery blue plants until they are three or four feet high. The next year's growth puts out the same primordial leaves, but long green needles in pairs grow out from the angles between these and the stem. The blue foliage persists on the plant, which is then prettily mixed blue and green foliage. Furthermore, the Stone Pine, particularly, and the Canary Pine, which are the most prone to do this, can react to grazing or other damage to the adult crown, by growing juvenile shoot replacements, and may grow juvenile sprouts on the trunk at any time.

The Stone Pine has been planted extensively in Italy and Spain but has a restricted natural range mainly in central and southern Spain and by the west coast of Italy, in southern Portugal and by the east coast of Spain. There are small stands in the Balearic Islands, and in Sardinia and Sicily. It was introduced to Britain some time before Turner was writing in 1548, and is infrequent in England and south Wales and scarce in Scotland and Ireland. That it needs hotter summers than it has here is indicated by the growth in southern California, where all the biggest I have seen grow. One planted in 1907 in the Huntington Gardens was 95/11ft in 1982 when two near the Capitol in Sacramento were 92/11ft and 85/15ft.

The biggest in Britain was at Embley Park near Romsey in Hampshire which was 75/12ft when it was blown down in 1986. The best now is the tree which spreads some of its crown over the main A40 in Crickhowell, Powys. It grows behind the old, high wall of Portmarr, and is 65/11ft and thought to date from 1820. The well-known tree near the Director's Garden in Kew has low, spreading branches and has to be taped at one foot, where it is 50/9ft. A tall tree on Bell Lawn is now 70/7ft. A big, spreading tree at Margam Park near Swansea is 65/9ft.

One by the drive to Bryanston School in Dorset was 56/11ft in 1983. One of the few old dated trees is at Fota Garden near Cork and planted in 1847, it was 66/8ft in 1987. Very slow growth is shown by one at Saltram House in Devon, 70/9ft in 1987, if it is the tree that was 60/8ft in 1910. A big, spreading low-branched tree at Dartington School in Devon was 70/9ft at three feet in 1984. One with two trunks in Hatfield Forest in Essex is 52/8ft + 7 and one in Elgin's Copse there is 50/13ft, but I have not seen it and can only assume that this is measured below low branches.

SCOTS PINE

Pinus sylvestris

No tree has a better right to the name 'forest tree' since it is the original 'fir' from which the word 'forest' is derived. Only by a nomenclatural quirk or two is it now called 'pine' and is the type tree of the genus *Pinus* while 'fir' is attached to the silver firs of the genus *Abies*. The Scots Pine has the widest geographical spread of any conifer with the exception of the Common Juniper. That tree uses the stepping stones of Iceland and Greenland to cross the Atlantic Ocean and spread right across northern North America. The Scots Pine is confined to the Old World, but within that it grows from central Spain and Scotland to Yakutsk in Eastern Siberia and south in Manchuria almost to the Pacific Ocean.

Over this great range, the species has evolved into many geographical varieties and at different times some authors have distinguished Scottish, Baltic, Crimean, Altai Mountain and other forms. The Scottish subspecies has been called var. *scotica* and var. *horizontalis* the latter typifying it from the level branches in the upper crown. In experimental trials it is notable in youth for its short and very blue foliage in comparison with plants from mainland Europe. After recolonising England post-Ice Ages, Scots Pine rapidly moved to Scotland, apparently en bloc, for it is now thought that there is no sound record in historic times of wild stands in England. The most southerly now is the Black Wood of Rannoch along the southern shore of Loch Rannoch. The large tracts of seemingly wild Scots Pine in England originated less than 400 years ago. The oldest are those on the Bagshot Sands areas in Berkshire and Surrey, arising perhaps from a nucleus of trees at Eversley Church and Bramshill believed to date from a few years after 1600. The New Forest pines are credited to seed or plants from Darnaway Estate in Morayshire, planted in 1776.

At Glasnevin Agricultural College where I took my forestry degree, the Scots Pine was known as 'the facile snare' because in one of our silvicultural works it was classed as 'a facile snare for the uninitiated'. This made the point that it was easy to raise and it established well on a wide range of soils and sites, including some of the most difficult, but on almost any it would be outgrown and outyielded by other species. It is unable to exploit better sites and even at its best is a smaller and slower growing tree than the other conifers used in forestry. The heaviest yield of timber is said to be carried by the stand at Shambellie in Kirkcudbrightshire. Planted in 1780 on a fertile site, this is peculiarly impressive with big, cylindric orange-red boles standing unusually close for any pine, but the individual trees are no bigger than 95/10ft, which is no great size for 215 years of growth.

Nonetheless, the facile snare is an important producer of high quality timber in certain localities. The stands in Windsor Forest have been selected and thinned for the best trees over many generations and turn out transmission poles for a special-ised market. These trees must be consistently very straight and only the best will be taken. In Ireland, the probably apocryphal story is told that foresters kept a few slightly substandard poles to add to each roadside stack in order that the inspectors would easily see and reject them. Having done that, they would, it was hoped, consider their job done and pass the remainder and the poles were kept for next time. The New Forest grows and re-seeds from some high quality stands. There are extensive productive plantations in Northumberland from the Hexham area to the Border.

There are scattered big individual trees in mixed woodlands in most counties, particularly in Sussex, but the only other part of England where Scots Pine is an important forest tree is the Brecklands in Norfolk and Suffolk. In the 1920s, the newly created Forestry Commission obtained large areas there of low grade heathland unfit for agriculture and therefore cheap. Funds were very limited and a source of local seed, plentiful and easily collected, was available from the Brandon

Hedges. These still exist each side of several miles of road in the Thetford and Brandon area, from a planting about 200 years ago of Scots Pines. They are widely spaced and for a long time cut over at intervals to make tall hedges, presumably to shelter former farmlands. Little thought was then given to the genetics of trees, and later, when this became important, it could be pointed out that the bushy form was not inherent in the strain but arose from the treatment of the trees, whose genotype would be unaffected. The stands grew quite well at first but growth in height began to culminate alarmingly early and the yield of timber was evidently going to be low. Some research into the origin of the hedges found that much of the seed probably came from the Hesse extractories and will have originated in the Hartz Mountains. The rather continental climate there may have been thought suitable for the Brecklands, the most continental climatic area in Britain, but this has not proved to be so. The facile snare had struck again, and as the crops were felled they were replaced by the Corsican Pine, which, though often difficult to establish, makes highly productive stands.

In Scotland, the Scots Pine still dominates productive forestry in limited areas, particularly in the Upper Dee Valley, Donside and in Morayshire, Nairn and parts of Inverness-shire. It also is the tree of the old Caledonian Forest reserves in the northwest, like Glen Affric, Benn Eighe and Abernethy and the finest old stands of all, Ballochbuie on the Balmoral Estate. Here big clumps along the lower slopes of Lochnagar present a view of coalescing great blue-green domes held on level red-barked branches on straight dark red stems. In the more open woods of the other

Scot's Pine (*Pinus sylvestris*):
Penrhyn Castle, Gwynedd

119

reserves, big old trees, many heavily branched to the ground, stand among smaller trees of all ages, which is the territory most appreciated by crested tits. Control of red deer is necessary to safeguard the recruitment of seedlings. The woods of Speyside around Loch Morlich are of this kind, too, and so, in a smaller way, are parts of Frensham Common in Surrey (without the crested tits).

The finest specimen is one reputed to date from 1792, some distance along the drive to Ballogie House near Ballater. It is 120/14ft with 40ft of clear, cylindric bole with uniform pink alligator-skin bark. A few exceptional old trees stand around the car park at Wishart's Burn a few miles west of Fochabers, Morayshire, the biggest being 100/14ft with a good stem. A similar tree on Baron's Court Estate in County Tyrone was 85/14ft with 23ft clear in 1976, and another nearby is now 115/12ft. In Spye Park, Wiltshire, 'The Raven Fir' was 60/18ft in 1970 with a clean, but forking bole, and another forking from the ground is 70/18ft at the part of the grounds of Kilravock Castle, Nairn, known as Leafy Turn. A very branchy old tree on the bank above the upper road in Belladrum, Inverness, is 108/17ft. At Longnor House in Shropshire, another branchy tree is 82/16ft at three feet, and one like it near Heaven's Gate in Longleat Park is 85/19ft at one foot.

Six trees planted in 1760 are in the garden at Brockenhurst Park in the New Forest. The largest in 1986 was 102/15ft but forks from its base, while two others have excellent, clear trunks, one of 85/10ft and the other 98/8ft. The matrix planting for high shelter in the first planting at Westonbirt Arboretum was done in 1829 in Down Covert, within and along Circular Drive. In 1989 there were 17 big trees, the biggest 92/10ft, near the entrance, and the tallest 102/9ft and 108/9ft near the centre. In 1969, a tree at Kidbrooke Park, Sussex, had 66ft of clear trunk and was 105/8ft.

Back in Scotland, a big rough tree in Abernethy Forest is 85/16ft, and a rather better one in the garden at Rossdhu, Dumbartonshire is 80/15ft. A few dated trees are, one in Dail Gheal at Novar, in Easter Ross, probably from 1750 planting and now 82/13ft by gravel-pits; one planted in 1811 in Happy Valley, Culzean Castle, Ayrshire, 98/12ft, clear for 40ft, and one of the same date by the Back Drive at Blairquhan, also in Ayrshire, 95/13ft.

Now James Paterson, indefatigable tree-hunter of Nairn has located near Lynedoch, Perth, 'The King of the Forest', 115/19ft, with a 20ft trunk before it divides into three stems, and Victoria Schilling reports one 132/13ft at Corby Castle in Cumbria by the riverside.

MACEDONIAN PINE

Pinus peuce

This is as imperturbable and healthy as any tree we grow. It has an in-built rate of growth of 18in a year, regardless of soil, site, altitude, exposure or disease. It grows its 18in in deep, fertile soil in a sheltered valley; in acid sand or limey marl and on the windswept top of a slatey, shallow-soiled Welsh mountain. In derelict gardens, or pineta where drainage has failed and trees die all round, the Macedonian Pine will stand there glowing with health and growing in its accustomed manner.

It is also a uniformly neat and attractive tree with a crown columnar in the lower and middle parts, with regular small branches upcurved towards their tips, and an acute conic top. In the oldest trees, it fans out in upcurved branches. It is clean and bright, the bark being smooth and dark grey ageing to pale, then whitish in small, smooth blocks divided by fine cracks. The shoot is bright apple-green and the leaves in dense bundles, bright green on the outside of the needles, lined blue-white on the inner sides. It is one of the two European five-needle pines, the Arolla Pine of the Alps being the other, similar in shape and foliage but duller and less tidy.

It is found in three small areas, on the border between Albania and Former Yugoslavia; in the western Rhodope Mountains of Bulgaria and along the border with Greece, in Macedonia. It was discovered by Grisebach in 1839 on Mount Peristeri by Lake Presba where former Yugoslavia, Albania and Greece adjoin, and introduced from the same place by Orphanides in 1863. Three trees from this seed were planted at Kew and surprisingly did not achieve their proper growth. One by the Isleworth Gate was 60/6ft in 1969 but is not there now, and two on the mound near the Palm House, numbers -561 and -562 were 50/6ft and 70/6ft in 1981.

Two other unusual merits in a pine, shown by this tree are the ability to grow in industrially polluted air, shown by one 70/7ft in Trentham Park, Stoke on Trent; and the ability to grow in shade. This was found by Major Richard Coke in his wonderful New Wood at Weasenham, Norfolk. One, planted in 1927 in the shade of a beech tree, (which was considerable until a branch was blown off it), grew at its normal speed and is now 85/5ft.

No tree outside Kew gardens is known to be of original origin, nor older than the 1878 pair at Westonbirt, but I have grave suspicions of the biggest of all, a superb tree at Stourhead. Not only is its unsurpassed size suggestive of a very early origin, but it is one of those mysterious trees that disappeared for a spell. There is no record of it, in any known book of trees or of Stourhead, or in lists of big trees. It is ignored by the quite long list of the conifers of note there in the *Report of the Conifer Conference of 1931*. It evidently sprang fully formed into being between then and 1957 when I discovered it at 95/10ft near the main path above the eastern bank of the Lake. It is now 115/13ft with many upper branches curving to the vertical to make a broad, conic top. Its closest rival is on the hill above Ochtertyre, near Crieff, and this is 105/13ft. It was only 70/9ft in 1955 so is evidently a little younger than the Stourhead tree.

The Westonbirt pair planted in 1878 stand about 20ft apart by the Willesley Drive which was made in 1876. They are near-twins, the same broad-columnar shape to an upswept top, both 8ft round, one 98ft and the other 82ft tall. The tree in the pinetum at Bicton, survived the 1990 gales to be 92/9ft and should be older

Macedonian Pine (*Pinus peuce*):
Stourhead, Wiltshire

than the Westonbirt trees for it was 42/3ft 8in in 1906, when one of the latter was 36ft tall. A tree in the Evergreens at Woburn will be older still, for it is a graft presumably because seedlings were not available, and from one of the first trees. It was 82/10ft in 1973. One in a group of conifers by a back gate into Scone Palace is 75/10ft and the group seems to date from about 1880.

In the far north, at Ardross Castle, in the pinetum, it can be seen that ten feet of girth does not require so long, and that there is another form of the tree, although rare. This pinetum was planted in 1900 and has four specimens. Two are the normal, neat shape with no low branches and are 98/9ft and 88/7ft. The other two have numerous quite stout low branches and broader crowns and these are 102/11ft and 82/11ft. A normal shaped tree of unknown age at Monteviot, Roxburgh, in the Pinery, is 95/11ft and one at Wootton Park near Dorking is 90/11ft. A fine pair in a strip of woodland with big conifers at Drenagh, County Derry, is 92/9ft and 85/8ft. In the northeast of England, Macedonian Pines are scarce but at Beaufront Castle, Hexham, a good tree is 80/9ft. At Brahan House, Easter Ross, in the old pinetum there is one 80/9ft, and in the Avenue planted in 1898 at Hergest Croft, Herefordshire, is one 80/9ft.

A survivor of 1916 planting at Wakehurst Place is 85/7ft and one of 1910 planting at Dawyck, Peebles, is 88/7ft but more rapid growth is shown by one of half dozen planted in 1926 at Bedgebury Pinetum in a wide group off Hills Avenue, which is 60/8ft.

PONDEROSA PINE

Pinus ponderosa

There can be no sight more inspiring, arboriculturally, than that of a Ponderosa Pine in the full vigour of late youth. At 40 or 50 years it is 80–100ft tall, a perfect cone of well-spaced whorls of branches curving up to vertical tips of luxuriantly long-needled brushes, from a stout stem tapering slowly and evenly to a long thick leading shoot. The stem can be seen through the open crown all the way to the straight, dominating leader. The tree is the picture of strong symmetrical growth, constant vigour and immense promise for the future. There are three such trees by the ride above the Valley Gardens in Windsor Great Park and another slightly smaller and younger and perhaps even nearer perfection, by a small ride half a mile to the north.

Along the floor of the Merced Canyon in Yosemite National Park, California, trees maintain very nearly this shape to 180–200ft. In Big Pine Campsite near Grants Pass in Oregon I made the tallest, a superb tree, 232/17ft, so the promise can be fulfilled in the wild, however unlikely it is to be realised so fully on the dry sands of Windsor. The tree has an immense range, covering virtually the entire Rocky Mountain system in the United States and extending into British Columbia in the lower Fraser River Valley and southwards into north Mexico. The populations in the central and eastern parts of the range (where it extends into the Black Hills of South Dakota) are the inferior, short-leafed and dark-barked Rocky Mountain Ponderosa, var. *scopulorum*, and, in the south east is the Arizona form, var. *arizonica*. This is a tree of excellent form and pale grey-blue foliage but slow growing in the United Kingdom as it needs greater heat. From here on it is the type tree from the western ranges, that features here.

It was, however, the Rocky Mountain form that was 'discovered', when Lewis and Clark first came across it in 1804 in the Dakotas. David Douglas saw his first in 1826 by the Spokane River, and, not for the first time (see Western Red Cedar and Western Hemlock) his botany let him down and he took it to be the, two-needled but not dissimilar from a distance, Red Pine. However, he kept a specimen and brought it back and the type was named by Lawson in 1836. By 1827, Douglas was collecting seed, although under what name seems not to have been recorded, and from this introduction, some of our finest specimens were grown. Douglas saw only the type, western form.

The Ponderosa Pine is closely related to the Jeffrey Pine, which largely replaces it above 6000ft in the south, but does not cross with it. Jeffrey Pine is genetically closer, in fact, to the Coulter Pine, with which it can be crossed. Ponderosa is distinct from both in its shiny, ridged red-brown shoot, although its other forms have smoother, blue-bloomed shoots like the Jeffrey and Coulter Pines. It also has very dark green leaves and smaller cones, and its male flowers are dark purple becoming bright before they open. The cones of Ponderosa and Jeffrey, but not of Coulter, Pine leave their basal whorls of scales on the tree, when they are shed, so complete specimens of mature cones can be had only by cutting them off the tree.

In Bowood Arboretum an original tree from David Douglas, planted in 1829, by 1984 was 135/14ft. It had a beautifully cylindric lower bole, arising from the ground without a trace of root-swell, but died in 1990.

Three trees at Powis Castle are thought to be Douglas trees although there seem to be no confirming records. The size of two of them does suggest that this is right. The one below the Castle is by the Welshpool Drive and is surely the one given in Elwes and Henry as 'Welshpool Gate'. There is no planting of old conifers near that gate. Their figures for 1908 are 105/10ft and the Drive tree today is 132/14½ft, less tidy than some but with a fine bole. Elwes and Henry did not see, or did not mention, the bigger tree up the valley above Gwen Morgan's Pool, although they did measure a Douglas Fir on 'Rabbit Bank' not far from it. The Ponderosa is 111/16ft with a good bole but rather storm-tossed top. The third is nearby, 124/11ft. At Bayfordbury, Hertfordshire, an 1837 tree is now 90/19ft.

A fine specimen on Policy Bank at Dawyck, near Peebles, is recorded as *Pinus jeffreyi* planted in 1838. Jeffrey did not discover nor send his noble pine until 1851, and the shiny red-brown shoots found beneath this tree when I first saw it in 1966 confirmed that it is in fact Ponderosa. It is now 115/11½ft and typically, has an impressive trunk, clear for about 30ft. The pinetum at Highnam, Gloucestershire, now

Ponderosa Pine (*Pinus ponderosa*): Powis Castle, Powys

Churchem Pinetum, has two dated old trees. The one planted in 1844 is a fairly rugged specimen 92/13ft and the one planted in 1856 is 105/11ft. At Eastnor Castle, the 'Pine Hill' has lost a specimen or two so it is not possible to fit the figures of the four big trees there today with earlier measurements. The best is now 118/11ft, which may be the same as the one 66/8ft in 1909, and another is 120/10ft.

It is unusual to find a big Ponderosa in a garden in a suburban street, and the one in Lexden, near Colchester, may have been in a park before the houses were built. In 1977 it was 72/11ft. One of the tallest and most shapely, with a spire top, is a fairly young tree growing fast at Rossie Priory, near Dundee. In 1931 it was 72/6ft and now it is over 130/10ft, figures which would fit a date of around 1870. A good tree is between the garden and the Den at Dupplin Castle, Perthshire, 115/11ft. Much further north, one at Brahan House in Easter Ross in a field above the house is 98/12ft and a splendid tree.

In the absence of dates for the trees mentioned at Windsor, which attain to 105/7ft with perfect shape, some similar but dated trees need citing. At Bodnant, in the Rock Garden near the gate, one planted in 1901 is 75/10ft having grown from a girth of seven feet in 1966. In the Hill Garden at Leonardslee, standing above the wreckage of most of the trees around it in October 1987, a superbly shaped tree, planted in 1910, was 75/5ft 4in in 1961 and in 1990, 111/8ft 9in. Even more rapid growth has been made by one of the group planted in Lyndford Arboretum, Norfolk, in 1950. By 1990 this was 82/8ft. Setting out in the same manner, one in the 1963 pinetum at Anglesea Abbey, Cambridgeshire, was 60/4ft 3in when 27 years old.

MONTEREY PINE

Pinus radiata

Seeing all those great dark domes and rugged, much branched and snagged trunks of Monterey Pines, from the middle of Kent to Hampshire and along the coasts to the west and north, it is hard to appreciate that they are all twice the size of any of the trees in the wild. The tree is an extreme example of the odd phenomenon that some trees grow better, faster and bigger the further they are from their native woods. Its natural range is very small, about 6000 acres at Carmel; a straggle of little woods for twenty miles along low coastal hills to the north, two southern outliers a hundred miles away and another on Santa Rosa Island. In the Carmel woods, by the Nine-mile Drive, the trees struggle to about 60/5ft before being killed by an evil-looking, brownish dwarf mistletoe. They grow better 60 miles to the north, in San Francisco, where in Golden Gate Park one with irrigation grew 52ft in five years. But, unaided, their growth in southwest England and southern Ireland is much superior to that anywhere in California, and in Australia and New Zealand it is better still.

In England and Ireland, young trees customarily add three feet a year, often four feet and sometimes more. One at Nettlecombe Court in Somerset holds the allcomers record for a conifer by growing nine feet in 1856 and stopping then only because a beetle chewed the leader. In Ireland, 70ft has been grown in 18 years; in Sussex, 80/7ft in 25 years, and 48/3ft in 10 years in Devon. But in Australia a whole industry is geared to the trees growing a steady six feet a year and so giving six-foot lengths totally knot-free between whorls. In the North Island, New Zealand, one reached 203ft in 41 years, a world record time for a conifer. In warm countries, growth is continuous and in some years it has been noted to have buds expanding in January in Cornwall. In Surrey, pollen is usually shed and growth started by the end of March, ending in September, often with a brief halt in July when a small bud is set, then resuming growth at speed.

Because of its history in the not so distant past, the Monterey Pine is a fire-climax tree adapted to regenerating after crown-fires. It does this by retaining the seed in the cones and the cones on the tree are rather massively woody. It is not so obsessive in this as the Bishop Pine where they remain for over 60 years, but holds them with viable seed for perhaps 20 years. When a crown-fire comes there are therefore great numbers of good seeds and the brief blaze does no harm to them protected by the thick scales, but the scales are left open and the seed is soon blown out to germinate on or in the newly bared soil.

With its branches laden with whorls of heavy cones, the tree is vulnerable to losing big branches in gales, and being so often planted for shelter in very exposed places and tending to make a broad, branchy tree, it has earned a reputation for not being windfirm. Nonetheless, when the entire 1910 pinetum at Leonardslee was blown flat in 1987, only the 95ft Monterey Pine remained.

The tree was discovered and introduced by David Douglas in 1832. No original tree is now known, but a cutting taken from one in Lee and Kennedy's Hammersmith Nursery was planted at Dropmore in 1839. Very broad and branchy, it was 90/19ft at three feet in 1970. After 1850 Monterey Pine was planted very widely and although it is less commonly seen in the north, the east and in Scotland, the trees that are there have grown as fast and become as big as all but the biggest in Devon and Cornwall. One of the fastest growing young trees is at Dundonnell, near Ullapool, among the most northerly (and westerly) of all Scottish gardens. When 35 years old, in 1986, this was 85/8ft. In the east and nearly as far north a 30 year old tree in the garden at Novar, Dingwall, is 62/3ft 9in. Further south, and still in the east, at Keir Castle, Dunblane, one of the first Monterey Pines was planted in 1851 and is 111/16ft, and another 1851 tree, at Kelburn Castle, Ayrshire, is 98/17ft. A little south of that, at Castle Kennedy, Wigtownshire, two were planted in 1849 and are 135/17ft and 111/16ft. A notably fine tree is prominent by the Lomondside road north of Luss. It is in Stuckgowan Hotel garden and 118/16ft dating from about 1855.

Of the biggest trees with single trunks, uncluttered with basal and low branches, or with only one or two easily avoided by a tape, the oldest is at Castle Horneck, outside Penzance. It is about the only tree in the small garden, and dates from 1850. It was 90/19ft in 1928 so had grown rapidly, but has rather shot its bolt and in 1979 it was only 98/21ft, an impressively massive bole with many moderate-sized branches. The best, cleanest bole of this size is on a lawn at Ballywalter House, County Down. This has no date nor early measurements and is 132/20ft, clear for at least ten feet. At Heckfield Place in north Hampshire, a tree with some low branches is 111/20ft; a similar one at Bowood in Wiltshire, probably of 1841 planting, is 85/20ft; two on the lawn at Woodstock, County Kilkenny, are 98/20ft and 105/19ft; at Kilruddery Park, County Wicklow, a broad tree is 80/22ft; a more branchy bole by the New Drive at Tregothnan, Truro, is 120/22ft, and a cleaner bole at Mount Stewart, County Down, was 100/21ft in 1976. One dying back a little at Emo Court, County Leix, is 102/21ft and another there is 111/18ft. A tall tree down by the Pumphouse at Belvedere House, County Westmeath, is 132/18ft.

At Northerwood House, Lyndhurst, a tall, fairly rough tree has a good stem through the branches and is 121/19ft. A broad, branchy tree planted in 1880 at Sidbury Manor, Devon, is 118/18ft and one with a few low branches and a good

Monterey Pine (*Pinus radiata*): Whiteways, Devon

stem at Charleville, in County Wicklow, which was 85/11ft in 1909 and 118/19ft in 1991.

A tree of high quality, its narrow crown and small branches owed to the big trees around it, is the tallest specimen found today, and also the tallest known in 1907. At Cuffnells, Lyndhurst, it is 142/12ft. Another, not unlike it but more in the open, is at Hillsborough, County Down, where it was planted in 1872. It was 138/13ft in 1982. The best clear stem, probably as a result of early pruning to give light to the shrubs around it, is one of five in the garden at Saltram House, Devon, 124/17ft, smooth and clear for 30ft. One in the same line has been pruned clean to 65ft and is 118/12ft. At Coollattin, County Wicklow, a tree 90/17ft is clear of branches for 16ft.

WEYMOUTH PINE

Pinus strobus

This tree has a sad story. When Europeans invaded North America, the Weymouth Pine covered vast tracts from New England round, to the west and south of the Great Lakes and, more mixed with other trees, along the high Alleghenies to the Georgia border. As these forests were explored, it was found that they contained specimens that were the tallest trees known in the world. In the valleys were trees to 250ft tall, and until nearly 1800, nothing like them was known. From the days of the first settlers, large areas were cleared to give room for crops and towns, and also for the timber. Here were seemingly endless woods of cheap but exceedingly valuable high quality timber. The habit of the tree is to grow a straight stem with well-spaced whorls of light, level branches to the top until after maturity, giving long, straight planks with small knots. The timber is light, straight grained and easily worked, so it was ideal for posts, beams and rafters as well as for shingles and laths and interior work. It is not very strong but it was no problem to use greater thicknesses where strength was needed and the whole house from shingles on the roof to floors, fittings and kitchenware could be made from trees on the spot.

By 1600, the Royal Navy was turning to the New World forests for possible naval timbers and the search was for tall trees for masts. Captain George Weymouth was sent to reconnoitre the woods of New England and returned in 1605 with seeds or plants from Maine and introduced the tree. It was named after him, but this was forgotten and before 1800 the English name was attributed by all authors to Lord Weymouth, the courtesy title of the eldest son of the Earl of Bath. He planted many woods at the family seat, Longleat, and it was said that he was the first to use this pine for plantations, and the date of introduction was taken to be 1705. But the late Marquis knew of no early plantings.

The rapid exploitation of the woods on the best soils and with the biggest trees was followed by a worse scourge. The German settlers, it is said, had nostalgic wishes around Christmas time for the pine they decorated at home, the Arolla Pine. So they imported large numbers of them. And these brought with them the White Pine blister-rust, *Cronartium ribicola*, to which they are accustomed and have developed great resistance. They carry it on their foliage and in their shoots but it

Weymouth Pine
(*Pinus strobus*):
produces timber which
is straight-grained and
easily worked

129

is rarely fatal to them. It is one of those fungi with a life-cycle involving two very different plants – the alternate host is the currant. The American White Pines had no exposure to this disease and no chance to evolve resistant strains, so were highly susceptible. And several currant species are common under-shrubs in the pine-woods of America. So the blister-rust spread rapidly and eventually reached the Pacific coast woods where there are several five-needle pines and the flowering currant is a common shrub beneath them. The Sugar and the Western White Pines are most susceptible to the disease. Damage in the eastern states is not today obvious to the traveller, but it must have had a big effect over the years.

In Britain, the Weymouth Pine will have been infected from a few imports of plants of Arolla Pine, but not from the usual imports of seed, as that does not carry the fungus. For a long time, the pine was a popular tree in collections and parks and grew rapidly to become some of the biggest pines growing here. Elwes mentioned in 1906 how subject the tree is to honey-fungus and blister-rust. A later footnote states that the blister-rust was first noted in 1892 at King's Lynn, but the account of the biggest trees has no mention of any being infected. By 1960 it was very different, and many big old trees were dead or dying, the black-barked, heavily branched trunks broadly streaked with white resin and many upper branches dying back. Today, few of these survive, but there are still some apparently healthy old trees and many thriving young ones, and only these will be cited here.

The outstanding specimen is at Chatsworth House in Derbyshire, the best of four in the pinetum and probably about 150 years old. It still has the conic crown of an immature tree and is adding to its height rapidly. In 1957 it was 118/7ft and by 1984 it was 144/9ft. Two others in the pinetum were 102/11ft in that year. In 1787 a group was planted near Cannop crossroads in the Forest of Dean. One died in about 1970 but there are four healthy and fairly shapely trees in 1988, one 130/8ft and one 120/12ft. The tree by the Circular Drive in Westonbirt Arboretum may date back to 1829 but not before that. It has looked ready to die ever since I first saw it in 1956 but is still there, far from beautiful and 80/10ft.

Rhinefield Ornamental Drive, in the New Forest, was planted in 1861 and began at its western and northern end with a group of Weymouth Pine and a few more on both sides. As is often the case, seedlings arose in and around the group and some today are obviously younger than the originals. The best of these is a very shapely tree on the eastern side, which was 85/4ft in 1962 and is now a splendid tree at 115/6ft. The big old trees have lost shape, and although generally healthy, have lost some big branches in gales. The biggest is further along the Drive, on the western side, now 124/11ft. Another, near the little bridge at the entrance forks at six feet and is 115/11ft near another 130/10ft. A solitary tree near the house at Blair Drummond in Perthshire is 85/11ft. One at Kitlands, below Leith Hill in Surrey is

85/13ft but is dividing into several stems. One below the Dolmellynllyn Hotel, with the two very Giant Sequoias, north of Dolgellau, is 95/11ft. A tree in a plot planted in 1907 at Avondale Forest Garden in County Wicklow is 105/7ft.

Some young trees to watch are: University Botanic Garden, Cambridge, planted 1964 and, after 27 years, 46/3ft; Churchill College, Bristol, planted 1961 and 30 years later 52/5ft; and one at Alice Holt Lodge in the arboretum by Station Ride, planted in 1953 and was 66/5ft 36 years later .

BHUTAN PINE

Pinus wallichiana

The Bhutan Pine is something of a firework of a tree. It rises rapidly and decoratively to a good height, sprays out as a climax, to die out and drop fragments and leave a passably pleasant aroma. Young trees often make leading shoots a yard long and grow 60ft in 30 years, straight to the tip of a shapely, narrowly conic crown, elegantly set with long blue needles hanging from the raised branches. Before it is 100ft tall, big branches have fanned out from the upper crown and soon after they begin to die back. Then the tree dies progressively from the top down, shedding hundreds of big cones all the time, and may die, leaving a carpet of the resinous, pine-scented cones.

It is more tolerant of town air and soils than are other five-needle pines and is moderately frequent in town and city parks and in small gardens on the outskirts of towns. It must be that some owners of small gardens cannot resist buying the attractive little plants and either do not know how quickly they will outgrow their space or, if they do know, wish to enjoy the years of splendid growth before the problems arise. As with Deodars, there is much to be said for planting and cutting in cycles of about 20 years. They are hardy northwards to Inverness in the east and Skye in the west and although there are few so far north, these include some big trees, like one at Aldourie on the banks of Loch Ness, 102/10ft.

The Bhutan Pine grows on the Himalaya at 8–10,000ft from eastern Afghanistan through Bhutan and perhaps further east and was introduced to Britain by A.B. Lambert in 1823. It was a standard component of pineta from about 1840 and its battered or dying tops are a familiar sight projecting from them today, although some of the trees have gone. None today is known to date from before 1831 and very few from before 1860. The expected span of life is about 150 years. Some of the old trees, dying back at the top, have grown several very large branches from low on the trunk and these bear the lower crown, usually quite healthy and able to sustain the tree.

The oldest of known date is at Hewell Grange near Stourport, planted in 1831. It was 85/11ft in 1974 with a good straight trunk and relatively shapely crown. In

Churcham Pinetum at Highnam, in Gloucestershire, the bigger of two trees dates from 1846 and was 66/10ft in 1983 with a good trunk and a few big low branches. In 1847 one was planted in Fota Garden, near Cork and this has many very low and big branches such that it cannot be measured at five feet and is 102/14½ft at three feet. At Kilruddery Park in County Wicklow a huge tree forks at the base and is 98/14ft with the minor stem eight feet round. Emo Court, County Leix has two splendid trees, one in the Grape Garden at 88/12ft and one in The Everglades, 85/12ft. One of these, and the Kilruddery tree have both increased their girth by five feet since 1904. At Powerscourt, County Wicklow, near the Golden Gate, a tree in an area where the big trees date from 1866, is 111/12ft. In Abbeyleix Pleasure Garden, County Leix, a similar tree is 120/12ft.

At Frogmore Mausoleum, Windsor, a tree with a stem of 23ft before it forks, was 92/12ft in 1982. Another good trunk is 20ft long on a tree at Whiteways House near Exeter, which is 108/11ft. Steady growth is shown by a tree on the hill at Ochtertyre near Crieffe, planted in 1888. It was 42/4ft in 1931 and 85/8ft in 1987. A big tree, very rough, with big, low branches, at Coed Coch near Abergele, is 118/13ft at two feet.

Two trees at Albury Park in Surrey set the pace for early growth when I saw them in 1954, splendid towers of trees, planted in 1921. The larger was 75/4ft when 33 years old and I thought this was the way that they should all grow. I have revised this since then, seeing that it was exceptional. That tree was 102/7ft when 65 years old. None found since can equal this for growth in height, but for girth it is well beaten by one planted at Churchill College, Bristol, planted in 1961 which is now 50/6ft.

Bhutan Pine (*Pinus wallichiana*): close-up of cones on branch

GOLDEN LARCH

Pseudolarix amabilis

Robert Fortune was the first botanist to see the Golden Larch when on his early
expeditions in eastern China before 1850 he noted dwarf forms of it in gardens. It
is native to only small areas in Chekiang and Kiangsi Provinces. He saw the wild
trees in the autumn of 1853, noting some 130ft tall with 50ft of scarcely tapering
trunk. He introduced it in the same year, but cones and seedlings were few and he
sent more during the subsequent years. The seeds probably all failed, but seedlings
sent in Wardian cases gave the first plants in cultivation. Lindley named the tree
Abies kaempferi in 1854 but Kaempfer never saw this tree, a confusion with his
Japanese Larch, which persisted until Gordon established the genus *Pseudolarix*
for it in 1858. Until 1989 the Golden Larch was regarded as no more than an aberrant
larch closely related to the true larches, *Larix*. But in that year, Frankis showed that
its peculiarities of short shoots showing annual increase and rings; male flowers in
umbels on leafy stalks; cones on separate branches, and scales, bracts and seeds

Golden Larch (*Pseudolarix amabilis*):
Jersey

being shed together when the seed are ripe, leaving only the central axis, make it remote from larches and close only to *Keteleeria* and the silver firs, *Abies*. It is now known to have a chromosome number of 2n=22 while every other member of the Family, *Pinaceae*, except Douglas Fir with 2n=26, has 24.

The Golden Larch is a difficult tree to establish in Britain, being tender when young and susceptible to summer drought. It is at best a slow growing tree, and a few of the older trees were blown down in recent gales. Growth in the United States shows that our winters are not the trouble so much as the lack of long, hot summers. It is, in America, successful only in a curiously limited area there, with 70ft trees only in New York State, notably in Central Park and in Hudson Valley gardens; fair trees on Long Island; in New Jersey and Delaware, and the biggest, 90/8ft in Philadelphia. There is no apparant reason why it should be so restricted and not thrive in further south.

Two trees are thought to be original Fortune trees from about 1854, both at Biddulph Grange, the recently rescued extraordinary garden in Staffordshire. In the poor sandstone soil, the low rainfall and long cold winters of the north Midlands, and in severe industrial pollution during most of their life, it is not surprising that the larger is now only 50/4ft. This is of little help in judging the ages of bigger trees. The only trees of recorded early planting elsewhere are one of 1858 at Tortworth Court, Gloucestershire, long gone, and one of 1872 at Scorrier House, Cornwall, which survived until about 1980 and was 70/8½ft in 1973. The biggest today is also near Falmouth, in Carclew and is 75/9ft. That indicates a very similar date of planting. At Leonardslee in Sussex, the tree on the bank below the new house was 60/6½ft before the gale of 1987 broke the top and main branches. That probably dates from early this century with growth like the larger of the well-known pair in Conifer Walk in Sheffield Park, Sussex. They were planted in 1919, the larger surviving only to be blown down in 1987, was then 52/6½ft.

Two at Wakehurst Place, Sussex, date from about 1915. One by the old entrance drive is, after severe gale damage, 13/5ft and one more sheltered near the lawn is 40/6ft. The northward limit is vague, as there is a young tree eight feet tall at Tillipronie in Aberdeenshire, and one planted in 1908 in the Royal Botanic Gardens, Edinburgh, is 40/5ft. In Ireland there are two in Mount Usher Garden, County Wicklow, 33/3½ft and 23/4½ft, and in 1980 the tree at Headfort, County Meath, planted in 1921 was 25/3ft.

The larger of two rather bushy trees planted at Bedgebury National Pinetum in Kent, in 1966 is 26/2½ft and one in the London University Botanic Garden at Englefield in Surrey, planted in 1963, is also 26/2½ft. A spreading young tree which makes strong annual shoots in the border beside Anthony Waterer's Walk in Knaphill Nursery, is 20/2ft.

DOUGLAS FIR

Pseudotsuga menziesii

A true aristocrat among the world's biggest and most important trees, the Douglas Fir made its entry into the horticultural world in an impeccably classic manner for a tree from the Pacific northwest. It was discovered by Archibald Menzies with the Vancouver Expedition in 1792, and introduced by David Douglas, the first great collector there, in 1826. It was, in the last century, the tallest conifer and second tallest tree in the world, with specimens verified to over 390ft and possibly a few over 400ft. Its very strong timber in vast quantities of long, straight logs is still the main source of the lumber industry in the western parts of North America. The fragment preserved at Quinault Lake in Washington, with trees 280–310ft tall and 20–25ft round, clear of branches for 200ft, is the most impressive of all stands of conifers.

In Britain, the young trees grew with a vigour unmatched by any conifer from other parts of the world and equalled only by the Grand Fir and Coast Redwood from the same region, and it was the first species ever to overtop the European Silver Fir. In 1931, the two species were level, with one of each recorded as 168ft tall. By 1955 both were 180ft but now many Douglas Fir are growing through the 200ft mark and, with one or two Sitka Spruces and Grand Firs, they make up all the tallest 50 or more trees. In Moniac Glen, west of Inverness, planted in 1882, Douglas Fir along the flat and one bank by the burn included 18 trees over 175ft and three of 200ft by 1983. Two trees by the gate of a cottage at Cannich a few miles away are over 170ft tall. At Broadwood near Dunster, Somerset, a long grove planted in 1874 has four trees over 175ft tall. Every year in stands like these, more trees grow past these heights and the numbers which are over 170ft or 200ft at any one time cannot be known.

Evidently, the criterion for selection cannot be height alone. Nor can it be the original Douglas seed trees, for there are numerous small groves and individuals widely scattered. Nor is superior girth adequate on its own, as many of the biggest boles belong to misshapen and broken trees. The best must be selected from those combining great size with exceptional form.

The most deserving of mention happens to be the tallest Douglas Fir, but of no great girth. This tree is splendidly seen from the Scottish National Trust property at The Hermitage just off the A9 at Dunkeld, although it stands in Forestry Commission land in Craigvinean Forest. It is a self-sown seedling from the three big trees at The Hermitage and arose among rocks by the Braan Burn in about 1887. In 1954, when its age was found with an increment borer, it was 165/10ft and perfect to its long leader, and I backed it as the first tree in Britain to reach 200ft as it is so well placed by water and in deep shelter. However, a squall down the valley broke the top, it seems, in around 1970 and it was the second tree known to 200ft by 1980.

Douglas Fir (*Pseudotsuga menziesii*):
Drumlanrig Castle, Dumfries

It has repaired itself completely and is about 205/13ft but exceptionally difficult to measure. The trunk tapers gently to the top, bearing small well-spaced branches.

The tallest tree, of any kind, in England is a Douglas in the Broadwood stand, right beside the road, 187/15ft, planted in 1874. It survived the January 1990 gale which cleared the other side of the road, the increased exposure causing it to become thin in the upper crown. The most impressive, massive, smooth bole is that of a tree in Belle Blair Wood, on the Dupplin Estate, a private wood by the A9 near Forteviot, Perth. The tree, 156/20ft, has a broad crown to the ground but no big low branches and the top is far from perfect althought the stem is superb. A similar, massive bole by the drive at Ardinaseig Hotel near Oban is 20ft round and clean for about 20ft but in the greater exposure than in woodland, the crown is somewhat rough with big branches and the height is only 130ft.

A tree by the river below Dunans House in Glendaruel, Argyll, is the biggest, taking height and girth together, and one of the finest. Very difficult to height, it is somewhere around 200ft tall, and has a bole 18ft round, tapering gently through regular branching of moderate size, to the long spire top. Of much the same volume, the biggest of several similar trees in The Georgia at Endsleigh Lodge in Devon, is 170/21ft. Planted probably in 1862, it has a branchy bole and a broad upper crown, like one next to it which is 150/19ft. A better tree to look at, by the drive into Belladrum near Inverness, has a long clean bole and a spire top at 170/19ft. The biggest fair girth at five feet is that of the tree by Dunkeld Cathedral, 22ft round. It has branches below five feet but they are very small and it does not fork, but the top was blown out at least 60 years ago and it has been around 105–110ft tall ever since. It was planted in 1846 as a gift to the Duke of Atholl and there is a story that it was a David Douglas original.

The biggest Douglas original is one of several in a group at Lynedoch, part of Scone Estate. Planted in 1827 it is 150/21ft and very branchy. The best is probably the Duke of Buccleuch's at Drumlanrig Castle, Dumfries. Planted in 1835 it was 135/17ft in 1984 and has a very black bark on a superb stem clear for about 30ft. It has a good top for its age and exposure. In a grove of originals planted at Corehouse in Lanarkshire in 1827, the best is 165/15ft with a long clean stem. Of several originals at Dawyck, in Peebles, one on Chapel Bank divides low and is a deplorable shape, but it is big, 105/20ft at one foot. Another, by the Dutch Bridge, is 160/14ft and a fine tree.

Among the big stems of top quality, the tree beyond the house at Castlehill, Devon, must be mentioned, 150/18ft and clear for about 30ft. A smaller but even finer one by the entrance to Glendye House, Kincardineshire, is 175/13ft and faultless and clear for over 50ft. The tree by the path to the Den at Durris House in the same county has an impeccable bole 18ft round, clear for 40ft. It was 165ft tall until a recent gale removed the top 25ft. Another great stem is by the drive at Glengarry Castle Hotel. Planted in 1867, it is 165/17ft.

Some bigger trunks of lower quality are, one by the ride at Sutherland's grove south of Oban, Argyll, which is 120/20ft and rough; one in the garden at Blair Drummond, Perthshire, 108/19ft, and one in the garden at Ballindalloch, Banffshire, 100/20ft. At Tregrehan in Cornwall there are two a little each side of 19ft, the larger one 130ft tall, both with excellent lower boles but branchy and broad in the crown.

Three more of the tallest with finely tapered tips good for many more feet yet are: one in the pinetum at Strone House, planted in 1875 and with a long spire, 180/15ft; one on the bank of a steep glen at Glenferness, Morayshire, a shapely 185/16ft; and the lovely tree at Randolph's Leap above the Nairn River, and next to a Sitka Spruce a few feet taller. The Douglas is over 195/15ft.

UMBRELLA PINE

Sciadopitys verticillata

The great southern proto-continent Gondwanaland broke up 150 million years ago and the tree families that had evolved there became widely scattered in the new continents, in Oceania, Australasia, the eastern edge of Asia and in America, with none in Africa or Europe. The Redwood Family, *Taxodiaceae* had already diversified into many highly divergent genera with little in common beyond their cone type and stripping red-brown barks. Today these are relict populations of only 14 species in ten genera and all but one of them, *Arthrotaxis*, with three species confined to Tasmania, have drifted into the northern hemisphere. A very recent study has removed nearly all of them and put them in *Cupressaceae*, and has given Sciadopitys a family of its own. This upsets the neat, if somewhat disparate concept of the Redwood Family, and we await further studies to re-assemble it before accepting that.

However, wherever placed, the Umbrella Pine is certainly a very odd man out. It has the bark and cones of a generalised redwood, but after that it is plain eccentric. Its leaves are of two very different kinds. There are elongated scales closely adherent to the shoot, each with a raised red-brown tip like a knob on the smooth pale ivory-brown shoot, and, borne by the terminal whorl of a dozen larger scales with much swollen tips, a crowded whorl of over 20 linear leaves 5in long. They are hard but fleshy and dark glossy green. Their upper surface has a deep, narrow median groove. In other trees this would be reflected in a marked keel on the under surface. In the Umbrella Pine. the under surface has a similar deep narrow groove and the two together almost divide the leaf lengthwise. This is now taken to be evidence that each leaf had been in fact two, and these have now fused into one. For a long time, they were seen as 'cladodes', photosynthesising shoots and not true leaves.

The Umbrella Pine is confined to Japan, in South Honshu, Shikoku and Kyushu. It was discovered by Carl Thunberg who spent 14 months of 1775–6 on Deshido mud island in Nagasaki Harbour as medical officer for the Dutch East India Company. It was six years since his predecessor, Englebert Kaempfer, had left Japan and started his tiny botanic garden near the gate on to the mud island. Thunberg refurbished this at first with plants raised from seeds he found in the forage allowed for the farm animals, as Kaempfer had done, but by now, travel restrictions were slightly less harsh. Thunberg was allowed on to the mainland around Nagasaki and went on the enforced annual pilgrimage to Edo. He was never in the native areas of the Umbrella Pine, but either found plants of it in local gardens, or, like Kaempfer, acquired foliage from the guards and interpreters, from which the first descriptions were made. It was still illegal to export any goods, and Thunberg did not collect any plants or seeds. The introduction of Umbrella Pine awaited Thomas Lobb, who in 1853 sent a tree from the botanic garden established at Buitenzorg on Java by Siebold, to Veitch's in Exeter. That survived only a few years, and the effective introduction was, as with so many trees from Japan, in 1861 when seed was sent by Robert Fortune and by J.G. Veitch.

Although very hardy and not markedly short-lived, there are no trees living today know to be planted before 1885 and only six before 1910. It is frequent in gardens

Umbrella Pine (*Sciadopitys verticillata*):
Langdale Chase, Cumbria

in southern and central Scotland; several are much further north, mainly in the west, to Armadale Castle on Skye, and Inverewe in Wester Ross, and a few in the east, to Brahan in Easter Ross and Drum Castle in Aberdeenshire, and Crathes Castle near Aberdeen. The biggest in Scotland tend to be near the west coast and in Central Perthshire. The best tree known to Elwes and Henry in 1905 was among the rhododendrons near one gate to Hempstead, Kent, now Benenden School, which was a shapely, slender 38/2ft and is now 75/5ft. The tallest measured recently is 75/5ft, planted in 1901 in the ravine at Bodnant. The biggest in girth is hard to decide as some are forked and need measuring below five feet, but the best is 40/6½ft at Armadale Castle with a 1916 tree at Headfort, County Meath, 48/6½ft in 1990 followed by the fine tree at Langdale Chase, Cumbria; 60/6ft, a tree at Castlewellan, County Down, 30/6ft and one at Kilmory Castle, Argyll, 36/6ft, and a 1906 tree at Avondale, County Wicklow, nearer 40/6½ft.

A fine specimen at Sheffield Park, Sussex, near the middle lake, dates from 1911 and is 56/5½ft and a sturdy tree at Penrhyn Castle, Gwynedd, in the wall-garden is 33/5½ft. A good tree at Leny House, Callender, Perthshire, is 44/5ft.

COAST REDWOOD

Sequoia sempervirens

The tallest tree in the world, since about 1890 when the taller Douglas Firs and Eucalypts had been cleared for lumber (and money), is fairly evidently not going to be amongst the tallest in Britain. It is easily surpassed in height currently by seven other conifers from the same region and even by one broad-leaf hybrid, the London Plane, in one place. Yet it has been here several years longer than three of the conifers.

The reason is that it needs very particular conditions to grow to great heights, and these are not found, more than partially, anywhere beyond its natural range, in the foothills of the Coast Range a few miles from the Pacific Ocean in California. Here, the key is the sea-fogs that drift in during the nights in summer and last through the morning. They bathe the tops of the 350ft trees in thick mist which condenses so that the tree does not need to conduct water from its roots up such great lengths of stem.

The native stands extend from some moderately sized trees seven miles into Oregon, south for 550 miles in California in a belt 10–20 miles broad, with a few gaps to some fine little groves to 190ft tall near Big Sur, and on to Salmon Creek Canyon. The stand farthest from the sea is an outlier in Napa County, 30 miles inland. The rainfall is about 70ins in the north with little in the summer and over most of the range there is none at all between April and November. Normally there is no frost, and summers are very hot. The tree's high needs for moisture are met much of the year by the sea-fogs. Hence, south of the Golden Gate, the tree is confined to seaward facing valleys, and the only ones 250–300ft tall are in the bowl of Big Basin and the nearby Henry Cowell Redwoods.

Nowhere in Britain has persistent sea-fogs, and nowhere has summer temperatures so high. Everywhere except a few localities by the coasts of Argyll and County Cork, has some frost in most winters. The natural range of the tree seems to extend no further northwards because of lower temperatures rather than lack of rainfall, which increases. Sea-fogs become few, but the tree can grow, if not very tall, in their absence. So it is altogether remarkable that we have some very big trees in every county in the British Isles. Cold, dry winds scorch their crowns regularly in the dry east and often in the west, too. This seems not to happen in California, for just after the rare, very damaging frosts of January 1989, I saw no signs of scorch around San Francisco or further north.

The nearest approach to the summer humidity of the natural range is found in our north and west, particularly in the glens of Scotland and in Ireland, and that is where our biggest trees tend to be. Growth, however, will be likely to be less rapid there than where summers are hotter. So the fastest growth is in the south of England, in sheltered, damp sites with a high water-table. The best example is the young avenue along the Rhinefield Drive in the New Forest. This applies to height growth rather more than growth in girth, which seems to be as rapid in the west and north. Height culminates early when the top grows out of cover and further growth is inhibited by cold or warm, dry winds in the east and by strong, salt-laden winds on the western seaboard. It continues only in the humidity and shelter of tall surrounding trees in deep, wooded coombs or at the base of a wet hillside. The tallest, 153ft, is in the deep ravine in high rainfall at Bodnant, Gwynedd, and half of the ten trees over 130ft are in sheltered Scottish woods. The majority of trees in eastern England have tops flattened at 80–110ft, depending on exposure. The failure of the top need make little difference to the increase in the girth of the trunk. A tree planted in 1867 at Blackmoor in northeastern Hampshire had its top blown or struck out by lightning before it was 15ft round in 1931. It continued this rapid growth in girth in an area far from the best for the species, on a bed of dry sands, but with the water of a moat-pond close by, and is now 21ft round, a huge tree for this region, but scarcely five feet taller than it was 60 years ago.

The best young trees are showing a rate of growth in girth almost equal to the young Giant Sequoias, and somewhat greater in height. But with age, both rates fall well behind. A 19 year old tree at Leonardslee, and a 21 year old tree at the University of London Botanic Garden at Englefield Green have mean annual increases in girth of four inches, and one at Broadlands, Hampshire is slightly faster, 63in in 15 years. A few trees 31 and 32 years old have mean annual increases of three inches, and one of 65 years was well over three inches a year. But for trees older than 70 years, two inches a year is about the maximum. The biggest, over 24ft round, date from around 1850 and so have mean annual rates of a little over two inches a year.

Growth in height can be very rapid in young trees. The best are around three feet a year: 70ft in 17 years at Albury Park, Surrey, and 105ft in 32 years for a tree in the 1955 avenue at Rhinefield, New Forest. Now 37 years old, it is 120/9½ft. Eight others with this rate of growth range between 13 and 37 years old, but none over 50 years old has maintained a life mean of over two feet a year. The strong decrease with age has caught up with them all.

It so happens that for this species there is a good set of dimensions of the earliest plantings, when they were between 25 and 33 years old. Robert Hutchison published the data for 60 trees, in 1877, and 25 were given dates of planting. Another 20 dated trees were listed with dimensions in 1891 when between 20 and 47 years old. So we have good sample comparisons between growth in the last century and growth in the last 50 years, of trees up to 50 years old. There is little difference between them, in height or girth, but the best modern figures are slightly above those of pre-1891 in both dimensions, and height growth in general is marginally greater. This is of particular interest in the light of the recent flood of spurious propaganda that our trees are being killed by acid rain. We can all see, from every roadside, that trees are growing luxuriantly, with long leading shoots and we know that old beechwoods have always contained some dying and dead trees. The whole campaign is based on poor observation, concentration on a few failing plantations, and sheer lack of botanical knowledge, but it persists, in the absence of verification.

The tallest tree in the world in March 1991 is considered by Ronald Hildebrant of Arcata, California, after much careful measuring, to be 'The National Geographic Tree' in Redwood National Park, which is at least 373/43ft. From a study of photographs of its top from varying angles, it may prove to be 376ft tall. The second and third tallest are in the same grove, 'The Harry Cole Tree', 370/48ft, and 'Tallest Tree', 368/45ft. The Redwood Highway, Route 101, heading north, enters tall groves at Benbow, where in Richardson Grove a tree on one side of the stores is 340/38ft and one on the other side is 328/28ft and all the dominant trees are over 300ft tall. A few miles on, it is The Avenue of the Giants where for 34 miles it is lined both sides, except for one small field, by trees 250–310ft tall and up to 47ft round. This length will never be widened or straightened. (Those in a hurry can use the freeway nearby.) About 60 miles further north, a few miles north of Orick, one of the best trees is only a short walk from a lay-by on 101, at Prairie Creek Grove. This 'Big Tree' is 320/59ft at six feet. Forty miles south of San Francisco, west of Saratoga, a much drier area catches the sea-fogs and grows immense trees, but standing further apart. Here, in Big Basin, 'Father of the Forest' is 310/47ft and

Coast Redwood (*Sequoia sempervirens*): Dropmore, Buckinghamshire

'Mother of the Forest' is 260/53ft. In nearby Henry Cowell Redwoods, 'Giant Tree' is 270/51ft and 'General Grant' is 250/41ft.

The Coast Redwood was discovered by a Portuguese missionary, Father Crespi, in 1769, presumably around San Francisco. Seeds or trees were taken to Portugal and some trees in Busaco are said to be of that age. Official discovery was in 1795, by Archibald Menzies, scientist and physician with Captain George Vancouver on the return south from Alaska. He sent foliage and cone specimens to Kew. David Don described the tree as *Taxodium sempervirens* as it is so like the only other species in the Redwood family then known, the Bald or Swamp Cypress, *T. distichum*, the one big difference being that it is evergreen. The priority rule in taxonomy ensures that the specific epithet remains with the tree to whichever genus it may be considered later to belong, so it is still *sempervirens* as a *Sequoia*. David Douglas wrote to Hooker at Kew in November 1831 saying that he had seen trees, apparently when working from Monterey in the summer, which he thought would be *Taxodium* species. He had repeatedly measured specimens to 270/32ft with 'some few upward of 300ft', adding that he possessed 'fine specimens and seeds also'. However neither specimens nor seed are known to have arrived, presumably being lost with hundreds of others and the journals of that tour, when Douglas's canoe was swamped on June 13th, 1833 near Fort George.

The introduction came about indirectly through Russia, who maintained a colony until 1850 at Fort Ross, 65 miles north of San Francisco, on the coast. Before 1840, the Russians had been growing the tree in the Crimea and Dr Fischer at Leningrad learned that there were none in Britain. He thought it only right that the country of Menzies and Douglas, the pioneers of the West Coast, should have some, and sent plants to Knight and Perry, London nurserymen, in 1844. Theodore Hartweg, who collected for Kew in 1846 in the Monterey area said that he did not send Sequoia seed, so any trees dating from before the 1850–1 collections of Lobb and Jeffrey, will be originals raised in the Crimea from Fort Ross seed and sent in 1844. Many are known to be pre-1850 plantings and many more are very likely to be.

Lord Grenville bought a tree in 1845 for 5 guineas and planted it by the lake at Dropmore, Buckinghamshire. It is a beautiful tree with regular, slightly drooped branches and a single stem to the tip. In 1982 it was 110/16ft having been 18/1ft when six years planted, and 94/11ft in 1907. At Claremont Garden, Esher, a fine tree with its portrait in *The Trees of Great Britain and Ireland* by Elwes and Henry when it was 98/13ft in 1907, is now 120/19ft and looks now exactly as it did then. At Stratfield Saye, home of the Duke of Wellington, one planted in 1848 was 64/6ft in 1877 and is now 120/20ft. At Longleat, Wiltshire, home of the Marquis of Bath, there are two very similar trees in the Pleasure Walk. One is recorded as having been planted in 1845 and was 62/8ft when 32 years old. This is presumed to be the larger one now, and is 105/21ft, while the other, almost sure to be of the same age, is 111/21ft. These are all in the relatively low rainfall and warm summers of southern England, and for their sites have grown well.

As expected, the biggest trees are in the cool, damp regions. One of the original trees planted at Fota, near Cork, in 1847, is 98/24ft, taped between big burrs. At Woodstock, Kilkenny, two trees, very probably originals, are 138/25½ft and 141/25ft. Two superb trees are among the variety of great trees on the slope between Loch Tay and the A827 at Kenmore, Perthshire, in Taymouth Castle Gardens, 132/24ft and 124/25ft, both growing fast. These may be originals, but could also be of post-1850 planting. At Caledon Castle, County Armagh, there are twelve trees over 20ft round, the biggest 121/24ft. At Rossie Priory near Dundee, in 1877 a tree 50/8ft was equalled only by the one at Longleat. In 1931 it was 82/15ft, and has maintained the same rate of growth to be 124/23ft in 1985. At Stuckgowan on Lomondside, on a steep bank above the A82, a tall tree in the woods, near a Monterey Pine, is 130/20ft. Near Perth, at Kinfauns Castle, one is 130/20ft. That these Sequoias do not have to be of 1850 vintage to be over 20ft round is shown by a pair inside the gate at The Gliffaes, Crickhowell. They were planted in 1885 and in 1984 they were 138/21ft 3in and 141/21ft. The tallest found so far is in the shelter of the chasm at Bodnant, Gwynedd. Along the bottom with its roots beside the stream, this tree, planted in 1887, is 153/16ft.

Back in the drier east, a grove of nine trees at Bowood Park, Wiltshire very probably dates from 1845 and has trees to 130/20ft and 115/21ft. Three trees around the Lake at Stourhead are also of this age and the biggest are one on the south bank, 132/19ft. Near it is one 130/21ft, while one by the drive to the House is 120/20ft. At Cuffnells, a clay hollow outside Lyndhurst, New Forest, a little grove planted in 1855 is a miniature Boulder Creek Flats with long clean trunks on trees to 140ft tall with one 21ft round. In the valley at Melbury, Dorset, a tree which was 85/15ft by 1906, and is probably from the original import, was 121/23ft by 1989 although rather exposed and scorching in winter now that so many trees have gone from around it.

The most extensive plantings are at Leighton Park, Welshpool. These started with what is now the Ackers Memorial Redwood Grove, part of the Arboretum of the Royal Forestry Society, when about 20 trees were brought from California on the deck of a ship in 1857. Now pruned clean for 60ft they range to 130ft tall and 17ft round, well spaced over the hillside. Below them many acres were planted in 1934 and are about 100/8ft, thinned several times. One was blown down before 1950 and lies as it fell, with whorls of branches down its length becoming trees 70ft tall.

GIANT SEQUOIA

Sequoiadendron giganteum

Of the many names used for this tree, 'Giant Sequoia' is probably the best for British usage and is now the preferred name in the United States, but 'Sierra Redwood', used by American foresters, has the merit of distinguishing this from the other Californian Redwood, *Sequoia sempervirens*, which grows only near the coast and is the Coast Redwood. The term often used here, 'Californian redwood', is ambiguous. At least it is better than 'Canadian redwood', which is often used by proud owners, when neither redwood ranges anywhere within 450 miles of Canada. The local Indians called this tree 'Wawona' and other Americans call it 'Big Tree' or 'Mammoth Tree', while in England it is familiarly the 'Wellingtonia'. The usual reason given for this name is that Lindley, describing the first foliage and cone samples in 1853, knew that this was the most massive and impressive tree in the world and thought it right that its name should commemorate the great Duke of Wellington who had died the year before. One writer has insisted, however, that Lindley casting about for a name looked out of his Dorset window and saw on the skyline the Wellington Monument, built in 1817.

Lindley in fact gave the tree a genus of its own, as *Wellingtonia gigantea*. The Americans, far from pleased that it was a British botanist naming their finest tree and that William Lobb had sent the foliage and seeds to England without their knowing, did not take kindly to the name and countered with *Washingtonia*. Luckily that was already in use for a genus of palm, and in 1855 the tree was considered to be in the same genus as the Coast Redwood which had been given the genus *Sequoia* in 1847, and so this new tree became *Sequoia gigantea*. By 1939 it was decided that it did merit a genus of its own, and the name *Sequoiadendron* was coined for it.

The first mention of the species is in the 1833 diaries of a traveller, J.K. Leonard. This received no publicity, and no location is given, but it may be assumed to be the Calaveras Grove, which is easily found beside the modern highway 4, California, at a lower elevation and further north than all but one or two. It was the first grove to be visited by tourists. The first identifiable individual tree was 'Hercules', one of the biggest in the North Grove at Calaveras, seen by John M. Wooster in 1850, when he carved his initials on it. Because of the nearby excitements of the goldrush, little notice was taken of this either. The tree was blown down in December 1861 and is still lying across the trail, at post 15. So, in 1852, when Augustus T. Dowd, a hunter employed by Murphys to feed the miners, followed a wounded grizzly bear well beyond his area, he came upon this grove, and led a party 20 miles under the pretext of showing them a giant grizzly. He was then regarded as its discoverer, and the biggest tree, the first he saw, near the entrance is called the Discovery Tree. It was said to be 300ft tall and over 24ft in diameter at the base.

The next year, in 1853, it was felled, leaving a six foot stump which was planed and polished for a dance-floor for 20 couples. The trunk was stripped of bark for 30ft and fixed around a former to make an exhibit, and two bowling-alleys were made on the peeled trunk. The bark was lost in a fire within a year, and the dance-floor is today rather rough and about seven paces across. It had been found to be 1244 years old. In 1854, 'Mother of the Forest' at the turn of the trail, was stripped of bark to 116ft for exhibition in New York and London. It stands today, stark and bleached by weather and blackened by fire.

Dr Albert Kellogg founded a California Academy of Sciences on April 4 1853 in San Francisco. He was given specimens of Giant Sequoia, probably by Dowd, and showed them at one of the first meetings, in the summer. By chance, William Lobb, collecting for Veitch's and taking a short break, was a guest at that meeting. He hurried off to Calaveras and collected specimens, quantities of seed, and two seedlings. The quickest journey he could book to England was overland through Guadalajara, Mexico and he arrived at Coombe Wood in December. He thought until his dying day that he would never be forgiven by the Americans for being the first to take their most famous tree into cultivation and to Europe.

However, another of those indefatigable Scots, this time a laird, John D. Matthew, from the Errol district in Perthshire, was collecting, unknown to Kellogg, Lobb or others, probably privately. Somehow he heard about the Sequoias at Calaveras, and, unlike Lobb, he knew that the first transatlantic steampacket was running that summer, boarded it and arrived at his home, Gourdiehill, in August 1853. He divided his seed among neighbouring lairds and, like Lobb's seed, it yielded many plants. Only the Scottish writer, Ravenscroft, seemed to know about this, and he lists the estates growing the first trees. Coming in the same year from the same source, the trees from this collecting by John D. Matthew, cannot be known from Lobb trees except by this mention, but they must be accepted as the true original trees. The biggest was at Megginch Castle, 108/27ft in 1986. but the giant specimen at Castle Leod, now 174/30ft, can justify the claim of Lord Cromartie's records to have been planted in 1853, if and only if, it were raised from Matthew seed, sown on arrival and planted out by that winter.

For many years after their discovery, loggers were clearing the more accessible stands at the lower altitudes, but the timber is weak and 'brashy' and big trees shattered when felled. So there was little profit from the industry, unlike the quality timber logged from Coast Redwood. It was therefore possible eventually to preserve, either in National Parks established, or by agreement with private owners, about 80 groves, and no felling has been done this century.

Some northern and middle groves are small or very small. The Tuolumne Grove, down a one-way loop-road off the road to the Tioga Pass has six trees, the top one a massive 255/62ft. Further south, the Mariposa Grove has over 200 trees, the biggest 'Grizzly Giant' at 200/73ft and over 3,500 years old. Towards the south are the two extensive groves, King's Canyon, with the stupendous 'General Grant', 255/80ft at seven feet and Sequoia National Park, where 'General Sherman' is 290/80ft at six feet. But 'Sentinel' by Giant Forest village car park, 257/69ft, and one in Ring Meadow nearby, 290/76ft stand clear in the open and are far more impressive. They are not, however, close rivals to 'General Sherman' in his eminence as the biggest tree in the world.

The tree is a fire-climax tree and these groves are all the result of fires. On these mid-slopes of the Sierra, the fire-cycle is 25 years, determined, as such cycles always are, by the time it takes for an area cleared by one fire to grow sufficient trees and shrubs to support the next one. This then burns out the shrubs again, and the Douglas and White Fir trees, since their bark is still resinous and fairly thin, but the Sequoias have by then thick, non-resinous, fibrous bark. The fire-thinning leaves the Sequoias now dominant although they grow less rapidly than the firs. They hold their foliage above the next shrub and young tree layer, and when 25 years later that burns, the rising heat opens the cones, which can hold their seed viable for that time, and the seed, shaken out by wind, falls on a clear, seed-bed of ash.

In cultivation after 1853, the biggest of all trees lost no time in showing that it was setting out to repeat its achievement in other regions. For a species reduced in modern times to a few relict stands on one side of one end of a single range of mountains, within a very limited altitudinal range, it is making the most extraordinary progress. It took only about 80 years to be the biggest tree, in volume of timber, in every county of the British Isles. One near Aberfeldy, Perthshire, 49 years planted was 21ft round, went on to be 26ft round in 73 years but then died, probably from honey-fungus. Other trees also from the original seedlots, and a few 15 years younger, are 30–36ft round in diverse regions from Sussex, through North Wales and Cumbria to Inverness-shire. On poor silt and sand at Bedgebury in Kent, one planted in 1926 is 20ft round when 54 years old, and on good soil at Rosemoor in Devon one 22 years old is 52/6ft 9in, and at Cracknells, Essex, it was in 15 years 30/5ft 8in.

Growth in height is not so spectacular, and is surpassed in speed by several conifers and broadleaves, at least to 150ft, and, at present, in total by three other conifers, all from western North America. A strong factor against Giant Sequoia in England is lightning-strike. The crown projecting above canopy-level and most other trees in parks and gardens is singularly vulnerable. Across the south and east of England all but a few Sequoias, our national lightning conductor, have their tops rounded off or broken at heights varying between 100 and 130ft depending on exposure. In Scotland, cloud-to-earth strikes are rare, and undamaged regularly tapered conic tops, some most shapely narrow spires to great heights, are the norm.

Because plants from the first two seedlots in 1853 were so abundant in the trade for the next ten years and because of the desire to grow this much publicised wonder-tree, lines and avenues of original trees were planted nearly as often as single specimens, in every part of these islands. And since the timber is worthless and the tree never blows down unless its root system is cut, eroded or flooded, they are still there and some are the most majestic arboreal features we have. Lightning and honey-fungus are the only hazards. The occasional tree is completely shattered by lightning and a few are killed by honey-fungus at random or just two or three in a line or group.

Because the tree grows so rapidly in Britain, it was already an odd fact before 1900 that we had a thousand or more specimens far bigger than any in the continent of America, east of California. Today every one of 102 trees in one avenue alone is twice the girth of any in that vast region, where one in the Tyler Arboretum, Pennsylvania, is 88/11ft and a very few are 50ft bushes. The greatest avenue of them all was planted in 1869 by Mr Walter of Bear Wood when he had 113 trees and planted 55 each side of the B3348 at Crowthorne, Berkshire, at 54ft spacing, with the spare trees behind at each end. The mean size now is about 125/24ft, most of them with tops rounded by repeated lightning-strikes, and a few, undamaged, tapering to 150ft. Two are 29ft round, but very conical. Wellington College nearby has a grassed avenue.

Minley Lodge near Frimley, Surrey, has a very widely spaced grass avenue of 38 trees to 125ft tall and 21ft round. Even more widely spaced is one of 28 trees at Hartley Wintney from Elvetham House to the A30, reputed to have been made from cuttings of the first tree at Stratfield Saye. Battered by lightning and storms, it has specimens to 125ft and to 24ft round. There are several avenues in and near Stratfield Saye. The longest is of 72 trees leading to a southern gate. Minsteracres Abbey has 63 trees lining the drive and a spur from it, standing in prominent lines on a brow as seen from the A68 switchback in Northumberland. Planted probably in about 1880, they range up to 120ft in height and one is 20ft round.

Many shorter avenues contain some very big trees. At Benmore, Argyll, the wide avenue, planted in 1870, has 14 trees and one is 165ft tall; the biggest is 21ft round. An undated avenue, probably of 1872 planting, above Diana's Grove at Blair Castle has one 162ft tall and another 25ft round, and is of 16 trees, well spaced. At Cowdray Park, a broad avenue of 18 planted in 1870 has one tree 30ft round and another 135ft tall. Near Comrie, Perthshire and formerly part of Lawers Estate, 23 splendid trees stand beside the woodland drive to West Lodge and are a public walk. The best is 144/25ft. By the entrance to Sindlesham House, Berkshire, there are 20 trees which date from 1871 and are up to 125ft tall and 25ft round. At Linton Park, Kent, an avenue of 32 trees was planted on a ridge in 1866 and has trees to 120/22ft.

Some lines are impressive and none stands out as well as the 13 planted in a shallow crescent in front of The House of Dun, near Montrose. They can, it seems, be seen from far out to sea. They look like originals of 1855–7 planting and are fairly uniform in size, to 102/23ft. On Myarth Estate near Crickhowells, a line of 10 trees on the bank above a public road is very tall. One is 165ft and the biggest is 27ft round. The 10 by the A835 south of Ullapool at Glackour are also tall, to 135ft and the biggest is 23ft round. A line by the River Walk at Oakley Park near Ludlow has 10 trees, all of which in 1960 were over 20ft round. Now the biggest is 27ft round and all are over 23ft.

Pride of place among the single specimens goes to the bigger of two at Castle Leod, Strathpeffer, as tallest, oldest and among the most shapely of all. It was planted by the great grandfather of the present Earl of Cromartie on his first birthday in 1853. The late earl assured me that this was so, and he will have known the date of birth of his grandfather from the family muniments, but this means that it could only have been a newly sprouted seedling from the Matthew import of August in that year. Whatever the case, it has long been by far the biggest tree in the world at that latitude, which runs through Siberia, Kamtschatka, Alaska and north Labrador. It is now 174/29ft with a long, conic spire. One of the known Matthew trees, planted in 1855 at Megginch Castle, is less shapely and 132/25ft. The 1856 specimen at Taymouth Castle Gardens is near perfection and is now 167/26ft. At Ardross Castle, Easter Ross, the 1855 tree on the flat far below the Castle is 138/28ft.

Many of the biggest trees will certainly be from one of the first two seedlots. Two very similar trees, both 36ft round with sharply tapering boles, are at Clunie

Giant Sequoia (*Sequoiadendron giganteum*): Powerscourt, County Wicklow

Garden near Aberfeldy and Princeland House, Coupar Angus. An extraordinarily rough, low-branched tree at Fasque House, Kincardineshire, is 37ft round. By contrast, a superb tree in a garden near Comrie is 168/31ft and a good tree at Glenlee Park, Kirkcudbrightshire is 165/24ft. A tree in the park below Powis Castle is 138/32ft and a more shapely one at Dolmellynllyn House north of Dolgellau is 148/30ft. Two of the 1856 trees by the drive to Penrhyn Castle, Gwynedd, are 154/19ft and 138/28ft. At Killinchrassie on Tayside, a fine tree is 124/30ft. At Scone Palace the tree at the top of the short avenue, dating from 1866 is 144/30ft.

In the garden of Achnagarry, a tree which has repaired its top after what looks suspiciously like lightning damage now 20ft down, is a splendid 164/24ft. Nearby at the gate of Glen Gloy Hotel by the A82, a tree with a perfect, very slender-conic spire is 160/20ft. Across the Great Glen at Balmacaan, Drumnadrochit, a sturdy tree by the east drive is 98/32ft and among a group of trees about the same height one is 170/23ft. At Coul House, Easter Ross, a fine 1856 tree is 155/24ft. Near Cawdor Castle a well-shaped tree is 165/25ft; at nearby Kilravock Castle, one is 148/25ft and in Morayshire, the adjacent county, at Altyre Estate, one of the 1871 trees by the farm is 141/28ft.

The tallest tree of any kind known in Northern Ireland is a Giant Sequoia at Caledon Castle, County Armagh, a fine tree at 165/23ft. In the Irish Republic, Powerscourt has many fine specimens. A line of 23 in the Dargle Valley, planted in 1861, includes No. 8 with a long spire, 141/26ft and No. 23, the biggest bole, at 130/29ft. A singleton of the same date below the Pepperpot is a splendid tree, 138/24ft. At the Waterfall, the bigger of a pair standing out in the grassy open area in front, is a shapely 150/24ft.

The tallest tree in Surrey is a Giant Sequoia by Polecat Lane, from Haslemere, under the south face of a high ridge, to Hindhead. Sheltered so far from lightning, which is frequent in the area, it has a Scottish-type spire and is 170/24ft. In the New Forest, a very similar tree towers dangerously 100ft above the canopy of oak and beech a short way down a cross-ride on the Rhinefield Ornamental Drive. Planted in 1859 it is 165/26½ft and has been more fortunate than its near twin in Bolderwood, planted in 1861, which was the same size in 1975 when lightning killed its top 20ft. The latter is now removed. Two exceptional trees in Devon are the larger of two at Woodhouse, Uplyme, at 155/25ft and one of several in the upper valley at Endsleigh, now 165/22ft. Then one should not forget the Duke of Wellington's own original tree, planted in 1857 at Stratfield Saye, which, outgrown by a slightly younger tree nearby, is 132/25ft.

SWAMP CYPRESS

Taxodium distichum

The Swamp Cypress at its best is an impressive, tall tree, its crown densely set with minute leaves, bright pale green or rich foxy brown, in season. At far from its best, it can be a low, misshapen tree with a corkscrew stem and twisted branches, a shapeless mass of thin twigs, bare for more than half the year. Young trees are usually shapely, densely twigged and conic but with an obtuse or rounded apex rather than an acute, spired top which adorns the much more open crown of its nearest relative, the Dawn Redwood.

Introduced in about 1640 by John Tradescant the younger, the Swamp Cypress was little planted for 200 years but is now frequent in England in parks and the larger gardens. It is not surprising that it is little seen north of the English Midlands or in Scotland and Ireland because it is accustomed over its extensive home range to long and very hot summers. It grows in brackish waters around the Chesapeake Inlet in Delaware south along the coast to mid Florida and along bottom-lands many miles inland, along the Gulf Coast to Mexico and 1100 miles northward along Mississippi bottom-lands to the lower Ohio River in Indiana. That is from the latitude of Gibraltar and south for 1000 miles. And yet there is one of respectable size (60/8ft) and shape, north of Perth, at Kinfauns Castle.

The classic conifer shape of a single stem persisting through a regular crown to the tip, has not survived in any of the biggest and, so, presumably oldest trees. It would be remarkable if it had, for these trees are all at least 230 years old, so far as can be estimated. For more than half that time they will have been projecting above the general level of tree crowns, vulnerable to every gale. Recent storms have shown the tree to be exceptionally windfirm (only one of the big trees was blown down) but several suffered damage from broken branches. The old trees tend to have several vertical branches making a variably narrow top, and this may well be what is left after the loss of spreading branches through the years. It gives them a respectable shape for such ages and heights.

Unfortunately, the tallest and biggest tree lost more than branches in October 1987. It lost some 40ft of its top. It still has a splendid trunk 19ft round, without swell from any low branch, but it had been 124ft tall. It rises from the bank of a small rhododendron-girt pool in Burwood Park near Weybridge, Surrey. Its crown always was rather rough, with big high branches, and looks much rougher, truncated as it is, but the bole is too good to ignore.

The nearest rival, and now superior tree, is at Dean Court, near Wimborne, Dorset. This was, in 1986, 108/19ft 5in with a broad crown and a less clean bole, but a very fine tree. The next biggest, at Syon Park, Middlesex, is a frankly ugly tree of quite deplorable shape. It is 75/19ft and can only just be measured at five feet before it erupts unrestrainedly into some twenty big vertical branches supported by a huge capital. It is out in the north park beside the Outer Lake. Syon has been famous for its big Swamp Cypresses for 150 years. Specimens were measured in 1837, 1904 and 1931 but there are still so many that only three can now be identified. Six are now 13ft round or more. One north of the Inner Lake is a fine tree now 102/15ft. In 1903 it was 90/12ft. One in Duke's Walk is 90/13ft 8in and this was 85/10ft 3in in 1903. Another in the north park, behind the Butterfly Garden

Swamp Cypress (*Taxodium distichum*):
Dropmore, Buckinghamshire

is multi-stemmed from eight feet, poorly shaped but very big. It is 92/17ft. These are all from plantings by Lancelot Brown in about 1755.

The outstanding big tree for shape is at Roezel on Jersey. It has a long twin spire to 111ft, a crown narrow all the way and a long clean trunk just over 15ft round. Its only rival has a bigger, better trunk but a less shapely, more branchy shorter crown and it is by the river at The Old Rectory at Much Hadham in Hertfordshire, 102/17ft with 35ft of good bole. It is next to much the finest Black Walnut known here and near two of the biggest Horsechestnuts and Yellow Buckeyes. A remarkably fine Swamp Cypress is at Gothic Lodge beside Wimbledon Common in Surrey and is jammed in a sort of courtyard, between two houses with scarcely room to breathe. Despite this, it grew from 90/11ft in 1904 to 90/16ft in 1979. Broadlands has two contrasting big specimens beside the River Test in Hampshire. In 1986 the more slender one was 118/16ft and the broader one 85/17ft. At Pusey House, Farringdon, Oxfordshire, an outstanding tree was 93/15ft in 1980 with a clear bole for eight feet. A tall and good tree prominent in the car park at Knaphill Nursery in Surrey has grown from 85/9ft in 1931 to 105/12ft today. Like the Wimbledon tree this is not only remote from any open water, but is also in Bagshot Sands, a notoriously drying soil.

At Pains Hill Park, Cobham, Surrey, two tall slender trees which were noted in 1904 still stand, some way apart on the bank of a lake. The larger, 82ft/10ft 4in in 1904 is now 105/13ft and the other, then 84/8ft, is now 102/11ft. They are a splendid pair with regular crowns. Dulwich Village near London has many good specimens of slightly less majestic sizes. One, prominent in front of the Art Gallery, is singularly shapely and 85/10ft, while the biggest is in the garden behind Ash Cottage and is 98/12ft. A big, somewhat battered old specimen stands in a swamp below a dam at Tilgate Park, Crawley. It was 83/11ft 8in in 1931 and grew well to be 82/15ft by 1982.

Brockett Hall in Hertfordshire has a long planting on one bank of the River Lee famous for the proliferation of big 'knees' and pictured in many books. In 1906 the biggest was 82/10ft and presumably the same tree, still the biggest, was in 1976 80/14ft. Another 'at the sheltered end' was 85/9ft and this is likely to be the tree 95/13ft in 1976. There were 16 more from ten to twelve feet round and 80–105ft tall in 1976. In Ireland, the biggest found is in the National Botanic Garden at Glasnevin, Dublin, at 80/9ft.

The Swamp Cypress came to the notice of botanists a good 60 years before any other member of the Redwood family was known. With its globular cones, lacking any projecting scales, it could only be thought to be a cypress. That the foliage was deciduous was either not appreciated or was thought to be of little importance in comparison with its being divided into two parted ranks, that is 'distichous'. So it was named *Cupressus disticha*. It was only after some other Redwoods became known, like *Cunninghamia* and *Sequoia*, (1702 and 1792), that it was seen that these were a family of their own, only remotely connected to the cypresses. The genus *Taxodium* was established in 1810.

COMMON YEW

Taxus baccata (plate 3)

The Yew has several interesting aspects, but the main ones revolve about the question of its potential length of life, and this is peculiarly hard to determine within any but the widest limits. Many factors conspire to make this so. First, the biggest, and therefore presumed oldest, are, wherever it can be seen, extensively hollowed by decay in the bole. No count of rings nor carbon-dating can include several feet of early growth. In the Bristlecone Pines of California and Nevada, completely sound cores are found in trees over 5000 years old, even if it needs a strong lens to resolve the annual rings. But the conditions there are so dry and harsh that decaying fungi cannot live within the live trees, whereas in the habitat of the Yew, they flourish in the normal high humidity. Second, the way round this which can be used in some trees, by cutting a primary branch, say 10–20ft up the trunk and adding the

10–20 years or less to the count of its rings, is not available in Yews. The primary branches are also very hollow, and, unlike in pines, beech, sycamore and others, a low branch on a Yew, if sound, could have arisen when the Yew was already very old. Their capacity to grow sprouts from the bole does not wane with age.

Other approaches to the question depend on knowing the sort of growth expected for a series of trees to attain their size. One way to do this is to plot the girths of all the trees of known date of planting and make a curve. Hundreds of oaks stand with plaques on village greens and in estates and gardens, and there is excellent cover for ages of up to 150 and a few beyond. A good series of curves can be plotted showing the mean rate of increase, the fast and the slow growers. (Girth is the only useful parameter over a long span. Height and spread culminate and then decrease with age.) The limits for the age of any oak up to about 15ft in girth are clearly seen. For Yews, this shows very little. There are only 50 Yews of known date and these are scattered from 30 to 1100 years of age. Not only are there too few to construct any useful curve, but the growth of Yew is seen to be so irregular, variable and anomalous, that no curve can be fitted to the figures.

For ages beyond known dates, oaks have such good curves that they can be extrapolated a long way. Further, by re-measuring old trees at known intervals, a series of undated slopes of growth can be plotted, each of which fits the age/girth curves at one place only. Therefore its age can be fixed to some degree of accuracy, and it allows the extrapolated sector to be confirmed and extended. No such work can be done on Yews. There are hundreds of measurements of big Yews, many from 1837 and 1897 and more from 1904 and 1950 but they must mostly be wildly inaccurate. Pennant and Daines Barrington started the tradition as early as 1769 when both independently saw and measured the Fortingall yew and recorded it as 52ft and 56ft respectively. The Yew at Tisbury has suffered severely. Successive attempts have been: 37ft (1834); 30ft 8in (1892); 35ft (1903); 29ft 10in (1924) and my 31ft 1in (1959) and 31ft 4in (1991). The tape must be threaded among some sprouts, but major discrepancies will be from the big breast of concrete put in at some unknown time. It seems to have been made to replace the fourth great limb which had broken out, and to be roughly the shape of the missing part. Depending on its date, this could make a difference of a few feet, but there is nothing to suggest that the trunk when whole was much bigger than it now is. Two trees at Cudham Church in Kent have long, smooth boles with which there seems no chance of significant error. But in 1896 they were said to be 28ft and 28ft 3in; in 1944 they were 27ft 6in and 26ft 6in, and in 1965 I made them 27ft 6in and 22ft 7in.

A marginal case is the Totteridge Yew (the earliest of all records quoted) whose figures of 26ft in 1677 and the same in 1777 could, as evidently rounded figures, hide an increase of several inches in 100 years. It was 27ft 7in in 1954, which could be in line with the previous figures. The Whittingehame Yew in East Lothian has recorded steady and very slow growth: 10ft 8in (1894); 11ft 3in (1931); 11ft 5in (1974) and 11ft 9in (1987). Equally cleanly rounded, the Stoke Gabriel Yew in

Devon has been: 15ft (1893); 16ft 8in (1944) and my own figures, 17ft (1959) and 17ft 3in (1982). At Church Preen, Shropshire, a tree with an old iron band holding the two stems together ten feet up, has a reasonably simple bole to measure at five feet and has a reasonably consistent record: 19ft (1780); 22ft (1893); 21ft 8in (1896 – improved precision?); 23ft 1in (1955); 22ft 6in (1962) and 22ft 8in (1985).

Short term increases in big old trees easily measured, show mean annual figures of mostly 2–5in over 25–35 years, but a very smoothly rounded bole at Bedhampton in Hampshire showed no detectable addition to its 20ft 2in in 21 years. The wristy bole at Durley not far away grew four inches to 23ft 8in in 19 years, and the clean boled smaller one at Hambledon, Surrey, added six inches in 25 years to be 20ft. In sum, the only conclusion from these figures is that big Yews are now taking four to more than ten years to increase by one inch in girth. Only two, and both younger and smaller than these, have shown more rapid growth (ignoring doubtful figures and trees with widely split trunks, which may increase merely by the division widening). These are at Southwick, Hampshire, adding 17in in 21 years to become 15ft 9in round, and at Pimperne, near the Dorset border, which added 13in in seven years, to be, unless I made an error, 13ft 9in.

So we turn to dated trees. The most intriguing of these is at Dryburgh Abbey, Selkirk. John Lowe writing in 1896 said that the monks planted one in 1136. He found the single Yew there in 1894 to be 11ft 4in round and ridicules the idea that so small a tree could be that old, and insists that the present tree was relatively recent. However, the Yew there in 1984 was 12ft 2in. It had added ten inches in 90 years and this rate of growth fits reasonably closely to 136in in 758 years, given a small increase with age. If this is so, we have a tree 858 years old and only 12ft round. The Yew at Hughenden, Buckinghamshire, is dated, in the church, to 1613. In 1980 it was ten feet round; one inch to three years. At Waltham St Lawrence, Hampshire, a 1655 Yew was 12ft 11in in 1966 and one planted in 1660 at Sutton, Sussex, was 12ft 3in in 1966.

It will be noted that these trees are all less than 13ft round, and the trees in which the interest resides are 25ft to over 30ft round. If the dated trees have achieved mean annual increases of one inch in two to three years, over their first 300 years, without any falling off at all at greater age, the 30ft trees would be 720–1180 years old. But it is fanciful to assume that there is no diminution, and the figures quoted show that the rate of big trees is often much less than half this and can be negligible. To grow the 17ft from 13–30ft must take many of them 1500 years and some will need more than 2000 years.

There is a fragment or two of evidence from annual rings. The Fitzhead Yew in Somerset had just been felled when I saw it. It had been noted by V. Cornish as 16ft round in 1944. The trunk had a big hollow centre, but a crosscut a few feet up showed 110 rings in one inch on the outside. That is one inch increase in girth in 12 years. The longest count of solid wood was 550 years, but this ended far from the centre. It was only a small tree, as churchyard Yews go. I was sent a polished sector from a Yew that had blown down in the furthest north stand of natural Yew on a rocky hillside near Ardnamurchan, Argyll. Growth at the extreme of the range might be slower than normal, but in humid woods in very high rainfall, probably not by much. From the centre, it is easy to count 220 rings to the bark. This is along a radius of five inches and the tree was about 35in round, giving a mean rate for life of one inch in eight years. Were it possible for it to have maintained this early growth-rate, it would still have needed nearly a thousand years to have achieved ten feet girth.

Now we turn from the trees themselves to more general and circumstantial evidence. There are hundreds of big Yews in churchyards, and only the Keffolds Yew above Haslemere is not, and despite no present sign or known history of a church there, the site looks right for one. All the others are in churchyards which are round or irregular, not post-mediaeval rectangular ones. This implies that they are at least about 500 years old. There is no tradition of planting a Yew when a church is built. It is stated that when the 12th century Cistercian Abbey was being built at Fountains, the monks used two old hollow Yews as shelters and tool sheds. One was still there until removed through a misunderstanding recently, and was 27ft round in 1961.

All the evidence leads inescapably to the position that the big Yews were not planted in churchyards. The church was built to be near the Yew. The site was already sacred, the meeting place of the elders and tribes. The church was placed so as to have the maximum shelter from the indestructible evergreen foliage, usually on the windward side of the porch or approach path. It was also placed near in order to appropriate the ancient sanctity of the site. Many of the oldest Yews are on a slight eminence above a stream and sheltered from the north and east. They have still an aura of being special to the ancients. Gregory the Great is said to have enjoined Augustine to preserve the old temples, and the trees associated with them may have been saved when there was no building, too. Additional reasons for the early Christians to enclose a Yew in their churchyard are the symbolism of immortality; the Roman use of Yew foliage at burial, and the use of male-flowering branches as 'palm', still the custom in Ireland. The provision of staves for longbows is not a valid reason. Bowstaves were imported from Spain and Portugal bound to the casks of sherry and other wines as import duty. British Yews yield knotty, inferior wood and only branches could be used. For a useful supply, many trees would be needed in each churchyard and probably 50–100 years between yields, but there is no sign or mention of this being done.

Since so many churches gain good shelter from their Yews, it might be thought that they would have planted them for that purpose. But although so rugged and reliable, Yew is so slow to grow, so prone to make lateral growth rather than height, that other species would be a better proposition, and the Yews will in fact have been used because they were already there and grown.

Yew timber is one of the strongest and most durable known. It is not these qualities that are the most important in making bowstaves. That depends on the clearly seen change in colour between the sapwood and heartwood. The bows need to be cut so that the compressible sapwood is on the inside of the curve and the highly elastic heartwood with great tensile strength is on the outside. It would be very difficult to fashion them like this without the clear colour change along the critical line.

The tensile strength and durability also are vital in the Yew surviving to such remarkable ages. The thin shells of hollow boles hold together and support long branches for centuries where no other wood could do either.

A number of individual Yews have been mentioned in passing, and a few more need special mention. Notably the one at Crom Castle, County Fermanagh, which has appeared by magic. Out in the swirling mists of the bogs this seems only natural, but it was a shock at the time. 'The Crom Yew' was written about in several Irish magazines, and there are two or three drawings of it, with accounts of its extraordinary crown, spread in a low canopy supported by oak posts and under which 200 guests were served with tea. In 1895 Lord Erne wrote that it had a 6ft bole, girthing 12ft at ground-level, and a spread 77ft in diameter. Elwes and Henry in 1902 quote Lord Erne and his 60 supports, so it remains a single tree, 'resembling an enormous green mushroom'. By 1983 I found it to be two very similar trees about 20ft apart, sharing the crown and supports. At three feet, they were 14ft 10in and 13ft 10in in girth, and so of similar, presumably exactly the same age. So where had the second tree been? If it had been there when the various accounts were written, why is there no mention of it, and how did the artists so signally fail to see it?

Gilbert White of Selborne measured the yew by his church porch in 1789, too late perhaps to include it in his *Natural History of Selborne*. At 3ft it was 23ft. By 1896 it was recorded to be 25ft 2in and in 1987 it was 25ft 10in. It swelled above this on one side with a view into a very hollow interior as many branches spread. It was blown down in the gale of January 25th, 1990 and re-erected within a few days. But it had a very small root system still attached and did not survive.

The fine Yew at Brockenhurst Church in Hampshire is best measured at three feet up, where it was 18ft 8in in 1896, and 19ft 2in in 1963 but 19ft 8in by 1972 and 20ft 2in in 1986 which seems to show a recent resurgence of growth.

The tree at Fortingall is still flourishing in its stone prison, built to deter souvenir hunters from cutting lumps from a tree they thought was linked to Pontius Pilate. It cannot be measured as it is one large fragment and two small ones, but the rough outline of the remains of the base indicate a diameter in line with the 52ft or 56ft girths of 1769. It is now considered to be 4–5000 years old.

The big Yew at Tandridge Church in Surrey has an important place in the development of the present ideas on the ages of such trees. It was Allan Meredith who saw in the notes on the history of the church the statement that the earliest foundations had a stone arch over a root of the tree, and realised what this meant.

The earliest church there was a Saxon one. So, about 1000 years ago, this root was of sufficient size to warrant stone vaulting. Hence, not only did the Yew pre-date the church, but it did so by an enormous amount of time. For the wall of the present church is 24ft from the trunk of the Yew. A root from a Yew would be of negligible thickness 24ft out, for many hundred years. For it to be big enough to need bridging over would surely need more than 1000 years and quite likely 2000 or more.

The tree is highly unusual in having the remains of a number of branches, on the side away from the church, that have bent down, rooted and come up as trees. The most remote, now just outside the churchyard edge, is 14ft round and at an angle as if it were once a layered branch. Two others 20ft and 25ft from the main trunk and about 8ft round, show clearly their old attachments at the base, corresponding with cuts on the nearest branches. One thin, much-rotted branch descends to the soil and creeps along it, with scars from the removal of several small stems.

The old tree is 62/34ft 3in and has four main limbs, spreading slightly from the base, and fully diverged at between six and ten feet up. The central one has only a sliver of ten feet of its exterior left on one side, the rest having rotted away. The hollow joins with the interior of the westernmost stem which is thickly walled round to the wide opening on the northern side and looks sound from the southern side, as do the two eastern limbs, but their centres join in the central hollow. From the south and northeast, the tree appears to have three diverging, massive and sound limbs, but this is not really the case.

WESTERN RED CEDAR

Thuja plicata

The Western Red Cedar ranges from the coast and islands of south Alaska to Mendocino County in northwestern California, and in a broad belt inland in mountains with high rainfall in Idaho, Montana, Washington and British Columbia. It was discovered by Nee who travelled with Malaspina in about 1791, on Nootka Sound on Vancouver Island and in the same place by Archibald Menzies in 1792. It was introduced in 1853 to Veitch's by William Lobb. David Douglas travelled and camped extensively in the woods in 1826 but failed to notice that it was a different species from that familiar to him on his 1823 expedition in New England, which was *Thuja occidentalis*.

Wherever the Western Red Cedar has the high rainfall and cool wet summers, it rapidly grows into a sturdy, well furnished, regularly conic tree. It shows its dislike of dry soils and exposure to warm or cold drying winds by making a slow-growing, scantily clad tree of little charm or use for shelter. There are big trees in the southwest of England, but they tend to run out of shelter and become thin at the top so they are not as tall as those in the glens of Perthshire and further north.

Golden-Barred Thuja (*Thuja plicata zebrina*): Bedgebury, Kent

North Wales also seems to suit this tree well, as does Ireland where big trunks are frequent and the crown shape is different. Like the Nootka Cypress in Ireland, the Western Red Cedar is less acute, often obtuse at the top, and very broad with big low branches, often bending to the soil, rooting and growing up as big trees in a ring around the main bole. This may be acceptable where there is a great deal of room as it gives a certain grandeur – a single-tree woodland – but it is usually preferable to have a good stem unencumbered by such parasitic extensions. They compete above and below the ground and make the main tree thin and eventually die back at the top.

There is little to choose among the biggest and finest specimens, either in size or form, but none is better placed than that in the minor dell below the Pepperpot at Powerscourt in County Wicklow. It is in a small, well-spaced group planted in 1867, next to a Giant Sequoia, a much bigger tree, and a splendid one, but not detracting from the *Thuja* as a monumental specimen of its kind. Its huge trunk tapers little for a *Thuja* and is clean and scarcely fluted for about 20ft. In 1989 it was 138/19ft 8in and growing very fast for in 1975 it was 100/17ft and in 1931 it was only 9ft 4in round.

A very similar tree stands on the broad margin of a road in Belladrum Estate, west of Inverness, on the edge of a wood. The date of planting is not known but will be near 1860. In 1987 this tree was 135/19ft 2in. The tallest of the species found is at Strone House, Argyll, where it was planted in 1875 among many other conifers on a narrow flat at the foot of a steep, rocky bank. The biggest of three there is a shapely 150/18ft 3in. Another of these best five is above the path up the valley behind the house at Castlehill in Devon. It is impressively smooth and massive from beneath and its height can be appreciated from along the valley. In 1989 it was 138/18ft. Marginally the biggest bole, and as good as any, is one among many huge Thujas and Giant Sequoias scattered, very irregularly, over the hillside at Balmacaan, just west of Loch Ness. It is 135/20ft and although another there, and one up the Glen at Glengarry Castle, are 22ft around, they can be taped only at three feet because of big low branches.

At Stourhead, Wiltshire, on the far side of the Lake, is the biggest of the very few known trees raised from the original seed sent by William Lobb in 1854. It is widely layered, and, deep in there, the real tree is 115/17ft. At Armadale Castle on Skye, a fine tree is 82/17ft 5in near the drive. A taller tree grows in the shelter of a small pinetum at Coed Coch, Abergele, Clwyd. This is 111/17ft 6in.

A remarkable planting, well visible from the re-aligned A9 south of Dunkeld, Perthshire, is the line on the Murthly Castle estate. There are 100 trees, 60ft apart, very regular in size and shape, with the biggest 120/13ft.

The Golden-barred Thuja, 'Zebrina', must have arisen within a few years of 1900 for although some say it dates from about 1870, the earliest dated trees are from 1902, including that at Dropmore in Buckinghamshire which had specialised in earliest plantings since before 1830. That tree was 75/7ft 5in in 1982. The tree that is prominent by the Lake at Stourhead was planted in 1906 and is 80/9ft 6in. Two outstanding specimens at Castlehill stand near together and nearly as big as any: 95/8ft 7in and 88/8ft 8in. One at Tottenham House, in Savernake Forest, Wiltshire, was 80/8ft 5in in 1984. In Ireland there may be another form (unless the climate is responsible for they are mostly much more golden) and have been called 'Irish Gold'. One at Stradbally House, Leix, is 85/8ft 8in and the taller of two at Woodstock, County Kilkenny is 80/8ft 4in round a forking stem while the other is 75/11ft 1in at four feet up, beneath a fork.

JAPANESE THUJA

Thuja standishii

The Japanese Thuja has foliage which when crushed emits the most delicious scent of any conifer. It is sweet and lemony, with an extra piquance; quite strong catchouk and a hint of eucalyptus. It is a distinctive tree, which after a little acquaintance can be identified from any distance although it is in general so like the Western Red Cedar. It has a broad conic crown with strongly developed low branches, which from a level start turn abruptly upwards, making U-shapes. The foliage hangs rather heavily but the shoot tips all arch over in a manner not found in other thujas. The foliage is speckled silver beneath and the bark has stringy strips between some very smooth areas which are a rich deep red or purplish red.

This was among the large number of plants brought out in the first serious direct imports from Japan in 1861. Collected by James Veitch, it was first marketed by Standish and Noble, the nurserymen of Ascot to whom we are eternally grateful for the raising of the glorious rhododendron 'Cynthia', which, when they fell out, neither Standish nor Noble could leave to the other. So the name had to be changed for one of them, and he called it 'Lord Palmerston'.

The Japanese Thuja is a tree of steady but slow growth, making most progress in western gardens with high rainfall and humidity. Yet the two biggest span a great part of the east-west possibilities, from Wicklow to Kent. In County Wicklow, a specimen in the Rhododendron Walk below the Dolphin Garden at Powerscourt is 66/10ft. The one in the garden at Benenden School in Kent was 72/9ft 4in ten years before, and should be its equal in girth by now. The next four biggest are very western. One at Patterdale Hall in Cumbria is 60/10ft but has to be measured at three feet because of low branches. Coed Coch in Clwyd has one with a longer clear bole, 66/9ft, the same sizes as one at Woodstock, County Kilkenny. The tallest is a fine tree at Tregrehan in Cornwall, which is 80/7ft 3in. A forking tree at Ochtertyre, Crieff, is 56/8ft 6in.

The oldest known, and presumably an original from 1861 seed, is in the east , at Linton Park, Kent. Planted in 1866, it was 72/8ft in 1986. At Leonardslee in Sussex, a group of three near the Hill Garden, lost one in 1987 but the remaining two are a fine pair, the larger 70/6½ft.

HIBA or THUJOPSIS

Thujopsis dolabrata

This Japanese tree has a high place among the conifers which are grown mainly for their foliage. Its hard, broad, flat scale-leaves are twice as big as those of similar foliages and their upper surface is rich mid-green with a high gloss. The tree always looks thriving and luxuriant. The underside of the leaf is equally attractive, with thickened margins of glossy yellower green around centres boldly marked in thick pure white in the shape of a hatchet blade. This is the origin of the epithet 'dolabrata' from 'dolabra', the Roman soldier's entrenching tool. There is no connection therefore with 'weeping' and the all too frequently seen 'dolobrata' is quite erroneous.

The Hiba comes in two extreme forms and a variety of near intermediates. The commonest form has a dozen or so stems of more or less equal size, perhaps with two, or just one slightly dominant in the centre. These will have bark shredding into fine strips and look as if they are scratching posts for a cat, as they may well be. The inner ring of stems is surrounded by an outer ring of somewhat smaller ones, which are rooted layers, and may have smaller, younger layers outside them. The whole makes a broad, domed or obtusely broad-conic crown.

The other extreme form is the tree form. This may always be the variety *hondai* from northern Japan and is much less frequent. It has a single, stout bole with short,

Thujopsis (*Thujopsis dolabrata*): close-up of stem

162

thick branches descending as they leave the trunk then curving sharply upwards bearing thick sprays of foliage sparsely and hanging vertically. Many trees are intermediate in habit, with a single bole branching low, forking or with two stems but these have the normal, spreading foliage. Whatever their form, the bright, glossy markedly reptilian scales give them great character.

Many trees have a spray here and there of foliage largely white or very pale yellow. These were planted as 'Variegata' which is an unstable form which has almost entirely reverted to green before the tree is of modest size. No big, old trees have been seen which have retained the variegation. An exceedingly attractive golden foliaged form is now sometimes seen but none is yet able to qualify for mention here.

The preference of this tree for a damp, mild milieu all the year round, is clearly shown by the location of the notable specimens. All are in Irish or other far western gardens with a high rainfall. The prize group is that at Portmeirion, Gwynedd, where some 20 big trees are spread along the hillside from the pinetum, above a pool to a line by a path towards the back. Several are 80ft tall. Near the pool one is 82/3ft 10in with a second stem 2ft 10in round, and another is 78/4ft 2in. In the pinetum, one is 80/3ft 9in + 3ft 6in. All are of this intermediate form, tall, with either a single stem or two stems, and normal foliage.

Woodstock, at Inistioge, County Kilkenny, has one among three, a many-stemmed tree 82ft tall above the far end of the lawn with the two main stems five feet round. The biggest bole is that of a grand tree at Tregrehan, Cornwall, 70/9ft, and has a trace of variegation. At Boconnoc near Bodmin, a good tree is 75/6ft and Trebah and Glendurgan on Helford River each has one 75/5½ft.

There are very few trees dated before 1900 and the oldest is at Hillsborough, County Down, which was planted in 1872, now at 70/3ft with many stems. In the Italian Garden at Bicton, Devon, one of the bushier kind, planted in 1873 is now 56/3½ft and once variegated. An 1882 tree at Arlington Court in Devon is over 60ft tall and has 70 layered stems. At Stonefield, Argyll, a big tree is 60/7ft at the main stem. At Derreen, County Kerry, two 50ft trees have been pruned to clean trunks, one for 40ft and the other for 30ft, both about 5ft round. These are true tree-form plants in foliage, too.

The variety *hondai* seen at Arduanie, Argyll, has very dense, crisped foliage on three trees to 46/4ft 2in and so the other tree form mentioned is probably not this but another northern provenance. A fine example is by Trident Pool in Powerscourt, 62/5½ft and the better of two of this form, out of five big trees at Kilmacurragh, is 46/7ft 7in. One at Kilmory Castle, Argyll, is 46/5½ft and two at Wray Castle by Windermere, Cumbria, are around 70/4½ft.

WESTERN HEMLOCK

Tsuga heterophylla

Nearly everyone knows that hemlock is a notoriously toxic herb, but remarkably few know that it is a genus of conifers related to spruce, certain to be frequent in their neighbourhood, and likely to be one of the biggest and best trees there. Any genus of conifer that has representatives in western North America has its finest species there. The hemlocks have four rather bushy trees in eastern Asia; a much better one in the Himalaya and two moderate ones in eastern North America. But the two in western North America are taller trees, and one of them is among the tallest and most shapely trees of the world. This is the Western Hemlock, growing all along the Pacific coast of Alaska and the islands, south to northern California with an inland population in the high rainfall areas of the central mountains from British Columbia to Idaho.

The biggest growth is in the Olympic and Cascade Mountains of Washington where trees to 260/30ft have been recorded. The tallest I found was 230/17ft below Mount Rainier. It was first collected as a foliage specimen on the Lewis and Clark Expedition in 1804 and described from this foliage in 1832. David Douglas must have lived under it during almost every journey, but he took it to be the Eastern Hemlock with which he had become familiar on his first, eastern trip, and did not send any seed. This was left to John Jeffrey who sent seed on April 24 from Vancouver Island, which arrived in August 1852. The date 1851 is usually cited, but although Jeffrey was on Vancouver Island in July and August of that year, he did not record collecting or sending seeds then. The British Columbia Expedition of 1860–1 sent quantities of seed, from which the majority of the earliest trees were raised, while William Lobb worked from 1852–4 to the south and east of the range of this tree and no seed is recorded from him. The species was therefore not commonly available until after 1862 and missed the great decade, 1850–1860, of pinetum planting in Scotland and was usually added between 1870 and 1890.

This hemlock is the ultimate climax tree in the rain-forests on the Pacific Slopes. It sheds great quantities of viable seed which grow fast and in deeper shade than any other conifer except shoots from already rooted stumps of Coast Redwood. Seedlings arise in rows along the tops of fallen logs and straddle them with their roots. They have a long-drooped leading shoot which allows them to work their way, undamaged, through over-shading branches. They also spring up in pockets of decay in the trunks of senile trees, and one growing from ten feet up on the 63ft girth Thuja in Hoh River Forest was over 100ft tall in 1973, while small seedlings are often seen in this country in forks and clefts. In Britain also, in woods managed on a shelterwood system, as at Weasenham in Norfolk and Kyloe in Northumberland, the ground is carpeted in seedlings which rise in dense clumps. Heavy thinning of these leaves superb clean-stemmed, shapely trees of great vigour to perpetuate the side-shelter and contribute to the dominant trees. I had the pleasure of being able to mark the thinning of such groups along the drive at Balmoral Castle and to leave beautiful trees 40–70ft tall which I now admire inordinately whenever I see them.

Western Hemlock is unusual in climax trees in starting away with great rapidity, and also unusual in conifers in its indifference to most soils. It just needs high humidity and high rainfall, the former being the more important, as the woods in Norfolk show. Trees a few years old will often make leading shoots three to four and half feet long on soils as different as light sands, heavy clay-loam and shallow or deep peat. They will grow well on loams over chalk and limestone, but not if rooting straight into them. They do not like to be near cities or towns in the south and east, but are luxuriant very near Perth and within the towns around the Highlands where damp, clean air and lack of drying east winds are probably the benign factors. They do not thrive at all in sea-winds by the east coasts but can be excellent near the shores of sea-lochs on the west coast of Scotland. Their peak areas are mid-Perthshire and Angus, Inverness-shire, Easter Ross, Argyll and North Wales.

As an extreme shade-bearer Western Hemlock retains its lower branches through life, unless very crowded. But it makes a strikingly good trunk if cleaned

Western Hemlock (*Tsuga heterophylla*):
Dropmore, Buckinghamshire

165

up. This should always be done in a garden starting when it is young. The bottom branches become a tangle anyway and those from above six feet bend down outside them. To have a good clear stem, and to grow other plants close to them, the stem should therefore be cleaned to at least 20ft.

There are only four trees known or thought to have been grown from Jeffrey's very small seed-packet of 1852. The first planted is the 1853 tree at Boturich Castle at the southern end of Loch Lomond. This is a fine specimen, although not as big as many younger trees, and was 130/13½ft in 1985. Another is the 1854 tree in the pinetum at Hopetown House near the Forth Bridges. Although well sheltered to a good height, this site is too near the east coast to allow the best growth, and in 1984 this tree was 100/10½ft. The other known Jeffrey tree was planted at Hafodunas in Clwyd in 1856. It grew well and was a superb tree, 120/14½ft in 1978, but was struck by lightning soon after, which removed about 20ft and left it 105/15ft in 1984. It failed to repair itself and was cut down by 1987. The fourth is a Jeffrey tree by inference because it was planted in 1859 at Dupplin Castle, Perthshire. It was 98/9½ft by 1931 and is presumably the biggest of these trees, among others, that was 148/13½ft in 1983.

The best trees in Perthshire include one at Hallyburton House which was already in 1907 ten feet round and in 1986 it was 144/15½ft; the two biggest trunks, one at Scone Pinetum, planted in 1866 and now 148/20ft and its near twin at Doune House, Dunblane, 150/20½ft both with many low branches; one planted in 1870 at Lanrick Castle near the bridge, 150/14½ft in 1988; a superb tree at Leny House, Callender, 150/15ft in 1984; one in a clearing in the woods at Culdees House, 138/15½ft a slender tree at Bonskeid House, Tummelside, 150/10½ft in 1990; an 1864 tree at Abercairny, Crieff, 132/14½ft in 1986, and many trees at Murthly Castle. The one by Roman Bridge, pictured in Elwes and Henry, I make about 160/14ft but another maintains that it is only a little over 140ft tall. The baseline is exceedingly difficult to establish as it is on a steep bank. On the Lower Terrace, a pair are 158/15ft and 155/13ft and the biggest of many giants by the East Drive is 150/16½ft.

In Argyll the biggest are one on a bank at Benmore, dating from 1870 and 164/15ft in 1991 and one at Strone House near the big Grand Fir, which dates from 1875 and is 148/16ft.

In Northern Ireland, a huge, low-branched but single-boled tree at Drum Manor, County Derry, was 108/19½ft in 1983. In North Wales a tree dated 1882 in the ravine at Bodnant is 141/14½ft.

In southern England, there is a cluster of big trees around Haslemere in Surrey, with one at Grayswood Hill now 102/16ft and several by Polecat Lane and in Honeyhanger, to 120/14ft. There are otherwise, singularly a few notable specimens in the top class gardens from Kent to Cornwall. In the valley at Wakehurst Place, Sussex, the very fine tree, with imposing views through its light branching for some 100ft of quality stem, is now 135/12½ft and at Stourhead in Wiltshire a similar tree, planted in 1871, was 135/13½ft in 1984.

The best height growth on a fairly young tree of known date is a highly creditable 140/7½ft for a 64 year old tree in the Miners' Bridge plots near Betws-y-Coed, and excellent all-round growth is shown by a tree at Cortachy Castle, Angus, planted in 1915 and 138/13½ft when 77 years old.

MOUNTAIN HEMLOCK

Tsuga mertensiana

On the moonscape lavas at nearly 6000ft in the Cascade Mountains of Oregon, the training ground of the moonshot crew, with no visible soil and in relentless exposure, only two species of tree can grow. These are the Lodgepole Pine and the Mountain Hemlock. The hemlock extends near the snowline along the main ridges far into Alaska, where it grows also down nearly to sea-level. Its range southwards from Oregon runs along the Sierra Nevada in California through Yosemite to peter out in scattered patches beyond, mostly at around 10,000ft. With a range like that, it is unexpectedly pernickety about where it will give of its best in Britain.

The favoured areas are few and limited, being Central Perthshire and Easter Ross with parts of Inverness-shire. Trees are growing in almost every county, but few of them are of much note outside those enclaves. The strong northerly bias is understandable but it is less easy to see what factors are involved. In its home range the tree is always accustomed to cool summers, high humidity and year-round abundance of ground moisture either from rainfall and snowfall, or in the southern areas, from snow-melt. In Britain, these places with the best trees all have cool summers and high humidity, but the rainfall is modest in comparison with western Wales and the western Highlands in Argyll and Wester Ross, where the specimens are not nearly so good. It may be that they need the winters to be as cold as possible, or the growing season shorter than it is in the mild west.

The slow, rather struggling growth in England, is of benefit to gardeners with limited space, since this tree, highly attractive in shape and foliage, is even more so with the dense crown that slow growth gives it, and it can be planted where bigger growing trees cannot. For, however slow it is, it nearly always makes a shapely miniature of the bigger trees and is only rarely bushy. So it makes a slender conic tree with pendulous foliage, variably blue-grey, useful on the poorest soil.

In the wild, many trees have dark green foliage, many others have pale grey-green and some are blue-grey. A selection in the trade of these last has yielded some very bright blue-grey forms sold as 'Glauca' but, as in the Noble Fir, these are the extreme forms of the natural population, where they occur at random, and have no common origin, so botanists prefer to call it var. *glauca*.

This species is the odd man out among the hemlocks in several features. Its needles are not flat but half rounded, and they have white bands of stomata on both

Mountain Hemlock (*Tsuga mertensiana*): Murthly Castle, Perthshire

surfaces. They radiate all round the shoot, giving the short shoots the aspect of the spurs on a cedar. It is the only species to have cones bigger than a thumbnail and cylindric rather than droplet-shaped. They are up to three inches long.

These features have led a few botanists to suggest that Mountain Hemlock is a natural hybrid between the Western Hemlock and the Sitka Spruce. It is more generally agreed that it has hybridised only with the Western Hemlock and then only very rarely. The history of the hybrid, Jeffrey's Hemlock, *Tsuga* x *jeffreyi* is even more bizarre than was John Jeffrey himself. The first specimen known was the only seedling to germinate from the first seed packet of Mountain Hemlock, collected in 1851 on Mount Baker in Washington State. The two species grow one above the other, often mixing at the edges, all the way from Alaska to California, and great quantities of seed of both hemlocks have been imported over the last one hundred years. However, not a single further hybrid was found until one arose from a packet of rhododendron seed, then one or two more from hemlock seed, well into this century. The hybrid itself was unknown in the wild until 1968 when Brian Mulligan found it in Washington and again, in 1970, in British Columbia. It shows no hybrid vigour at all and inherits its habit unchanged from the Mountain Hemlock but its foliage is dull grey-green on both sides, flattened and sparse. The cone is like the Mountain Hemlock but a little smaller.

The Mountain Hemlock was discovered in 1827 on Baranof Island, Alaska, by the German botanist K. Mertens circumnavigating the world in a Russian expedition. It made a poor start here, though, because after Jeffrey's 1851 seed yielded only the hybrid, his second seedlot, sent from the Oregon Cascades in 1852, was no more successful, and no plants were known to have been raised. It was left to William Murray, collecting on Mount Scott in Oregon for Lawson's Edinburgh nursery in 1854 actually to produce trees.

The premier planting is on the Middle Terrace at Murthly Castle in Perthshire, where four trees were planted in 1862, and one added in 1863. These could well have been from the 1854 seed grown at Lawson's, for seedlings make a very slow start and are tiny bushlets for many years. The 1863 addition grew to be the prize exhibit as it is much bluer and more pendulous than the others. It was praised by Elwes and Henry, and prominent in the fine portrait of the group that illustrates the species, taken in about 1906. It is now 105/11ft. One of the other four was blown down in 1989 when it was 102/10ft, and the biggest remaining is now 95/11ft. Two short lines are below, on the Lower Terrace, one of them probably of the same origin and date as the five, since it is 92/12ft and the biggest trunk known, and five presumably younger as they are six to eight feet round. Another short line north of the Lime Avenue has four trees to seven feet round.

A tree planted in Diana's Grove at Blair Castle in 1872 is 105/7ft and shows how this species, in Perthshire, has a long, slow start and then grows quite fast, for in 1931 that tree was only 33ft tall. At Port-na-Craig near Pitlochry, a good tree is 68/8ft; one at Keir Castle is 70/8ft and one at Meikleour near Blairgowrie, is 66/8ft. Fairburn Castle in Easter Ross has a tree in the pinetum 82/11ft; one in the Old Garden 118/8ft and one near the Castle 85/9ft. At Dochfour by Loch Ness there are two very good trees, 75/8ft and 80/8ft. Also in Inverness-shire, a tree at Reelig House is 56/8ft and one at Doune House, Rothiemurchus, is 72/8ft.

The biggest outside these favoured areas, is in the Dee Valley in Aberdeenshire at Craigdarroch Hotel, Ballater, 82/8ft and Balmoral has one 52/7ft. One in the Monteviot Pinery, near Jedburgh, Roxburghshire, is 66/11ft. In the west of Scotland, the biggest is at Strone House, Argyll, 72/6ft. In England, one at Streatlam Hall, Durham is 56/9ft and one in the west, at Monk Coniston, Cumbria, is 62/9ft. Further south the only notable tree is a beautiful, pale, slender-spired shapely one at Dropmore in Buckinghamshire, planted in 1906 and 80/4ft in 1982.

CALIFORNIA NUTMEG

Torreya californica

Two features of the crown save the California Nutmeg from being a dull, dark and uninteresting conifer. Rising from a usually broad base of level branches, it nevertherless culminates in a slender spire with very short, level shoots. Or, if it is a forked tree, as many are, in two equal spire tops. In addition, the level branches hang out their lesser shoots in dense rows. This arrangement brings much credit to the Brewer Spruce and Dovaston Yew, but has done little as yet for the California Nutmeg. This is no doubt because the tree is rather seldom seen. The Torreyas are in the Yew family, and so are more primitive than even the Monkey-puzzles and Redwoods and are single-sex trees. There are five species, two in China, one in Japan, one scarcely surviving by a short stretch of river between Florida and Georgia, and this one in California, the biggest, as one would expect, and the most widespread. It grows in two areas separated by the wide Central Valley; scattered in gullies in the Coast Range for 100 miles north and 100 miles south of the Golden Gate, and for 300 miles along the lower foothills of the Sierra Nevada, with many stands by Route 49 and the road to the Yosemite entrance at Portal.

It was introduced by William Lobb in 1851 and is today quite uncommon in big collections and very scarce outside them. Of the 20 biggest, five are in Ireland,

California Nutmeg (*Torreya californica*): Tortworth, Gloucestershire

seven in far-western coastal Great Britain and three in western inland gardens, leaving six in the north or the east. So, while not extreme in the matter, this is another of those conifers happiest in very high rainfall, cool summers and mild winters.

The oldest and biggest in girth is a Lobb original planted in 1852 at Fota Garden, County Cork. It is now 50/12ft and a very sturdy, thriving tree. The second oldest, and presumed also to be from the original seed, was planted in the sheltered, damp pinetum at Poles, near Ware in Hertfordshire, in 1858. A slender tree, the tallest yet seen, it has fine spire top and in 1969 it was 73/6ft 8in, a little crowded but growing well. The next oldest was planted in 1861 on a lawn behind the mansion at Tortworth Court in Gloucestershire. A little thin from the lack of trees giving close shelter, it is a thick-boled, squat tree at 40/9ft.

A big tree at Tregothnan in Cornwall, although less exposed, shows signs of stress, or perhaps of old age. It is undated but very probably of pre-1860 vintage, and 66/10ft 8in at six feet. One at Castlewellan, County Down, well sheltered on a bank is of very similar age and size and 66/11ft but in full vigour. At Stonefield in Argyll, the tree has been lying down for many years, so it does not compete in height, but it has grown faster than most. Now 42/10ft 3in it was 3ft 10in in 1931, and was leaning even then. It was probably planted, therefore somewhat after 1900.

A close pair of big trees at Streatham Hall, on the campus of Exeter University, may be original trees since they are in a planting with some 1856 trees. They are big enough, although the girths are both slightly inflated, one by low branches making the measurement at three feet up, and, in the larger, by the stem forking at ten feet. They are 70/9ft 10in and 66/10ft 7in respectively. In the previous 21 years they had added, in the same order, 26in and 28in, which figures do not conflict with an 1856 planting.

BROAD-LEAVED TREES

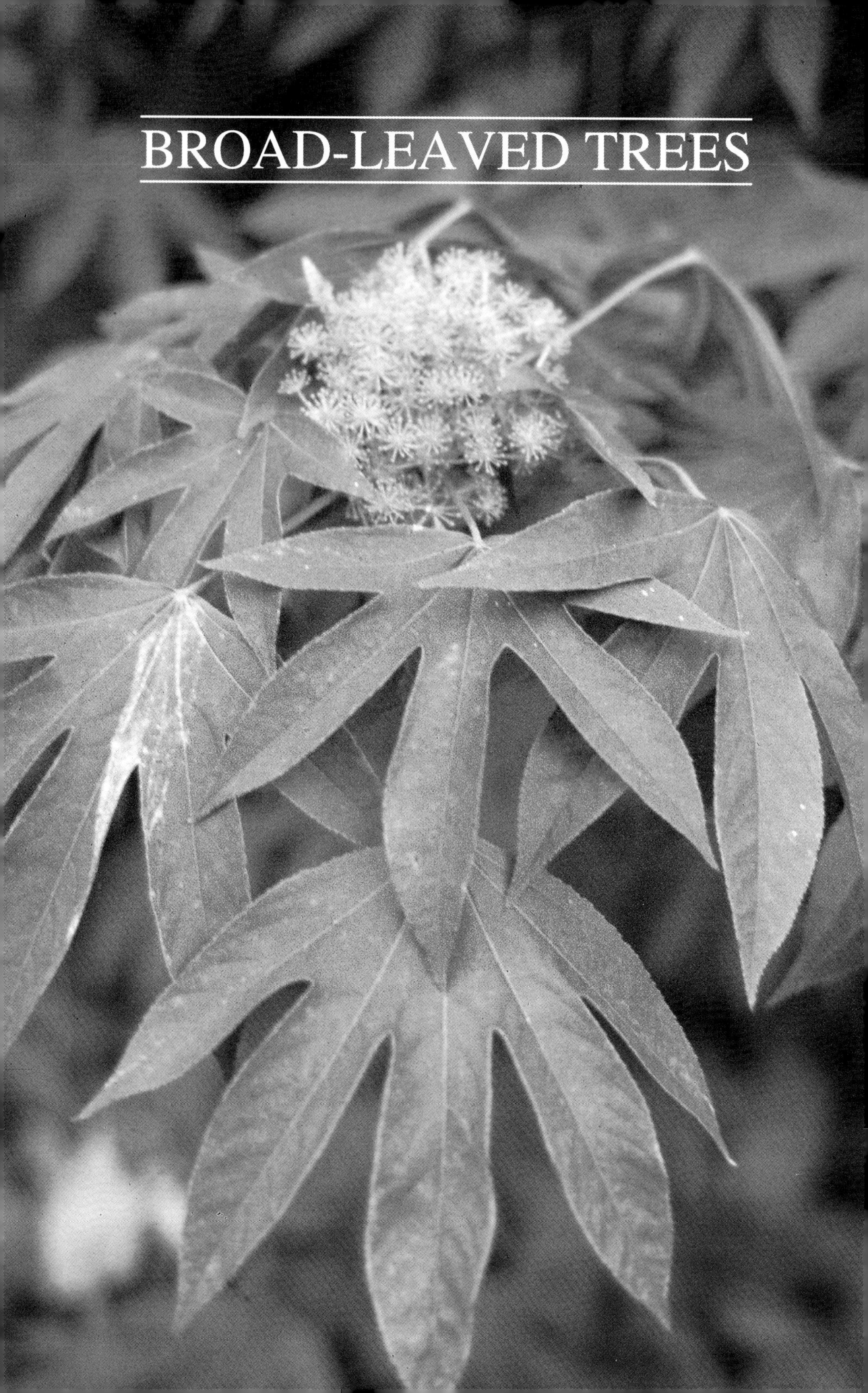

FIELD MAPLE

Acer campestre

The vagaries of continental drift and Ice Ages with their subsequent rises in sea-levels, have left the British Isles with but a single species of maple. It is unfortunate that this one, although a respectable tree and vaguely pleasant in many ways, should be among the few in this huge and varied genus to be so very ordinary. There are about 150 species, and the great majority of these are in eastern Asia, from the Himalaya to China, Korea and Japan.

Even that great repository of the Tertiary flora in the west, North America, has only 13 species. These include two of the biggest trees, the Silver Maple and the Oregon Maple. The latter also has the biggest leaves in the genus. By a stroke of luck in the wanderings of populations, the genus in America also includes the beautiful Striped Maple, a snakebark and a remote outlier from all its close relatives in China and Japan. America has also the only maple in the world with a pinnate leaf, the Ashleaf Maple which there they call the 'Boxelder', which has a unique range from New York to California and southern Mexico. And it has two of the best maples in the world for brilliance of autumn colours.

Europe has only ten species, with nine natural hybrids involving particularly the Sycamore and the Montpelier Maple. The Sycamore is one of the biggest of the maples, but the biggest leaves outside America are on the Caucasian Van Volxem Maple, just beyond the boundaries of Europe. The one feature that is at its best only in European species is big flowers. The Norway and Italian Maples have bigger

Field Maple (*Acer campestre*): the only native species of maple in the British Isles

petals than any others, the former with umbels of bright acid-yellow flowers and the latter with hanging racemes of pale yellow.

The Field Maple is depressingly moderate in all departments. It often belies its American name of Hedge Maple and grows into a high-domed tree of 60ft or more, and over 80ft in Scotland and Ireland. Its flowers are small with dull yellow-green petals and hide among the well-opened foliage. The leaves are small, or at best, medium-sized on sprouts. Their autumn colours are usually pleasant but unexciting yellows, only here and there some trees turn a striking bright gold and then orange. Even more locally, there are trees turning dull crimson and purple. The dark green summer foliage is enlivened by glimpses of the wings of the fruit turning crimson, but it all hardly adds up to a thrilling tree. Just a useful one for filling in a background. Its one unusual feature, shown mainly in hedges where it has been cut back frequently, is that the shoots bear corky wings.

The Field Maple occurs over most of Europe from southern Sweden to central Spain and in Asia Minor and Iran, and even in the Caucasus Mountains, although it is plainly not a species of Caucasian origin. It migrated into England fairly late when the land-bridge was mostly a chalk ridge. It spread on lime-rich soils so it extended only as far as Durham and Cumbria, but has long been planted further north and west and in Ireland.

Only four dated trees have been found, the oldest being one planted in Kew Gardens in 1927. For a native and widespread tree this is a sign that planting a specimen has rarely rated any attention or interest, for there is nothing to suggest that it is a tree with a short life-span, and big pollards and trees imply that it can persist for a long time. However, there are very few specimens worth going far to admire. One exception is a fine tree on a bank behind the Dower House at Chilston Park in Kent, 70/14ft. Another is in the Policies of Kinnettles Castle in Angus. This is not only 88/8ft but it has 26ft of clear stem. On the Island in the Demesne of Abbeyleix in County Leix, the bigger of two trees is 88/11ft and one in the Demesne of Birr Castle not far away is 80/6ft at two feet. The high water-table by the lime-rich rivers of central Ireland plainly favour good growth.

A broadly crowned low tree by Ewelme Church in Oxfordshire in the Rectory garden is of note for having been passed by Henry in 1908 as a Montpelier Maple, and thus having its girth noted 76 years before 1984, when it was nine feet round. It has grown slowly and could well date from around 1700.

CAPPADOCIAN MAPLE

Acer cappadocicum

The Cappadocian Maple cannot be said to be sufficiently well known to have a true common name – the one used here is nothing more than a borrowed anglicising from the botanical epithet. This is rarely a happy contrivance, and it may be hoped that the name 'Coliseum Maple', now used in the United States, will be adopted. Both names refer to the once Greek Province of Asia Minor. The native range of the tree is remarkable in that it is the only tree to extend from that region, through the Hindu Kush and along the Himalaya to China. In the west, it inhabits the Caucasus Mountains and the Elburz Mountains and in the far east of its range it is a distinct variety, var. *sinicum*, a smaller tree with a rough, scaling bark.

It was introduced in 1838, probably from India, and in 1850 from the Caucasus Region, and became quite a frequent component of the plantings of arboreta before 1880. The big trees, most often seen in western gardens with high rainfall, date from about that time. It is rather less common in the eastern areas, except from recent plantings of the highly attractive form, 'Aureum'. It is sometimes seen in roadside planting and in front gardens, but its enthusiastic suckering makes it unsuitable for

Cappadocian Maple (*Acer cappadocicum*): Westonbirt, Gloucestershire

such confinement. It is a typical Caucasian tree, exceedingly healthy, with smooth, glossy foliage and vigorous.

Its ability to grow suckers is equalled only by the Caucasian Wingnut, and is much greater than that of any other maple. Small tufts of leaves, usually bright red, emerge over a wide expanse and, unless prevented from doing so, soon make a thicket hiding the tree. The species was unique for many years in being the only one in which the tallest known specimen was a sucker. This was one of a ring of similar suckers round a tree dating from 1850 by the old Main Gate into Westonbirt Arboretum. It was 85ft tall when the crown of the tree was a dome 82ft tall. The main stem has since died and the suckers remain. The best defence against such excessive growth is to plant the tree in a meadow grazed by cattle or on a lawn mown regularly.

The best feature of the tree is the unfailing autumn colour. Late in October, the crown of densely borne foliage turns a bright butter-yellow and may hold on to achieve shades of orange. It is a valuable feature in Westonbirt where scattered big trees form a background to the predominant reds and crimsons of the other maples.

The bark is particularly smooth, without fissures or ridges, only shallow flutings smoothly rounded. This distinguishes the tree from other maples except Lobel's, which is very closely related and has a few teeth on the lobes of its leaves; variably strict, upright habit, and, best of all, bright blue-white young shoots. The Cappadocian Maple always grows a broad dome of a crown, about as broad as it is tall, and reaching down to within five to ten feet of the ground. The lower branches are level and sinuous. No tree has a long clear bole and more than eight feet clear is rare. Since early vigorous growth tails off considerably and few specimens are more than 120 years old, there are no grand specimens to celebrate, but smoothly rounded boles over eight feet round are curiously impressive, even when not very young.

The best is in the lower garden at Westonbirt School which is 66/10ft near another, 66/9ft. Half a mile away, in a field by the A433 beside the Arboretum, there stands a good tree 60/8ft, and this is like one in The Downs at the Arboretum, at 82/8ft. By the Circular Drive another of the 25 big specimens in the Arboretum is 62/8ft with a twisting trunk, but the best in shape as well as in position, and a great sight in autumn colour, is by the Waste Gate, and is a regular dome, 60/8ft. One at St Pierre Hotel, Chepstow, that I have not yet seen is 82/10ft. The species flourishes in Scotland and one of many good trees in the Den at Dupplin Castle, Perth, is 46/9ft. Two in the roadside hedge of Munches, by the A710 south of Dumfries are 52/8ft. One surviving in Osterley Park, Hounslow, is 58/9ft and one by the drive at Howick, Northumberland is 40/9ft. A broad, low tree on a bank below Gatton Park School at Reigate is 50/9ft.

Measured low, a few are over 11ft round, as at Dollar Academy, Fife, 46/11fft at three feet and by the drive at Hafodunas, Clwyd, 52/11ft at one foot.

Plate 1

Nikko Fir *(Abies homolepsis)*: Bedgebury, Kent

Cedar of Lebanon
(Cedrus libani):
a must for the Georgian mansion

Plate 2

Chinese Fir
(Cunninghamia lanceolata):
Bedgebury, Kent

Maidenhair Tree: Gingko *(Gingko biloba)*:
original tree (1761), Royal Botanic Gardens,
Kew, Surrey

Plate 3

Hybrid Larch *(Larix* x *eurolepsis)*: female cones

Maritime Pine *(Pinus pinaster)*:
Holme Lacey, Herefordshire

Common Yew *(Taxus baccata)*:
Brockenhurst Church, Hampshire

Plate 4

Sugar Maple *(Acer saccharum)*: close-up of branches and leaves

Common Alder *(Alnus glutinosa)*: a tolerant and versatile tree

Sweet Chestnut *(Castanea sativa)*: Castle Leod (1550), Strathpeffer, Scotland

Plate 5

Fernleaf Beech
(Fagus sylvatica
'Asplenifolia'*)*:
close-up of leaves
on branch

London Plane *(Platanus* x *acerifolia)*:
Ely Cathedral, Cambridgeshire

Plate 6

Grey Poplar *(Populus* x *canescens)*:
Birr Castle, County Offaly, Eire

Maryland Poplar *(Populus* x *marilandica)*:
Peper Harrow, Surrey

Plate 7

Western Balsam Poplar *(Populus trichocarpa)*: close-up of leaf

Turner's Oak *(Quercus x turneri)*: Royal Botanic Gardens, Kew, Surrey

Plate 8

Small-leaf Lime *(Tilia cordata)*: three close together, neat and shapely

English Elm
(Ulmus procera): maybe
brought by pre-Iron
Age tribes from a local
variant in southern France

LOBEL'S MAPLE

Acer lobelii

Lobel's Maple is a tree of unusual shape, great vigour and a few puzzles. It is native to southern Italy and seems to be one of only two tree species which are naturally fastigiate, the other being *Malus tschonoskii*. Its branches are nearly vertical and often devoid of laterals themselves for six to eight feet, although there are a few specimens which are relatively normal in shape. Young trees, which are strictly fastigiate, do broaden considerably with age. There is no mistaking the species, whatever its shape, because the young shoots are bright blue-white with bloom unlike those of any others in this Norway-Cappadocian Maple group, but found in a few rare Asiatics like *Acer giraldii*.

It is named after Mathias de L'obel as is the genus *Lobelia*, and he was a Flemish botanist and physician to King James I. Its date of introduction is oddly attributed to three different, but anagrammatic dates, 1683, 1836 and 1863, of which the last looks the most convincing in the light of the biggest trees today. It is strange how often a Lobel Maple is growing in a small thicket of root-sprouts of Cappadocian Maple. The two are closely related, and Lobel's has been demoted by some to be a variety of the Cappadocian despite the distance between Italy and the Caucasus Mountains, but the suckers are so often of the variety *rubrum* with leaves flushing bright red and margins remaining red, that these trees must surely be grafts. I have not heard of anyone admitting making such a graft, and if Lobel Maple does have a natural population with more than widely scattered individuals, it should not be necessary.

The oldest known dated specimen was planted in 1896. It is in the University Botanic Garden at Cambridge and is 72/7ft. The next oldest is at Westonbirt Arboretum, in a forest of Cappadocicum suckers and dates from 1922. That is now 92/7ft and this is more in line with the rapid growth expected. It also remains very slender in the crown. Another there, in the maple collection off Broad Drive, was planted in 1936 and when 46 years old was 72/5ft. Another example of quite rapid early growth is the tree planted at Rosemoor, Devon, in 1975, which when nine years old was 33/1ft 3in and when 14 years old was 46/1ft 9in.

Easily the greatest specimen found so far stands a little below the drive to Eastnor Castle in Herefordshire. It is about 90/12ft, slightly hemmed in and with signs of failing at the tip, but still an outstanding tree. When found in 1970, it was 85/11ft. There are two close groups of big trees, presumably planted to form striking features, around the beginning of this century. One is at Ashridge Park, Hertford-shire with three trees, 80–85/8–8½ft, and the other at Heckfield Place in Hampshire with four, 80–85ft forking or dividing low, one nine feet at three feet, one six feet dividing; one five feet forking, and one single-boled, four feet. In the Royal Botanic Garden, Edinburgh, a tree now 70/8ft was 56/5ft in 1954, so this will also have been planted around 1900. Two more, of similar age, are in Battersea Park, London, 72/8ft and 70/8ft. One at Colesbourne in Gloucestershire, probably dating from 1908, is 60/7ft.

Near the entrance drive to Heligan House in Cornwall is a somewhat battered tree, 80/7ft, recognisable as a Lobel Maple only by the shoot and foliage. In Ireland, there was a good tree, 80/6ft in 1968, at Gurteen le Poer in County Waterford. More recent records are one at Abbeyleix, County Leix, 85/5ft in 1985 and one in the River Garden at Birr Castle, County Offaly, 70/5ft in the same year. In Cannizaro Park, Wimbledon, a tree forks low and is 56/6ft at three feet. At Thorp Perrow in Yorkshire, one in a 1937 Jubilee Planting is now 62/5ft. In the Heather Garden at the Hillier Arboretum in Hampshire, one planted in 1954 is now 70/4ft.

OREGON MAPLE

Acer macrophyllum

Even a small young specimen of the Oregon, or Bigleaf, Maple, looks set on being a majestic tree. It is not only the big leaves, the biggest of all the maple, and the foot-long flower racemes like bell-rope woolly handles, but the bark is soon interestingly ridged with orange-brown fissures, evidently making ready for rapid expansion in the trunk. The shoots are not as stout as would be expected with such leaves, and the large sucker-like bases on the leaf stalks, which can be a foot long, clasp in opposite pairs around the shoot hiding it.

Although this is the biggest maple, in stature as well as in foliage, in the world, with a tree in Washington State 155ft tall and a hulk in Stanley Park, Vancouver, I make 32½ft round (the National Champion is 37ft round, in Oregon, but looking at its picture it forks too much and too low for me to accept), the few growth records in this country are not exciting. But it does make steady progress, and trees planted in the last 25 years in city parks and in car parks are growing well in these less-than-perfect sites.

The Oregon Maple was discovered, like so many trees growing near the Pacific shores of North America, by Archibald Menzies in 1792–3, sailing with Vancouver's squadron. It should then conform to the usual story and have been introduced by David Douglas on his first trip to the west, and indeed it is often credited to him, in 1827. But some give 1812 and some also 1824. It seems that the Lewis and Clark Expedition of 1804 collected specimens and seeds, and some plants from these were being grown in east coast nurseries. The 1812 date may relate to John Fraser's last journey to the Carolinas in 1809 if he returned by a northerly route, but the 1824 date is certainly Douglas on his first collecting trip for fruit trees in New England in 1823. He brought back Oregon Grape in the same way, from Lewis and Clark.

Oregon Maple (*Acer macrophyllum*): Kensington Gardens, London

The oldest tree, with a known date, was an 1850 tree in the Pagoda Vista at Kew, which was 70/8½ft in 1967 but has since disappeared. From calculations only, the next oldest is the one towards Hollybush Gate, Circular Drive, Westonbirt. It is now 90/11ft and periodic measurements since 1967 show a slow, consistent fall from just over one inch to just under one inch a year. Since it was 9ft 2in in 1967, it should date from about 1870. Several should be somewhat older, if girth be a reliable criterion, but they are all in the Irish Republic, and it may be that the tree makes extra vigorous growth in that region. The best is a remarkable tree at Marlfield in County Tipperary which was not only 62/12ft in 1968 but had a clean trunk for eight feet. In the quadrangles of Trinity College at the very hub of Dublin City, two in the Front Quad are 50/11ft and 52/11ft, although with low branches and many swellings on the trunks, while a somewhat better tree in the New Quad is also 50/11ft.

In the far south, the notable specimen is at Trebartha in Cornwall which is a shapely tree now 82/8½ft. In the Midlands, a fine specimen each side of the drive to Arley House near Bewdley have good cylindric trunks for over six feet and are 70/8½ft, and one towards Tortworth Court house is 60/8½ft. In the southeast, the best is a vigorous, handsome tree in St Clere Arboretum at 700ft on the North Downs near Wrotham, Kent. In a clay area now sheltered by trees planted in 1905, this is now 66/7ft and, having added three feet since 1969, it must have been planted around 1935.

Towards the north, one at Castle Milk in Dumfries was a good tree, 72/6½ft in 1985 and one in the Royal Botanic Garden at Edinburgh is 85/7½ft. Out to the west, on Arran, a tree at Brodick Castle is 66/8ft. Four trees are much further north, in the garden of Newton House towards Lossiemouth in Morayshire. The best in 1980 was 62/5½ft. The National Botanic Garden at Glasnevin near Dublin has a specimen which has always been labelled 'Aureum'. No one else seems to grow, or even to have heard of, this variety, but its foliage has a good tinge of yellow. It is 40/5ft, growing slowly.

NORWAY MAPLE

Acer platanoides

This tree has a somewhat inapt English name since its broad range across Europe from the Caucasus Mountains westward, intrudes only minimally on the southeastern corner of Norway. Unusually, there seems to be no alternative name. However, the botanical name may cause real confusion. It will have seemed a good description to Carl von Linne in 1758 when he coined it, since the foliage was the only one on a maple then known to resemble that of the London plane. Linnaeus was not to know that the Scots were soon to refer to the Sycamore as the 'plane', and the Americans were to call their Eastern Plane the 'Sycamore', so that to call the Norway Maple the plane-like maple, even if in Latin, was to add a third species to the tangle.

Early writers were often casual in their use of English tree names, rendering their works of little use in unravelling the histories of some trees in cultivation. There is no unambiguous reference to the Norway Maple before 1683 although the tree had probably been cultivated, if uncommonly, long before then. It was George Sutherland who recorded it first when he listed all the trees that he moved in 1683 from the botanic garden at Holyrood Palace to a new garden beneath Edinburgh Castle, where Waverley Station is now. There are now no trees of known planting date much over 100 years old, although several are much bigger than those and will be much older, but it seems not to be a very long-lived tree and probably not one dates back to before 1800.

The tree is an enormous asset to tree-planters concerned with landscapes and amenity in a range of sites from city parks to open downland, village greens and sandy heaths, because it combines healthy, vigorous growth on all normal sites with two annual periods of prominent beauty. Although sometimes said to need a chalky soil, Norway Maples grow just as fast in light sands and seed themselves freely on them, and are also much at home in fairly heavy clays. One planted in the Leyshon maple glade at Westonbirt, on a light clay grew six feet each year for three years. At the end of that burst of vigour, it was snapped off in a high wind. In early spring, occasionally in late February and usually before mid April, bright acid-yellow flowers with big petals open on copious umbels before the leaves begin to unfold. The tree is then spectacular in a wintry landscape. Extensive planting by the Ministry of Defence on Salisbury Plain transforms that area. The hint of green in the flowers becomes more marked as the leaves unfold after a week or two, and matches their yellow-green, so the display is prolonged. In full leaf, the tree is nothing particular. The leaves are elegant individually but in rather heavy masses. This changes in mid October when they turn bright butter-yellow and then to orange-brown if they persist. There are always some trees around in which many outer leaves turn scarlet. The fruit ripens and remains with big, flat wings, very green until they fall, but the umbel bearing them often lasts through the winter, nodding at the tip of a shoot.

The Norway Maple shows every possible arrangement of the sexes on the tree. A few are single sex trees, a few have branches of each sex, and some have whole umbels male or female. In some umbels some flowers may open as female then become male. There is very little variation in the time of flowers and leaves opening, but in autumn a few trees colour before the rest and often these show more red. It is, in fact, a uniform species with little variation in shape or size of leaf or shape of crown.

Of the several seedling colour variants selected for garden use, two are horticultural disasters which should have been put straight on the bonfire. Naturally they are popular, and form dark pools in many new plantings, like black holes into which light goes, never to emerge. The worst is 'Faasen's Black', and 'Goldsworth Purple' is little better. This was given to Wisley Gardens in 1936 and was a seedling from a 'Schwedleri'. Schwedler's Maple itself is good in autumn as its leaves turn orange and crimson, but freakish in spring, when its flowers look brown as their dull yellow, small petals blend with dark red discs and umbels, and the leaves emerge red-brown. In summer, it is dull green, tinged dark red. It arose in Germany in 1870 and is frequent here on village greens. One on Main Ride in Westonbirt is 102/9ft.

In 1888, van Volxem's nursery sent 'Stollii' to Kew. A splendid but very rare form, this has double-sized leaves variably shallow-lobed. Two big trees of this have been found recently. One is at Birr Castle, by a farm road in an area known as Killean, and is 56/10ft. The other is on the south bank in the eastern part of Alexandra Park, St Leonards, Sussex and is 95/10ft.

Returning to the type tree, Westonbirt has a fair proportion of the best specimens, as well as the oldest of known date. That is an 1876 tree by Willesley Drive, 82/10ft, and the two tallest are of the same date by the Waste Drive. One above the gate is 105/11ft and the other, one of several along the bank there, is 105/8ft. A good one by Pool Avenue is 82/10ft and could date back to 1855 but no further, like one of those by Holford Drive, 95/9ft. The biggest bole is at Hafodunas, Clwyd, 85/14ft near one of 70/11ft, although one at Elioch, Dumfries, is 75/17ft and disqualified by being a double trunk.

A fine tree at Pampisford, Cambridge is 85/10ft and was 66/4ft in 1906. A sturdy tree at Castle Fraser, Aberdeenshire, is 85/12ft and another northerly big tree is at Doune House, Rothiemurchus, near the group of 200ft Sitka Spruces. It is 80/12ft. A tree by the farm building at Eastnor Castle, Herefordshire, is 75/11ft and one at Batsford Park, Gloucestershire, is 98/10ft. At Canford School near Poole, Dorset, a tree in the pinetum is 90/11ft. The biggest of three in the Park at Belsay Castle, Northumberland, is 70/11ft. None of these has a long bole or clear trunk and mostly they branch below eight feet. They all appear to be healthy and growing fast, so the fact that none is effectively bigger than 14ft round, in a popular tree available for at least 300 years, is a good indication that it has a relatively short life-expectancy.

The curious form, 'Cucullatum' has been around since about 1870 but decidedly sparsely. It grows a slender, upright crown bearing nearly circular, crinkled and hooded leaves with seven to ten veins fanning out from the base to end in shallow, acute lobes. Five of the biggest are by The Waste and Broad Drive, in Silk Wood, Westonbirt, dating from 1876. The tallest there is 102/8ft. A group of five around 70/7ft was in the northeastern part of Kensington Gardens in 1978. The bigger of

Norway Maple (*Acer platanoides*): Westonbirt, Willesley

two in the Royal Botanic Garden, Edinburgh is 85/7ft. One at Emo Court, County Leix, in the Grape Garden, is 82/8ft. The bigger of two at Osterley Park, Hounslow, is 70/8ft. One planted in 1880 in Alexandra Park, St Leonards, is 60/8ft.

SYCAMORE

Acer pseudoplatanus

For such a common, everyday tree, the Sycamore lives in quite a web of confusion and controversy. The common name in England and Wales, 'sycamore', means 'fig-mulberry' (*Sycos* or *Ficus*, the fig; *morus* the mulberry), and was erroneously transferred from a Levantine tree with edible fruit of that name in translations of the Bible. A better, and accurate name is the seldom used 'Great maple'. In Scotland, however, the tree is the 'Plane' to which confusing usage, Linnaeus referred in his name 'pseudoplatanus'. The circle is completed by the Americans calling their eastern plane, the 'sycamore'. They distinguish our sycamore as the 'European sycamore' or the 'Sycamore maple'.

A few authorities have considered this tree to be a native of Britain. Yet most see it as a hill and mountain species that would not have been growing on the coastal plain or low chalk hills from which it could have spread to Kent as the post Ice Ages warming developed, even if it has subsequently spread into the relevant area of France. It has been suggested that it was introduced by the Romans, but it is hard to see why they should bother as no part of it can be eaten, and our native Field Maple gives timber of similar qualities. The more likely idea is that it came during part of the long period when France and Scotland had quite close relations. This is in line with the presumed oldest trees being in Scotland and the reputed oldest, at Newbattle Abbey, near Edinburgh, being planted during the Reformation. This puts the date of that tree as around 1550.

The tree is anathema to many conservationists and they rejoice in rooting it out of native woodlands. It is certainly too competitive on fertile, base-rich soils and its prolific seeding and heavy fall of persistent leaves enable it to become rapidly the dominant tree. Against this, it does nourish a vast population of aphids in late spring and early autumn, and small mammals proliferate on the woodland floor, and bees come far for the abundant nectar. More important, as a pioneer or subsequent tree on high sites, on poor limestone or chalk soils in great exposure, and in industrial pollution, it has no equal in providing rapid and effective shelter. Furthermore, and astonishingly in a tree of Central European mountains that has never seen the sea, it stands straight and tall in extreme maritime exposure where native trees can hardly stand up at all.

Sycamore (*Acer pseudoplatanus*): Newbattle Abbey, Scotland

The timber is among the very best we can grow. Hard and strong it can be sharpened to a point in skewers; planes very smooth and takes polish. It can be scrubbed daily without the grain picking up. Being nearly white, it is therefore ideal for kitchenware and working surfaces, and it takes no taint and little stain from food nor does it give any taint. It can be dyed for use in marquetry when it is called 'harewood', and turns excellently. It has good sounding qualities and is used in string instruments, where the prized ripple-grained pieces are used for fiddle-backs. Large logs with wavy grain fetch high prices for making furniture.

Although big trees are everywhere, there is an unexplained regional distribution of both the really big trees and those with high quality, long boles. There are a few in Kent, more in Lincolnshire and east Yorkshire, more again in Cumbria, but the greatest concentration is in the Lothians and from Stirling to Perthshire.

The Newbattle Abbey tree, possibly dating from 1550, was a superb tree when it was photographed in 1904. It was then 95/16ft with a clear stem of 16ft. In 1990 it was still a beauty although somewhat thin around the top. It was 85/18ft and the small increase for 86 years suggests that it is near its end. It is quite otherwise with the giant tree at Birnam, Dunkeld, Perthshire. The second of the 'Birnam Oaks' this is by the Tay in a little park behind the Birnam Hotel. It has a great dome of a crown, 105ft high; big, luxuriant leaves which in some years escape the tar-spot fungus which infests the other Sycamores there, and outsize fruit and seeds. A seedling I raised added six feet to its height in its third year in my Surrey garden. The trunk of the parent is scarcely six feet, a waist between branch buttresses and the swell of a vast root-system which is like a wooden wall along some 20ft of a bank above a lower path. At five feet up it was 20ft round in 1906 and now is 25ft. It was 22ft in 1956 so it maintains a fairly steady growth, as far as re-measurements of such a trunk can reveal.

The fine tree between the drive and Drumlanrig Castle in Dumfries-shire is similar but fully in the open, yet with a narrower crown, its trunk running a little higher before the branches spring. It was 102/18ft in 1904 and 111/21ft in 1970. It has kept up somewhat faster growth than the Birnam tree and by 1984 it was 23ft round. The doyen of the Kent contingent of Sycamores is at Cobham Hall, towards Rochester. This very imposing tree was 105/16ft in 1906, the biggest noted at that time anywhere south of Cumbria. By 1965 it was only 19ft round and when last seen, in 1982, it was 120/20ft and somewhat thinly foliaged. Another nearby was 98/15½ft and both were outstanding for height and good form for southern England, as was one at Godinton Park, Ashford, Kent, 70/19ft in 1983. A remarkably broad-crowned, symmetrical tree is in the Grammar School grounds at Louth in Lincolnshire, 70/16ft.

At Plas Newydd on Anglesey, a tree 62/22ft can be measured at the statutory five feet by threading the tape above and below huge branches which spread level for a great distance on all sides. Situated on a small rise, great vistas of the mansion, the Menai Straits and distant Snowdonia can be seen through its crown. At Tynninghame, East Lothian, a vast tree is in the field below the house and can just be measured below the lowest branches, at five feet. It is 105/24ft. At Yester House in the same county, a fine tree by the drive was 70/17ft in 1987 and at Newliston House, Midlothian is one 60/20ft. In Ayrshire, the 'Dool Tree' by the House at Blaiquhan, one of the few of these grim natural scaffolds to survive, is 36/17ft and a splendid tree below the house at Bargany is 85/19ft. In Renfrewshire, Ardgowan has one 72/20ft. In Argyll, by the sea at Gareloch, a spreading tree at Drymsynie House is 85/24ft, measured below branch-swell, at four feet.

Perthshire has many exceptional Sycamores. In Taymouth Castle Gardens beside Loch Tay, a grand old specimen is 98/19ft. A short one at Fingask Castle is 40/20ft and one at Kippenross House, Dunblane, is 98/20ft.

SILVER MAPLE

Acer saccharinum

Two hardy maples have distinctly silvered undersides to their leaves: the Silver and the Red, in a little section of their own with their flowers bunched at the nodes on very short stalks. The flowers open well before the leaves, in March or April and mature early into fruit by June and are then shed. The other maples that flower so early, like the Italian and Ashleaf, ripen their fruit through the summer and shed them in early winter. Although the Silver and the Red Maple flower abundantly, they are only rarely seen to bear fruit in this country, probably because of our cool, short summers.

The Silver Maple is easily distinguished from the Red by its larger leaves, deeply and angularly lobed and deeply toothed. It also has unambiguously five-lobed leaves where the Red has a round-based leaf with three main lobes and an optional pair of small ones towards the base. The bark and crown are also very different. It is a little unfortunate that the Silver maple must be called *A. saccharinum* as this invites confusion with the Sugar maple, *A. saccharum*, both from the meaning and from the alphabetic division coming after eight identical letters. For a long time the Silver was *A. dasycarpum* which avoided both factors. The Silver Maple does yield maple syrup and sugar, but it is the Sugar Maple which is the one used commercially.

The Silver Maple is native to an extensive area from southern Ontario and Quebec to Oklahoma and the Gulf Coast, throughout which it has summers much hotter and longer than ours. Yet, unlike many trees from that kind of range, it is not greatly affected by latitude, and there are big trees in the far north of Scotland, although fewer than in southern England. It was introduced in 1725, probably sent by the Bartrams to Peter Collinson. It is fast growing and short-lived, and no tree is known with a date before 1876 although a few may be a little older than that.

Because of its easy establishment and very rapid early growth in a variety of indifferent soils, the Silver Maple was often planted by arterial roads and in town and city parks. It made the required early show of light attractive foliage but as the height was near its maximum the tree began to fall out of favour for roads. It acquired the reputation of losing the high, arching branches. This did it no good with the authorities planting roads but it is a factor only on stretches in high exposure.

Its record in the gales of 1987 and 1990 was not at all bad. The tallest then known were at Westonbirt where one was blown down in 1989 and two more in 1990, but the tallest remains today, 105ft. The big planting of nine trees on Haste Hill near Haslemere was effectively destroyed, but the biggest trees at Kew and at Osterley Park were unharmed.

The Silver Maple has a long season of attractive growth. It starts in March or before, with clusters of dark red flowers closely held in pairs at each node. By May the emerging leaves are rich orange-red before maturing bright pale green above and silver beneath. They darken somewhat towards autumn, when they turn pale yellow and then biscuit before some have flashes of scarlet, and some purple. Sprout shoots show best a mixture of scarlet, crimson and purple which is seldom seen in mature crowns.

In the wild, there is much variation in the depth and breadth of lobing, and individuals from near the extreme of this form are seen planted as 'Laciniatum'. But the most extreme form is a clone 'Weiri'. This has very slender, spikily toothed lobes and also dark brown shoots and a markedly more pendulous habit. It was found in 1873 by Dr Weir in the Genesee Valley near Rochester, New York. It is now popular for planting in parks and malls, and grows nearly as fast as the type tree. Neither is long lived, as they tend to break up when about 12ft round the bole and 100 years old and there are no venerable and huge specimens.

At Sandford Park, Cheltenham, planted in 1925, there are two big 'Weiri', 85/9ft and 88/8ft in 1989, and a type tree 108/11ft, with very good growth for 64 years. A 'Weiri' at Anglesea Abbey, Cambridge, planted in 1929 was 72/7ft in 1973 and 95/9ft in 1990. An undated 'Weiri' in Jesus College, Cambridge is 88/8ft. One planted in 1975 at Stratfield Saye, Hampshire, was 52/2 when 11 years old. Among the best of the type trees is the survivor by Willesley Drive in Westonbirt. Planted in 1876, it is now 105/10½ft. The biggest specimen is in Kew Gardens near the Japanese Gate and is 95/13ft and an exceptionally fine tree, still growing fast, as it was 92/11ft in 1965. Two other exceptional trees are at Osterley Park, Hounslow. One near the House is now 92/12ft, and the other in the West Prospect, is 105/11ft. In the pinetum at Wisley Gardens, two planted in 1926 have done well in the poor bagshot sands and

Silver Maple (*Acer saccharinum*): close-up of leaves

187

in 1991 they are 108/10ft and 105/9ft. At Christ's Hospital School, near Horsham, a drive curving up to the School was lined by Silver Maples, measured in 1989. The best of 13 big trees was 105/10ft by the southern gate; 85/10ft by the top gate; and 80/12ft, 85/11ft and 85/11ft between them. As far north as Ardross Castle, Easter Ross, a tree on the lawn is 42/9ft and in Bute Park, Cardiff one is 80/9ft. Young trees showing good growth are: Hester Park, Cheltenham, 1954 planting, 52/4ft in 35 years; Chase Cottage, Haslemere, 1966 planting, 66/4ft in 20 years; Cracknells, Essex, 1970 planting, 42/3ft in 15 years.

SUGAR MAPLE

Acer saccharum (plate 4)

This most attractive tree is decidedly underrated in this country, and to some extent in its own. There, the astonishing blaze of fall colour from Nova Scotia to the Gulf of Mexico is usually credited mainly to the Red Maple. The northern three-quarters of this vast tract, however, is also Sugar Maple country and although it is rather less overwhelmingly abundant than the Red, it is the Sugar Maple that, to my eye, supplies the real fire. It is more uniform in its colour and is a brilliant flame-scarlet with an orange tinge that outshines the various scarlets, crimsons and purples of the Red, and is more often seen in streets and gardens. Its leaves are also much larger and are held better. It ranges from Cape Breton Island to Kansas and is thought to have been introduced in Britain in 1735.

In Britain there is, or has been, a conspiracy of silence about the excellent growth of this tree, and it has been quite wrongly classed as one of those eastern North American trees that cannot make much progress in our short, cool summers. It no doubt would grow better if we had the real summers with five months around 90°F to which it is used, at least from Ontario to Kansas, but, like the Red Oak and Silver Maple from almost the same regions, it can manage very well with what it finds here, even in mid-Scotland and in Ireland. Not only that, many specimens show bright, if rather brief orange and scarlet in the autumn.

The cause of this tree cannot have been helped by the most outstanding specimen by far, standing behind a label proclaiming 'Norway maple'. This was at Bulstrode Park, Gerrard's Cross, and when I found it in 1967, belying its substantial cast-iron label, it was 90/11ft. When I returned to report its progress in 1982, it had been blown down some years previously. The differences between Sugar and Norway Maples are not striking, singly, but they add up to a tree of a different aspect, especially when in leaf. The Sugar Maple bark is never a crisscross of fine, brown ridges. It is dark grey with large plates separated by coarse, rough edged fissures. The leaves differ in having deeper cut lobes and, a fine detail, but a useful one, only the lobe tips taper finely into whiskers, the big teeth have minutely rounded tips.

The underleaf is pale enough often to give the tree a dappled effect from a distance, but, my prime spot-feature which very rarely fails – on the green shoot there is a band of purple-red at the origin of each pair of leaves. Another point is that a Norway Maple of any size above the sapling will carry bunches of big green fruit well into the autumn. Sugar Maple rarely fruits in Britain and it would shed any it had by midsummer. The difficulty in separating these trees when in the nursery must account for the rogue Norway Maples in some American plantings, particularly the two in the Sugar Maple avenue to the Gateway Arch in St Louis.

With the loss of the Bulstrode Park tree, the biggest Sugar Maple is a shapely tree at Belton Park, Lincolnshire, in the paddock, now 72/9ft, but there are taller ones. Among the 20 specimens of varying size at Westonbirt Arboretum, the one leaning somewhat out over the northern sector of Circular Drive is 85/5ft, and one by the Willesley Drive was 90/5ft in 1982. There are three good, big trees at Eastnor Castle, Ledbury, on the slope above the storage-barn, that on the lower part is 50/8ft and the upper two are 70/6ft and 70/9ft, in fine shape and growing fast.

Scotland has many moderately big trees, with one at Moncrieffe House, Perthshire, 72/8ft in 1982 when one at Kailzie, Peebles, was 65/5ft. At Montreve House, Fifeshire, a tree was 60/5ft in 1983, while at Gask House, Perthshire, there are two, one very tall and slender, 88/3ft and the other 60/6ft, and in the west, at Crarae, Argyll, is one 46/4ft. In Ireland, the biggest is starting to die back and is 70/8ft at Mount Usher, County Wicklow. Most extraordinary is one on the Isle of Lewis in Stomoway Woods, 53/7ft.

It must be said that the Sugar Maple does not seem to be at all long-lived, for none of the seven recorded in 1907 is still extant, although only one, nine feet round was likely to be mature. Growth is not as fast as in many maples when young, and a tree planted at Bedgebury National Pinetum in 1934 attaining 50/6ft when it was 54 years old has done well. Of the few dated trees, only one in the Ten Acre West at the Hillier Arboretum has grown faster. This was planted in 1954 and was 42/4ft when 31 years old.

VAN VOLXEM'S MAPLE

Acer velutinum var. *vanvolxemii*

The Caucasus Mountains are a great bulwark against a northerly influence on a wide tract on their southern slopes from Georgia to Armenia and northern Iran, which has the Black Sea on its west and the Caspian Sea on its east. This singularly favoured but not very extensive region is a refuge for a sample of the old Tertiary flora, the only one in the vast area between eastern North America and eastern Asia. It has only one endemic genus of tree, *Parrotia*, but to a remarkable extent the species it grows of widespread genera are very superior trees.

This is most notable in alders, oaks, wingnuts, limes and maples. The Caucasian features are great vigour of growth; extreme good health and freedom from pests; usually stout, shining, smooth shoots, but a few quite hairy, and substantial; big leaves, usually glossy and hairless. Some of the herbaceous plants are likewise vigorous and healthy, with a tendency to gigantism. The origin of these plants can often be assumed at first sight.

Among the best examples is Van Volxem's Maple. From a moderate distance it could pass for a robust Sycamore with big yellow-green leaves. The Sycamore does grow in the Caucasus Mountains and has much of the typical Caucasian appearance and constitution, as, to a lesser extent, does the Norway Maple also. But Van Volxem's Maple differs in important details from the Sycamore and is in another section of the genus. Its buds are sharply conic and dark brown where those of the Sycamore are ovoid and bright green. The bark of Van Volxem's tree remains smooth and dark or silvery grey to the greatest age so far attained, where that of the Sycamore at moderate age becomes pinkish brown and breaks into small, thick scales. Most convincing, however, is the arrangement of the flowers. They are not in big catkin-like racemes, but in big, erect, many-branched umbels.

The foliage is like that of the Sycamore but usually much bigger, and more yellow. The leafstalk can be almost one foot long, quite stout and yellowish green and the blade six inches long and up to eight inches across. The tree was discovered by Mr van Volxem, a nurseryman, presumably Dutch, who collected this maple and two others and introduced them through his nursery. He sent this one to Kew in 1873. The original tree is still in the maple collection there but is uncharacteristically small, only 65/7ft today. An introduction by Gordon Harris in 1979 has yielded trees with singularly vigorous early growth. Very few trees were raised last century and the tree is still rare so there is only a very small number of specimens about which to enthuse.

Two of the best are at Westonbirt Arboretum in Silk Wood, in Willesley Drive, and in the maple collection each side of Broad Drive. Both these drives were first planted in 1876 and it is probable that both the trees were in the original planting and therefore raised from the original 1873 seed. The one by the Willesley stands many yards in from the Drive edge, among background trees. This has caused its side-branches to be shaded out and eventually shed, leaving a smooth, pale grey trunk rising to 55ft before it forks. The tree is 92/9ft. It was 50/4ft in 1921 and 80/8ft in 1976. The other, in the maples on the east side of Broad Drive, has no constraint on its west side and has foliage to ground level and a broad crown. It is 90/9ft. In 1967 it was 65/6ft.

A near twin of the larger Westonbirt tree in size and probably in age, is in the Royal Botanic Garden in Edinburgh, prominent on a corner in the Leith Place entrance area, with a seat round its stout eight foot, smooth trunk. It was 44/6ft in 1955 and is now 72/10ft. At Tortworth Court in Gloucestershire, where Lord Ducie made his arboretum to rival that of his friend William Holford at Westonbirt, two trees by the drive were 60/9ft and 50/7ft in 1973. From the Gordon Harris seed of 1979, Mr Harris has a tree which ten years from seed was 33/2ft and Hugh Johnson of Saling Hall, Essex planted one in 1980 and in 11 years it was 36/2ft.

YELLOW BUCKEYE

Aesculus flava

For a tree of such superb qualities, the Yellow Buckeye has been shamefully neglected, not only in Britain but, far more grievously, in its home country. In the United States it seems never to be planted, although the coarser, less attractive European Horse-chestnut lines streets all across the north. In the woods on the Allegheny Mountains, especially from Virginia to Tennessee there are glorious trees to 140ft tall and with pole-like stems for 60ft. In Britain it has at least been planted sparsely in big gardens and in parks, especially in those established around London around 1840.

We have the excuse, denied to the Americans, that the seeds cannot be stored and it was very difficult a hundred years ago to have them collected in October in America and sown in November here. So nearly all our bigger, older trees are grafts on Horse-chestnut, often with an unsightly union at five feet. Home collected seed has not, in my hands, yielded a single plant. The first trees were received in 1764 and this will be plants lifted by one of the Bartrams and shipped to Peter Collinson at Mill Hill. Seeds were never sent in the days before dormancy was understood and refrigeration was available.

This tree has foliage that makes that of the Horse-chestnut look crude and dull. The leaflets taper to a long stalk and to a fine tip and are finely and regularly toothed. Their upper side is bright, glossy green, with numerous pale yellow, straight parallel veins, and in autumn turns orange, scarlet and crimson. The flowers are not exactly a blaze of colour, as they are pale yellow and narrowly tubular, but they look unusual and pleasant among the bright green leaves. The variety *virginica* has red, pink or cream flowers and occurs wild only at White Sulphur Springs, West Virginia. It does not appear here under its proper name, but one of the biggest specimens, 72/11ft in Bath Botanic Gardens has been labelled var. *purpurascens* for at least 30 years, and although not yet checked in flower, it seems reasonable to suppose that it is var. *virginica*. More positively identified is a tree I found labelled *Aesculus x carnea* in 1979 in the garden of the Bishop's Palace in Chichester. Since the foliage showed that it was a Yellow Buckeye, I asked a gardener if the flowers were red, and was assured that they were. It was 60/7ft.

The best tree found is in the semi-private, residents' park at St Margaret's beside the Thames in Twickenham which is 75/10ft with a long bole and well-placed on a lawn. If it is a graft, the union is not evident. A taller tree but less splendid is one of two at the Old Rectory, in the river-garden, at Much Hadham, Hertfordshire. It is 85/9ft and was grafted at three feet. The second tree is 72/7ft, grafted at two feet. The only other specimen noted much over 70ft is one at Holland Park, London, which suffered breakages in the 1987 gale but one stem reaches 85ft and the trunk is seven feet round at four feet.

In Hyde Park, London, a slightly crowded, erect tree at the Magazine by Serpentine Bridge, is 70/6ft, and in Victoria Park, Hackney, the best is 72/7ft. At Bromham Hospital, Bedford, a tree dated 1896 is 46/7ft, at four feet, which is below the graft. Of two trees at The Gliffaes, Crickhowell, grafted at four feet, the larger is 60/7ft, and a fine, rather erect tree at Denman College near Abingdon, Berkshire, also a graft at three feet, is 60/7ft at four feet, under a branch. In the Abbey Gardens, Bury St Edmunds, a tree grafted at three feet is 65/8ft.

That this species can tolerate highly polluted air is shown by the three trees around 40/7ft in the gardens near the lake at Trentham Park, Stoke on Trent. They must have made much of their growth when the Trent nearby was a river of oil and the air was like that in the engine-room of a diesel ship. It is also happy enough far to the north. Small trees are found into Easter Ross, and at Drum Castle, near Aberdeen, a good tree is 60/6ft. At Kinfauns Castle, outside Perth, one is 70/7ft.

Yellow Buck-eye (*Aesculus flava*): Royal Botanic Gardens, Kew, Surrey

HORSE-CHESTNUT

Aesculus hippocastanum

No tree could try harder than the Horse-chestnut to be accepted as a native of Merrie England. It ornaments almost every village green, rectory lawn and ancestral lawn or park, as well as city and suburban parks. It convinced the Post Office sufficiently to appear in a series of stamps with three other species, as 'British Trees'. But it will not do. It is as exotic as the Laburnum. It is native only to three small populations on high mountains where the borders of Greece, Former Yugoslavia and Albania converge, one population in each country. And it was unknown to botanists until 1596 when foliage and flowers were sent to the Dutch botanist Charles de l'Ecluse, working in Vienna as Carolus Clusius. Plants were sent to France in 1603 and to England in perhaps 1612 or 1615.

It is a remarkable tribute to the tree's adaptability that coming from southern mountains, it grows to great size in every part of lowland Britain. It is unfailingly floriferous, bearing thousands of foot-tall panicles of flowers in our variously cold, cloudy and wet or warm and sunny springs. There is never a bad year for Horse-chestnut flowers, only some extra good ones now and again. The tree also seeds itself quite freely in open woodland. The conkers rarely fail to germinate. The flowers are worthy of study in that only one of the three on each branch of the panicle open at a time, spreading the period in full flower and giving each flower space; it has a big patch of rich ochre-yellow at the base of the upper petal. By the end of a fine day this patch is bright crimson, the change arising from the flower having been pollinated and signalling to bees that they are no longer required.

A few of the very old trees have branches spreading far and drooping to the ground where they root and proceed further afield. A curiosity of this is that no tree is seen in the process of doing this. They have all done it long ago. None is known with long branches drooping and yet to reach the ground.

The popularity of the tree for public parks is in one way unfortunate. The heaviest falls of rain occur in thunderstorms on summer afternoons, when the tree is in full leaf and the maximum number of people are in the park. Many may shelter under the leafy crown, which has the sudden added burden of the water. Horse-chestnut wood is weak, and frequently a large branch will break off, which can be dangerous. The timber is soft as well as weak and light, and the combination of these and a smooth fracture make it a good wood for toys and artificial limbs.

All the family, *Hippocastanaceae*, have leaves and shoots in opposite pairs. A young seedling shows a pattern of growth very unusual in a hardwood, with an unbranched annual leading shoot above a pair of branches, the leaves plainly opposite and decussate, that is each pair is at right-angles to the pair above and below. The flower panicles are terminal, so the axis of a branch ceases to extend once it bears a flower. Because of this, the crowded sprouts growing from the area around the tip of a stem or big branch cut back, bear no flowers until they have grown well out and separated. This has inspired recommending cutting back crowns of trees in suburban roads to obviate the hazards of missiles intending to knock conkers down.

There is a great variation in the time of leafing out, and to a lesser extent, in flowering. Most localities have a tree or two that expands its buds when the others are dormant, in early March, and has leaves fully expanded and flower-buds erect and clear when the others are barely at the opening 'sticky-bud' stage. Similarly in autumn, a few very early trees (possibly not the same ones that are early in spring) colour in early September, and usually turn crimson, while the normal trees remain green until mid October, when they turn gold and orange-brown.

Longevity or lack of it is peculiarly unpredictable and a sad shortage of planting dates for the biggest trees adds to the problem. The position is that a short avenue exactly 299 years old was apparently complete, and now it is 326 years old only one has been lost, so this is certainly potentially a long-lived tree. No specimen can be more than fifty years older than this group, yet many trees are much bigger without dates. The lost avenue tree was 18ft round in 1963. The seven remaining trees have girths ranging from seven to fifteen feet, which helps not at all in estimating the ages of those known of over 20ft. The avenue trees are variably crowded and small-branched. At the same time as there being known and suspected trees 300 years old, it is common to see trees coming to bits and removed when they are far from old.

Growth in girth is apparently of the unusual pattern found in Scots Pine and Common Lime, that is a rapid start of well above one inch a year, declining rapidly after 100 years or so to small fractions of an inch. Examples are 18 years for 24in; 20 years for 28in; 24 years for 46 and 50in, but 70 years for 75in; 104 years for 120 and 135in and 128 years for 108 and 128in. Then trees 14–17ft round have added between three and six inches in 15–18 years. So it is hard to say how old a big tree may be.

The oldest dated trees, were planted in 1664 at Busbridge Lakes near Godalming, in an avenue. They are closely spaced and so not very big, but they are very tall. The biggest is 130/15ft and the next biggest is 120/12ft. The next oldest dated tree was planted in 1735 at Broadlands, Hampshire, and is 88/15ft. One dating from 1756 at Alresford House in Hampshire is 72/9ft at three feet but its trunk has been confined by huge layered branches in a ring. At Castle Ashby, Northampton, a similarly layered tree but with fewer and less confining layers is 100/17ft. The champion for layers is an extraordinary tree, more a woodland, near the gate to Headfort School near Maynooth, County Meath. This has a wall of foliage beside the verge, but the stem is 90ft away. It has a six foot trunk above which a dozen big branches arise in a cluster, and four of them arch shallowly then extend nearly level to dip down to root 75ft out. From there on they grow several big stems, some spreading level again, some curving up.

Horse-chestnut (*Aesculus hippocastanum*): Hurstbourne Priors, Hampshire

The finest Horse-chestnut all-round is that near the church at Hurstbourne Priors in Hampshire. One of those trees in which the great size is not at first apparent because it is so well-proportioned, it is 120/22ft with a cylindric clear trunk for 13ft. It has increased two feet in girth in the last 40 years. The next best was, until 1987, in front of West Dean House, near Chichester, and is similar but not so tall. It was 85/20ft with a splendid bole clear for 15ft. Two exceptional trees are in the garden by the river at The Old Rectory, Much Hadham, Hertfordshire. The better is 120/19ft and the other has a branch at six feet and is 120/19ft at four feet. At Preston Hall, Midlothian, a big tree near the garden is 85/19ft, and one at Canford School in Dorset is 92/18ft.

Among the biggest trees spoilt by heavy, low branches, one at Moncrieffe House, Perth, which was 19ft round in 1883 is now 88/22ft at three feet, widely spreading but not layered. Another like that is in the outer Park at Syon House, Middlesex. This was 15ft round in 1905, and today is 65/20ft at four feet. A tree in a garden at Seend, near Newbury, was 36/25ft at one foot in 1987 but a poor shape.

Some smaller trees of superior form with long trunks are: at Walcombe, Wells, Avon, 98/17ft; at Kilkerran, Ayrshire, above the House, 108/17ft (which was 85/14ft in 1906); at Badminton Park, Gloucestershire, in the garden, 102/17ft and, a finer tree, 105/16ft; at Culcreuch Castle, Stirlingshire, 90/16ft; a broad tree near the House at Spetchley Park, Worcestershire, is 70/18ft. A widely layered tree by

Crathes Castle, Kincardineshire, is 85/15ft and another at Barrington Hall, Essex, is 65/14ft. A very shapely tree at Townhill Park, Hampshire, is 75/15ft. The old pollard in the courtyard at Cawdor Castle is 62/17ft, its branches springing from six feet up.

The double-flowered Horse-chestnut, 'Baumannii', found in Geneva in 1819, has flowers congested with petals which remain in place, brown, as the flower fades, instead of falling to reveal the young fruit, becauses it is sterile and has no ovary, stamens or fruit. At other times of year it is known only by being grafted at the base, and by local reputation for being useless for conkers. The outstanding planting is a line of seven in Henrietta Park in Bath, 80–90ft tall and ten to twelve feet round. In the same city, one in the Royal Crescent is 90/11ft. Roseberry Park, Epsom has five 40–55ft tall and six to nine feet round. The biggest is at Westonbirt Arboretum in a group near the Centre, and is 100/13ft.

INDIAN HORSE-CHESTNUT

Aesculus indica

It is ironic that the Himalayas which had been thought erroneously for a long time to be the home of the Common Horse-chestnut, was all the time home to a very different and more attractive species. This grows from Afghanistan along foothills, mainly east of the Indus, at 4000 to 10,000ft, east to Nepal. Trees there in the last century were often found 150ft tall and 40ft round, but it must be doubted if any of great size has survived the recent wholesale destruction of forests in much of this area.

The Indian Horse-chestnut has many features lacking in the common tree which make it a better tree for many purposes and particularly recommend it to those concerned with city parks. Its leaves unfold a pleasing orange-brown and when mature they have long, elegant, slender leaflets on dark red stalks, and they hang to reveal a pale silvery underside. The flowers are on panicles over a foot long and open with the lower petals pink, often making the whole flowerhead appear pink from a distance. Furthermore, the flowers open in July and August, when those of the Common Horse-chestnut have long faded and when the parks are most used. This also means that the conkers are quite unformed at conker-collecting time and the trees escape bombardment and climbing. When the conkers are shed, in late November, they are shining coal black. The leaves show rich brown to orange colours in late October.

The conkers sown as soon as collected in the winter, readily yield strong seedlings early in spring. The tree is very hardy and tolerant of city airs and soils. It seems to have only one failing, and that is found only in a minority of specimens. It can break low down and early into many stems without a strong central axis. In

Indian Horse-chestnut
(*Aesculus indica*): a tree
ideal for city parks

some situations this big spreading bush of fine foliage and numerous flowers is acceptable or even useful but where a real tree is required early attention to pruning to make a clean stem should result in a good tree, and is usually a wise move anyway.

My sources do not say when or by whom this tree was made known to botany but they all say that it was introduced in 1851 by Colonel Henry Bunbury to Barton, Suffolk. It is not yet common but it has been planted in all parts of these Islands and shows no preferences for or against any of them. The strong preponderance of London and the south of England in my register of specimens, where 129 out of 151 are from that region, may reflect the distribution of gardens where unusual broad-leaf trees were being planted before the tree was easily available, more than it does the regions where it grows well.

In about 1933, Sydney Pearce, who was Curator at Kew, raised some seedlings presumably from seeds from the trees in the collection around the Tea-house, and in 1935 planted three of them by the path from the Main Gates. One of them, on the north side of the path, was particularly floriferous and shapely with dark green leaves on yellow-green stalks and long panicles pink in bud. It is now 'Sydney Pearce' and 45/7ft. Grafts from it are growing in a few gardens, including Torosay Castle on Mull.

The biggest specimen is in a group of four by the Coach Path above the house at Endsleigh Lodge, Devon. It is rather a rough tree with big low branches, 82/10ft, and is at least a single stem while the other three fork low. The best stem, clear for six feet, is in the garden at Hidcote in Gloucestershire, a fine tree at 60/9ft. Very similar is a tree at Lindridge in Devon, a huge, regular dome, crowded with flowers when I saw it, also with six feet of clear stem and 56/8ft in 1989. In the same class is a splendid tree but less free from its neighbours, at Townhill Park in Hampshire,

70/9ft with a good bole. Near it is one, 40/6ft, peculiar for being a graft set at over seven feet up on its rootstock, a practice not to be recommended.

One of three trees at Glendoick, Perth, planted in 1923, is 70/8ft. One at Highdown in Sussex planted in 1924 was 50/5ft in 1983, showing that the tree can grow on chalk. A less shapely tree planted in Frogmore Mausoleum grounds in Windsor in 1897 was 75/10ft, measurable only at one foot, in 1982. In Cannizaro Park, Wimbledon, one at the top of the bank was 80/8ft in 1988. Of many in Westonbirt Arboretum, the best stem is that by Loop Walk, 70/7ft and a more branchy tree by the eastern part of Pool Avenue is 75/7ft. The two siblings of 'Sydney Pearce' at Kew planted in 1935 are 56/7ft and 46/6ft. A type tree on the lawn at Killerton planted in 1930 is now 52/7ft at three feet, with low branches. One at Jenkyn Place, Bentley in Hampshire, planted in 1952 is 42/5ft.

JAPANESE HORSE-CHESTNUT

Aesculus turbinata

The Japanese Horse-chestnut is the only one of the world's species to share two important features of foliage with the Common Horse-chestnut. These are the glutinous bud-scales and the complete lack of stalk on the leaflets. Other Asiatic horse-chestnuts have well-stalked leaflets and so do all but one of the North American species, and that one, the Ohio Buckeye, has definite stalks, but short. The Japanese tree has one feature all its own – its huge leaves. As it is so like the familiar species, the leaves on strong growth, about twice as big, give the observer the odd feeling of having shrunk himself to half size. He also may feel the urge to snap a leaf off and use it as a parasol or umbrella as the banana leaf is used in hot countries.

A big leaf may have a main stalk 17in long, stout, a third of an inch in diameter at the big, sucker-like base. With the biggest pair of the radiating leaflets each 18in long, pointing somewhat forward, the whole leaf-blade can be over two feet across. The autumn colours are orange-brown with the midribs at first picked out in white. However, there is nothing striking about the flowers or the conkers. The panicles are low and bluntly conic, about four inches each way and the conkers are small and dull brown. The bark is pink-grey and smooth, with lenticels and a few corky-sided vertical fissures, distinguishing the tree usefully in winter from the common tree. The leaflets differ not only in size but in a broad, triangular tapered tip as opposed to the sudden contraction of the common tree leaflet from a very broad end to a short, acute tip.

Bruce Jackson in his *Trees of Westonbirt*, written in 1927, says that the Japanese Horse-chestnut was introduced 'about 45 years ago'. That puts it in 1885, yet a few lines later he dates the tree on the mansion lawn at 1883 and makes no connection between the dates. Nor does he speculate on the date or origin of the tree by Circular Drive which was bigger than the lawn tree then, as it is today, and, he said, differs slightly in its foliage. The lawn tree has lost part of its crown in recent years and is 50/8ft but the tree in the Arboretum is fully crowned although a little hemmed in, and is 72/9ft. William Holford and his son, George, were evidently fond of the species and there are several others. There are three by Pool Ride, dating most likely to around 1910; a pair below the clearing on the south side of the eastern end of Willesley Drive, both 72/6ft; one on the north side, 70/5ft, and one, probably 20 years older, is in the Aesculus group near the present gate into the Arboretum, a fine tree, 82/7ft.

The Earl of Ducie, at Tortworth Court, was naturally not far behind, and planted one in the Dell in about 1890 which was 55/8ft in 1980. The biggest surviving at Kew, a graft, in the collection, is 62/7ft. At Headfort in County Meath there was one 65/7ft in 1980. At Birr Castle, County Offaly, growth has been a little slow and the tree planted in Lilac Walk in 1933 is 44/4ft but that is vigorous compared with one in the Royal Botanic Garden in Edinburgh which dates from 1910 and is only 46/3ft. I collected a few conkers from the two trees at Tortworth in 1964 and by 1987 one was 36/3ft at Alice Holt Lodge. A northerly tree is at Innes House in Morayshire which was 52/3ft in 1980. In the Golf Ground extension at Wakehurst Place, planted after 1915, a strongly branched tree is 50/7ft. In the collection at Thorp Perrow in Yorkshire planted in around 1930, a tree is 70/6ft.

ITALIAN ALDER

Alnus cordata

The Italian Alder is native to Corsica and southern Italy and was introduced in 1820. Despite its southerly origins, it grows remarkably fast into a fine tree at least as far north as Aberdeen. It seems as little concerned about climate as it is about soil, for it grows well on chalk and light sands, although rather better on clays and in damp areas. It is superior in form, foliage and growth to all other alders except, of course, the one from the Caucasus region, *Alnus subcordata*, and it has a larger fruit even than that. It has copious long and bright yellow male catkins from a very early age, and they are usually the first alder catkins to open, often in February. The prettily cordate leaves are rich glossy green above, while beneath the midrib has little patches of pale orange-brown hairs projecting perpendicularly.

The best Italian Alder is at Westonbirt Arboretum in Gloucestershire by Skilling's Gate into Silk Wood. It stands in a dry valley which until 1974 was the boundary between Gloucestershire and Wiltshire and beneath which run the headwaters of the Bristol Avon. Water runs above ground only rarely in times of great flood, but the tree will surely have access to subterranean water at all times, in the

Oolitic limestones where the stream runs. It is 112/10ft which makes it the tallest specimen yet recorded and the biggest in girth except for a hulk 13ft round at Tottenham House in Savernake Forest, Wiltshire. It is not quite straight, leaning out a little from nearby lesser trees and slightly sinuous further up, but it still has a shapely, conic top and regular branching beneath. Its date is not recorded, but it must be in or after 1876 when planting in Silk Wood was begun. It was 89/8ft in 1963 so 2ft in 25 years agrees with this date.

Another fine specimen at Westonbirt is in the old Arboretum, in Victory Glade and this is of known date, 1928. It is of excellent shape and is 85/7ft. This one was 62/5ft in 1965 so is growing at the same rate as the big tree and helps to confirm the assumed date of that tree.

Another pair of noteworthy specimens is growing at Smeaton House near Haddington in East Lothian. The larger one is near the gate to the lake, across the Park from the House. It is a fine tree, 95/8ft, but does not hold its good shape to the top. It was 80/7ft in 1966, so is growing at the same rate as the Westonbirt trees and should date from around 1880. The smaller tree by the House is of better shape and has luxuriant foliage. It was 72/7½ft adding 16ft to its height and 18in to its girth since 1966.

Italian Alder (*Alnus cordata*):
Smeaton House, East Lothian

On the Fen in Cambridge is a fine line of eight big Italian Alders grew until 1992 near a wet ditch. The biggest was 72/8ft. In the University Botanic Gardens across the road, one planted in 1953 was 56/5½ft after 26 years, and in Oxford University Botanic Garden one planted in 1930 is 80/7ft.

There are two big and luxuriantly foliaged, if not particularly shapely trees, in the Cathedral Close at Canterbury. The larger of these is one of the biggest in the country, 65½/10ft and the other is 62/8ft. A splendidly sturdy specimen is in Calderstones Park, Merseyside, not tall but with a fine bole. It is 62/9ft. In Battersea Park, London, a small group around a lake has four big trees. The two largest are 85/8ft and 72/8½ft.

COMMON ALDER

Alnus glutinosa (plate 4)

The Common Alder is appreciated by birdwatchers and riparian owners more than by the generality of gardeners and landscapers, except those committed to the use of native species. As a garden tree it is far surpassed for versatility, tolerance of difficult soils, vigour and, usually, stature; for shape, catkins, fruit and foliage, by the Italian, Grey and Red Alders. But it is in a class of its own as a source of seeds for birds and as a defence against the erosion of waterside banks.

Its small pseudocones are borne in greater numbers than the fruit of any other alder, and the seed they yield are alone in being a main resort of feeding flocks of small finches in the winter. These are among the most attractive of all small birds, in plumage, habits and voice. A good waterside stand of alders can attract mixed flocks of several hundreds of redpolls and siskins but often with a few goldfinches and linnets, and in the western Highlands, some twite. As a rule the combined flock feeds together, hanging on the bunches of fruit, quietly winkling out the seed with a little vague twittering and the occasional 'fayee' call which is common to all the species of the genus *Carduelis*.

Every so often, perhaps about ten minutes, they undergo, like cliff-nesting colonies of gulls, a 'dread', a panic evacuation for no discernible reason. It is thought to be like a fire-drill, to keep them alert for danger and practised in evading it. The flock erupts from the trees with a buzz and babble of their mixed calls, then separates into species flocks, bouncing around gaining height. The redpolls, in tighter formation, raise a loud chorus of their flight-note, 'jidgit' while the siskins straggle more and pour out a mixture of the flight-note, 'see-oo', the 'fayee' note, and a strange low buzzing. Circling, breaking and re-forming, the flocks suddenly go silent and pour back into the trees.

Waterside trees grow beside ditches, streams, rivers and lakes of all sizes where there is movement of water to keep the oxygen level high. They do not thrive by stagnant pools with little or no throughput of water although they may persist there a long time after the stream has been diverted or has failed. They also grow well in swampy woods provided these are near a river with a good flow. They can grow equally well in the rich soils of a marked springline even if it is in a wood. The best specimen in Britain was growing, until 1987, in such a wood at Sandling Park near Hythe in Kent. It was 102/20ft with a long, smooth clean trunk like prime oak.

On the bank of a river or lake, the roots grow a little way out into the water as a thick pad of hard, dark red thongs, trapping passing silt to build the bank out and strongly resisting damage from floods, waves and wash from water-traffic. They are an ideal riparian tree, providing food for finches, perches for kingfishers, stems for willow-tits to peck out their nest-holes, and root-tangles to hide the homes of otters. And they did these services along many of the most attractive valley-bottoms in the southeast of England, until the water boards became obsessed with the fear of floods and began driving big yellow machines along small rivers and destroyed long stretches. Worse, it was said that once they had spent big money to acquire the machines, they needed to keep them working and let them roam into areas in no real need of the work. That was when drainage and riverside clearance were at their most damaging and before conservation of valuable habitats was regarded as respectable beyond the ranks of the then derided pioneeers of a 'green' approach to anything.

Now these days are largely gone and some imaginative schemes for managing water-courses are in place. Over-zealous rushing the water to the sea is usually now seen to have been short-sighted. For fifteen years (to date) there has rarely been enough water, and with over-abstraction from the aquifers which ought to feed the springs giving rise to the streams, water-courses are shrinking and drying up. Unfortunately, the change of use of valley-bottoms from pasture to arable, has meant that the abundant fertility once conferred by floods and exploited in the old water-meadow system, cannot be used to advantage, and top-soil and water are still sent as hastily as possible to the sea. Which is one of a million or two flagrant examples of the short-term gains of 'the market', mortgaging and pillaging future wealth.

Common Alder had an important place in productive forestry when wood was used for specialised purposes, mostly now replaced. In large sizes it was used in making gates for locks and docks and in waterside pilings, and possibly it is still in small quantities. It is peculiarly resistant to alternate wetting and drying. For the same quality, it was the wood for mill-girls' clogs and smallwood today goes into the backs of scrubbing brushes and stiff brooms and duck boarding. For these smallwood pieces, coppice stems were grown and alder coppices very well, cut stools growing new shoots three or four feet long for some years. These and the smaller trees were also important for producing high quality charcoal, as needed for gunpowder.

There are very few dated trees of any age and none of more than 70 years growth, and the growth-rates indicate that since girths over ten feet are very scarce, the normal life-span of a maiden tree is not above 150 years. However, there are a few much bigger boles, on pollards or hulks in remote native stands and occasionally in gardens, and some may exceed 200 years of age. In health, the tree is fairly wind-firm so the loss of big trees is largely due to the end of their natural life.

With the loss of the Sandling Park tree in the 1987 gale, there is no specimen known worth spending the time to find. Near where that stood, a young tree of excellent shape and vigour, doing its best to be a replacement, was 46/2ft in 1980 and its progress will be interesting to watch. The oldest dated tree is in the University Botanic Garden in Oxford, planted in 1920, and when 69 years old it was 72/7ft. When 50 years old it was 65/5ft, giving a rare insight of a steady rate of growth over two periods. One in Stonepit Wood in Borde Hill, Sussex, was 82/7ft in 1987. In Acorn Bank garden in Cumbria one is 75/9ft. In the roadside border at Flitwick Manor in Bedfordshire, a stout-boled old tree is 70/13ft. The biggest is a hulk in an ancient woodland reserve on Dundonnell Estate in Wester Ross, 17ft round. In the same region, at Torosay Castle on Mull, a good tree is 70/7ft. In the University Botanic Garden in Cambridge, a small group planted in 1952 has trees of 56/4ft and 50/4ft.

SILVER BIRCH

Betula pendula

The Silver Birch is much the better of the two birch tree species which were among the first woody plants to recolonise Britain after the Ice Ages. The other one, variously called the Downy or White Birch, *Betula pubescens*, has an untidy, shapeless and twiggy crown, the Silver birch has fine long-pendulous shoots hanging from elegantly arched branches on a straight stem, persistent to the tip until maturity. It is lucky that the botanist, Roth, who used this feature for his specific distinction, published his name before Ehrhart's *verrucosa*, based on the warted shoots, or the awful name 'warty birch' would be heard more often than it is. The name bestowed by Linnaeus before either of these names, *alba* was declared a *nomen nudum* or *ambiguum* since the description that was published with it failed to distinguish the Silver from the White Birch and was used for both, which defeats the object of botanical naming.

The Silver Birch has exceptional value in gardens. It grows very fast in its first 20 years. It will often reach 60ft, as long as it is planted when only one or two years old, before its roots have wandered far beyond the volume of soil that is moved with a tree at transplanting. It is very easily raised, and often raises itself, thriving on any well-drained soil but also on the less heavy clays. When taller, it provides

Silver Birch (*Betula pendula*): close-up of catkins on branch

the high light shelter that is needed by rhododendrons and many other shrubs which may be damaged by late spring radiation frosts. The light tracery of twigs keeps the night-time temperature one or two degrees (on either scale) above that of open ground. The light summer foliage prevents sun-scorch. The one disadvantage is that on the light sandy soils in which rhododendrons and azaleas are often grown, the roots of birch are exceedingly invasive and dry the soil in summer. Therefore the trees must be as sparsely placed as will give adequate shelter.

This tree is highly attractive to birds. The foliage in spring and in autumn carries a large population of aphids, the first crop of which feeds nestling tits and warblers. The autumn crop feeds the adults, the warblers building up reserves of fat for their migration. The fruits are abundant and their seeds much sought by small finches, especially by redpolls and siskins but also by goldfinches, twites and blue tits. The crowns in hill country often harbour nesting colonies of redpolls, and the decaying upper stem and branches are feeding and nesting places for great spotted woodpeckers, even in semi-suburban areas. Rotting bases and stumps are bored for nests by willow-tits.

A lawn must remain an open glade and free of trees in the middle, but a fringe of Silver Birches encroaching is fine. The white-barked stems must not be spoiled by low branches and a mess of old twigs on the trunk. The trees need to be cleaned of all side-shoots as early as possible, allowing sun and wind to play on them as well as making the trunk fully visible. The effect of a group of birches so treated would be magical, but they are always left half hidden behind dying twiggery and the stem is given no chance to grow and smooth over branch-scars when the branches are still there. A laird in a Perthshire castle saw in 1975 a seedling springing up in the flower bed beneath his bedroom window, and cleaned up the stem. After 18 years the tree was 46/1ft 8in and pruned to 25ft clear. It looked a little sparse, but it has great promise of making a striking white trunk before long.

As a pioneer tree of rapid growth, the Silver Birch is not likely to live to an advanced age. No dated tree is known earlier than 1905, but that means little since so few are of known age. It is assumed that in England the trees die back and are broken down when they are less than a hundred years old, and may do so any time after 60 years. In Highland glens, whilst selecting big trees with very rough bark towards the base to try to find curly-grained wood (known as 'maser birch' in Scandinavia where it is valued for making drinking-cups), it was found that healthy trees were up to 220 years old. In England mature upper branches are much bored by woodpeckers as, although the timber is so strong and elastic in use, it decays rapidly when dying on the tree. Branches may be heard falling from birches more often than from other trees. They are quite light by then, and seldom do any harm.

The Silver Birch has chances to show its pioneering quality when fires on southern heaths clear areas of trees. The birches spring up in dense swathes and clumps, and these, frequent on Frensham and Chobham Commons in Surrey, for example, are sure signs of past fires. They do not thin themselves naturally to any extent, until overcrowding causes deaths which leave gaps for Scots Pine and Oak to invade the stand. Similarly, the A93 from Ballater to Balmoral is lined by some exceedingly closely packed birches, arising after fires no doubt caused by the criminal habit of so many motorists of throwing out lighted cigarettes. All cars have internal ash-trays, but some people have not the wit or decency to use them. The Silver Birches look very attractive at present, but cannot remain very long in such good shape. The banks of heathers behind them will invade the area until it is flammable again, and unless motorists join civilisation, the birches will start again.

With a tree so fragile and short-lived, outside Scotland at least, it is asking for trouble to enthuse about a big specimen that has not been seen for more than a few years, and risky in many cases when it was seen this year. There is an interest in how big birches have grown, but not many people would go out of their way to see a tree with only a minor probability of it being there. I mention only a few particularly good trees which seem to be far from approaching senility, and some of the best young trees of known date.

At Castle Leod in Easter Ross, a tree in the field beyond the 1550 Sweet Chestnut is 70/10ft with a splendid bole. At Battlesby, Perth, a superb tree, apparently quite young, is 80/7½ft with a clear stem for 30ft. At the edge of the garden of Etal Manor, Northumberland, a self-sown seedling is 85/7½ft and very fine indeed. A tree in the Arboretum at Lyndford, near Thetford, Norfolk, is of good form and 85/7½ft. At Megginch Castle, Perthshire, one planted in 1921 by the drive is 85/7½ft. Sandford park, Cheltenham, mostly planted in 1925, has a fine tree at 72/6ft. In the University of London Botanic Garden at Sunningdale, a shapely tree was 80/4½ft when 42 years old.

HORNBEAM

Carpinus betulus

The Hornbeam is a pleasant, if rather dull tree of more interest for its remarkable timber than for its adornment of the landscape. It is at its best in spring, when densely hung with short male catkins, individually pale brownish yellow, but looking more yellow in the mass, and in late autumn when the foliage turns from yellow to old gold and often orange-brown. It has a similar 'juvenile cone' to that of the Beech, so a hedge clipped within its limits retains pale brown dead leaves throughout the winter. The trunk and bark have an unusual aspect as the mainly smooth dull grey bark is streaked and patterned in dark grey and the stem is corrugated by deep flutes between rounded ridges giving a 'wristy' or 'muscular' appearance.

The timber is the hardest of any European tree, the strongest and, after the Box, the heaviest. It is readily workable by sharp tools, except where cross-grained, but this dulls their edges quickly. There is no colour difference between sapwood and heartwood, so it is not used for bow-staves, but its bony hardness and its great strength give it many specialist uses. Before cast iron replaced it, Hornbeam was the timber that could best take the strains required of cog-wheels in mills, and the teeth constantly meshing could remain smooth and efficient. This smooth, imperceptibly wearing quality is still used in the train of members of the mechanism of piano keys and hammers, the delicate balances of which have to return to position precisely when actuated ten times a second. The keys themselves were often hornbeam suitably dyed. Pulley-blocks and roller bearings, cams, yokes for cattle, skittles and bobbins were other uses. The centre of a butcher's chopping-block is made of small blocks glued together to make a surface of end-grain which resists wearing while the outer parts are of beech or some other wood which wears slightly and leaves the centre convex.

The wood is close-grained and dense, making it an excellent fuel and the source of some of the best charcoal; and small-wood when too small for turnery for tool-handles, pegs and chessmen, was first class oven-fuel. Despite all these qualities of hardness and strength, the wood when on the tree is very prone to fungal decay. Old trees are soon hollow, and dying and dead branches are frequent. Maiden trees are probably not long-lived, being very seldom more than 12ft round. But pollards can be much bigger and have been known to be 30ft round however hollow they are and must be some 300 years old. As with the Yew, the great strength of the timber will hold the outer trunk together and support the branches, long after the centre has decayed.

The Hornbeam was a late arrival here, entering about 5000 years ago as the last remnants of the land-bridge were eroding away. It had no time to spread far in England beyond the south-east, and is not thought to be native beyond Cambridge and Oxford with probable outliers in Somerset, Monmouth and Herefordshire. The only areas where it is the dominant tree in woods, and then possibly owing to a long history of management, are Hainault, Epping and Hatfield Forests, all in Essex. As a shade-bearing tree, late in the natural succession, it is an understorey in the other parts of the south-east. It is, however, completely hardy, and has been planted on a small scale right through Scotland to Sutherland.

Planting dates before this century hardly exist, so it is a splendid slice of luck that the biggest maiden tree has a date, and so it is the oldest known as well. It is in front of Hurn, or Heron Court, Christchurch in Hampshire, and was planted in 1740. It allows just enough space for a clean measure at five feet between the top of the root-swell at three feet and the bracket of the lowest of the huge limbs into which it divides above five feet, and is 60/15. In 1906 it was 70/10½ft so it is maintaining, to date, its annual increase of somewhat under one inch a year. The only other old dated tree was planted at Bitton Rectory in Somerset in 1817. It had noticeable branch-swell to a little below five feet and was 75/8ft in 1908 and 60/10ft at four feet in 1959 but was cut down a few years later.

A very hollow hulk in Easton Park, Dunmow, Essex, was 65/31ft in 1949 but burned down in 1956. Its owner, the Hon. Maynard Greville maintained that it took a new lease of life after the explosion of a bomb dump close to it when the Park was a wartime airfield. He thought that this could have aerated and added nitrogen to the soil. In Hatfield Forest not far away, the biggest pollard now is 60/16ft. A decrepit ruin in Lullingstone Park, Kent, all open-work and burrs, was 50/15½ft in 1982. A hugely spreading tree with a clean, apparently sound bole, is at Patshull House,

Hornbeam (*Carpinus betulus* 'fastigiata'): Oxford bypass

Albrighton, Staffordshire, and is in 1991 65/12ft. A similarly sound, but less spreading tree north of the lake in Syon Park, is now 70/11½ft and a good tree in the Botanic Garden in Bath is 85/11ft. Several good trunks are about ten feet round and the best are: in University Parks, Oxford in the north border, 80/10½ft; at Orchardleigh near Frome in Somerset, 75/10ft with a big crown; at Tatchfield Mount in Hampshire, 77/10ft and, the best in shape, at Bishopsthorpe in York, 88/10ft.

In Scotland, the biggest is in a tiny village, Acharn, on a little road that winds along the north side of Loch Tay. Practically on a moorland margin of the road, it is 70/11ft. Murthly Castle has two, 75/9½ft, close together at the Castle end of the monumental conifer avenue, East Drive. Abercairney, also in Perthshire, has one 36/9½ft and Fyvie Castle, Aberdeenshire, has one 72/9½ft by the drive.

The cultivar, 'Fastigiata' arose before 1880 in Germany and starts life as a slender, ovoid-columnar tree, much narrower and more columnar than the quite dispensable, untidy 'Columnaris'. A few of the early grafts of 'Fastigiata' received were allowed to grow unpruned and have made broad, upswept bushes, branched down to the ground, like two off the Broad Drive in Westonbirt, planted in 1929. Normally the lower branches are cleaned off and the trees have a good clear leg and so they grow into the splendid dolls house specimens so much admired. Their cause has, I believe, been well served by two groups, one of two trees and one well beyond them of eight, skilfully spaced and sited on the false summit of Bix Hill as the A423 climbs on to the chalk above Henley. This planting was the work of the regrettably short-lived Roads Beautifying Association. The northern inner bypass at Oxford, along the part of the A40 known as Sunderland Avenue, has half a mile with three rows of superb trees to 44/5ft and is spectacular throughout the year, pariculary in winter, with its close tracery of straight, slender shoots.

The earliest known trees are two in the National Botanic Garden at Glasnevin, Dublin, planted in 1888 and now 60/7ft and 62/6ft. At Kew in the collection, one tree planted in 1894 is 65/9ft at three feet and a more shapely one dating from 1919 is 56/6½ft. A broad tree is an imposing presence in a corner of Branklyn Garden in Perth. It has been allowed to keep its branches down to five feet and is 62/8ft and one in Howard's Field at Wisley starts branching at one foot, below which it is 52/7ft. One at Colesbourne, Gloucestershire, planted in Ring Meadow in 1902 cannot be faulted and is 85/5½ft. A group of five fine trees near the end of the garden at Bulstrode Park is composed of uniform trees about 70/4½ft.

SWEET CHESTNUT

Castanea sativa (plate 4)

The Sweet Chestnut contributes substantially to the arboreal landscape in the lowlands as far north as the coastal part of Sutherland, which is creditable for a tree whose natural range is entirely south of the Alps. It is, moreover, like the similarly but somewhat less southern, Turkey Oak, a big tree throughout, adding to the number of interesting, huge and rugged old specimens everywhere. It grows rapidly in youth as a shapely conic tree with a sturdy stem and numerous, regular, upraised branches and begins to spread its crown and thicken some branches in a less regular crown by the time it is a hundred years old. Height growth then has to a great extent culminated, but the increase in girth of the stem remains rapid until senility and decay set in. It grows more rapidly than the Common Oak but does not live quite so long, so the biggest trees of each species are about the same size.

A well-marked feature of the Sweet Chestnut is the spiral assumed by the ridges in the bark. This does not begin until the tree is some one hundred years old and eight to ten feet round, when the silvery grey bark has little more than cracks, which are vertical. With increasing age, the bark becomes pale brown and strongly ridged, a distinct spiralling setting in. The spiral may lean to the left or to the right, perhaps more often to the right, and increases in angle with the passing years. In the oldest trees, the ridges are lying over at about 45 degrees from the vertical. The timber beneath remains straight and vertical in grain in most trees.

The Romans are credited with introducing the tree, but this would seem to be based on the occurrence of husks and nuts found in middens in places like Hadrian's Wall. That may only mean that they imported chestnuts among their stores, and no doubt walnuts, too. They probably did not expect to be in Britain long enough to harvest from trees that they planted, but with the nuts around in quantity, probably stolen by kitchen minions, this could have led to a few escaping and growing, in Roman times.

The arrangement of the flowers in this tree is unusual and has been poorly observed so the description in most books is quite wrong. It is agreed that the prominent male catkins arise from the distal buds of the previous year's growth. It is not true at all, although often recounted, that the female flowers are on the same stalks at the base of the males. The female flowers are borne on few-branched peduncles of the current year, and each branch terminates in a small bunch of cord-like erect stalks. The little knobs on them are flower-buds, unopened and in most years aborting. In good, warm seasons, however, these open as a spike of white male flowers, weeks after the normal males have withered, giving the tree a second and very different flowering.

When jays have taken all the acorns they can, burying them in their territories to enrich them for possible snowy times, some of them turn to collecting and burying Sweet Chestnuts. This does not seem to have become sufficiently wide-spread or common to be an important factor in the ecology of the tree or of the jay, but it may yet spread. The absurdity of the stance of those rabid conservationists who debar the planting of exotics like the Sweet Chestnut, is apparent in the light of the fact that chiffchaffs and all other migrants returning from Africa spend time in the Sweet Chestnut woods or similar, and have been many months in a vast mix of tropical hardwoods, none of which grows here. A slight addition of southern European trees in our countryside can only make the birds feel more at home.

The Chestnut of greatest renown is that near the church at Tortworth in Gloucestershire. It is one of only two trees marked on the one-inch Ordnance Survey maps, the other being the Major Oak in Sherwood Forest. It is reputed to have been a boundary-marker in the reign of King Stephen and so to have been a prominent tree in the twelfth century. This is attested by a marginal note in Peter Collinson's copy of Evelyn's *Sylva*. The evidence for such great age, provided by the tree itself, is far from convincing. It nearly fills its compound with a crown of stems arising from supine and probably rooted, hugely rotted branches, breaking off the remains of the trunk in a ring. In 1891, Robert Hutchison gave a figure of 47ft for the girth. Two of the branches, now partly torn out, may at that time have been integral with the trunk, but it is impossible today to see how such a high figure was achieved. It had evidently deteriorated sharply since 1766 when Strutt found it had a ten-foot bole, 50ft round at five feet and bore three limbs, one of them 28½ft round. Strutt's drawing was unrecognisable as the tree by 1900, but the three branches will be those resting on the ground today.

Today, a tape can be threaded around, above most parts of branches at one foot, and it reads about 33½ft. A path weaving at three to five feet up below some big branch-timber could be a better measure, but that is no more than 37½ft. Were Strutt nevertheless correct in 1766, the tree could be believably around 1000 years old at that time. But, as the tree at Rossanna, cited later, shows, 37½ft can be grown in about 300 years, so if the reputed age be accepted a large segment must have vanished since Strutt's day.

There is no problem in fixing the precise date of the survivor of two trees at Castle Leod, Strathpeffer. It is there in cast iron in front of the tree, '1550' on a large plaque, itself of great age, and is confirmed in a document in the muniments room in the Castle. That makes it the oldest tree of any kind in Britain with a known date. (The 1126 Yew at Dryburgh Abbey must wait until more evidence to confirm the strong supposition that this is the right tree, can be adduced.) This tree, with the spirals of bark ridges at about 45 degrees, on a bole 13ft long, is now 88/25½ft, in full health. It was 21½ft round in 1908 and the growth is slow compared with most of those in England, which is a consequence of the cool summers so far north. Until a gale in 1979, there was another 1550 tree beside it, but smaller, being 20ft round in 1966. Neither showed any sign of crown die-back then, and neither does the one there today.

The next oldest with a date, a little vague but near enough to take this place, is a low, broad tree attributed to 'about 1570' at Balmerino Abbey in Fife, and 42/20ft. An avenue in Greenwich Park, London, is dated as 1664. It contained several broad, low, twisting branched trees, mostly dying back in 1955 when one was 23ft round, and fewer in 1975 when another was the same size. The next oldest dates from 1718, at Rossanna House near Ashford, County Wicklow, where it is now regarded as a 'John Wesley' tree. It was 29½ft round in 1903 and is now 70/34½ft, a life mean of over one and a half inches a year. This is slightly increased by having to be measured at around four feet and by small burrs and sprouts being circumnavigated, but it is a grand tree.

Bigger trees than any of these are known in two places, both of unknown date. The biggest is at Canford School near Poole in Dorset. This is a hulk with little crown left but much of its foliage on sprouts along the short trunk. It is 56/44ft after recent clearance of the biggest sprouts, and is largely a conglomerate of burrs. It was recorded as 39½ft round in 1953, but comparison is difficult and in 1967 it was only two inches less than it is today, so there is no good basis for calculations of its age. The other is at Melsor Hall in Northamptonshire and this is a better quality hulk with fewer sprouts on the bole and more around the base. It is 62/36ft.

The biggest of several big trees at Thenford Hall near Brackley can be measured only at three feet where it is 32ft round and it is 72ft tall. At Howletts Park near Canterbury in 1983 there was a good specimen, 75/32ft. At Broxbournebury, Hertfordshire, a tree which was 24ft round in 1908 was 88/30½ft in 1988. In Bushey Park, Middlesex, one beside Glazebrook Road was a good hulk, 36/30ft in 1981. One of the best specimens, with a sprout-free, clear ten foot bole is in a field close to the A272 at Moor Farm, Cowdray Park, east of Midhurst, Sussex. It is 75/30ft, having added 21in in 15 years. The St Pierre Hotel at Chepstow, Gwent has three trees over 22ft round. The biggest in 1988 was 60/30ft.

Croft Castle, Herefordshire, has a famous planting of Sweet Chestnuts, once reputed to have been raised from nuts salvaged from the wrecks of the Armada in 1592, but probably planted in fact around 1750. The pattern of trees, in lines, could still, as has been suggested, have marked the disposal of the ships. One line is particularly impressive for the size and closeness of the trees, and in 1960 I laid a 100ft tape along the best part and found that in this length there was more wood than air. That line has 14 trees and the two biggest in 1984 were 75/28½ft and 70/28ft. These will be the ones noted in 1871 as 20½ft and 20ft. One in the main avenue was 70/28ft and one by a wall in Home Park was 56/28½ft. At Betchworth near Dorking, there are many big trees and two in a rough line of several near the track by the golf course are 28½ft round much sprouted stems. At King's Walden in Hertford-shire, a line of 11 trees has an end tree 65/28½ft and one four trees from it 60/26½ft.

The line of trees by the drive to Stourhead House is not a great feature but the second tree is a big one, although with only a small, short crown, like the others. It is 42/26½ft. A sturdy, rugged but clean-boled tree at Studley Royal, Yorkshire, prominent in the meadow below the Chapel is 52/26½ft with a bole eight feet long. At Hanworth Hall, Norfolk a tree was reported in a magazine in 1933 as 105/38ft with a fine long clean trunk. This had to be seen, as no tree measurements can be taken on trust. It turned out to be 85/25½ft in 1969 with a ten foot bole and today it is 26½ft round.

The award for the best stem had long been a runaway win for the tree in the garden at Chatsworth House, Derbyshire. This superb stem on a tree 80/18½ft and as smooth and cylindrical as a Corinthian column for 40ft. With a relatively small crown, it could not be expected to be growing fast and had in fact added 28in in 77 years. It was blown down in 1990.

SOUTHERN CATALPA

Catalpa bignonioides

It could be said that we were unlucky to receive the Southern Catalpa 159 years before the Northern Catalpa. A tree whose original range stayed on the plains of the Gulf Coast was unlikely to be as successful or widely useful as the closely related species native to the harsh continental winters of Indiana and Illinois. John Catesby, when he sent the tree from Mississippi or Louisiana in 1726, will not have known anything about another species, but as it turns out his species is, it seems, actually the hardier and has some advantages in its appearance. In North America, both species are planted in all parts indiscriminately, north to the Canadian border, and seem to show no difference in adapting to the varied regions.

In Britain, the Southern Catalpa is frequent in towns and cities across the south, infrequent in the Midlands and rare and small in Scotland and Ireland, showing sensitivity to cool summers. The warmer cities like Bath and, overwhelmingly, London have most of the best trees, except for one outsize tree, 36/10ft in Bute Park, Cardiff. North of the Midlands the Catalpas are small, tend to be bushy and are foliage trees rather than flowering trees. The best in Scotland is in the wall-garden at Culzean Castle, Ayrshire, 40/4ft.

At Syon House, Brentford, an old tree has long been collapsing into the lake, and if this is, as I like to think, the one mentioned by John Loudon in 1837, it is much the oldest, for it was then some 35 years old, to judge from its size. The next oldest are probably the line in Palace Yard, by Bridge Street, and they are, or were in 1969, the biggest, but their future is likely to be short. In 1969, four of the five were around 11½ft round and one was 11ft. They were presumably planted when the Palace was finished around 1857. I have been unworthily deterred from measuring them lately, as it required permission from the Lord Privy Chamberlain then, and the added security now would be formidable.

Southern Catalpa (*Catalpa bignonioides*): a frequent site in towns and cities across the south of England

There are at least seven big, low-crowned broad trees in Kew Gardens, but only two are dated. One planted in 1879 northwest of the Temperate House is now 33/8ft. Bigger ones are on the other side of the Temperate House, 30/9ft; on Bell Lawn, now 42/10ft and the other dated tree, planted near Victoria Gate in 1914 and now 36/9ft. Outside Rochester Cathedral a tree which is considerably decumbent, is 40/9ft. In Bath Botanic Garden, a tree near the great Golden Catalpa is 40/9ft but has been dying back lately.

As a decorative tree, the Catalpa has the severe limitation that it is gaunt and far from shapely until mid-June when the foliage unfolds, and reverts to that state in early October when that is shed, without even the benefit of worthwhile autumn colours. In the hotter parts of America the crown can be identified from a distance by a distinctly yellowish cast to the leaves after midsummer, and a passable gold is achieved before they fall.

GOLDEN CATALPA

Catalpa bignonioides 'Aurea'

Anyone less than captivated by the briefly displayed charms of the Common Catalpa or not swept off his feet by the sight of golden foliage, should steer clear of this tree. It can have very splendid gold leaves, bigger than grow on any other tree, but it has all the failings of the green-leafed form and at least four more of its own. It is less hardy and more prone to damage to its new leaves in late spring frosts. These are rare in late June, but have occurred. It is also caught in a double bind. It needs full sunlight to develop its best golden colour, but it needs midday shade or the leaves may scorch. It is very expensive and very slow. And then it may well flower. Few things are more insipid than a scatter of white flowers in front of golden foliage.

No specimen has been noted further north than two in the Jephson Garden in Leamington Spa. Around London, small trees, big splashes of gold, show here and there where there are or were small nurseries. This form was on sale by 1877 and its date or place of origin are not known but it will have arisen in a Dutch or German nursery most likely.

The one very large and impressive specimen is at Bath, in the Botanic Garden. It has a huge spread from long branches leaving the trunk at three feet and reaching out many yards, parallel with the ground. It was 30/7ft at three feet up in 1984, an enormous butter-yellow cloud – for three months.

Golden Catalpa (*Catalpa bignonioides* 'Aurea'): Hilliers Arboretum, Hampshire

HYBRID CATALPA

Catalpa x erubescens

Several slightly different hybrids have arisen in nurseries between the Southern Catalpa and the Yellow Catalpa, *C. ovata* of China, which was sent by Robert Fortune in 1847. The hybrid trees in Britain are sometimes known as 'Tea's Hybrid', the name common in America, because this clone, 'J.C. Teas', arose in the nursery in Bayville, Indiana, owned by Mr Teas. There was no doubt about the Chinese Catalpa being one parent because the seed was picked from it, and the leaves inherit the prominent lobes of that species. The father species is harder to determine, and since Indiana is in the natural range of the Northern Catalpa, it was assumed that the other parent is the Southern Catalpa.

This tree was raised in 1874 and was sent to Britain in 1891. I nourish a theory that the first grafting material was acquired by Bide's Nursery, trading in Farnham, Surrey, until fairly recently, because so many of the biggest trees were in or near the Farnham district. One was in a garden laid out in 1900, and was a hugely spreading tree when it was felled by new owners in 1984, nine and a half feet round at three feet. Another, at Wrecclesham was a splendid, long-boled tree, 62/9ft when it was blown down in 1987, and the annual rings showed a planting date of about 1904. That gale also took a good big tree in Aldershot and, at Petworth in Sussex, the tallest of all at 80/8ft, but only trimmed some of the top of one in Alfred Road, Farnham, which is 55/9ft.

Other than my assumed Bride's trees, there are only three big trees. At Townhill Park, Hampshire, a broad tree with big branches was 36/10ft in 1983 and one hopes it is still there. At Hergest Croft, Herefordshire, near the tennis court, a fine tree is 60/9ft and in Sydney Gardens in Bath, another excellent tree, 60/8ft, stands near a railway bridge.

NORTHERN CATALPA

Catalpa speciosa

The Northern Catalpa overlaps in its southernmost native area in Arkansas, the range of the Southern Catalpa, which was introduced to England and to cultivation in 1726. The two were not distinguished until the differences were noticed by Warder in 1854 but he did not publish, and it was 1879 before Sargent made it known and used Warder's name, *speciosa*. The combined species have a wide range from the Gulf Coast up the Mississsippi Valley to Illinois and Indiana so any planting made before 1879 could have been of either species unless the origin were known. This may explain the statement in an American work that the Northern Catalpa was being cultivated by 1754, and does explain its being grown in France in 1802. But although Catalpas were commonly planted in southern England, no tree of the Northern was known before Sargent sent seed to Kew in 1880. Today, however, I am convinced that there is one, first noted as a big tree in 1945, which must pre-date the Sargent trees.

Adequate data from growth is available neither here nor from American trees, to indicate the date of this tree in Radnor Gardens beside the Thames in Twicken-ham. In the much hotter and longer summers of New York one in the Vanderbilt Garden is 95/10½ft , two by the Capitol at East Lansing, Michigan, are 56/19½ft (at three feet) and 80/11ft, but none is dated, and growth will certainly be faster than in London. The Radnor Gardens tree is 65/11½ft, two feet bigger in circumference than any other in Britain. It had added 15in in the previous 23 years, which is slow. This suggests that it could have taken more than 100 years to have been ten feet round in 1967 and so to date from before 1860. At the least it surely predates the Sargent seed. Furthermore it is a graft at six feet on Southern Catalpa, with a good but very evident union between the smooth, flaking pink and brown rootstock and the craggy fissured dark grey of the scion-wood. So it was not a seedling. This does not affect the estimates of age above. But it does suggest that seedlings were not available and that Sargent's seed was not yet being grown, while raising the unanswerable question of where the scion-wood came from.

Northern Catalpa endures severe winters in much of its natural range and colder still in many parts where it is much planted today around the Canadian border. In

Northern Catalpa (*Catalpa speciosa*): Royal Botanic Gardens, Kew, Surrey

France it was reported to survive a frost of -26°C, so it is extremely hardy. But these trees enjoy long, hot summers, and in Britain we rarely have one. The mild winters of Scotland are not enough in the absence of hot summers for the tree to be grown except very rarely north of the English Midlands and all the bigger trees are to the south of that region. A tree did survive in Edinburgh for at least 36 years but seems to have died soon after. The biggest northerly tree now is 11/6½ft in Mourne Park, County Down. Of the rest, few are noteworthy but one at Broadlands, Hampshire, was 20/9½ft in 1986; one at Aldershot in Hampshire beside the church near Manor Park is 40/7ft; one in the American Garden at Bicton, Devon, is 55/6ft and one planted in 1900 at Bisterne, Hampshire, is 56/9ft. There are good flowering trees in several London parks and a few suburbs, and a notable planting alongside Southwark Cathedral.

KATSURA TREE

Cercidiphyllum japonicum

This tree is not only elegant and attractive in general, but is botanically eccentric and enigmatic. Its origins are obscure, as it is only distantly related to any other plant. On one interpretation of its floral structure it is a relic of a whole Order of plants not connected with any other known. More usually it is held to be in a Family of its own but within the Order *Magnoliales* and perhaps in the Family *Magnoliaceae*, but equally likely to be in the Trochodendron Family or nearer to it, within the same Order. It is, in any case, extraordinarily primitive, and although a broad-leaf tree, it has, like the *Trochodendron*, *Tetrecentron* and *Drimys*, the wood structure of a softwood, with the tracheides which predate the evolution of the vessels and fibres of the hardwoods. Even then, this wood is said by some to be more primitive than that of conifers, and also of the Ginkgo.

In Late Cretaceous times, the genus *Cercidiphyllum* was widespread across Asia, Europe and North America until late Tertiary times. It was known to Siebold in Japan before 1850, probably only from foliage samples, but even he did not manage to bring the tree out of the closed country in either of the boatloads of plants he succeeded in spiriting away. It was only after the opening up of Japan to the west in 1854 that the Katsura was introduced to the United States, by the American Ambassador, Thomas Hogg, in 1865.

It was first received in Britain when seed was sent, presumably by Sargent of the Arnold Arboretum, to Kew in 1881. Little or nothing is recorded of the early growth in Britain because, by some mischance or oversight, it has no entry in Elwes and Henry's great work. However they must have seen it on several of the estates they visited after 1900. Early growth is often rapid, so the specimens would not have been of negligible size.

There are very few dated plantings and the oldest is a group of five planted in 1905 by a trout lake at Frensham Hall, Shottermill, Surrey. In 1966 the best of these were 56/6ft and 65/4ft. At Battlesby near Perth, 14 were planted at about the same time as those, but it is known only that this was after 1901 and it could have been well after. The best now is 56/4ft. The tree remained scarce until after 1930 and judging by the growth of trees from after that time, there are very few likely, on grounds of size, to be of earlier planting. Until recently, Westonbirt could be said to have been the headquarters of the tree in Britain. Where the 14 at Battlesby were the biggest planting until then, Westonbirt soon had clumps in all parts of the Arboretum and Silk Wood, and there are more than fifty sizeable trees, almost as many as all the other gardens combined. These groups and a few single trees include no trees dated before 1931 and only a few clumps known to date from 1935 and 1936.

The Katsura was regarded as endemic to Japan and the biggest broad-leaf tree there until Ernest Wilson found it in west China in 1910. Some specimens he found were the biggest broad-leaf trees in Asia, presumably outside the tropical rainforests. Wilson measured one tree 130ft tall and another 55ft round. He thought the Chinese form was distinguishable from the Japanese by several minor details and by growing normally on a single stem. He named it var. *sinense*, but in cultivation and on later examination of foliage specimens from each country, they are not now

Katsura Tree (*Cercidiphyllum japonicum*): Benmore, Argyll

regarded as separable. Since the array at Westonbirt includes many trees with single stems right to the tip and many in which the leaves turn bright red in autumn (another feature given to the Chinese form) a rumour developed that the Westonbirt trees were of Chinese origin, but there is no evidence known to confirm that.

In North America, the distribution in general and of best growth and specimens, closely parallels those of the Dawn Redwood, with trees seen from Montreal to Georgia, but very few on the Gulf Coast, and the finest plainly from Massachusetts to Pennsylvania. These include trees of 90/6ft at Smith College, Northampton, Massachussetts; of 85/10ft at the Barnes Arboretum, Pennysylvania, and a vast bush, planted in 1898 in the Morris Arboretum, Pennysylvania and 82/20ft at one foot. This shows a liking for hot summers with high humidity and plenty of rain, but not in excess, and an ability to tolerate very cold winters. In Britain, where no summers are as hot or long, and no winters as cold but summer rain is normal, the Katsura should be able to grow moderately well in all parts, and this is the case. There are trees to 46/5ft + 5 (two stems) as far north as Novar, near Dingwall, Easter Ross; to 66/4ft in the dry of East Anglia at Sandringham, and to 70/6ft + 6 at Ashbourne Hotel near Cork, in the cool, mild wet of southwestern Ireland.

At Westonbirt, the tallest is in Victory Glade, a forked tree, 82/5ft + 4; a tree single stemmed to the tip is beside Circular Drive, 70/5ft, and another towards the eastern end of Main Drive is 70/6ft. A group on Morley Ride, planted in 1935 has trees of 66/3ft and 56/5ft. A single tree by the Visitor Centre was planted in 1969 and in 19 years had grown to 42/3ft. In the Hillier Arboretum, one of two very similar trees planted in 1954 was 50/5ft in 1991. Equally rapid growth is shown by a sturdy, single-boled tree towards Battleston Hill in the RHS's garden at Wisley, Surrey. Now more than 52/6ft, this was 36/3ft in 1968 and so will date from about 1950.

Some other large specimens include a forked tree by the Mansion Pond at Wakehurst Place, Sussex, 62/7ft + 6; a low-branched tree at Hergest Croft, Herefordshire, 82/7ft at three feet; a good tree at Minterne, Dorset, 52/6ft and another at Leny House, Perthshire, 60/6ft. In the garden at Etal Manor, Northumberland two trees stand adjacent in a glade, both with single stems but one, 50/6ft, has an inherently sprouty trunk, and the other, 60/5ft has an exemplary clean one. I suggested that annual use of secateurs would ensure a very superior matching pair.

TURKISH HAZEL

Corylus colurna

It may cause surprise, not to say alarm, in some quarters, to see a hazel in the list of contents of a work devoted to fine, big specimen trees. The American hazel is an unashamed shrub, and the European Common Hazel is little better, but from the Balkans eastward, through the Himalayas to China there are hazels of respectable stature. They are classed as three full species, but they are little more than the Turkish Hazel differing only in fiddling little details. The Turkish Hazel itself is named less from its occurrence in the modern Turkey of Asia Minor, but from being native to the old Turkish Empire in Former Yugoslavia and the Balkans. It is found in Asia Minor and in small stands on the southern flanks of the Caucasus Mountains to Georgia.

The botanist Clusius, Charles l'Ecluse, introduced it to western Europe from Istanbul in 1582 and the first trees in Britain are thought to have been grown by John Rea by 1665. The English name may also owe something to imports by the Turkey merchants in Aleppo who may have sent nuts or plants around that time. The oldest trees are at Syon Park, Brentford, which have never been given a date but from their size in 1908 and today may have been planted around 1830, but had they grown in youth as some are now growing, it could have been nearer 1850. None other is known with a date before 1900. Since there is no sign of the other five trees listed by Elwes in 1908, it could be a tree with a short life, but the big trees today are mostly looking very healthy and only three have died or died back since I have known them.

The small number of reasonably large specimens suggests that few were planted in the last century, but since 1900 it has been quite popular and since 1950 has been adopted by municipal planters in streets and parks. In this they may have been inspired by the excellent trees to be seen in many cities and parks in eastern North America. A big recent street planting lines both sides of a main street in Letchworth, and most parks in London now have a number of trees. It seems to prefer the hotter summers and low rainfall of the eastern parts of Britain, for while frequent from Dorset through Yorkshire to Edinburgh, it is very scarce, if present at all, west of Herefordshire and only two have been noted in Ireland. The specimen furthest north is a far-flung outlier at Dundonnell in Wester Ross. It is 100 miles further north than the next most northerly seen, in the University Botanic Garden in Dundee, and it is in a far western area of cool summers and very high rainfall. It prefers not to notice and from a 1956 planting it is 26/3ft in 1991. There are several in southern Scotland, in both the east and the west.

It is easy to see why the tree is coming into fashion. In winter its flaky brown and grey bark is unusual and its neatly conic crown of sturdy branches, level in the lower crown and rising to make a narrow top, is attractive and keeps clear of street

Turkish Hazel (*Corylus colurna*): Syon House, Brentford

furniture. It has big catkins, extending and yellow very early in spring, usually before March, and in summer a leafy crown of dark green, shiny substantial foliage with dark red petioles. It is not a great show in autumn, but it grows with considerable vigour on almost any soil, including a chalky one, and with paving over its roots.

The finest specimen is in Syon Park, Brentford, on the north of the lake. It has a broad, rounded top now, but a splendid clean trunk for 15ft and is 70/10ft. One in the wilderness by Church Walk is 60/7½ft and another in the Rose Garden is 52/6ft. Two more may be as old as these. One in the northern border in University Parks, Oxford, is a broad-crowned tree with many low branches and is 60/9ft, and the other is in the Abbey Garden at Bury St Edmunds. This has two stems and has long borne the label telling us that it is the American hazel, *Corylus americana*, which is a shrubby little bush, small in all its parts. This veteran is 60/9ft + 6½. A 1900 planting at Colesbourne in Gloucestershire, has one tree 75/5ft and another nearby probably of the same age was 75/7ft in 1984. Hergest Croft, Herefordshire, has the tallest, in 1985, which was 88/6½ft and Brocklesby Park in Lincolnshire had one 84/6½ft in 1977. In Wakehurst Place one survived the gale in the Shrubbery near the Mansion and is 70/5ft. At Avondale in County Wicklow a tree by the path to the house is 75/3½ft and of fairly recent planting.

In the botanic gardens the trees are liable to come under expert scrutiny, and one in the Royal Botanic Garden, Edinburgh, has recently changed its identity to the Himalayan form now called *Corylus jacquemontii* and is 75/7ft but one Turkish Hazel is 72/6ft. Not far away, at Smeaton House near Haddington, two in the Park are 60/5½ft and 50/6½ft. At Owston near Doncaster, one was 40/7½ft in 1977.

Of the younger specimens, my favourite, at Kew, is as near perfection as can be required. Unfortunately its label lacks a date, but in 1979 it was 30/2ft and 12 years later it was 40/3½ft. It is on the lawn a little south of the Palm House. At Forde Abbey near Chard but in Dorset, a tree planted in 1947 was 60/5ft by 1988. One of the same date in the University Botanic Garden at Oxford was a little slow to start and was 36/2½ft when 31 years old but has done better since and when 42 years old it was 46/4ft.

DOVE-TREE

Davidia involucrata

The discovery, re-discovery, naming and introduction of the Dove-tree is the most romantic story in the world of trees, and has a sting in its tail. It is pure bathos that this tree has been given a demotic popular name, which I refuse to repeat, when it has two good names, Dove-tree and Ghost-tree, and a third even better, Davidia, commemorating its discoverer who was one of the most enterprising and skilled of all the plant collectors.

Jean Pierre Armand David was a Basque, born in France in 1826. In 1851 he was ordained as a priest in the Lazarist brotherhood and in 1862 he was sent to their mission in Peking, as a teacher. In his spare time, he collected zoological, botanical and geological specimens and sent them, with studies on other subjects, to the Museum d'Histoire Naturelle in Paris, as requested before he went to China. The material was so diverse, beautifully preserved and new to science that the Museum Director, Henri Milne-Edwards, implored the Superior General of the Lazarists to allow him time devoted to collecting. He was allowed to make three journeys, one to Mongolia, one to the Tibetan border and one to Central China. He discovered the deer named after him, 1500 new species of plant, and the Giant Panda. This was on the second expedition, in Sichuan, and he even managed to have a live panda shipped out from this exceedingly remote, inland area, to arrive in Paris in good order. It was on this journey, based on Mupin, near Tibet, from 1868 to 1869 that he discovered the Davidia. He sent herbarium specimens from the tree in flower to Paris and they caused a minor sensation and were the type specimen for naming the tree, *Davidia involucrata*. But he sent no seed.

No one else saw a tree for 19 years, when Augustine Henry, in the same manner as David, was given permission by the Customs Service with whom he was a doctor specialising in medicinal herbs, to take two big tours at the request of Kew. One took him north of the Middle Yangtse and the other south. It was on this one, in Hupeh, where the border with Szechuan curves from east to south, that Henry came upon a single Davidia in full flower, in 1888. He could not return for the fruit, so, again, only dried specimens of flowers and foliage arrived at Kew. Henry's tree was 1000 miles east of Mupin. Sir Harry Veitch of the Royal Exotic Nursery, Chelsea, had refused in 1893 to join Kew in sending a collector to China, but after eventually seeing Henry's specimen, agreed that this was worth the risk and expense to bring back. At Kew, Ernest Wilson, then 22, was chosen for the task in 1899.

By this time, Pere David had been back in Peking for 30 years. The location of his tree was unknown, and he was in his last year. The only way now was to find Henry's tree in Hupeh while Henry was still in China, although 1000 miles from it, at Simao in Yunnan. Wilson arrived at Hong Kong in June 1899, left his equipment there and went via Tonking, the Red River, on small native boats and sedan-chair to arrive at Henry's house in October. Henry was out collecting and returned next morning and spent some days in instructing Wilson in collecting techniques, Chinese botany and Chinese ways. He sketched on a postcard a map of where the tree was. The map showed the Yangtse across the top, three named districts, the Kuan River running south with an unmarked line parallel to it, one village and three houses – in an area the size of France, with no scale, and a vaguely placed 'Davidia'.

Wilson set off back to Hong Kong to collect his gear, round to Shanghai; and 1000 miles up the Yangtse to Ichang, arriving in February 1900. After practice runs there, he bought a river-boat to ascend further to Badong where he took on six armed guards because of bandit activity and on April 25th came to Ma-huang-po where they remembered Henry. He even found a few residents who remembered where his Dove-tree was, and they took him the two mile walk to the spot. There was the stump, near a house built the year before, with its roof made from the Davidia timber. At first, Wilson resolved to go to David's tree at Mupin but did some local collecting first and three weeks later found a 50ft tree in full flower. He then decided to comb a hundred mile radius for more and found ten. He carried on collecting, returning for the fruit in the autumn and sent large quantities to Veitch's which arrived in the early spring of 1901. Wilson returned to see them in April 1902 and not one had germinated, but in May he helped to pot up 13,000 plants.

But, after all this effort, these were not the first. Unknown to Wilson and Veitch, Paul Farges had sent among his collections in the Ichang area, 37 seeds to Vilmorin's Nursery in 1897 and one of these had germinated in 1899. Botanically, the interesting part is that all these trees differ from David's tree, which is the type specimen, and has soft white down on the under surface of the leaf. These have a shiny smooth under-surface, as well as much shorter peduncles and more purple smoother bark. They also grow faster. They are the variety *vilmoriniana* and are evidently the form in the east of the range, south of the Yangtse whereas the type is restricted to the western part, north and west of that river. Wilson did eventually introduce David's type tree on his second journey from 1903 to 1905 during which he travelled 13,000 miles and included the mountains of the Tibetan border.

Specimens of the Vilmorin variety outnumber those of the type in gardens today by about five to one, with the type nearly restricted to the gardens of prominent horticulturists who dealt with Veitch's early in this century. Plants seen for sale today are always the variety, and a few early plants of the type were grafts on to Vilmorin rootstock. The type can show bright autumn colours, orange and crimson, occasionally, while the leaves are usually bigger. Both have a reputation for delaying flowering for many years but the first flowers on the 1902 seedlings opened in 1911 and the single 1899 tree at Vilmorin's flowered in 1906. It is probable that flowers arise on arching laterals rather than more upright stems, and the crowns of young trees are rather fastigiate for several years. The leaf shape is more variable in the variety and some are found, particularly in North America, with ovate-lanceolate foliage. At Birr Castle, they succeed in raising cuttings from strong sprouts on the trunks.

Among the type trees, one of the best is in Loop Walk, Westonbirt Arboretum. Oddly this is not the one known to be from Wilson seed of 1904, which was nearby in Clay island and died in the 1976 drought, but a much bigger tree whose origin was unknown to Jackson when he wrote the Catalogue in 1926. It also showed signs of distress early in the drought and was given regular bowser-loads of water. Its crown died back badly but has regrown well since and the tree is now 80/6½ft. At Tregrehan in Cornwall, a low-branched tree, measurable at around three feet, was 50/6½ft in 1971 and is now 46/9½ft, which shows exceptional growth, but seen in leaf in 1991 it was allotted by David Hunt of Kew to the variety. One in the wall garden at Heligan also has low branches. Measured at two feet, it is 40/9½ft. At Minterne, in Dorset, two trees planted in 1929 are 72/5½ft and 46/5ft. A shapely tree at Fosbury Manor in Wiltshire is 70/5ft. In north-east Scotland, one planted at Blackhill, Morayshire, in 1931 was 52/5½ft in 1986. A few other gardens have big bushy multi-stemmed trees, as in Wakehurst Place, Sussex, and Penjerrick in Cornwall, but all the other trees are fairly young and small.

The variety *vilmoriniana* is just as bad at making big bushes and the best real tree is one of two at Trehane in Cornwall, 56/9ft near another 50/6½ft. One at Werrington Park, also in Cornwall, is 62/8ft and one at Tregothnan is 46/6½ft. At Hergest Croft, an original tree from the 1902 seedlings, planted in 1903 is 52/6½ft. At Ashbourne, County Cork, a tree with a damaged top is 7½ft round, and in Northern Ireland, one at Rowallane, County Down is 33/7ft. In north-east Scotland a tree at Crathes castle, Kincardineshire, is 33/6ft at three feet, and well south of that, a fine tree at Dalmeny near Edinburgh is 46/6ft. At Bodnant, Gwynedd, one in Chapel Walk is 52/6ft, presumably of the same age as one the type nearby planted in 1908 which is 52/6ft at three feet. At Stourhead, by the gate, one of the variety

Dove-tree (*Davidia involucrata*):
its origins are in China

is 52/6ft. At Warren House, once part of Veitch's Coombe Wood nursery where the Wilson plants were raised, there is only one of this variety and this is only 33/3½ft. The four of the type have done no better, the largest being 50/3ft. Despite the two forms being the same size at Bodnant, and very little different at Warren House, the young trees generally show superior growth on *vilmoriniana*, as at Vyne House near Bristol where both were planted in 1948 and the variety was 42/3ft 7in in 1984 when the type was 23/2ft 6in.

A big tree at Dartington Hall was a 1902 original and 50/7½ft at one foot in 1968 but the crown died soon after and today a basal sprout is 30/2½ft. At Birr Castle a tree with a yellowish underside to the leaf was grown as var. *laeta,* but died after 1966. A graft from it is growing in the National Botanic Garden in Glasnevin and is 42/5½ft. The name *laeta* is now regarded as a synonym for *vilmoriniana.*

TASMANIAN BLUE GUM

Eucalyptus globulus

Hard winters in 1962 and since have made the Tasmanian Blue Gum of historic interest only as a spot plant in municipal park annual bedding schemes, in Great Britain. But not in Ireland where it is the fastest growing tree of all and where there are some very big trees. This is of great interest climatically, demonstrating dramatically the warming effect of a hundred miles and less of the Irish Sea. For there are only two trees known to survive in Cornwall, in Falmouth, where before 1962 there were dozens of good specimens there, and a few in Devon. Until 1987 there were six trees, to 80/8ft by the road to the shore at Abersoch, but they were all killed.

So now there is no established Blue Gum in Wales. Yet within sight of Snowdonia across the water, Blue Gums abound in gardens in Bray and Killiney and soon after planting they are over 100ft tall. There are none apparent north of Dublin until much further north where similar trees grow between Belfast and Strangford Loch, while the biggest of all is north again, in County Antrim. And, nearer Britain, the Glens of the Isle of Man grow 100ft trees also. This is an extraordinary occurrence and is due entirely to the warming of the destructive eastern winds as they cross the narrow Irish Sea.

The Tasmanian Blue Gum grows in southern Tasmania, where it was discovered in 1792, and also in a small area of Victoria. In the land of giant gums it is a minor

Tasmanian Blue Gum (*Eucalyptus globulus*): juvenile and adult foliage

player, said to be only 180ft tall, but it puts up an astonishing performance in warm countries and was soon the tallest tree in most of them, to 250–280ft. It was introduced to California in 1856 and sold on a large scale by a Mr Nolan of Oakland who received seed in 1861. It is a wonderful tree for the coast and the southern Coast Range. So wonderful that Mr Nolan will not lightly be forgiven by Californians. Flowering and seeding without pause it has swamped the native vegetation for hundreds of miles and is ineradicable. Even as far north as the Noyo River, the bank below the US 101 bridge was a silvery blue mass of seedlings growing six or eight feet a year when I saw it in 1975 and must be assumed to be a forest 120ft tall now, unless steps have been taken. On the Campus at Berkeley, a close plantation made in 1877 has dominant trees 210ft tall and a singleton outside is 160/23ft.

It was introduced to Britain in 1853 when Mueller sent seed from Mount Butler to many European botanic gardens. The biggest here today was planted in 1857 and is surely of this origin. Memories of better days include a tree put out as a spot plant in Ventnor Park from 1969 seed which was 63/5ft nine years later and one at Sidbury Manor, Devon, despite having been badly broken back to 26ft was 52/2ft when ten years from planting.

The 1857 tree in Antrim is at Saint Macnissi School at Garron Point. It forks from the base and was 75/13ft at four feet in 1911 and a great tree, 102/25ft, in 1982 looking good for many more years. At the Eccles Hotel at Glengarriff, County Cork, a tree which was 138/19ft in 1968 is much in need of a revisit. Seedlings from it were springing up at six feet a year. At Clonmannon, County Wicklow, a tree dating from about 1890 was 52/4ft when 15 years old and now it is over 100 years old it is 111/15ft. At Rossdohan, County Kerry, a self-sown tree was 46/2ft when five years old. At Glencormac in County Wicklow, one of a group is 140/13ft and another is 124/17ft while above the car park one 92/12ft has 33ft of clear trunk.

In Barony Glen, Isle of Man, one was 111/10ft in 1978 when one in Laxey Glen was 120/13ft when 58 years old. In the garden at Ballywalter, County Down, one of four big trees was 115/17ft in 1982. There is one in County Dublin in Dr Robinson's amazing garden at Earl's Cliff on Howth head. Planted in 1970, it was 50/4ft in 1989.

This species is one of the few that is readily recognisable. Its eight inch sickle-shaped leaves are like those of the excellent Mountain gum, *E. dalrympleana*, which is hardy in the south and west of England and Scotland and grows as fast, but that has small flowers and capsules in threes, while the Blue Gum has very big solitary top-shaped fruit bloomed bright blue-white. The ground beneath any tree more than a few years old is liberally strewn with these unmistakable indicators.

BEECH

Fagus sylvatica

Few sights in the tree world can be more inspiring and beautiful than the sunshine on the smooth, silvery trunk of a beech, towering through the brilliant green of its foliage newly unfolded. Nor, in Britain, is any woodland more grand than that of a well-thinned stand of old beech, the apparently cylindric boles rising maybe 60ft without a branch, whether in late spring beneath translucent green crowns; in autumn beneath yellow, orange and russet, or in winter with the colour on the floor and the crowns bare.

There is an unexpected amount of interest attached to both the growth and the ecology of such a common, familiar tree. It was a latecomer in the post Ice Ages recolonising of England, perhaps crossing along the last parts of the chalk ridge, and had time to spread only as far as south-east Wales and north perhaps to the Vale of York. It has been planted abundantly to the farthest corners of these Isles and withstands any degree of cold to which it is subjected, and a great deal of exposure at height. The form is almost always branchy and poor in the west and stands of high quality stems are largely confined to within the natural range, on the South Downs and Cotswolds. But a few good stands and several excellent individuals grow from Yorkshire through southern Scotland to the Firth of Moray. The best stand was at the foot of the South Downs near Arundel at Slinden. This was planted in 1730 and underthinned for 200 years. Then a heavy thinning, leaving only the best stems, to spread their crowns and yield top quality seed, made it a wood of remarkable beauty with long, smooth, clean boles for 60ft on trees to 135/10ft. It was blown down in October 1987.

Growing so well on chalk downs, even exposed at 740ft at Chanctonbury Ring, Beech were often assumed to need chalk or limestone soils which dried out rapidly. In fact, neither is true. Many miles of tall Beech hedges line the roads on Exmoor and Dartmoor and huge shelterbelts make much of the landscapes in the Southern Uplands of Peebles and Roxburghshire, all are on acid soils. Those in Devon are often peaty, with ladder-fern, cinquefoil and other acid-loving plants as ground flora. Many beechwoods in the Weald and in Wales have whortleberry beneath, or are being invaded by rhododendron.

The Beech is a very thirsty tree. It is happy on these acid sites because it has plenty of water in well-drained soil or on banks beside ditches. It cannot stand water-logged or continually wet soils, but on dry soils its roots will penetrate powerfully to a depth where it can find water. In chalk, which is the greatest aquifer and is always fissured, the roots go down to where the fissures are full of water. On sands, they go down to the water-table and on the light, acid sands in the New Forest they fan out above, but will not enter, the clay lenses or beds. Where these are not far down, the trees are vulnerable to being thrown by the wind. Hence the familiar hugely spreading but thin root-plate standing over a pool of water. In years of severe drought, like 1976–7 when the water-tables sank many feet, Beech were dying from drought in many areas, and were still dying five years later. This was seized upon as evidence for the absurd idea that acid-rain was killing them, although other Beech in every neighbourhood were, and still are, growing luxuriantly.

The Beech bears more shade than any other native tree except the Holly and the Yew. Beech can grow up under any species but none can grow up under Beech. Therefore the climax wood will, in the absence of other factors, everywhere be Beech. But the inability to grow in wet clays precludes Beech from replacing Common Oak and Hornbeam in clay vales. It will form the climax only on light, well-drained soils – if the Yew has not got there first in numbers, and if the soil is not so light and dry that it is a heath of birch, sallow and pine – and the Beech cannot compete.

The annual pattern of growth is unusual and shared by some oaks; the big terminal bud erupts into a long shoot – one and a half to two feet – in two weeks in early May, and hangs there, drooping and grey with silky hairs, static until July when its terminal bud shoots out an additional one to one and a half feet. By September the new shoot has straightened. This means that summer rain is important or the roots need to be near the water-table.

Another unusual feature, and also shared to some extent with some oaks and the Hornbeam, is that the shoots of young trees bear juvenile foliage, indistinguishable from mature shoot leaves until the winter, when they remain unshed and dark brown until spring. This is exploited in the use of Beech hedges for winter shelter and colour, but there is more to it than there may seem to be. There is a 'juvenile cone' about six feet across at the base and tapering to a point about nine feet up, within which all the leaves, whatever the origin or age of the shoot, behave in this way. This can be seen clearly where a hedge is allowed to grow beyond the 'cone' either upwards or laterally. The projecting shoots stand out quite bare in winter. If an old trunk should grow a low sprout, as is usual on the Fernleaf Beech, those sprouts or any part of them within the 'cone' retain their leaves. In these cases, the 'cone' above six feet or so will all be within the width of the trunk, so shoots at these heights will shed all their leaves. This was elucidated by a Danish botanist with the memorable name of Count Muckadell di Schiaffalitsky.

Most beechwoods have a long history of management. In the Chiltern Hills this was, in the far past, dysgenic – the best trees were harvested and the misshapen and inferior trees were left to yield the seed for regeneration and the quality of the stands deteriorated sharply. Some of the generally very poor quality of stands in the south-west of England and the west generally may be from this cause, too. In the Cotswolds and South Downs areas it was usual to thin out the poor trees early and to keep at least some of the best until they had shed seed. In either case, no trees grew their full span of years. So, despite the tree being native, there are very few woods with a full range of ages and the senile and decrepit trees are in parkland or a few corners of neglected wood. A well-known exception is Burnham Beeches, Farnham Royal, where the trees were all pollarded about 200 years ago and have, for a long time now, been left uncut until they collapse.

It is evident, however, that beech is not a long-lived tree and although there are known exceptions, the normal span is about 250 years. Unlike the Oak, which takes an inordinate time to die, the beech does it over a weekend. Several species of fungus are usually established in decaying parts of the butt and roots, and at some point these tip the balance, and a tree seemingly in full health on Friday has collapsed into a pile of rotting wood by Monday. With honey-fungus, all the foliage will die in a summer week and the tree stands bare. All this is the natural end for a beech, but that has not deterred proponents of the Acid Rain is Killing Our Trees crusaders from publishing pictures of dead beeches captioned 'killed by acid rain'. With the normal cut-off of 250 years, and a large number not lasting as long, it follows that the trees from the great era of beech planting of 1730-1780 are at, or nearing the end of their natural span, so that in many landscapes of that period, dead Beeches are a common sight.

All of which makes it very hazardous to cite a list of the biggest, and therefore oldest, specimens in any expectation that many will remain to be admired a few years hence. However, while knowing that the most thriving tree today can fall to pieces tomorrow, it is certain that a few at least will grow well for a long time yet, and the sizes which have been attained and the locations where it has been achieved, could be of interest even when the trees have gone. Although no maiden tree has been found lately as much as 23ft round, there are 16 over 20ft and 28 over 19ft, all very big Beeches, and those with clean boles of any notable length look absolutely massive. Not all 28 can be noted here, because, apart from the need to watch the boredom threshold, room must be made for the entry of some smaller trees which have other points of interest.

The prime stem, among the top half dozen of all hardwood trees, is on the north side of the A31 a quarter of a mile west of the Jermyn's Lane turn to the Hillier Arboretum west of Ampfield in Hampshire. It is 30ft down the shallow road bank and is now somewhat obscured in summer by seedling birches. It stood proud to be admired from passing holiday traffic until the 1987 gale spoilt it. It is 115/13ft and is as smooth and round as a factory chimney for 52ft, seeming a perfect cylinder, the slight taper that must be there offset by the eye's natural over-compensation for foreshortening by height. At 52ft the stem forked into two fairly close vertical stems, one of which was torn out at its origin. It must have been quite old, because it was written of well over a hundred years ago as the noted 'Blacksmith's Gun-barrel'. By good fortune, it was either spared or overlooked during the two wars.

Sydney Park in Bath has several superb stems of Beech. By the north-east entrance, one is 92/15½ft with 30ft clear, and by the southern entrance, one is 108/14½ft with 40ft clear. At Tottenham House in Savernake Forest, the best of several fine trees is 120/15ft with a single bole 56ft long, clear for 40ft. The biggest girth for a

Beech (*Fagus sylvatica*):
Pendogwm, Montgomery, Wales

maiden tree currently known is that of a tree in the Park at Tullynally Castle in County Westmeath, an altogether remarkable specimen. It is 132/22½ft and the massive bole continues about 60ft bearing moderately sized branches from 20ft. Another in the Park is 138/19½ft and one below the Castle is 120/20ft, both of similar shape. The next biggest are Penjerrick in Cornwall, near the garden gate, with many branches from near ground level and 75/22ft, and a hugely impressive tree near the northern gate to Mote Park, Maidstone, clear for 20ft and 105/22ft, while one at Yester House, Haddington, East Lothian has two other notable features. In a big wood near the river, it was probably planted in 1680 and would, in that case, be the oldest dated beech. It has grown rapidly, instead of falling to pieces, in the last 20 years, probably because it has gained much space from the collapse of neighbouring trees. In 1967 it was 20ft 2in round, and in 1987 it was 120/22ft with 20ft clear, smooth, silvery bole. Another of this size by the garden fence at Preston Hall in Midlothian is 100/22ft with a fine bole well into the crown.

The oldest dated trees are, another at Yester near the House, known to be from the 1680 planting and now a rather rough tree 85/19½ft; one of several in a 1690 avenue at Arniston Hall, Midlothian, now 85/20ft; one in a line at Broomhall, Fife, planted in 1730, now 120/17ft; and a superb tree in a wood by Blair Drummond House, Perthshire, from a 1750 planting and now 108/20ft. In 1972, a tree dated 1717 was at Kilkerran House, Ayrshire, 98/17½ft. Probably older than any of these but undated is a vast tree by Loch Fyne at Ardkinglas House, reputed to have been the gathering place for the clans and now 85/20ft with low branches. The 'Five Men of Moidart' standing out on the edge of grazing-land by the Loch should have an origin tied to Scottish history to go with such a peculiar site and the name; probably an early 18th century planting. The biggest two are 17ft round. A tree in a roadside copse near Cawdor Castle, at Earl's Mill, was noted long ago and, now 65/19½ft, it must be very old.

Some other trees over 20ft round are: in the garden of 'Powis' in Sidmouth, 80/21½ft; at Knightshayes in South Park, 92/20½ft; at Jardine Hall, Dumfries, beside the drive, 80/20½ft with a good bole; and by the Den at Durris House, Deeside, 98/20ft. Some other slightly smaller trees with outstanding boles are: at Panmure, Angus, by the Old Gate, 92/17ft clear for 20ft; a superb tree outside the garden at Haddo House, Aberdeenshire, 75/19ft; by the Lake Walk at Birr Castle, County Offaly, 105/18½ft, clear for 15ft; the best of several similar at Tynninghame, East Lothian, 115/18½ft clear about 30ft; at Glendoick, Perth, 102/19ft; at Newbattle Abbey, Midlothian, 95/19ft; at Tal-y-Garn, Glamorgan, 92/19ft; at Killinchrassie, Tayside, 105/19½ft with eight feet clear in the garden and, more branchy, 88/20ft in the Broom Park; outside the pinetum at Abbeyleix, County Leix, 130/19ft.

The tallest are one in a wood near Hallyburton House, Coupar Angus, 150/16ft, near another 105/18½ft; at Beaufort Castle, Hexham, 144/18ft and at Ebworth near Stroud in the Cotswolds, 138/11½ft, beside a tree of 93/16ft which has low branches spreading 100ft. A superb tree outside the wall-garden at Conon House, Easter Ross, is 130/14ft with a smooth bole to a great height, and at Stourhead one by Obelisk Ride below the house is 130/17ft.

A few old beeches have branches layered at a distance, some then sending up vertical stems. The best known last century is that at Newbattle Abbey, of which the original trunk has long decayed away, and surrounding stems are nine and seven feet round. At Tregrehan, Cornwall, the main stem is 60/14ft. At Kilravock Castle, Nairn, the main stem is 92/17ft. 'The Wooing Beech' at Sandon Park, Staffordshire, is 80/14ft and a layered beech at Mount Congreve near Waterford, is 85/16ft. An extraordinary old tree on a mound at Pollok near Glasgow, rests its branches all round the mound and is 22ft round at six inches.

The Beech hedge for a third of a mile along the A93 at Meikleour between Perth and Blairgowrie is the highest clipped hedge in the world, trimmed up one side to 85ft and 100–105ft tall. The trees are three to four feet apart and a short length has a second row across a small ditch. No forester would 'sheugh', or heel in, trees in that way making suspect the story of the origin of the hedge, if not the date, 1745. The trees were said to be ready for planting in the wood behind when the workers were called away to kill and be killed by fellow Scotsmen in the mayhem of that year.

FERNLEAF BEECH

Fagus sylvatica 'Asplenifolia' (plate 5)

This graft-chimaera of continental origin has its outer tissues derived from a form with deeply laciniate, slender-acuminate leaves and interior tissues of normal beech. Some epicormic buds from the normal Beech are often started into growth by damage to the crown, particularly by any cutting back. Many of these bear ordinary Beech foliage, but others are affected to varying degrees by the fernleaf tissue. They often bear some leaves lobed like oak-leaves and others more deeply cut. Undamaged shoots in the most common form of the several grown, grow successively more slender and deeply cut leaves as extension growth ends in midsummer, the last ones being mere strips, unlobed and like very slender willow leaves. The crown is notably dense, not only because the shoots are close and slender but also because the tree has a great tendency to sprout fine shoots from the branches and the bole. These evidently arise nearly always from the external tissues as they are generally fully fernleafed.

The probable original tree is at Knaphill Nursery, Surrey, by Anthony Waterer's Walk. It was planted in 1826 and is 72/14ft with a good trunk holding a big, domed crown. None is bigger at the standard five feet. A splendid tree at Tal-y-Garn in Glamorgan is 85/13½ft. The tallest is a tree at Busbridge Lakes House near Godalming, Surrey, which is 110/13½ft and the next is 105/10½ft at Hallyburton House, Coupar Angus, Perthshire. A fine, domed tree at the Holbourne Museum in Bath is 88/13ft. At Errol House, Perthshire, a good tree is 80/13½ft. At Lydham House, Shropshire, is a tree 82/13ft.

The only avenue seen is one by the drive through woodland to St Martin's House near Perth with seven trees each side, the biggest 9½ft round and some 80ft tall.

DAWYCK BEECH

Fagus sylvatica 'Dawyck'

The estate of Dawyck, near Peebles, was owned by the noted family of Nasmyth until around 1900, when it was bought by F.R.S. Balfour. In about 1860, a wood of beech had been planted on the hill behind. Among the young trees, one was found which was growing strictly fastigiate and was dug up and replanted by one of the gates into the garden near the house. In 1908, Balfour showed the tree to Elwes or Henry, who measured it in 1912 and found it was 48/4ft 2in and was convinced that it was much older than Balfour's estimate of a planting date around 1860. Today, with many young trees to measure, we would accept that date with no qualms, and it agrees with the story. About 1907, Balfour distributed grafts to Kew and to some of his garden-owning friends, and also to the Hesse Nurseries in Hanover. But in Britain the tree was said not to be in the trade until Hillier's was selling it in 1937, and their first public planting was of that date round the Basingstoke bypass.

The Dawyck original was 88/8½ft in 1984 but the tallest was one in Wakehurst Place which could have been a Balfour gift to Lord Wakehurst in 1907. It was 100/8ft before it was blown down in 1987. Another of this origin may be Lord Ducie's at Tortworth Court which was 92/7½ft in 1980, and two at Exbury at the approach to a bridge may have been a gift to Lord Rothschild in that year. They were 80/8ft and 72/7½ft in 1987. The Balfour tree at Kew was planted in 1910 near the Azalea Dell end of the beech collection and was 85/5½ft in 1984. Lord Ducies' great rival and friend George Holford at Westonbirt would be expected to have acquired an early specimen but the oldest known there was planted in 1922 near the old Main Gates and moved in 1928 to the Willesley Drive where it is now 90/6ft. The four big trees in Nymans Garden before the 1987 gale were not quite big enough to have been early Balfour grafts, and the two surviving in the Magnolia Garden are now 88/5½ft and 80/5½ft.

Dawych Beech (*Fagus sylvatica* 'Dawyck'): Thorp Perrow, Yorkshire

An imposing group of trees at St John's College, Cambridge, is made up of two in St John's Road, 75/4½ft and 66/6ft and two in Bridge Street, 72/6ft and 72/5ft. Belvidere in Buckinghamshire has a fine tree, 90/5ft in 1990.

The Dawyck Beech is sufficiently uniform to make a formal line or avenue but not too strictly formal as its outer shoots often curve out and down from the crown a little untidily. An avenue at Stowe School is highly effective with eleven trees each side and the best now 62/5ft. Another happy use of the tree is to utilise its formal shape with its foliage of the common woodland beech to mark the change from woodland to designed garden without the contrast being too stark. It is also a good alternative to the Lombardy Poplar, and with superior foliage and autumn colour, as a group of spire-crowned trees in a glade or clearing, or, as at Exbury, to mark the approach to a bridge.

It is a pity that the general public so seldom sees that this tree is not a Lombardy Poplar. I once spent many minutes trying to convince some builders lunching in a garden that they were sitting under two fine Dawyck Beeches. I made no progress until I managed to find a few beech-nuts growing on their Poplar. There is a fine Dawyck planted in the apex of the triangle where the A31 begins its life as a spur from the A3 to the Hog's Back outside Guildford. It is very prominent, now 62/5ft, and will date from around 1938, but I have heard it described as a Poplar a few times and never by its true name.

PURPLE BEECH

Fagus sylvatica 'Purpurea'

Astronomers have their theoretical, and probably actual, black holes, bodies of such unimaginable density that even light cannot escape from their gravitational pull. It pours in but none ever comes out. The arboreal world has its own black holes and the biggest are called 'Purple Beeches'. These light-sinks absorb good daylight and return nothing, since black, even if stained a little with a muddy sort of purple, cannot be counted as 'light'. In the generally low light levels of this country, these are the archetypal blots on the landscape. It is inevitable, it seems, that the few trees that have a positively malign effect on their surroundings should be the most popular for public plantings, so churchyards, war-memorials and village greens are deep in the gloom of Purple Beeches, aided at lower levels by the shapeless Pissard's Plum. It is equally to be expected that where levels of light are lowest, as in Scotland, this beech should be particularly common in its worst forms. One estate in Aberdeenshire, which I prefer not to specify more closely, has a long curving approach planted each side with what I think must be 'Swat Magret', the blackest of them all.

Purple Beech (*Fagus sylvatica* 'Purpurea'): Coole Park, County Clare

The village of Bramdean on the A272 in Hampshire is a pretty enough place to see in winter, but it should be avoided in high summer. About 175 mature Purple Beeches can be counted along about a mile of the main road, and more spread along side-roads and out into the surrounding country. I read once that we owe this to a farmer who owned the land and who recovered unexpectedly from a serious illness. His reaction was to realise that had he died, no one would have anything lasting to see to remind them of his having lived, so he planted these trees to ensure that we should all know. Well, we do know now, but some of us wish that he had preferred Lombardy Poplars.

The standard excuse for accepting these dismal blotches is always to point to their remarkable colour as the leaves unfold and they live up to the popular name 'copper beech'. It is a most peculiar pinkish brown, not the full blooded copper of a phase of the Plumleaf Thorn in autumn, and pleasant as it may be, it is out of place as the colour of the crown of a huge tree. In any case it lasts but a few days before its inevitable decline.

There are a few clones in which the full summer colour is such a rich dark red that it is clear of the dark muddy brown-black tints that deface the more commonly grown trees. One is 'Rivers Purple' of which the stock tree, a graft, was in the Sawbridgeworth Nursery, 66/13½ft at three feet, above which it divided into three stems, in 1984. A specimen in Monteviot Pinery, Roxburgh, is 85/14ft. The rather splendid 'Brocklesby' I know only from seeing the original in Brocklesby Park, Lincolnshire, and a few labelled trees at Kew, perhaps a little more red than 'Rivers Purple'. The original was 82/15½ft in 1977.

All the trees of selected forms must be grafts, but many 'copper' beeches are seedlings and so vary widely in their colour. It is no longer possible, so rife is the contagion, to raise a bed of all green seedlings. Beds in forest nurseries are heavily speckled with pale pinkish and dark purplish plants. Most of these will grow out of it to become respectable beeches, but the dark ones may not, and are likely to be segregated by the forester for decorative planting or given away. Despite the unnecessary pigment seeming to mask the chlorophyll, these trees grow at about the same rate as the green ones. One at Alice Holt Lodge in Hampshire planted on the lawn in 1924 is 63/9½ft in 1991.

As in the green form, old trees are vulnerable to breakage and to fungal decay. Several of the biggest have gone since I first measured them. The biggest now are one at Melsor Hall in Northamptonshire, 72/20ft and one at Syston Park in Lincolnshire which was 62/21ft at three feet. At Beaufort Castle, Inverness, a tree was 85/19ft. The tallest and among the best was 124/17ft in Chart Park, near Dorking, but that was in 1984, before the gales. More safely sheltered is a fine tree at Dalguise near Dunkeld in Perthshire which was 100/13½ft with 35ft clean, smooth trunk, like that at Mottisfont Abbey which is 100/15ft and unusual because so many of the big trees have fluted trunks with big swellings at branch-scars.

One of that sort at Doune House, Rothiemurchus, is 95/17ft but a smoother bole graces a fine tree at Dale End Park, Ironbridge, which is 92/15½ft, the same dimensions as one in Chatsworth Park in 1984.

GOLDEN BEECH

Fagus sylvatica 'Zlatia'

This is another tree which has been around for 100 years but whose time has not yet come. Just as a green beech displays in its new foliage an unmatched shimmering brilliance, this golden variant is for some weeks a fresh, bright, but soft golden yellow lighting up its surroundings. Quite soon a tinge of green begins to spread, among the first leaves out, but this shows off to advantage the still bright yellow newest foliage. Since beech make all their first growth in about three weeks, the crown fades to green unless there is a second spurt of growth in July.

Because of this, the tree is often rather dismissed as a fleeting spectacle, usually no better than a Common Beech. But this is to underestimate it. A hint of the gold enlivens the foliage through the summer in most trees, while some specimens, like the two in The Downs at Westonbirt Arboretum, contrive to have their outer crowns fresh gold all summer, as may all those growing very fast and fully in the open.

The Golden Beech was put on the market first by Spaeth of Berlin in 1890. It had been found as a single tree in Serbia a few years before and they had to build up a stock of grafted trees. Plants from Spaeth were very important additions to the

Royal Botanic Gardens at Kew and Edinburgh and the National Botanic Gardens at Glasnevin from about 1880 to 1910, and to private collectors of new and rare trees. The first two received trees in, or soon after, 1890 and so did a few private gardens, but the first trees are of unrecorded dates, and the oldest of known date is the smaller of two at Kew, planted in 1903. It evidently remained scarce in the trade until about 1960 particularly, and still is today. In all the 1700 gardens and parks I have scoured in varying degrees of intensity for interesting trees, only 21 have one, and only ten of these have trees which must be of pre-1960 planting.

Since the varieties of beech with foliage in which the chlorophyll is heavily masked by dark red or purplish pigments are found to grow as fast as those with good green foliage not so encumbered, it would be grossly unfair if the highly desirable Golden Beech were not also at least as vigorous as these. In three of only four older dated trees, they are comparable, and in one, the growth is superior to almost any other form of beech. But in this very small sample the variation in growth in girth is too great to allow close estimates of age from girth, and the biggest undated trees, which might be thought to derive from very soon after 1890, may not be so old.

The biggest was at Hollycombe in Sussex in 1981, when it was 82/11½ft at four feet. It forked above this and had an extensive crown. The presumed 1890 tree in the Royal Botanic Garden, Edinburgh, is 80/9½ft and a shapely tree. It was 56/6½ft in 1967, which accords quite well with its assumed age. In Kew, the oldest dated tree was received in 1903 and by 1984 it was only 66/6½ft, but an undated tree nearby was then 72/7½ft and may be older. One at Nymans in Sussex, planted in 1912 in the Arboretum below the Terrace (an area much damaged in 1987) was 82/8½ft in 1985. An undated

Golden Beech (*Fagus sylvatica* 'Zlatia'): often dismissed as a fleeting spectacle

tree by the entrance to Sezincote Garden in Gloucestershire was 75/6½ft in 1988. Another, at Lindridge Park near Ashburton in Devon, was 75/8½ft in 1989.

The best growth record is for the larger of the two on The Downs at Westonbirt Arboretum, both planted in 1934. This tree, when 33 years old, was 48/5ft; when 41 years old it was 62/6½ft and at 58 years old it was 75/8½ft. The other one is now 72/7½ft. They are widely apart in the open field and have nearly globular crowns.

COMMON ASH

Fraxinus excelsior

The Common Ash has somehow become a byword in country literature and among poets, for grace and elegance although in my view it is an exceptionally coarse and dull tree. Probably the poets are to blame with their 'Lady of the Woods' encomia, for many nature writers accept such often repeated judgements uncritically. It is admitted that very occasionally a beautiful ash is seen with a long, clean trunk, nearly cylindric, pale grey with very even, shallow ridges in a network; this is a splendid sight, but few are like that. Normally, ash are short-boled, heavily branched, much forked and graceless. Nor do autumn colours come to its aid, for apart from a few trees showing a brief flash of gold, the great majority shed their leaves still green. That sheep may relish these leaves does nothing for the tree.

One difficulty for the Ash is that it is a gross feeder and to be at its best it needs a scarce kind of soil. It must be highly fertile, base-rich and well-drained but always damp. This is found in limited areas on the margins of valley-bottoms in limestone or chalk districts. Foresters consider that meadowsweet or ramsons (garlic) are the indicators for the growth of top quality Ash. This is prized for superior sports goods, hockey-sticks mainly, now that aluminium has supplanted wood in tennis racquets. For the required great elastic strength, growth must be rapid and evenly sustained, as a year or two of slower growth and closer annual rings leads to brittleness. Thinning must be regular and, in this light-demanding tree, heavy.

Second quality Ash, unfit for sports goods, grows on land typified by dog's mercury. This is often much shallower soil and is widespread in limestone hills and on chalk slopes, which is where most woods of pure ash are found. Being shallow it is more liable to dry out, and growth is slower and less regular. Meadowsweet is common in Highland glens along roadside ditches. These receive copious water from the hills behind and the acid run-off from the peats dissolves the minerals and nutrients of the lower slopes and becomes base-rich. These stretches are often only ribbons, too restricted to be used for plantations,but may contain some big specimens.

Ash, however, spreads extensively on soils which are not well suited to it, and it does not add to its reputation on them. It grows slowly and is often of deplorable form as it is afflicted by one pest and one disease. The pest is the Ash bud moth. Its pleasant name, *Prays curtisella*, fails to compensate for the damage it does. It eats out the terminal buds, and ash being an opposite-leafed and branching tree, this means a wide fork developing below each infected bud. The plant becomes branchy and bushy. The disease is bacterial canker of ash and is often very severe on shoot, branch and stem, making them ugly as well as stunted. Together, these render great areas of wild ash woodland unattractive scrub, useful only in being the preferred nesting place of the lesser whitethroat.

Clays are not ideal for ash, but they tend to remain damp and to have moderate to good nutrient status, so some good trees grow on them. Some are seen in city parks, especially in London, and in gardens in clay areas.

As a light-demanding tree, ash has an open crown, since good foliage will not grow in the shade of the upper crown. Ivy enjoys the light available and is not shaded out so it tends to ramp to a great height. Since ivy is a plant of soils with a high lime content, it is common in the better ashwoods, and the trees may be heavily garlanded. This is of no concern to the tree until it becomes senile and lets in even more light, after which the masses of ivy add greatly to the top-hamper of the tree and hasten its downfall in a storm. But this is only towards the end of the natural life of the tree and, not being parasitic, the ivy's roots are spread widely near the soil surface and barely compete with those of the ash. The ivy adds enormously to the wildlife value of the woodlands with its evergreen shelter, its nectar-rich late flowers and its succulent fruit through the winter.

From the rapid early growth on good sites and from the fact that trees over 12–13ft round are unusual and bigger ones very scarce, it can be reckoned that the normal life-span of ash is less than 200 years, and the biggest, other than the few great hulks, are about 250 years old. In this it is similar to beech, although a few of those live longer, but the similarity is instructive in that, in contrast to ash, the dense, shade-tolerant crown of beech shades out ivy and only a few straggles of climbing shoots grow up lower stems, yet the ash, much encumbered, lives about as long.

The finest Ash was, in 1976, at Tynan Abbey, County Armagh, at 90/26ft with a trunk about ten feet long and a reasonable crown. If that is no longer extant, the crown passes to one at Tullynally Castle, County Westmeath, still in Ireland, but in the Republic. This is in the Park, 98/23ft, and another in the woods is not far behind, with a better trunk, 108/20ft. A remarkable tree stands out in a field at Innerwick, halfway up Glen Lyon in Perthshire. This grand old tree was 98/22ft in 1983.

Common Ash (*Fraxinus excelsior*): the
best specimens grow on highly fertile,
well-drained soils

The biggest girth is that of a heavily burred hulk, 40/29ft at Clapton Court, Somerset. Allan Meredith found a tree 26ft round at six feet up at Talley Abbey, Llandeilo, but I have not seen this and know nothing of its form or condition. At Cotesbach, Leicestershire, a hulk with barely half remaining was nonetheless 40/21½ft in 1981. At Holywell Hall, Lincolnshire, a rather battered tree is 52/19ft with the stem dividing low, and at Hurstbourne Park, Hampshire, a good tree is 105/19½ft. At Birr Castle, County Offaly, in Mount Palmer there is one 92/18ft, and Michael Heseltine has one at Thenford House, near Banbury, 72/18ft. At Kildangan, County Kildare, one by the drive is 40/17ft while at Abbeyleix, County Leix, is a splendid tree 102/17½ft.

Among the trees of highest quality but lesser stature, one at Finnebrogue, County Down, is 115/12½ft with a clear stem for 45ft. At Rossie Priory, Dundee, a superb tree below the drive is 124/9½ft with a bole clear for 60ft. A handsome tree by the gate at Harrington House, Lincolnshire, is 108/11½ft with a clear trunk for 30ft. A tall specimen near the entrance to Cockington Court, Devon is 121/13ft.

HIGHCLERE HYBRID HOLLIES

Ilex x *altaclerensis*

The origin of this remarkable tough, vigorous and varied group of hollies, so important in gardens and parks now, was involved with the development of glass and glazing methods in making glasshouses and orangeries attached to mansions around 1800. The tax on glass began with the window-tax in 1696 and on glass itself in 1746, which was increased until 1808 and reduced only in 1825. The glass was of poor quality and glazing-bars were broad, so there was not much light for flowers. Fowler's Orangery at Syon Park in 1820 led to Paxton's conservatory at Chatsworth and elsewhere after 1840 but until then the orangeries relied mostly on shade-tolerant plants and the Madeira Holly was a favourite for winter decoration with its abundant large red berries. The plants were grown in tubs which were wheeled out on to the terrace in summer to make room for a display of flowers.

Hollies are very difficult to multiply by cuttings or grafts, so new plants were raised by sowing the berries. The seeds inside these berries had all been pollinated when the plants were out on the terrace. The bees can, in England, only have been visiting flowers of the Common Holly. The plants raised were all hybrids between that and Madeira Holly. Around 1838, Loddiges Nursery began distributing plants raised at Highclere Castle in Hampshire and Loudon described them as var. *hodginsii* and sent them to Lawson. One of these became the common form, a vigorous male with purple shoots taken now as the type Highclere Holly, and the

Highclere Hybrid Hollies (*Ilex* x *altaclerensis*): close-up of branches, leaves and berries

other, with green shoots, is 'Hendersonii', but there was confusion for years between these as both have been spread at times under the name 'Hodginsii'.

The hollies have no real claim to the classic name *Ilex* as this was used by the Romans for the Holm Oak. The holly was likened to the juvenile and lower crown leaves of the oak. When Linnaeus simplified the classification system in 1753 he established the genus *Quercus* for oaks and the Holm Oak became *Quercus ilex*, which left the name *Ilex* free to be used for the genus of hollies.

Most of the biggest hollies in parks and gardens, are 'Hodginsii'. It has few equals for withstanding both salty maritime winds and industrial pollution. It is therefore invaluable for shelter and ornament in sea-front gardens and in city parks. Its broad, flat leaves, variably toothed and spined or entire, have a distinctive gloss, giving the tree a grey cast. As a male, it bears no berries but many foliage variants are female. The males have big, purple-tinged flowers opening from purple buds, wreathed densely along outer shoots, so it is decorative in late spring.

Westonbirt Arboretum has numerous big specimens along both Main Drive in the Arboretum and Willesley Drive in Silk Wood. Several are 55/4ft and some are the superior form once distinguished as 'Nobilis' with bigger, regularly toothed leaves on rich purple shoots.

At Ballamoar, Isle of Man, one is 75/5½ft. Rapid growth is shown by one at Coleton Fishacre, Devon, which was planted in 1932 and was 72/3½ft in 1984 beside another of the same age, 62/4ft. In the Holly Walk at Kew Gardens, one at the north end, west side, is now 60/6ft. One above the pool at the eastern end of Bodnant, Gwynedd, is 60/4½ft. In the Derby Arboretum, laid out by Loudon, one is 50/4ft and in Calderstones Park, Merseyside, one is 46/6ft. A tree in Jesmond Dene, Newcastle, is 56/4½ft. A good companion to 'Hodginsii' in a planting of Highclere Hybrids is 'Camellifolia', contrasting with it in many features. 'Camellifolia' is female, bearing plentiful, large scarlet berries; it is formally conic in crown with level tiers of branches, and its leaves are highly glossed bright green, elliptic-oblong to five inches long and entire or with an occasional small, spined tooth. It is seen often in city parks and large gardens. A good one, 46/3ft, is at Kinfauns Castle outside Perth; four to 40/3ft are in Lincoln's Inn Fields, London; the best of three in Waterlow Park, London, is 42/4ft and Calderstones Park, Merseyside has one 52/3ft and another 30/4ft.

BLACK WALNUT

Juglans nigra

This tree shows that it is an aristocrat by its combination of stature, form and foliage. A good specimen, over 100ft tall, will have a long, clean trunk almost perfectly cylindrical for 15–30ft, holding a high domed crown of radiating branches with leaves to 20in long of the brightest fresh green. The name 'black walnut' arises from it being first found in the woods of the Alleghenies and coastal plains of the early colonies in Virginia where, among the host of tree species, there was one other walnut. The striking difference between the two that is evident as you walk the woods is the bark. One soon has deeply fissured dark brown to quite black bark and the other has pale grey, smooth plates separated by pinkish fissures. That was called the 'white walnut' or 'butternut'.

The Black Walnut ranges from Long Island and southern Ontario to mid-Texas and South Dakota, a vast region with long, hot summers of a kind unknown in Britain. Some trees with a similar native range, like the Red Oak and Red Maple manage well without their accustomed summers and grow much the same from Kent to the Highlands, while others like the American Plane and White Oak can scarcely be grown in Britain at all. The Black Walnut, like the Sweetgum, *Liquidambar*, is between these extremes. It thrives to a great size where our summers are warmest, in the southeast, along the south coast and in East Anglia, and fades out north of the Midlands. It is a small struggling tree in the north of England and in Scotland. It can be said that no good specimen grows north and west of a line from Gloucester to York. Until 1990 there was a brilliant exception to this. A very good tree, 60/10ft, was growing at Brahan House, Muir of Ord, Easter Ross, until it was blown down. This showed that the effects of local microclimates can be strong and unexpected. The Firth of Moray has two arms – the Beauly and Cromarty Firths – that are either side of Brahan about five miles away, and the narrow strip of coast of this region has early and relatively warm summers.

The nearly globular, two-inch fruit, freely borne in the south, are pale green and rough with fine, hard crinkles. They are solitary or sometimes in pairs, but one individual beside Albury House in Surrey has them in bunches of four to five. This has been distinguished as var. *alburyensis* and is exceedingly rare. Apart from the original tree, now 75/12½ft, there is a graft from it on the terraces there, 50/3ft and one at Kew Gardens, planted in 1960 and now 30/3ft. The fruit is of little interest here for the nuts, although in America they are edible and sweet, but the hard, rough husk has two interesting features. When scratched it emits a strong sweet aroma, and the juice it yields gives a dark brown dye which is fast in water.

The male catkins extend from buds grown the previous year and are conic until they extend to be thick cylinders four inches long and yellow in bunches of three to five. The female flowers are terminal on the new shoot, in fives although only one or two mature into fruit. The best growth is on deep, fertile soils, mainly on clays but also on lighter clay loams, and usually not far above the water-table.

The tallest, biggest and best Black Walnut is in the garden of the Old Rectory at Much Hadham, Hertfordshire, standing on a little island in a minor tributary of the River Lee. It was raised from one of Bishop Henry Compton's original trees at Fulham Palace and dates from 1820. There seem to be no early records of its size but in 1983 it was 120/21½ft so it had by then a mean annual increase of one and a half inches in girth. It has a good clear trunk for about 15ft and a high, spreading crown on big upcurved branches. The next best is at Mote Park, Maidstone, Kent, in the middle of a big hayfield in the valley beyond the house and below the woods. The 1987 gales removed nearly all the big exotics in the wood above, which included very big Cucumber Trees and others, but caused no harm to this tree out in the field. It is recorded as dating from 1805 and in 1905 it was 102/12½ft. In 1990 it was 85/20ft exactly. It has the appearance of a pollard, having five limbs arising from a bole of ten feet.

A notable old tree has its own compound at Marble Hill, Twickenham, and a plaque. It is 108/18½ft and its crown spreads down nearly to the ground although it has about eight feet of bole. It was 98/14ft in 1905, so it has added barely half an inch a year since then, which is slow. But it is the same rate of growth as one at Syon House, Brentford, in Old Show Ground, which is now 70/14ft and was seven feet round in 1849 and ten feet in 1903. Another with a low, spreading crown from a short bole is the larger of two on the lawns below Antony House in Cornwall. That is 56/15½ft with about six feet of trunk and one of its branches snakes down almost to the ground about 30ft away.

In the summer, the big crown of bright green much divided leaves of a Black Walnut is well seen from the road to Albury near where that leaves the A25, over the Gate Lodge. It has a short bole in a copse beside the garden, and is 85/16ft, having been recorded as 88/9ft in 1904. At Bisham Abbey near Marlow, a shapely tree with a long trunk is 111/14ft. A very similar, tall tree in Battersea Park near the playground in the northwest, is 111/10½ft with about 20ft clear. The University Botanic Gardens of Oxford and of Cambridge have, very properly, good trees which are close rivals, both with clear trunks both growing fast, and both 11½ft round. The Oxford tree is 100ft tall and has increased its girth by 30in in 35 years, while the Cambridge tree is 80ft tall and has added 24in in 17 years, so it should make up in girth now for its lesser height.

A fine, sturdy tree at the Rectory in Middle Woodford near Salisbury was planted in 1832. It is now 70/16ft and has a bole of nearly ten feet before it divides into five limbs. In the Bishop's Garden at Wells Cathedral a nicely black barked tree is 70/12½ft with 12ft clear before two minor branches arise. Roath Park in Cardiff has a good tree, 75/10ft.

In Scotland, now that the Brahan tree has gone, the best is 60/4½ft at Blairhoyle, Lake of Menteith, and quite a young tree. Further north, a younger tree at Darnaway,

Moray, carries the flag, but is only 23/1½ft, at Bradbush. In Ireland the biggest of very few are one planted in 1929 at Birr Castle, County Offaly, in Mount Palmer, 60/5ft and one at Abbeyleix, County Leix, 65/3½ft.

Among recent plantings, the tree at Wimpole House, Cambridge, planted in 1940 seemed quite a vigorous tree at 50/5ft in 1987 until I saw one at Churchill Hall near Bristol which was planted in 1961 and was 52/5ft in 1991.

COMMON WALNUT

Juglans regia

The Common Walnut has been prized as a fruit tree and moved around for so long that, like the almond, the natural limits of its range are hard to determine. It has, to me, the unmistakable features of a member of the Tertiary flora of the Caucasus and Black Sea regions. It is exceedingly healthy and vigorous with stout shining shoots and large, smooth, leathery, almost oily leaves. If that region is where it arose, it moved far from it unaided before man took a part in its planting, for it is found native in Greece, Albania and Serbia, through Iran and the Himalayas to Burma and western China, and probably in Japan. The Americans call it 'English Walnut', which is plainly an understandable error by the early settlers when finding the Black Walnut and Butternut growing in their woods, and 'Persian Walnut', which is correct.

The Romans, with their appetite for the fruits they knew at home, certainly brought them to England, and whether they planted them themselves or their kitchen minions did so, the walnut was introduced during one or both of their occupations. Linguistic evidence for this is seen in the name, for 'wal' is Anglo-Saxon for 'foreign', so the tree was known then as a newcomer. Like the sweet chestnut, the fruit is in need of hotter summers to ripen fully than it can have in Britain, and to reach the size that the Romans were used to, but the tree grows splendidly even as far north as Easter Ross and the Isle of Skye.

The present distribution of trees of good size, and the paucity of good stems can be put down to the very high prices paid for high quality timber. It is written that sometimes timber firms encouraged schoolchildren to scout for good trees. I doubt if that were ever true. I know that when a tree of quite good size and quality was blown down in a Hampshire village around 1970, we could arouse no interest at all from local firms and cast as far afield as Crewe. They said they could not come all that way for a single tree. So it went for firewood or local amateur cabinet work.

It does seem, however, that earlier there had been much felling of good trees in areas where they were concentrated: in parts of southwestern and southern England, particularly in Somerset, Devon and Gloucestershire. The tree is still locally common, in those parts, as it is in Lincolnshire, east Yorkshire, the Midlands, and East Anglia, but rarely other than short-boled with big low branches.

There is only a handful of dated trees and all but one are less than 70 years old and show moderately rapid growth, as is expected from a Caucasian type tree and are seen only on base- rich, deep, damp soils. A selected fruiting clone, 'Lady Irene' in Crittenden garden in Kent had three-foot-long shoots all round its lower crown, but even that was only 42/3ft when 36 years old. However, an orchard of fruiting clones at Brook Farm, Boxted, Essex, all with Black Walnut rootstocks, had 40-year old trees mainly 45/5ft which is more as expected. Progress thereafter can be gauged only by the re-measurement of big trees. The only old tree with a date, at St John of Jerusalem's near Dartford, Kent, is reputed to have been planted in 1632 but as it was only 70/13ft in 1965, either the date is suspect or growth becomes excruciatingly slow with great age.

Re-measurements over more than 20 years are very few because the big trees noted at the beginning of this century had nearly all gone by 1960, and today only one survives. The three available sets of updates suggest that the biggest trees grow slowly, but much faster than the possible 1632 tree. A splendid tree at Laverstoke Park, Hampshire, had added four feet to its 14ft girth in the 70 years before it was blown down; one of the many trees in the far north at Gordon Castle, Morayshire, added two feet in 50 years, and the superb Gayhurst tree, to be celebrated below, added three feet in 76 years.

It is indicative of a fairly sharp cut-off towards senility that only one of the fifteen trees cited between 1901 and 1908 is now alive. They were 12–17ft round, and for a tree of reasonably rapid early growth, this means that the life-span is relatively short. There were, in 1955, two very big trees in Pilton Churchyard in Northamptonshire, but by 1972 both had been destroyed, one 18ft round, by lightning and the other 21ft round, by fire. Both were very hollow hulks. The limit in girth seems to be at 21ft, although we have two specimens today in excellent order that, with luck, will exceed that. It is probable that they are 350 years old or more.

The distribution of the biggest trees today is very odd. A large proportion is found between Yorkshire and Easter Ross. The tallest stands beside the fattest, in the same garden and only two others are first class specimens. Pride of place must be given to the Gayhurst tree, beside the drive to the House near Newport Pagnell. It has the appearance of a prime oak with a massive cylindric lower bole for ten feet. It was 80/17ft in 1907 and it was a surprise to find it at all in 1984 when it was 65/20ft and a fully crowned, healthy tree, not the abbreviated hulk it so well might have been.

This remained unequalled until 1990 when Mrs Welleer-Poley wrote from Boxted Hall, Suffolk, to say that she had a bigger one. It is on a long bank facing the Moated Hall and is 88/21ft with a complete, if much fluted trunk, clear for 13ft, and a full, healthy crown of huge, spreading branches. Furthermore, the next tree on the bank, although a much smaller one, is the tallest known, 105/12½ft. This took the place of the fourth of the top class specimens, as the tallest. This is in Perthshire at Garth House, on that remarkable brae facing south over the Tay below Aberfeldy where there are so many outsize trees. This fine walnut is 98/12½ft.

The only good walnut seen lately in the former stronghold in the southwest is at Rosemoor Garden near Torrington, Devon, 60/11½ft. In East Anglia there was, in 1965, a hugely spreading tree 60/16ft at two feet, with low branches, at the West Suffolk Hospital in Thetford. In the northwest, there is a good tree 75/13ft at Lydham Hall, Shropshire, and two at Holker Park in Cumbria, 60/10ft and 60/9½ft, but it is in the northeast that they begin to cluster. In Yorkshire, a broad tree at Ribston Hall was 52/15ft in 1973, when one at Grantly Hall, Ripon, was 70/11ft. In 1993 two large trees at Newby Hall were 62/10½ft and 72/10ft. In Northumberland, a tree at Beaufront Castle, Hexham, is 50/14ft and in 1977 a tall one at Alnwick Castle was 80/8½ft.

Far more are in Scotland, into the fairly remote north at Easter Ross, where one in the wall garden at Novar, north of Dingwall, is 46/11ft; two at Brahan House, Muir of Ord, are 72/10½ft and 56/10½ft, and at Coul House a tree is 40/8ft. Even more remote in the north, one in Stornoway Woods, Isle of Lewis, is 33/9ft. To the east, and very nearly as far north, a broad tree at Cawdor Castle, Nairn, by an approach road, is 62/15ft at two feet, with a forking stem, and at Moy Hall, Morayshire, one is 72/9½ft. A tree at Crathes Castle, Deeside, is 56/8½ft. In Perthshire there is not only the tall tree mentioned at Garth House, but also two at Fingask nearly as tall, 92/12ft and 92/11½ft; one in The Den at Cardine House, 70/10ft; one at Cluny Garden near Aberfeldy, 65/9½ft; one at Logie Lodge, 46/10½ft and on the border with Angus one at Farrell Main, Kinnaird Castle, 56/12½ft.

Common Walnut (*Juglans regia*): close-up of fruit and leaves

Midlothian is rich in very big common hardwoods and Preston Hall just north of the A68 near Edinburgh has two big walnuts, 80/13ft and 56/12ft. A line beside a drive, continued along a hedge at Panmure, Angus, is an unusual planting with 14 trees, with a mean size around 60/7ft but number eight is 85/9½ft. Ireland has a few big trees in the Midlands. By a drive to Kildangan House in County Kildare a tree with a good clean trunk is 65/9ft. Below the castle at Tullynally, County Westmeath, a low-branched, widely spreading tree is 72/13ft at three feet, and a similar specimen at Emo Court in County Leix is 75/12½ft at three feet.

CASTOR ARALIA

Kalopanax septembobus

This strange tree, so gaunt with coarsely ridged bark and sparse spiky shoots in winter, is transformed in the summer to a well-clothed, glossy-leafed tree that looks as if it has been moved out of a tropical planting in a city office atrium. Towards autumn it projects from the tips of its branches ivory white flowerheads on which the little white flowers open at the tips of radiating spokes up to a foot long. It is an added eccentricity that such a tree should grow to its greatest size and perfection in the north of Scotland or at an altitude of 1,000ft in the Southern Uplands.

The flowers in their big umbels, and the black berries into which they mature, show that this tree is in the Ivy Family. Like some other rather bizarre trees, it is native to Japan, although this one is also found in Korea and scattered from western China to Mongolia. It was introduced by Carl Maximowicz in 1864, and has never been other than scarce in cultivation, nor acquired a general popular name. I regret that when required to give it one for use in a book, I coined the contrived sounding 'Prickly Castor-oil tree' unaware that there was already a more civilised name 'Castor Aralia' in use in America.

There are two extreme forms of this tree and so many intermediates between them that a few of which are hard to place. But the type and Maximowicz's variety (var. *maximowiczii*) are fortunately the usual forms and very distinct, such that in the absence of the intermediates they would surely have been established as full species. Both, probably, were sent by Maximowicz but because so many in the wild cannot be allotted firmly to one or the other, the ranges of the forms have not been defined. Wilson sent the trees at Kew from western China, and these are very much of the type form. They have five-inch leaves, nearly circular with five shallow, broad lobes and on five-inch petioles. In the best Maximowicz form, the foliage is much bigger altogether, eight inches across on stout, hairy red-brown stalks four to eight inches long and deeply cut into five long-pointed lobes.

New shoots, notably in the variety, have soft-pointed bright blue-green spines, and on old wood, persisting on the trunk, where they are sharp but very small at the tip of small rounded blisters likely to snag only the least wary tree-measurer.

Although quite rare in our gardens, there are trees in all the regions and Maximowicz's variety slightly outnumbers those of the type, particularly in Scotland, so it is probably the hardier. All have been allotted to one form or the other, only a few being at all doubtful and any of those with distinct separate lobes as opposed to point-tipped projections from a broadly rounded leaf, have been put with the variety. All those in the north of Scotland are plainly Maximowicz's.

Of the type trees, much the biggest was at Emmett's, Ide Hill in Kent, which was 65/10½ft in 1984 and was blown down in October 1987. The group of four Wilson trees at Kew all suffered some damage at that time, and perhaps in a severe cold spell since, for two of them have died back to 50/4ft. The best is now a two-trunked tree, 56/5ft + 5 and healthy. The tallest is now at Warren House, part of the old Veitch nursery at Coombe Wood, Kingston, Surrey, 72/5½ft. A fine tree at Lythe Hill Park, Haslemere, is 66/5ft. One in Aldenham Woods, Hertfordshire is 62/5ft; at Croome Court, Worcestershire, one is 56/6ft and at Brockenhurst Park, Hampshire, one is the same size. A pair in Greenwich Park, London, were about 50/5½ft in 1984. In Wales, a tree in Dyffryn Park near Cardiff is 48/6½ft and in Scotland the tree in the Royal Botanic Garden, Edinburgh, is 42/5ft.

The Maximowicz variety is growing in several gardens in Wester Ross. The most northerly is in Leckmelm, by Loch Broom near Ullapool. It may well be the most northerly specimen in the world, and it is a big one, 50/8ft at three feet. On Deeside near Banchory, west of Aberdeen, by the road through Durris Estate, a finer tree with a single long trunk is 56/7½ft. Dawyck Gardens, near Peebles, at 1000ft, has two, the better one on Policy Bank is 60/5½ft, and Stobo, across the valley,

Castor Aralia
(*Kalopanax
septembobus*):
close-up of leaves

which shared the Dawyck larches of 1725, has one 60/5½ft. At the opposite end of the country, almost in Cornwall, a pair of trees by the stream in Endsleigh, Devon, has one forking stem 60/10ft and a single bole tree 46/7ft. Ramster near Chiddingfold in Surrey has a handsome tree 56/5ft and at Nymans, Sussex, a sturdy tree by the pergola, is 36/6½ft and flowers heavily in most years.

SWEETGUM

Liquidambar styraciflua

The Sweetgum is best known among gardeners for its brilliant, if erratic, autumn colours, but it is also outstanding throughout the summer as a shapely tree among the very best for handsome foliage. The leaves are then large, glossy, a good green, and star-shaped, fairly densely held but well displayed. A well-grown tree retains a regular conic form with an acute apex well into maturity, its lower branches of moderate size, level then gently upswept and its upper ones rising progressively more acutely with their height of origin. Without foliage, it is a gaunt, rather spiky tree as it grows few minor shoots, but the luxuriant foliage hides this open crown structure completely in summer.

As a native to eastern North America, from Long Island, New York to the Gulf Coast in eastern Texas (with an outlier from southeastern Mexico through Guatemala, where it is largely evergreen), the tree shows some sensitivity to lack of heat in the summers in this country. Trees over six feet in girth are confined to south of the Thames, except for one in Malvern, Worcestershire. Those in Scotland are not above 30ft tall, although there is one of 20ft as far north as Innes House, Morayshire. It is very rare in Northern Ireland and while quite frequent in the Republic, the bigger trees are confined to counties Cork and Kerry in the far southwest. In Wales it is scarce and the only one of noteworthy size is at Tan-y-Bwlch, Maentwrog, 56/5ft. It was introduced in 1681 when it was received by Bishop Compton at Fulham Palace, from his collector/missionary John Banister, in the Alleghenies.

The great variation among individual trees in the time, intensity and hue of autumn colour has been much written about. Planters were advised against mass planting and avenues because they would not give a simultaneous and uniform display. There is, however, much to be said in favour of the different effect of varied colours over a long period, and now that cloned selections are available the question need no longer arise. Unselected trees vary according to inherent factors, to the weather and often a little to the site, but not in my view to the soil.

One noticeable phenomenon is that the first trees to colour fully have generally small leaves, turn clear scarlet and are not growing fast. Many of the young specimens have corky flanges on their bark. I think these have been raised as cuttings from low sprouts or from root-suckers and they never will grow fast or bear big foliage. The leaves turn deep red before falling. Seedlings tend to have big leaves and a more vigorous, open crown. These colour later and more variously. They show yellow and orange first and then bright scarlet in mid-season, or a minority keep green leaves until late in October when a proportion, scattered through the crown, turns yellow. By the time these have become red, some of the others are yellow, and when these turn red, the first ones turn plum-purple. The tree is mottled with all these colours until a November frost causes all the leaves to fall. This mottled yellow, orange, red, dark red and purple is the general colouring in Texas and the deep South, perhaps in areas with a hot, dry summer, while in the Alleghenies and the north, uniform scarlet is usual.

As in all autumn reds, the onset and duration depends on the amount of sunshine received. In the climate of Britain this is variable in different years. A good, sunny summer and long sunny autumn will give the best show of scarlet. It is often said, about maples, too, that a sharp frost will bring up the bright colour. This is probably not true. It has been stated that the brightest colour comes from large changes in temperature between night and day. In Britain these occur in high pressure spells and these mean sunny days and cold nights, which are favourable for colour, but more than a tinge of frost will shrivel the leaves. The best colour is on vigorous trees and these often include those on fertile, damp sites around lakes. These can be marked frost-hollows but even a small lake holds enough heat to take the edge off a slight radiation frost, so the best trees for colour should be those in a valley and close to a lake.

No tree is currently known with a documented planting before 1900 but many of the biggest are in gardens where planting dates from before 1850 and are probably at least as old as that. Sweetgum is probably not very long-lived for none in the United States is recorded as quite 20ft round yet. In Britain, ten feet is almost the limit so far and losses among the big trees noted in 1907, and even much more recently, have been high. Recorded growth of dated trees is never more than very moderate. Among the most vigorous, one planted at Kingston Lacey in Dorset in 1908 was 56/7½ft when 75 years old; a 1928 tree at Wilton House was 56/5½ft when 59 years old and the only one showing any sign of urgency is in the University Botanic Garden in Oxford, 53/5ft when 39 years old.

The problem of the inconsistent colours in autumn was, in gracious days, resolved as far as inherent ability is concerned by the prospective purchaser cruising the nursery lines at the appropriate time and tying a personal label on chosen trees, which would be lifted after leaf-fall. By the time that this practice was restricted at best to a few old and valued customers and unavailable to the public at large, trees were starting to be grown in containers and could be purchased and planted out when in leaf. Now that the disadvantages of large plants in containers are more appreciated, all this becomes unnecessary. Reliable and consistent results are given by a few selected clones. 'Palo Alto' was raised in Saratoga, California and was among the first, but may need hotter summers than ours and has not impressed here.

'Worplesdon' may be better, but the outstanding clone to date is 'Lane Roberts'. This was among a few trees sold by Hillier to Lane Roberts, which Sir Harold noticed as outstanding when he later visited the garden and asked for some scionwood from it. It has extra large leaves, a broad conic crown and vigorous growth as well as autumn colours about as scarlet as the best unselected trees, and, of course, as a clone, all will colour simultaneously on one site. The dates of origin of none of these seems to be on record, but the oldest tree of 'Lane Roberts' must have been planted a little before 1950. It is in Roath Park, Cardiff and is 50/5½ft. The well-known tree on the lawn in the Hillier Arboretum was planted in 1954 and is 42/4½ft.

There are two specimens which stands out in quality and in size from the others. One is in the South Arboretum at Stratfield Saye and could well date from 1800, when the now blown down big Tupelo was planted. This Sweetgum has a straight very solid trunk for nearly 20ft before bearing a near-vertical side-branch and another 20ft before dividing to lose the straight axis. The tree is 92/10½ft with a symmetrical crown culminating in a flat dome. The other is on the lawn north of the Lake at Syon Park, Brenford. This is 102/10ft and has a clean, although slightly

Sweetgum (*Liquidambar styraciflua*):
Stratfield Saye, Hampshire

waved and leaning trunk for over 50ft. At that point it divides into three widely angled branches, the base of a high, irregular, rather open dome.

The runners up include a second tree at Syon Park, on the same lawn and 95/8ft which anywhere else would be the tallest Sweetgum in the place; a well-crowned tree at The Rookeries a little west of Dorking in Surrey, 95/7ft in 1983; one in the woodland at the west end of the West Prospect at Osterley Park, Hounslow, which is 92/6½ft; a fine, prominent tree in the northern part of Alexandra Park, Surrey, is 85/5ft, and one at Escot in Devon, smaller than the very big one that was there in 1965, is 85/6ft. The species is vulnerable to windthrow and Kent lost a tree 85ft tall with a splendid long clear stem at Mote Park some time after 1965, and the survival of an equally imposing tree at Linton Park, 88/7ft clean boled to 45ft in 1984 is doubtful.

Two very good trees in the pinetum at Wisley Gardens are very alike and both 65/5ft. They were probably planted in 1926 when the pair of Silver Maples nearby was planted. A choice tree well placed in the open for admiration on all sides is in the Winter Gardens at Malvern. Now 65/6½ft, this has grown unusually fast in the 17 years since it was 54/4½ft.

CHINESE TULIP-TREE

Liriodendron chinense

The extraordinary wealth of tree species in eastern North America, survivors from the Tertiary, pre-Ice Ages flora, owes its existence to the orientation of the mountain ranges there. The Alleghenies system runs nearly north to south, like the Rocky Mountain system in the west. In both cases, as the ice approached from the north, the plants could migrate southwards and stay in their preferred climate until the ice retreated and then migrate back. None of the species was lost and the east preserved its huge array of broad-leaf trees and the west preserved its conifers and added some from Mexico.

Across the Eurasian land mass the Alpine Mountain uplift from Portugal to Burma had raised high chains of mountains running very largely from west to east, adding, in the west, to the Mediterranean Sea and forming an impassable barrier for plants. During the Ice Ages the plants west of Burma had no access to the possible refuges of Africa or India. It is only from Burma, through China to Japan that north-south mountains gave routes and refuges to the south.

So the old flora of North America has no parallel west of the Far East, except a curious area of Tertiary plants in the Caucasus and Elburz Mountains which escaped glaciation, and there is a huge gap across the world, lacking these species and genera, but a close parallel between the floras of America and China. One of the best of the hundreds of examples is the Chinese Tulip-tree. It was found in 1875 in the Lushan Mountains but was effectively unknown until Augustine Henry refound

Chinese Tulip-tree (*Liriodendron chinense*): discovered in 1875 and introduced in 1901

it in 1888 on his travels south from Ichang on the Hupeh-Sichuan border, where he found his *Davidia*. Wilson, when searching for and collecting from the Davidias, came across it and introduced it in 1901.

Very close botanically to the American species, it may be regarded as a shade more primitive, because its normal crown leaves have the deep lobing found often on sprout leaves of the other, the middle lobe tapering towards its base, a form discarded in the mature crown of the American tree, in favour of shallow, broader lobes. New foliage of the Chinese tree emerges reddish orange on glaucous shoots, adding distinction to the tree. The leaves can be eight to ten inches, a size equalled in the American tree only on strong sprouts. Their undersides are variably silvered. The flowers are smaller and have much less green on them, and are mostly a feeble pale brownish orange. The bark difference may be due to none of the trees here being yet more than a third of the age of the oldest of the other. It is pale grey and very shallowly ridged. In Ireland where most of the best of the relatively old Chinese trees grow, the boles have a strange trademark. They grow big discs of black algae prominent on the pale bark. Growth of the best trees is decidedly slower than in the American species, and none has been found to add as much as two inches a year. The most rapid are one in Lyndford Arboretum in Norfolk which was planted in 1960 and when 23 years old was 42/3½ft and the bigger of two at Fota Island near Cork, mentioned below.

Borde Hill in Sussex had two of the biggest trees until the 1987 gale blew one down and took the top out of the other. They were both planted in 1913 and had reached 85ft. The survivor, in the North Garden, is now 60/8½ft. Two at Exbury, below the upper pool, were both damaged in the gale and may have begun to die back at the top before that. One is 88/7ft and the other, broken to 70/7ft. One at Ashford Chase near Petersfield in Hampshire has not been seen since 1979 and it was a fine tree then, 80/8ft so it is hoped that it is still there.

The Irish contingent is led by the bigger of two in Mount Usher garden at Ashford, County Wicklow, now 75/8½ft. It looks as if it is very vigorous, but in 23 years it added only 29in to its girth and 13ft to its height. The other is 70/5ft. The Fota tree, mentioned above for good growth, was planted in 1936 and is 85/7ft. In 21 years it had added 41in to its girth and 39ft to its height. A smaller tree there, now 50/5ft is probably of the same age and growing more slowly, as in 1966 it was almost the same size as the other. There is a good, slender specimen in the Pleasure Grounds at Abbeyleix, County Leix, 82/5½ft and in the National Botanic Garden at Glasnevin near Dublin a good tree is 70/5ft.

TULIP-TREE

Liriodendron tulipifera

It is fitting that the most euphonious of botanical names should belong to a tree of great stature, luxuriant foliage and remarkable flowers. The Tulip-tree makes very rapid growth on good, fertile sheltered sites, not too acid nor liable to drying out quickly, but only in those regions with warm summers. North of the English midlands it is slower, does not become very big and is shy in flowering, but it is still a splendid foliage tree. On any site it is slow to reach its flowering age, which is seldom less than 25 years from planting. Until maturity approaches, it is more valuable as a foliage tree than as a flowering tree for although the flowers are big, they do not show much being among fully unfolded leaves, and mainly green themselves. The best way to appreciate the beauty of the flowers is to float them on a bowl of water on a table. Only on the oldest trees are the flowers numerous and conspicuous.

The flowers show that the tree is a magnolia, and very primitive indeed. It differs from the true Magnolias in having buds formed from stipules, and in the lobed leaves. As in others in the Family, the flower is bowl-shaped, because it evolved before there were precision flyers like bees and flies to pollinate it, and it had to cater for the more blundering beetles. It has no differentiation between the rings of sepals and petals, so they are referred to collectively as 'tepals'. The broadly bilobed leaves are similar to those of Ginkgo and Bauhinia and an occasional leaf on a young Bigleaf storax, but otherwise of a shape not seen in our trees.

The Tulip-tree ranges from Ontario to Louisiana and grows there in a very different shape from how it does here. As a young tree with us it is a shapely but usually quite broad conic tree with the main stem persisting rarely more than 20ft. In America it grows like a hybrid poplar, narrowly conic, very open-crowned with sparse whorls of slender, raised branches, and a pole-like stem straight to the tip 100ft up. With age, in Britain, the crown grows ever more broad with heavy, irregularly set branches and many domed sub-crowns. In the best stands in America, particularly in Pennsylvania and Delaware, even casually by roadsides, the slender, conic light crown may be maintained to 150ft, clear of branches and like a machined pole for over 100ft. These are regrowth stands, cut over maybe as little as 60 years before. Old survivors in estates and occasional reserves now preserved do, if in the open, have some big branches, but if in woods they may be 20ft round and clear for 30ft. One in Tyler's Wood, Winterthur Garden, is 180/16½ft and with few branches until it spreads a big but fairly narrow and upright crown at about 80ft.

The tree was introduced by the early settlers in Virginia, perhaps around 1630. John Banister sent it to Henry Compton, Bishop of London, at Fulham Palace before 1680 but only one tree is known today to be of this sort of age. This is partly because it was very rare for a long time, since even today, when seed-dormancy and germination techniques are understood better, and transport is rapid, wild seed gives very poor rates of germination, as it does in America, and in 1680 it will have been worse. It is also partly related to the tree rarely living very long, being fragile. There are two trees, one of which is known to date from 1685 and the other, much bigger, should be older, but so many of the large trees known earlier have disappeared this century that it must be classed as a short-lived tree.

The fastest growth in girth in a young tree is almost three inches a year, shown by two specimens. One at Coleton Ralegh in Devon was planted in 1926 and was 62/13ft by 1984. The other is at Lanhydrock in Cornwall, planted in 1933 and 80/10½ft in 1987. At least two inches a year has been added by the tree at Killerton, planted after 1925 to replace the big old tree that died before 1960. The young tree was 95/12ft in 1992. Two trees planted in 1932 in Rosemoor Garden near Torrington promise well, being now 85/9ft and 82/8ft. A younger tree at Stourhead, planted in 1962 was 25 years later 50/4½ft. All these examples are in the southwest, and of the 17 biggest old trees, seven are in the southwest of England, six in the southeast. Although this reflects the warmth-dependent growth, it is not at all representative of the distribution as a whole.

In Scotland, a tree at Dollar in Fife is 62/9ft; at Doune House, Perthshire, the best is 88/8ft and further north, on Deeside, one at Durris House is 50/5ft, and further again, at Reelig House, Inverness-shire one is 80/8ft. At Novar, Easter Ross, there is a forked tree of 56ft. More unexpectedly, two more are way out to the west. On Mull, Torosay Castle has one, rather broken now, 56/15ft, and Dundonnell, Wester Ross, has a rugged old tree 70/9ft at two feet. In Northern Ireland, Hockley Manor, Armagh, has one 80/18ft at two feet, and at Sheldon Abbey, County

Tulip-tree (*Liriodendron tulipifera*): a tree of great stature

Wicklow in the Irish Republic, a widely forked tree dating from 1770 is 80/13ft +11.

The oldest dated tree and one that might claim to be the biggest is at Esher Place in Surrey, standing behind a plaque saying that it was brought from the Carolinas in 1685. It is a grand old tree, with a spreading, thin-topped crown, 70/30ft, forking very wide by eight feet, but the same size at three feet and five feet up, scarcely distorted by the vast bracket to one stem, swelling out above six feet.

A more shapely claimant to the title is an undated, and scarcely known tree in the old wall garden beside the pinetum at Golden Grove, Carmarthen. I was told about it when I was there in 1982, so it was known at least on the estate, but there is no mention of it in the literature. It was 80/26½ft, and although a broad tree and growing a few sprouts, the bole is a respectable cylinder for eight feet, which makes it a clear champion, and a wonderful specimen. The next biggest was, in 1985, in Leigh Park, Havant, Hampshire. This must be the one that Elwes and Henry put in 'Hale Park, Havant' as it fits the size, and there are no trees of interest at all in Hale Park. If this was the one, it was 75/18ft in 1879, and 105/21½ft in 1985 with a good, clean bole.

In adjacent properties on Leith Hill in Surrey there were, pre-gales, and with any luck there are still, two of the finest Tulip-trees. At Kitlands, the tree 111/20ft in 1987, is remarkable for both its long-conic-topped columnar crown and its clear trunk of ten feet. The nearby tree in Leith Place was 95/20½ft and broader in the crown but very nearly as good. Taplow House, Taplow had, in 1974, two as big, and one of them as good. This was 120/20ft with a fine bole, and the other was 80/20ft, dividing into three trunks at six feet up.

At Melbury in Dorset, a tree by the Chapel is 72/20ft with a bole beset by sprouts. At Stourhead, the great tree near the southern shore of the Lake, is 120/20ft at three feet, spoiled only by the fork at three to five feet. At Haffield House, Herefordshire, a tree with low branches is 108/20ft measured round the main stem above the branches. At Glendurgan, Cornwall, two trees planted in 1832 were 111/20ft and 108/13ft in 1984, both with heavy branches in the lower crown. A shapely tree at Priory Court by a corner on the hill down into Bradford-upon-Avon, is 108/16ft.

COMMON MULBERRY

Morus nigra

This species has no place in a book devoted to inspiring and noble specimen trees, as it has never managed to make anything of the kind. A sprawling low tree on a short, bent and burred stem is as much as one can expect of it. I drag it in willingly, however, because who wants a book, or person, to be boringly predictable? And it is a splendid subject with which to break the monotony as it has two features of compelling interest. One is that although it has been in cultivation as long as any tree, propagated and spread for a few thousand years over much of the temperate world, it has, uniquely, remained invariable everywhere at all times. There is not a single cultivar. At least, even Gerd Krussmann, who hoarded every scrap of information on varieties that he could find all his working life and detailed thousands in his works, had none at all for Black Mulberry. Only the 1990–91 edition of *The Plantfinder* spoils this by citing two, 'Chelsea' and 'Wellington'. This invaluable work does not describe plants, so I do not know how they differ from the type nor how permanent they are likely to be. Since there are many gardens in Chelsea which pride themselves on supposedly very old trees, I suspect that 'Chelsea' has been propagated for its fruit, deemed to be more luscious than those on other trees.

The second feature is that the Black Mulberry has an unassailable reputation for growing very slowly to a great age, and I think this is spurious. I set about it some years ago, very convincingly in the pages of *The Garden*, but, as is to be expected, this had no apparent effect and the stories go on, so this is a chance to repeat it. In my early tree-watching days, I accepted these myths like everyone else and saw no reason to question them. Then in 1966 Maxwell Eley showed me round his garden at East Bergholt and I emerged from under a big rhododendron to tell him that the mulberry I had just measured was nearly seven feet round and was the biggest I had yet seen. He was interested and said, 'So, how old would you reckon it to be?' I had by then formulated my 'one inch a year' rule for growth in girth of normally vigorous trees, a hasty mental computation started with the 82in and doubled it at once for slow growth. Then I added 50 years for it being a mulberry, and another 50 vaguely taking account of the King James plantings, and rounded up for luck, and said, 'Well, I suppose it will be about 300 years'. He did not actually snort, being too kind for that but he looked down at me from his six feet four and said, 'That tree was planted on the day I was born. And I am sixty-four'. The likelihood that the Black Mulberry would be a tree of rapid growth should have been obvious from its apparent origin in the Black Sea region, although its natural range cannot now be known more than vaguely, and from its luxuriantly leafy crown.

It is therefore highly significant that no tree more than 11ft round was known to Elwes in 1912 and none as big is known today. All the reputedly very old trees that Elwes found were in poor shape and small. For a tree to date from the King James inspired plantings of 1605 to be only ten feet round its mean annual increase would have to be less than one inch in three years. This is not credible for a healthy tree with the densely leafy crown of a mulberry. The majority of the good, measurable trunks I found for years were close to five feet round and if the East Bergholt tree were any guide, these would be less than 60 years old, and the biggest were less than 100 years.

Dated trees largely bear this out. An 1845 tree at Wray Castle in Cumbria is only 33/4ft, but this tree is at the extreme of the northern range of the tree in Britain. Two 1897 trees at Wells Cathedral are 26/6ft and 30/5½ft; Christopher Lloyd's tree at Great Dixter in Sussex planted in 1910 is 30/6ft and two 1938 trees at Stanway in Gloucestershire are 26/4½ft and 28/4ft. All these show a mean annual increase close to the expected one inch a year. A reclining tree at Jenkyn Place in Bentley, Hampshire, planted in 1946 is 26/4ft and one as far north as the Mirfield Community in Yorkshire is three feet round after only 29 years, so that rate can be exceeded.

The clue to the supposedly ancient trees, planted by Shakespeare and sat under by Milton lies, I think, in the traditional method of propagation. This was by truncheons. These are five-foot lengths of mature branches sunk two feet into the soil. Innumerable sprouts emerge from the inevitable burrs and soon make a leafy, fruiting, low tree. This was much preferred to growing seedlings, which remain slender, unimposing and fruitless for many years. The sprouty burrs spread a little over the crosscut top, but do not seal it and it decays after some thirty years. The spray of now quite big branches around the top of the truncheon begins to open out until some rest on the ground. The tree is now '300 years old' and fit for Shakespeare. Soon, the decayed bole either gives way, or is regarded as unsightly, and another truncheon is made from a branch and the cycle is renewed. Two truncheons were planted at Alice Holt in 1954 and are now venerable trees about 25/3½ft at two feet, and have long been fruiting. One planted in 1952 at Snowdenham House near Bramley, Surrey, is 36/3½ft and much decayed.

It is thus easy to see why there are no big mulberries, and there never will be. They grow fast and have short lives. There may be a few genuinely old trees, but

Common Mulberry (*Morus nigra*):
close-up of bole

they will be only a ring of branches around where the long departed old stem had stood. It is worthy of note that in these cases there is nearly always a mound in the centre. It looks as if these were attempts to hold the old stem together by partially burying it, and supporting the inner parts of the collapsing branches. The tree at Broadlands in Hampshire with the date '1605' on its label is, I am sure, giving the supposed date of the introduction of the tree, like that on the '1754' Ginkgo nearby, rather than the date of planting. The mulberry is broken, decayed and only eight feet round.

The Black Mulberry is grown in North Wales and as far north as Cumbria in the west, and to York in the east. Few indeed are worth celebrating or even mentioning. The best I have seen is at Weathersdane near Wye in Kent, which is 28/10ft at one foot, where it is a clean, rounded trunk. The tree with the biggest spread seen is at Cliveden, Buckinghamshire, 30/7½ft, which can be measured only at six inches because of low branches which give the crown a width of 60ft. A good tree, measurable at the normal five feet is 52/6 in the gardens of Buckingham Palace. Another is at Athelhampton in Dorset, 33/6½ft. One measurable only at two feet at Sullington Manor in Sussex is 46/8ft.

COIGUE

Nothofagus dombeyi

This might be better placed under the name 'Dombey's Beech', but since the Chilean Spanish names have been used in this book for the Southern beeches, consistency will be maintained. The tree, in any case, is the choicest evergreen broad-leaf over much of Britain and the most rapid in growth. It grows in Kew and the far southeast, but is tender in the northeast and achieves its outstanding rates of growth only in Dorset and to the west, and best of all in Ireland, north and south. It revels in cool summers and a high year-round rainfall. Given those, it rapidly shows its superiority over other broad-leaf evergreens like the Holm and Lucombe Oaks.

The foliage is black from a distance, and dense, but it is held well and the leaves, one to one and a half inches long, are glossy and prettily toothed. The flowers add greatly to the attraction as they are made up of three scarlet protruding stamens. The bark is also unusually interesting visually as it matures from dark grey to brown ridges, which strip with age showing orange and then dark crimson beneath. Plants are thin and straggly for several years and begin to thicken their trunks with their customary great vigour only when the small, ascending branches have built up dense systems of foliage. Most of the big trees bear a few big, rising branches at wide intervals on the lower stem although a few, like the one at Bodnant, hold a dozen or so more spreading, on the basal length and are very big bushes.

The species was introduced in 1916 when F.R.S. Balfour of Dawyck received a quantity of seed and sent it to Kew. Only four seedlings were raised and only one of these seems to have been traced. In 1973 it was 65/6½ft at Trewithen, near Truro. Kew had more seedlings in 1922, planted one or more itself and gave one to Captain Collingwood Ingram at The Grange, Benenden, Kent. The 1928 pair at Mount Usher were probably of this origin, too. After another import to Kew in 1930 the tree became more widely planted. Now there are trees from Dundonnell in Wester Ross, Crathes Castle in the east, and Brook Hall, County Derry, in Northern Ireland, scattered rather thinly to Cornwall and Kent.

The progress of the four biggest trees at Mount Usher has been remarkable. The two 1928 trees were 72/8½ft and 85/8½ft in 1966 when 38 years old. When 47 years old they were both 88/10½ft. When they were 61 years old, in 1989, they were 102/13ft and 115/13½ft. A third tree by the river was 56/6½ft in 1966 and 88/10½ft by 1989, and one by the gate was 75/10½ft in 1989. Two by the River Walk were 62/5½ft and 62/4½ft in 1989 so will be worth watching. Muncaster Castle near Ravenglass, Cumbria also has many fine specimens. One off the drive was 75/6ft in 1971 and is now 102/10ft and another the other side is now 89/9ft. At Winkworth Arboretum in Surrey, one planted on the top of the bank in 1937 was 42/4ft in 1960 and 85/9ft

Coigue (*Nothofagus dombeyi*):
Muncaster Castle, Cumbria

in 1991. At Hillsborough, County Down, a big, spreading tree but with a good stem was 85/9½ft in 1976 and six years later was 92/10½ft.

A splendid tree planted at Minterne in Dorset in 1934 was 62/6ft when 33 years old and in 1988 it was 105/10½ft. At Rowallane, County Down, one tree was 65/7ft in 1966 and was 82/10½ft in 1991 when another is 85/8½ft. In Roche's Arboretum in Sussex, a slender young tree in 1967 was 52/3ft and now, in the remains left by the gale of October 1987 it is 95/7½ft. At Bulkeley Mill in Gwynedd, a good specimen was 50/3½ft in 1960 and grew to be 82/8½ft by 1984. Both Crathes Castle and Brodick Castle have trees of 72/8½ft. A tree planted in 1936 in Crarae Garden, Argyll 42/3½ft in 1969 was 72/8ft in 1987. The outsize bush in Bodnant Garden is in Chapel Walk. Measured at one foot from the ground it was 58/8½ft in 1966 and 72/10½ft in 1976. Today it is 98/14ft measured round the forking stem at five feet. One in the Savill Garden, Windsor Great Park, was 56/3½ft in 1975 and 98/6ft in 1990. In Michael's Walk at Birr Castle, a tree planted in 1932 was 48/4½ft in 1966 and 75/7½ft in 1989.

ROBLE

Nothofagus obliqua

The full name, 'Roble Beech', might be better for this tree. 'Roble' is Spanish for oak and was given to the tree by the Spanish invaders and settlers as it was the common countryside tree in the manner of the oaks in their homeland. But it is a beech. It is one of that group of beeches which evolved in Gondwanaland before the super-continent broke up and took various species to New Zealand, Australia, Tasmania, New Guinea and southern South America. They are very beech-like in their fruit; three nutlets in a woody capsule with tubercles or little spikes on the outside of the four valves. (The peculiar lack in the English language of a commonly understood term to describe little conic or flattened projections from a surface is a perennial trial to botanists. The favoured course is to write 'awl-shaped', although few readers will have seen an awl, and many of the objects are not truly that shape, anyway.)

This southern hemisphere group of over 20 species has recently been augmented by new species found in Papua New Guinea and only eleven are growing outside a few specialist collections. Six of these are evergreen and one partially so. Six are from South America, four of them deciduous; three from New Zealand, all evergreen or semi-evergreen, and one each from Tasmania and Australia, both fully evergreen. Their generic name 'Nothofagus' means 'false beech' and this was probably a slip, now irremediable, for 'Notofagus' meaning 'southern beech', the collective common name for the group.

The Roble is the most commonly grown species in all parts of Britain, even locally in small forest plots. In Chile it extends north into the region of Mediterranean climate, beyond others of the genus there. So some provenances at least withstand dry, hot summers, and range south to 41 degrees. It is among the hardiest. In Britain, very severe frosty periods can kill young trees to the ground, but no established trees have suffered more than some die-back in the crown. Its slender branches and very rapid growth render it susceptible to breakage and many of the tallest trees have lost upper branches.

There have been three main introductions of this tree, the first by Elwes in 1902, the next by Balfour of Dawyck in 1917 and then Harold Comber of Nymans sent a quantity in 1926. Several of the big trees are probably originals from Elwes's seed but only three are properly dated, two at Kew and one at Tortworth Court and none of these has been visited for 13 years. One assumed to have been an original was by the drive at Grayswood Hill in Surrey, and was 80/9ft in 1982 but was wrecked by the October gale in 1987. The validity of accepting the biggest trees as coming from Elwes's seed has been fatally weakened by the discovery that the biggest, in the Sunningdale Nurseries, is not after all one of these, although it was 75/11ft in 1975, but is a Balfour tree of 1917. The known original at Tortworth was 85/8ft in

1976, and the two dated at Kew were 82/7ft in 1987. In the Wilderness at Nymans one of the six was 105/8ft in 1985, and at South Lodge, Lower Beeding, Sussex, the biggest of eight similar trees almost sure to be of Comber's 1926 origin, were 115/8ft and 105/8½ft when they were all blown down. At Trewithen near Truro one was 82/9ft in 1985 and may survive.

There are many records of extremely rapid growth by young trees, and these are mostly more notable for growth in height rather than in girth, which is the reverse of the case in the Rauli. The youngest example, however, shows great vigour in both dimensions. At the London University Botanic Garden in Englefield Green, on Bagshot Sand, it was 92/6½ft in 27 years. On the same soil, in the Valley Gardens, Windsor Great Park, a tree grew to 70/3ft in 14 years and to 92/5ft in 26 years but blew over when 98/6½ft and 37 years old. In the Lyndford Pinetum near Brandon, Norfolk, a tree planted in 1960 was 80/6ft when 30 years old.

Some fine specimens remain to be mentioned. A notable one at Kew between the Cumberland Gate and Palm House Pond was planted in 1936 and in 1991 was 88/7½ft. Another at Bulkeley Mill near Llanrwst, Gwynedd dates from 1926 and was 85/9ft in 1984. A 1933 tree at Blairquhan, Ayrshire, was 85/8ft in 1984. A 1925 tree at Weasenham, Norfolk was 88/8ft in 1990. The biggest tree is undated, at Ashbourne House near Cork, and was 98/10½ft in 1987. At Muncaster Castle in

Roble (*Nothofagus obliqua*):
Killerton, Devon

Cumbria there are groups and lines in all parts, some of them dated, but the best group is undated, in the 'private garden' where one tree by the gate is 98/6ft and another is 102/7ft. A third has exceptionally large leaves. A Comber tree in the Royal Botanic Garden in Edinburgh is 62/7ft. At Benmore, Argyll, a group has trees to 95/7ft. A fine specimen at Stowe School by the cricket-ground is 85/8ft and one at Mount Usher, County Wicklow, is 88/8½ft. At Rowallane, County Down, one is 72/9ft; at Howick, Northumberland, a tree is 85/7½ft.

RAULI

Nothofagus procera (N. nervosa)

The Rauli is the best southern beech we can grow for handsome foliage, spring and autumn colour, and for sheer sturdy vigour. Its leaves emerge orange-brown before turning bright, light green and maturing darker. Then in October they turn yellow, orange and often crimson. They are the biggest of the genus that we can grow, although variable in size within and between individuals. They are usually over three inches long and on some trees five or six inches, very evenly finely sharp-toothed and with a classic 'carpinifolia' pattern of numerous, straight, parallel and prominent veins. The southern beeches are singularly obliging with their numbers of vein-pairs, a feature which is usually either unreliable or has too much overlapping between species to be of great use. In *Nothofagus*, however, they are positive and reliable in distinguishing the common deciduous species. The evergreen ones have no visible veins, anyway. Antarctic beech has three to five; Lenga, (*N. pumilio*) has six to seven; Roble has eight to eleven and Rauli has fifteen to twenty-two.

Rauli has been planted in small numbers in most of the important tree gardens in the British Isles and in small plots in some forests. It was introduced in 1910 by R.F.S. Balfour of Dawyck who sent it to many gardens from 1914 onwards, and in 1913 to Kew by Bean.It is hardy everywhere generally but there have been losses during the most severe winters, when trees in their first two or three years can be killed back to ground level. They will often re-grow shoots three feet long in the next year, but some of these fail soon after. In Chile it grows above the Roble in cooler sites, and from its behaviour in Britain, this may well be because it needs the higher rainfall, for in the dry east of England it succeeds only on damp sites, and away from those it is less hardy than the Roble. With few exceptions, the big and fast-growing trees are in high rainfall areas of the west and in Ireland.

The shoots are lightly covered in long hairs and are much the stoutest among the southern beeches we can grow, and the buds the biggest. Unused to the warm periods normal during the British winters, these buds show an alarming propensity to swell and prepare to shoot in March, two months before it is safe to do so. Returning cold weather usually stops this in its tracks, but late frosts will still burn back early shoots causing temporary damage. In other respects the foliage is extremely healthy and it is only the stem which can run into trouble. On sites at or towards the foot of long steep slopes, sharp frosts have caused some canker leading to dieback. Great spotted woodpeckers have in the last thirty years taken to emulating their American relatives in sap-sucking. They do a much neater job, making smaller holes without wide entrances but about as deep. Not only is the purpose obscure but it is not known whether they return to the holes and if so when, because no one has yet seen one at work. It is known to be the work of this species only because it is seen on trees beyond the more limited ranges of the other two woodpeckers here. Although a few native trees are affected, like the Common Oak, Broadleaf Lime and even the Box, it is, oddly, a few South American trees which are favoured most, beyond the North American Red Oak and American Linden, which are also victims in places. The tree more used than any is the hybrid Nymans Eucryphia. The Rauli is less often afflicted and so is the Coigue or Dombey's Southern Beech, but one of these, at Nymans, is the only tree I have seen worked so extensively as, apparently, to kill it.

With its stout, strong branches, the Rauli does not suffer the breakage frequent in the Roble, but it is much more susceptible to being blown down. The gales of 1987 and 1990 removed at least nine trees out of the small number at risk. These included four among the biggest, notably trees of over ten feet in girth at Caerhays

Rauli (*Nothofagus procera*):
Benmore, Argyll

Castle and at Wakehurst Place, and one whose vigour made it a regular subject for measurement, at Winkworth Arboretum. It had been planted in 1937 and ended its life fifty years old, having been 92/8½ft three years before.

The late Earl of Bradford showed keen interest in southern beeches, planting many species on his properties at Weston Park, Staffordshire, and the Tavistock Woods in Devonshire, as well as helping to inspire, organise and partake in a seed-collecting tour in Chile. Two trees he planted in the Tavistock Woods were raised in 1960, planted in 1961 and nine years later were 50/2ft. One was 65/3ft in 1977 but both succumbed to very severe frosts a few years after that. A tree in a little Forest Garden at Rheidol in Powis, one of the many such groups planted by Frank Best when he was Conservator for Wales, was 60/3ft when 15 years old; a ten year old tree at the London University Botanic Gardens in Englefield Green was 40/2ft planted in 1989, and one in Aberdeen University Botanic Garden, planted in 1970, was 52/4ft when 17 years old in 1987. At nearly 1000ft altitude in Vivod Forest Garden, another Frank Best planting, was planted in 1953 and was 85/5ft in 1988. Desmond Clarke, the editor of the revised editions of W.J. Bean's *Trees and Shrubs Hardy in the British Isles* planted one in his garden near Haslemere in Chase Lane, in 1956. When 30 years old it was a superb tree, 52/5ft.

Many of the biggest trees now following have made similarly great growth, as is evident from their planting dates where known, or, in the undated trees, from earlier measurements, a few of which will be added. The greatest tree of them all is by the drive near the castle at Brodick Castle on Arran. It is of unknown date but was 60/9½ft in 1957 and in 1988 it was a sturdy and luxuriant 98/13½ft. The next biggest is at Mount Usher in County Wicklow in the Nothofagus Grove. The two great Coigue beside it were planted in 1928 and the Rauli will most probably be of the same age. It was 52/6ft in 1966 and by 1989 it had attained 105/11ft. A tree of unknown but similar age in the wood on the hill at Frensham Hall in Shottermill, Surrey, should by now be equally big. In 1981 it was 92/10½ft.

In eastern England, the biggest is an original tree planted in 1915 at East Bergholt Place in Suffolk. This garden is on the shore of an estuary and in a very narrow zone which is milder than the rest of East Anglia. The tree has a large, domed crown on a good stem and in 1972 it was 85/9½ft, but was blown down in 1987. At Muncaster Castle on the coast of Cumbria, a specimen planted in 1923 in the garden terrace is now 80/10½ft. An undated tree at Minterne in Dorset was 52/5ft in 1967 and 88/8½ft in 1988. One beside the drive through Durris Estate on Deeside was 42/4ft in 1955 and 70/9½ft in 1987. A tree at Benmore, Argyll, in a 1937 planting, was 53/4ft in 1966 and 70/9½ft in 1983. At Powis Castle on the hill in the Garden, a tree is 95/7ft and at Rowallane, County Down, one that was 44/6½ft in 1966 is now 65/9ft.

LONDON PLANE

Platanus x *acerifolia* (plate 5)

This is the first intercontinental hybrid tree to have arisen, whatever the details of its somewhat obscure origin. Its parents are the great Oriental Plane and the Western Plane which the Americans prefer to call 'Sycamore'. The Oriental Plane grows from the Balkan Mountains through Asia Minor to Iran and has long been planted in Kashmir, where it is called 'chenar'. The Western Plane has the reputation of being unable to grow in the cool summers of Britain, and although that is now seen to be not quite true, it remains that despite numerous introductions since 1637 none had been noted as surviving and none of any significant age is known. Hence it has been said that none could ever have flowered in Britain, so the hybrid must have arisen in a warmer climate, probably in southern France or in Spain.

The issue is much confounded by botanists not distinguishing the London from the American Plane until this century, and even until quite recently the London Plane form 'Augustine Henry' was being sold as a Californian species. Early references to Western Plane growing in England refer, where any description is given, to London Plane. This hybrid was also treated until about 1850, as a variety of the Oriental Plane. Confusion was such that even the great Augustine Henry listed in 1906 some of the great specimen London Planes as Oriental and one Oriental as a London Plane.

Stephen Spongberg in *A Reunion of Trees* (1990) traces the origin of the London Plane to the younger John Tradescant bringing seed or cuttings of the American Plane to Lambeth in 1637. He was already growing Oriental Plane in the garden. Hybrid seedlings arose and he gave some to Jacob Bobart at Oxford University Botanic Garden. Unfortunately, Spongberg goes on to speculate that Bobart planted one in Magdalen College in 1670 and says that this is the oldest. But that tree is now given the planting date of 1801 and numerous trees older than that are known. Also Desmond Clarke thinks that Bobart's herbarium specimen shows that it could be the American species and suggests that any hybrid planes that Bobart had could have been acquired from a European botanic garden.

The alternative account of the first London Planes in Britain centres round Bishop Gunning who was at Ely from 1674 to 1684. He is thought to have planted during that time the enormous tree at the Bishop's Palace across the road from the Cathedral, and to have been concerned with the great tree in Ranelagh Park, Barnes, and possibly others at Woolbeding, Sussex and at Peamore, Exeter. Certainly the Ely tree is the biggest, although far from the best one known. It is a trifle disturbing that although Gunning was at Oxford in Bobart's time, the tree has grown since 1904 sufficiently to throw doubt on its reputed age, although this might be because it divides low and its girth is increasingly augmented by branch-swell.

With both parents trees of noted longevity and size, together with hybrid vigour, which is very evident in the rate of growth, it is not surprising that London Plane after 250–300 years has yielded some of the biggest trees in the land and threatens to carry on to far greater sizes over a long period ahead. It is probable that in a 100 years time all our biggest trees will be London Planes and the two redwoods. The oldest planes, whatever their exact ages may be, and many are at least 250 years old, are all in full vigour with no signs of incipient decrepitude. Some young trees in cities are attacked by anthracnose, *Gnominia*, put down to early season warmth in streets. This kills the emerging flowers and shoots, but no old tree seems to have been affected.

The tree has many merits for use in city streets, and a few demerits. It will grow fast in poor, made-up soils with brickbats, rubble and clay, little inconvenienced by compaction or by the entire root-run being paved over. It virtually never sheds branches in gales and is exceptionally windfirm. In the 1987 gale, a number were blown over in London parks, where their roots were under tarmac. It responds rapidly to pruning of any severity and in the south of France where shoot-growth is extremely vigorous, this is used by cutting the canopy over the street back to the stem in autumn to give winter light and sun. In early summer the canopy has begun to grow out again and by midsummer it is shading the street.

The less desirable features are that without pruning, a plane will outgrow the space available and shade windows of many storeys. In the hot year of 1976 with drought, planes shed piles of big, curved, hard plates from the bark making walking under them very difficult. The tufts of fine hairs on the seeds break into tiny fragments which can cause irritation to eyes when the fruit distintegrate in gutters in winter. The roots can lift paving and in Philadelphia where half a million planes line streets, a high proportion of the claims for personal injury received by the City authorities is due to the uneven sidewalks caused by London Planes.

Although so well known for its ability to withstand smoke and poor soils in cities, the London Plane grows into a bigger, finer tree in the countryside. Where it has the space, it develops an immense, domed crown which increases slowly in height. In woodland where lateral growth is restricted, growth in height remains more vigorous and the tallest broad-leaf trees in Britain are the group of planes in high beech and oak woodland at Bryanston School, in Dorset.

The Ely plane must come first as the biggest, the most famous, and the possibility of being an original tree. Its trunk is so misshapen that several people could stand inside the tightly drawn tape within the concavity on one side, but this is not caused by decay. It has smooth, healthy bark and although arising from the largest of the three limbs being offset from the other two, the six feet of trunk is otherwise reasonably circular. The crown is complete and vast and the tree measures 120/30ft. The main doubt as to its 1685 origin is that the girth was 20½ft in 1904 so it has added 9½ft in 86 years. At that rate of growth it could have been planted as late as 1775 and still have been 20½ft by 1904. The Ranelagh Park tree has a better trunk, dividing into three at 15ft and nearly cylindric, although it has a flared base and flutes from this are smoothing out until eight feet up. It is 132/26ft and was 25ft 4in round in 1903. On the same basis as the estimate for Ely, this suggests a planting around 1700 and could be taken as a fair confirmation of possible 1685 planting.

The finest specimen of all, however, has no recorded nor anecdotal history at all, and is known to very few. It is at Lydney Park, Gloucestershire. It was noted, but not measured, during a meeting there of the Royal Forestry Society 20 years ago and not measured until I saw it in 1983. Just inside the gate to the Deer Park, it is quite superb. It is 110/28ft and has a bole of 15ft of near perfect cylinder, unmatched by any tree of this size.

The tallest London Plane, and tallest broad-leaf tree in Britain is one of three among five planted in 1740 by the river towards the road at Bryanston School, Blandford Forum, but I would not like to say which one. They are nearly impossible to measure in the summer with tall trees blocking most lines of sight, and in winter it is hard to decide which is the truest top in the high domes seen through other shoots. At the first visit I had one 153/18½ft and two 150/18ft and 150/19ft, but next winter it seemed that they were 155–160ft tall. Another in the same group is 138/22½ft.

The ugliest London Plane, a delightful monster, is by the A419 at Chilton Foliat and was valued enough as a feature, if not a beauty, to have a plinth made to preserve it when the road was widened. Despite what must have been a grievous loss of feeding roots, its strange truncated crown showed no stress. It has a splendidly cylindrical bole 26ft round, rising about eight feet and degenerating at once into three conical stems which taper and divide to make a little crown barely 50ft tall.

The biggest trunk of all is disqualified by being a fusion of two. This is on the lawn at Mottisfont Abbey near Romsey and is 120/38ft, and highly elliptical. The two stems, parting at ten feet up, can be visualised as having centres eight feet apart as they reach the ground. The intriguing part of this is that trees do not fuse. If they do, then where are examples of the process partially completed? Where are there trees just beginning to fuse? None is seen here, and in the crowded stands of immense redwoods in northern California, there is always room to squeeze between the closest pairs. Coppice shoots crowded round the edges of stumps of oaks, ash and willows are never seen to be fusing. So it cannot happen. Yet there is an engraving in the house at Mottisfont, I am assured, that shows these two trees about eight feet apart. Two other planes on the lawn are normal and splendid trees, 115/23ft and 125/24ft.

The finest plane in or near London is by the Festival Walk at Carshalton. It is 140/22½ft and has a trunk about 15ft smoothly rounded. A rival at Montpellier Road, Twickenham, has been spoiled by needing shortening back but it is still 108/20½ft with a superb trunk for 40ft. A plane with half its extensive crown over the main road through Witley in Surrey, stands on the edge of the Rectory garden and is now 128/22ft with a short trunk. At Wootton House near Dorking a plane 102/22½ft is attributed by some to John Evelyn's planting when he lived there. Since Evelyn died in 1706, that would, if true, make it among the oldest planes.

ORIENTAL PLANE

Platanus orientalis

If the tree chosen for adorning so many city squares and streets had been the Oriental Plane instead of its hybrid, the London Plane, many urban prospects would now be immensely more attractive. That the squares might be severely restricted in their open places and the streets impassable to traffic, need not concern us. That is a trifle that a little early training could avoid. In place of the coarse, heavy foliage of a rather garish green, there would be canopies of delightful, airy, star-like leaves of pale green turning bronzed russet in autumn.

Although the Oriental lacks the hybrid vigour of the London Plane it is sturdy and vigorous enough for the purpose, and probably as resistant to urban air and paved root-runs, and is even more reliably healthy. That it was not planted is due to the great reputation the London Plane acquired soon after the early plantings, for growth in sooty air, inspiring its adoption by the city and park authorities. The use of Oriental tails off north of the Midlands and it is scarcely seen at all in Scotland. The other factor against it is the received idea that it grows huge and spreading branches from near the base.

The best known specimens mostly have this feature. One at Woolbeding in Sussex has several layered branches resting on the ground up to 90ft long, and trees at Melbury Park in Dorset and elsewhere are heading that way, but it is far from an invariable feature. One of the oldest and finest specimens, one of several Oriental Planes that Henry took to be London Plane, now 85/20ft at Bisterne in Hampshire, has a superb bole spoiled only by a few branches which could have been removed with secateurs when it was young. A tree at Kew, southeast of the Palm House, 98/12ft, has a grand clean bole for 15ft. It may have been pruned.

The tree is native to the eastern Mediterranean shores and islands, and the Levant, but has been spread by cultivation far beyond its original range. It is not native to Kashmir but has been there so long and is so successful that, as the 'Chenar', it is popularly supposed to belong there. The date of introduction to Britain is not known precisely but it was being grown here by 1562. There was complete confusion among the three planes, Oriental, American and London, until Henry sorted it out in 1911. Early records of the American Plane belonged to the London Plane, and that was regarded as a form of the Oriental, and even Henry called the famous Ely plane 'Orientalis' and, as stated above, the Bisterne Oriental, the 'London'.

A few young, dated trees have grown fast enough to make the London Plane look over its shoulder. From a 1915 planting, a tree in the garden of Buckingham Palace is 50/12ft when 63 years old, and another at Glendoick near Perth is 82/11½ft. The much faster growth of two planted in John's Mall in Birr town, County Offaly, in 1950, to 50/10ft and 36/9ft when 37 years old, cannot be discounted entirely by their stems being singularly conic.

Oriental Plane (*Platanus orientalis*): sturdy and vigorous enough to withstand urban air

The giant of the species is close behind the house at Rycote Park near Thame, Oxfordshire, on a shallow mound and draping big low branches all over it, but with about six feet clear. This was 70/28½ft in 1983. The next is by the drive to Woodstock Park House near Sittingbourne in Kent. This is very similar to the Rycote tree and was 92/27ft in 1982. It is somewhat affected by a swelling when taped at five feet, and is only 21½ft round at six feet. The excellent tree at Weston Park, Shifnal in Staffordshire had no such problems and was 75/24ft in 1977 but was cut down in 1988. At Duntish Court in Dorset the tree cannot be measured at five feet, only at one foot, and is 92/25ft. The biggest at Corsham Court in Wiltshire is a straightforward 92/23½ft although it has big, low branches. In Melbury Park, Dorset, the tree on the bank of the lake has huge, recumbent branches, but an incipient fork in the stem which rather spoils its 75/21ft. The tree in the Ranelagh Park at Barnes has the form of leaf which has been separated as 'Cuneata' but is now usually lumped with the type. Clad in ivy, it is 88/19ft. Being very near the more famous old London Plane, it does show that the Oriental can do well in the conditions regarded as the preserve of the other species.

HYBRID BLACK POPLARS

Populus x *canadensis*

Early in the eighteenth century, not long after its introduction, the Eastern Cottonwood from the eastern half of the USA hybridised spontaneously with the Black Poplar, forms native to western Europe. Several clones have been selected and introduced and have made big trees. As clones of a hybrid between single-sex species, these are all

Hybrid Black Poplar (*Populus* x *canadensis*): distinctive crown forms

either male or female. This, together with distinctive crown forms, is a prime aid in identifying them.

BLACK ITALIAN POPLAR 'Serotina'

The first of these hybrids to be planted widely, arose in France soon after 1700 and was brought to Britain in around 1780, where it was soon commonly planted in preference to the native Black Poplar. It was favoured because it grows even faster, to greater heights, with a long stem clear of burrs and often of branches. It is straight, even if leaning, giving good timber-lengths, and is male, and so does not strew the neighbourhood with cotton-wool covered seeds. It makes an immense tree in less than a 100 years but thereafter it is liable to severe loss of branches in storms, and is not long-lived.

'Serotina' is particularly serotine – it is the last tree in leaf in the landscape. The red male catkins are out by May or before, but the foliage unfolds towards June, red-brown fading over two weeks to quite a pale greyish green. It is sparsely spread over the big crown, which rapidly matures from an open, somewhat narrow and upswept cone of whorled branches, to a big dome of strong, upcurved branches making a wide, very open goblet shape, on a long, clean trunk. The whole tree in exposed positions has a tendency to be noticeably swept but it stands up well. In my student days in Ireland I was shown an avenue of 'Serotina' bordering a narrow road across a lowland bog. The two lines leant uniformly and strongly towards each other over the centre of the road. Some years later, I was talking trees in the lounge of a hotel when a man excused himself for intruding having overheard us, and asked if we could settle a problem that had bothered him for years. An avenue of poplars along a road across an Irish bog leant towards each other and how could that be? It was years later that I learned that road footings sink gradually into bogs, this would bend the trees towards the centre line, and no vagaries of wind need be invented to cause this.

Because of the fragile crown and short life-span, the biggest trees that I knew have now gone, and the survival of those not checked for many years must be doubtful. Two young trees showing exceptional growth are of more potential interest to the next generation of tree-measurers. At Merthyr Mawr, Glamorgan, a good tree planted in 1936 was, when 44 years old, 105/11ft. In the University Botanic Garden at Cambridge, one of several similarly aged trees, planted in 1957 was 32 years later 70/9½ft.

One of the best clear stems is in a field at Chelsworth in Suffolk, a remarkable tree now 138/25ft and without branch or blemish for 30ft. At Munden House near Watford, a tree in the garden was 118/14½ft clear for 55ft, and if that survives, it will be a stirring sight. In a small wood at Abbeyleix House, County Leix, the larger of a pair is 150/17½ft. One near the lake at Bowood House, near Calne, Wiltshire, is 150/16ft. At Huntington Castle, County Carlow, a tree by the river is 130/15ft. Several big trees hang precariously on to life by the River Cherwell in the University Parks and Mesopotamia in Oxford. The biggest in 1989 was 111/15½ft.

Black Italian Poplar 'Serotina'
(*Populus* 'Serotina'): the last tree in
leaf in the landscape

MARYLAND POPLAR 'Marilandica' (plate 6)

This is probably a backcross between 'Serotina' and the Black Poplar, dating from about 1800. It is female and inherits from the Black Poplar much of the density of shoots, making as a young tree a densely domed crown. With age it becomes more like 'Serotina', usually with a good, straight stem but rarely as long. Sometimes the female flowering and snowstorm of cottonwool seeds is the best indication of which it is, but the foliage can give a hint from the very markedly flat-based triangular leaves with jagged toothing. It has been planted in a number of urban parks but big trees decline rapidly and some are now only stumps.

The earliest known specimen was planted at Kew just after 1843 and is a fine tree, surviving the recent gales almost unharmed, and it has a sturdy trunk pruned clean of small shoots. In 1907 it was 90/9ft while in 1967 it was 102/16½ft and it is now 120/18ft. An even better tree, and bigger but of unknown age, is at Peper Harow, near Godalming in Surrey. Its trunk leans a little, but is very clean for 15ft before the first branch, and being 130/20ft it is an impressive tree. It was 16ft round in 1959. Another tall tree is a seedling from the Kew tree, probably therefore a hybrid, at Augustine Henry's old home, Colesbourne, near Cheltenham. It is one of a pair in the Ring Meadow, in which the trees date from 1903 and is 132/9½ft. Even taller is one thought to date from 1825, found by Michael Lear at Osterley Park, Hounslow, and 144/14½ft in 1991.

RAILWAY POPLAR 'Regenerata'

The English name is my fault. Soon after I had learned how distinct this tree is from the 'Serotina' with which I had been classing specimens, there was excitement in finding new examples. I noticed that unusual numbers were growing near the railway lines from London, out of Kings Cross in the north and out of Waterloo to the south. They were around sidings, coach sheds and allotments as far out as Haslemere in the south. Later, I saw how they were also frequent in the Regent's Park area of London, and around the hop gardens of the Wey Valley above Farnham, Surrey, and the cressbeds in Hampshire. I had published the name and it was too late to amend it once it had been adopted in the revision of Bean's *Trees and Shrubs Hardy in the British Isles*. This was too flattering to worry about, although with the passing of time it becomes less apt as the railway trees, planted around 1900, decline and are not being replaced.

'Regenerata' means 'vigorous' and was quickly recognised as a fast growing tree in smoky atmospheres. It arose in 1814 at Arcueil in France, a spontaneous seedling cross between 'Serotina' and 'Marilandica' and was introduced some time around 1870. It is very different in detail and in many grosser features, from 'Serotina'. Its trunk bears many branches and snags and its upper crown is of slender branches arching out and dangling long fine shoots, the reverse of 'Serotina' which has stout branches, incurved, bearing raised stout shoots. 'Regenerata' is female, and is highly distinctive in April with bright green, small fruiting catkins hanging like caterpillars in close rows. In Riverside Garden beside the ring-road in Salisbury, planted in 1913, the bigger of two is 90/15ft. This girth is equalled only, rather oddly, by another in Salisbury, in a garden by the water-meadows, belonging to a house in Harnham Road and easily seen from the car park of a hotel there. It is 124/15ft. The tallest is in Boultham Park, Lincoln, and was 132/14½ft in 1983. Examples in public places like this are always in danger of severe lopping on the grounds of safety. This has befallen several once tall trees by the Serpentine in Hyde Park and Kensington Gardens. One in the former, re-growing strongly now, is 85/13½ft. Rapid early growth is shown by one in the poplar collection at Alice Holt Lodge, Hampshire, 34 years old and 90/6½ft and one in the extension at Wisley Gardens, Surrey, 11 years old and 46/3½ft.

EUGENE'S POPLAR 'Eugenei'
    A seedling found in a bed of silver firs in the nursery of Simon-Louis Frères at Metz in France in 1832 was named after the infant son of the founder, Gabriel Simon, Eugene, then three years old. It is thought to be a cross between a Lombardy Poplar and 'Regenerata' and inherits a measure of the erect habit of the Lombardy. The original tree grew very fast and was 80/9ft in 25 years and 150/23ft when 72 years old. It was introduced to Kew and Glasnevin and probably to Edinburgh, in 1888. It is distinguished by being a male tree with strongly raised whorls of light branches making a conic crown with smaller leaves than the related hybrids. It is sometimes seen in roadside plantings and some of the larger gardens but remains uncommon.
    The smaller of the two original trees at Kew had to be removed in 1984. The larger, which was 90/5ft in 1912 when 24 years old and 118/11ft when 78 years old, is now 135/12½ft. At Glasnevin, the largest of three original trees is 115/9½ft while at Edinburgh the specimen is now 115/14½ft. At Colesbourne, three were planted in 1903 and the two biggest when 81 years old were 141/14ft and 138/12½ft. Young trees making good progress include one on the lawn at Alice Holt Lodge, planted in 1952 and 102/8ft when 38 years old; one in the University Botanic Garden at Cambridge, planted in 1963 and 70/6½ft when 26 years old, and one in the extension at Wisley, planted in 1978 and 36/3½ft when 11 years old.

ROBUSTA POPLAR 'Robusta'
    Simon-Louis Frères are also to be congratulated on raising what is in many ways the best of these hybrids. It arose in 1895, a seedling from a selection of Eastern Cottonwood that they had made, crossed with pollen from the form of Lombardy Poplar which they had also raised at their Plantières nursery. It is thus of similar parentage to Eugene's Poplar, and it was thought that this could have been the pollen parent, at first. It is outstanding for its speed of growth, young trees making shoots seven or eight feet long when growing in deep, damp alluvial soil in warm areas; for its profusion of big, rich red male catkins, sufficient to identify it in April; the bright orange of its unfolding leaves, and all summer for the luxuriant big leafage.

In this last, it follows its female parent, as it is very like the southern form of the Cottonwood of South Carolina and Georgia. It is common in small field-edge plantations; beside motorways and in valley-bottoms and was the choice for the home production of matchbox timber, mainly in East Anglia and Herefordshire. When the match company stopped buying the wood, the main market was pallet wood which was less profitable, and little more planting was done. However, the biggest areas of Robusta in Suffolk have become the site for the only colonies of breeding golden orioles, an exciting newcomer to the regular breeding species. The nesting, now about 30 each year, was threatened by the felling of these rapidly maturing poplars and lack of replacement, so some of the mature stands are now preserved and more young ones planted.

Big old trees are very scarce, few being planted in gardens since they were probably thought to take up as much room as the hugely spreading 'Serotina'. In fact, their crown is only broad-columnar and with their orange spring colour and splendid glossy foliage they make great specimens in a large garden. Few of the fastest growing trees on the best sites have yet made notable specimens. The biggest is at Dyffryn Park near Cardiff, 111/13½ft and probably about 70 years old. One at Colesbourne, planted in 1912, was 108/11½ft in 1983, when one in the garden at Bowood was 111/11½ft. One at the top of the Serps Pinetum at Wakehurst Place is 90/11½ft. In a plantation in Foxley Park, Hereford, planted in 1952 there were trees to 105/5ft in 1975 and a small wood at Snowdenham House, Surrey, planted in 1952 had trees to 98/6ft at 24 years and 105/7½ft by 1987. One at Forde Abbey, Crewkerne was 85/5½ft in 27 years.

GREY POPLAR

Populus x canescens (plate 6)

This tree is considered to be a natural hybrid between the Aspen and the White Poplar. As such it is unlikely to be native in Britain when the White poplar is mainly an Asiatic tree and ranges no nearer than south and eastern Europe and North Africa. It will have been introduced very early, probably by tribes colonising in the wake of the retreating ice and needing a tree of strong growth on poor sands and glacial outwash, useful also for shelter by its suckering. It certainly has great hybrid vigour, far outgrowing either parent. It seems also that the introductions were of few clones, for almost all the trees here are males. The cross could easily have arisen here, as the White Poplar will have been valuable to early settlers for its ability to spread thickets of suckers in coastal sand. The aspen will have been within pollen-range in many areas.

The biggest trees now are in wide valley bottoms in chalklands and in lowland limestone, notably in Hampshire and Dorset and in central Ireland. It thrives also in base-rich soils in Highland glens, often by roadside ditches, and one remarkable tree grows on the seashore at Dunrobin Castle, Sutherland. Just about on the line of spring tides, its roots must mostly be in salt water, but that has not stopped it growing to 75/13½ft. In such a position, as in the wide valleys of Hampshire, it shows great resistance to breakage by storm, and old trees usually maintain a full crown until they are blown down. It is noticeable also that many of the tallest trees are in the north of Scotland, so the origin of one parent in hot countries has not affected the hardiness of the hybrid.

Growth is usually fast in early years. At the University of Surrey Campus, a tree 22 years old by the entrance is 72/6ft and one by Terry's Pool is 60/6½ft when 23 years old. This sort of growth may be maintained for over 50 years as in a tree at Abercairny in Perthshire. This was 88/5ft in 1962 and by 1986 it was 105/8½ft. Some very big older trees keep up a good rate, but others relapse into decidedly slow growth.

The top specimen all round is at Birr Castle in County Offaly. It grows on the little floodplain of the River Camcor a little above where this enters the Little Brosna in the complex of waterway arrangements around the Lake at Birr. Its date is not known, but it was 88/12ft in 1910 and its subsequent growth suggests that it dates from around 1800 and made slower growth before 1975 than it has since. It was 105/16ft in 1966; 124/18ft in 1985 and is now 150/19ft. It has a clear, almost cylindric trunk for 20ft.

Nearby at the boathouse are two smaller trees, the larger 120/16½ft. John White reports a big boled tree in the University Parks in Oxford, 88/18½ft. Two very tall trees are at Ardross Castle, Easter Ross, by the river entrenched deeply below the Castle on a path to the bridge. One is 144/12½ft and the other 135/11½ft.

Back on the Irish limestone plains, a good tree at Abbeyleix, County Leix, was 124/11ft in 1984. Also in Ireland, in the Wicklow Hills, a tree by Weir Lodge on Powerscourt Estate is 105/11ft. A fine rugged tree at Castlehill, Devon is 98/13½ft. What appears to be a younger, faster grown tree at Hutton-in-the-Forest near Penrith, is 105/12½ft.

BLACK POPLAR

Populus nigra var. *betulifolia*

This majestic tree has recently aroused great interest among some field botanists and is being saved from oblivion especially by Mr Edgar Milne-Redhead, who has assembled a great deal of data from his own observations and those of a network of correspondents. Its trouble was that it was neglected by planters after about 1800 in favour of the Black Italian hybrid poplar. It was planted in numbers but only as the male form, known as the Manchester Poplar, in the cities of the northwest. As a countryside tree, it was disappearing. It was not generally recognised where it did occur, but was taken to be the Black Italian.

This is unforgivable once the very clear differences are seen. The true Black Poplar has a trunk and stem with big burrs and the ridges in the bark are less prominent and shorter, not persisting for any great length; the big branches arch out and down, then sweep up holding dense bunches of shoots; the leaves unfold in April and are only briefly red-brown before turning bright green, and, moreover, about half the trees will be female. And there lies one reason for its falling out of favour, for in midsummer the females blanket the neighbourhood in cotton wool. This will not do in cities and parks, but the tree is too valuable for its high resistance to polluted air to be avoided, so the male clone, 'Manchester', was selected and propagated, but that was not adopted for general countryside planting, as the Black Italian is superior in rate of growth and in its clean, upswept crown. But it has a shorter life, disintegrating rapidly when mature, while the Black may persist for more than 200 years.

The Black Poplar's status as a native has been questioned and is hard to determine but it is the western form of the European Black as found in France, although, curiously, it was first known and described as this variety from a tree found in the Hudson Valley, New York, by Andre Michaux soon after 1800. The tree had obviously been known in England from the earliest times but it had not been noticed that our trees had softly hairy new shoots, leaf-stalks and flower-stalks where those in Germany, eastern Europe and Russia are glabrous.

Although it does not customarily grow annual shoots of four or five feet, as its hybrids may, the Black Poplar can grow strongly, and with its dense foliage, can build up a big bole at least as fast and occasionally even faster. One in the University Botanic Garden at Cambridge, planted in 1957, made 49in in girth in its first 16 years and was 85/7½ft when it was 32 years old. At Templeton College, in Kennington, Oxford, a tree 14 years old was 50/3½ft, but the fastest is one in Cracknells garden at Hadleigh in Essex, taking only ten years to be a bushy crowned tree 52/4ft tall. A handsome, shapely selection from Holland, 'Vereeken', in the Populetum at Alice Holt Lodge, is now 37 years old and 85/7ft with an open, upright crown.

Before 1912, there were many big trees noted in Scotland as far north as Morayshire with most south of the Forth, but today none is known. The biggest are in Shropshire and Powys and in a broad belt south to Dorset and Somerset and in London and East Anglia. Within those areas it is at best locally fairly frequent, but beyond them it is scarce. The two biggest and best are beside a stream behind Longnor House in Shropshire, and in 1984 these were 124/20½ft and 98/24½ft. At Leighton Hall nearby, another very fine tree was 124/17ft in the same year. A well known veteran on the edge of the playing-field at Christ's School in Brecon is 110/21½ft with a big upright branch leaving the trunk at six feet. A prominent feature of the A39 in Somerset is the Black Poplar at Cannington, now in a tiny park between the old road and the cut-off straightening it. It has a trunk of some 20ft and is 88/19ft, and one across the old road in

Black Poplar (*Populus nigra* var. *betufolia*): Morden Hall Park, London

a yard is 82/17½ft. A good tree, 98/17½ft, towers from the town car park by the river at Newtown in Powys. In Oakley Park, Ludlow, by the river Teme, a tree which was 100/16ft in 1908 was 100/18½ft in 1971, which suggests that it had become very slow in its growth in maturity and could date easily back to 1700.

LOMBARDY POPLAR

Populus nigra 'Italica'

The Lombardy Poplar has the distinction of being the one species of tree recognised by the British Army. All the other trees are submerged under 'bushy-topped' or 'conifer' but 'poplar' stands apart and refers to the Lombardy Poplar. It is being trivial to spoil this clean-cut classification by worrying that to the military, a Dawyck Beech or two, or a Cypress Oak will be cheerfully accepted as a 'poplar', as they too often are by the general public. There are three frequent forms of Lombardy Poplars, and two more seen locally. Here, we are concerned with the conic or multiple, narrow-topped male tree which is the usual kind seen. The female 'Giant Poplar' will have a section of its own. That leaves us with four apparently distinct forms of true Lombardy. The most common can be called the Original Form, the familar slender columnar-conic tree with a narrow apex. Mixed with it and seldom distinguished from it is the 'Plantier Poplar' one of several seedlings which arose in the Simon-Louis nurseries at Plantières near Metz which was marketed in 1885. It has hairy young shoots and leaves but is more easily known as a leafier tree with a broader top, of several vertical stems. Then there is an unrecognised form which I notice in and around south London which is like the original form except that it has curling small shoots on the exterior of its crown. Lastly, a much more obvious and frequent form which has escaped being named. I saw it labelled 'Elegans' in Ottowa Botanic Garden, but that name belongs to a tree like the Plantier Popular, raised in New York, and broader than the Lombardy. This tree is in fact so much narrower as to be almost absurd, a pole with small vertical leafy shoots close to it. All the first ones I found were 102ft tall which was odd, but I now know many taller as well as young ones.

The original Lombardy Poplar seems to have arisen in the Po Valley soon after 1700. It was introduced to France in 1749 and to England from Turin by the Earl of Rochford to St Osyth Priory in Essex where he planted several cuttings in 1758. Two with decayed trunks were there in 1911 and one was still there in 1984. Loudon found one at Whitton, 115/19½ft in 1838 and as the Duke of Argyll, who planted it, died in 1761 this may in fact have been the first tree. It has been noticed that this tree, so striking in the landscape, did not appear in paintings or landscape drawings made before 1800 and it was not in the market before 1775.

Although one 1758 tree is still alive, and re-growing strong shoots from a much broken and divided stump, this is a short-lived tree in general. Elwes tried to find trees mentioned by Loudon 70 years before and found none, nor did he find several others recorded well after that. Of the eight he noted himself or cites from 1879 to 1911, only the St Osyth tree may stand today. Two of the trees were killed in the exceptionally hard winter of 1881 which killed or damaged great numbers in eastern and southern England. No such winter losses have been reported since. It is remarkable that the tree lives as long as it does, for so often it is seen isolated in fields or towering out of shelter, a standing invitation to lightning and gales.

Tall trees are safe enough except in great gales when nothing except a Giant Sequoia can be said to be safe, but only if they are left alone. The sad thing is that those in charge of trees in public places are easily scared into believing that a tall poplar is a danger to the public, or, even if they know better, that other people will think they ought to be doing something about it. So they do, with three disastrous results. First, the tree is instantly rendered hideous, a truncated bunch of mutilated spikes. Second, new shoots emerge in bunches and within a few years the tree is casting more shade and is more top-heavy than it was, and much more dangerous. Third, the severed tops, unlike lateral branches cut in the approved Shigo manner, cannot grow protective tissue over the wound. So the bases of the now heavy brushes of new shoots decay and fails to hold them. The widely erudite and massive Dr Alex Shigo revolutionised tree surgery with his studies on the structure of the origins of branches and the reactions they make to different methods of pruning. Briefly, a tree has built-in defences against the loss of branches, a normal and natural occurrence as a tree matures. A branch originates from within the tree as a cone-shaped body and when the branch is broken or cut, this is isolated from the trunk by a barrier of wood tissues resistant to the passage of fungi. The base of the branch is prevented from rotting the trunk. At the base of a growing branch there is a visible collar and this is the source of the scar tissue that grows across the wound and seals it externally. All cuts must be made just outside this branch-stem junction and the scars will then be grown over most rapidly and fully, without the use of a sealant. All progressive tree-surgeons have been Shigo oriented for years now, and breaking his rules is fraught with danger. This covers all lateral branches, but obviously the main stem itself has no such defences. So when cut across it remains open and liable to decay.

A superb line of 52 Lombardies was beside the A330 at Holyport, Berkshire, spaced 15ft apart. All but one or two runts were narrowly topped, shapely conic-columnar trees and carbon copies of each other, with tufts of shoots at the same height and same angle. In 1978 ten of the best chosen almost at random were 105–108ft tall and eight to ten feet round, but were showing signs of die-back and deteriorated rapidly and had to be felled within a few years.

Letchworth town centre has a fine planting around and across the square, made in 1913, slender and shapely and around 100ft tall with the biggest now 115/8½ft and 115/6½ft. A long avenue across a field in the park at Revesby Abbey, Lincolnshire, was planted in 1968 and now has trees to 65/5ft. The oldest dated planting is the avenues in the 35 acres of endless, packed, jumbled and leaning headstones of some 40,000 graves in the weird Abney Cemetery at Stoke Newington, London. The avenues were planted in 1840 and the biggest that is easily measured is 108/10ft.

Older, no doubt, and far grander, are the trees on the Fen, each side of the Causeway in Cambridge. In spite of their age, size and open positions, so far as I could see in 1994, not one had come to grief in the past ten years. I measured 19 in 1984 and found the biggest to be one on the east Fen, 130/11½ft and two on Coe's Fen, 108/12ft and 111/13ft. The larger of a similar pair in the middle of Farnham, Surrey, in the Gostrey Meadow is 105/13ft. John White finds one in the University Parks, Oxford, to be now 108/13½ft. Manor Park in Aldershot has several, one of them 108/12ft.

Few were blown down in the 1987 and 1990 gales, considering the number at risk, but unfortunately those few included the tallest in London and Britain, 132/12ft in Marble Hill Park, and the tallest in Surrey, 118/10½ft at Oxenford Grange, Elstead. One in Henrietta Park in Bath was 121/13ft in 1984 and a good tree at Newby Hall in Yorkshire was 118/8ft in 1989 and should still be there. One loss mourned was the wide group of nine trees to 108ft tall in the dell at Cannizaro Park, Wimbledon, because it was a superb example of the use of such groups in landscaping and garden design. Four trees on a grass bank in Leigh Village in Kent are missed because they were all over 100ft tall and up to 13ft round.

Lombardy Poplar (*Populus nigra* 'Italica'): generally a short-lived tree

There are many dated trees or groups which show good growth, as well as those already mentioned. E.A. Bowles's tree at Myddelton House, Enfield, dates from 1906 and was 117/10½ft in 1976. The trees in Sandford Park, Cheltenham, were planted in 1925 and the best in 1978 was 118/7ft. A 1930 tree in Randall's Park, Leatherhead, was 90/9½ft in 1979 and one of the same date at the Windlesham Arboretum was 111/8ft in 1984. A 1938 tree at St Osyth Priory was 85/8½ft in 1984. One of a group at Churchill College near Bristol, planted in 1961 is 100/7½ft. A group at Templeton College at Kennington near Oxford was planted in 1974 but cheated as they were then 25–30ft tall. My prophesy of a crippling check in growth for a decade was as wrong as it could well be and the trees were to 60/5ft in 1987.

The extra slim and fastigiate form can be seen quite often once the eye has learned to pick it out. The first I saw were at The Hendre near Monmouth were there are 16 good specimens now 110–120/6–9ft. Horsham Park had a good group of four to 118ft in 1982. Cockington Court, Torbay, has two, one of them 118/5ft in 1984, and two at The Courts in Avon in 1988 were 115/5½ft and 111/4ft, dimensions that plainly reflect a peculiar shape.

The Giant Poplar, *P. nigra* 'Gigantea' is of unknown origin, and again remains generally unnoticed as a distinct entity until its peculiarities are noted, after which it will be seen in small numbers everywhere. It divides into three or four slightly spread trunks within a few feet of the ground so its crown increases in breadth with height, all the way. It has coarse, untidy lesser branches, but most striking in late spring it is strung with copious, big long, curved female catkins, followed in summer by masses of cottonwool seeds. On Coe's Fen in Cambridge there is one 105/11ft and by Loch Earn at St Fillans a roadside tree is 72/9½ft. In 1985 Fawley Court near Henley had two, 105/12ft and 100/10½ft.

WESTERN BALSAM POPLAR

Populus trichocarpa (plate 7)

A Balsam Poplar is a frequent sight in suburban gardens, planted for the pervading sweet scent in April, but soon regretted. When it begins to grow seven feet a year it overtops the house and shades most of the garden. If it is a female, of which there is an even chance, it will blanket the neighbourhood in cotton-wool in June. Male trees drop myriads of catkins, mostly for some reason half-opened, in April, and, male or female, the rampant root-suckers colonise the garden. On a shrinkable clay, the roots will endanger the foundations of the house. Understandably these suburban trees disappear at least as fast as they are planted.

As a park tree, the Balsam Poplar, although untidy not only in dropping pieces, but also in numerous snags and small branches randomly bunched on its trunk, is ornamental, easily raised and resistant to city air. In full leaf it is very attractive as the big, long-triangular glossy leaves twist to show their undersides which are as white as if painted, and in autumn they are bright gold for about a week. The size of the leaf is proportional to the vigour of the shoot. Those on the leading shoot are therefore the biggest and as the summer advances and growth accelerates, the size of leaf along the leader increases towards the tip.

The seed, as in other poplars and willows, has to be sown within a day or two at most after being shed. Even today this is scarcely possible as a means of introduction from the west coast of America to Europe and this has to be done by sending cuttings. Even that was not available to the early collectors in the west, like Douglas and Lobb, before cold storage. So although this Balsam Poplar is common in valley bottoms from Alaska to south California and was seen by all the collectors, it is the only big tree that had to wait until nearly 1900 before it was cultivated in England. It was sent from British Columbia in 1892. One at Kew survives from an1896 planting, but it has not made the most of its time and is now only 80/6ft, a size comfortably exceeded by some trees elsewhere planted after 1950.

One advantage the Balsam has over the fast growing hybrid Black Poplars, apart from its superior foliage, is that it will grow as fast as anywhere in the cool summers and acid soils of high rainfall areas like the Highlands of Scotland. Until its height culminates, the crown is fairly narrowly columnar tapering to a conic top. After that, it grows big, more spreading branches near the top but it does not assume the hugely rounded dome shape of the Black and most of its hybrids. The life span is short and many have died or broken up in storms when younger than the oldest at Kew, so, despite the furious rate of growth, none has attained any great dimensions. This is also true to some extent in the native range, for although it is the biggest broad-leaf tree in the Rocky Mountains, and at the turn of the century trees were reported to be 200ft tall, and one was more recently recorded as 230/32½ft, the biggest today seems to be one in Seattle, 152/22ft.

A list of the biggest trees is a very temporary statement, and greater interest may attach to the growth rate of smaller young trees. The tallest are in a small group in a slight depression near the River Spey at Wester Elchies in Inverness-shire. Here two trees were 135/8½ft and 132/9ft in 1989. In 1984 a tree on the lawns at Bowood House in Wiltshire was 135/10ft. Several big old trees in the University Botanic Garden in Cambridge have declined over the years and left the biggest in 1987 as one 112/11ft. At Newby Hall gardens in Yorkshire, one is 115/9½ft. H.J. Elwes planted one at his home, Colesbourne in Gloucestershire, in 1900. In 1984 this was 118/8½ft.

It is poplar canker that causes deterioration in the crown and various selections have been made which show resistance to this disease. They may grow into bigger trees than any we currently have, but they are still scarce in gardens. One known as 'NWA' is very vigorous and healthy in two poplar collections. At Thorp Perrow in Yorkshire one planted in 1951 is now 100/8½ft. In the Alice Holt Populetum, one planted in 1954 is now also 100/8½ft. Rapid early growth of some unnamed clones includes one at the Hillier Arboretum 56/5ft in 14 years; one 60/4ft in 11 years at Wisley; one 112/6ft in 28 years in the Kingscliffe plots in the Quantocks and one at Ardkinglas Castle, Argyll, 108/9ft in 30 years.

CAUCASIAN WINGNUT

Pterocarya fraxinifolia

No tree in the relict Tertiary flora on the southern flanks of the Caucasus Mountains is more typically Caucasian than the Wingnut. It has abounding vigour and good health, stout smooth shoots and very large leaves, shining bright green. It also has two botanically eccentric features. One, shared with a small number of other trees, is that it lacks winter-bud scales. It passes the winter instead with two small leaves coated with dense orange-brown hairs, folded closely over the shoot-tip. Only one of the eight species of wingnut has normal buds, the Japanese *Pterocarya rhoifolia* with big shiny pale green bud-scales, which it sheds early. The other oddity is shared with the *Metasequoia*, but is apparently unique among broad-leaves, and that is non-axillary lateral buds. Since this is not mentioned in the standard works nor any other I can find, it could be that some broad-leaves beyond my ken grow in this way. This wingnut has its lateral buds on long stalks arising at angles from well above the axil.

This tree is in the class of the Cappadocian Maple in its rapid disappearance behind a thicket of suckers. Being so much more vigorous, however, the wingnut suckers can soon be full-sized trees, and a single plant can be a segment of forest. It can be hard work making one's way to the centre to measure the original bole or group of boles, and when one arrives it will often be a disappointment, since with the intense competition of its own suckers below and above the ground, it or they are often relatively puny. The invasive suckers are a big drawback in gardens, and can be controlled only by mowing, diligent cutting back, or by grazing with cattle. The nuisance is halved when the tree is planted by a waterside. It has the advantage of growing a nearly instant copse, if that should be needed, and is also a means of abundant propagation. However, better plants, easier to move, are raised from cuttings of strong shoots taken in late June.

This tree was introduced to France in 1784 but it is thought not to have been in Britain until a little after 1800. It is infrequent but present in many parks and gardens north to Perthshire and in Ireland. It does not do well in shallow or drying soils, thriving best in medium loams and clays with access to water, in a damp hollow, a high water-table or open water nearby. It is generally hardy but a late spring frost can scorch new foliage badly.

There is no difficulty in choosing the best and biggest trees, and the Strangeways family has them all on its two estates in Dorset. The prime one of these is in the valley garden at Melbury Park. The planting date is not precisely known, but it is known that by 1866 the tree was 30/4½ft and, for this species on that site, it will have been planted in about 1820. Growing in a mown area, it has no visible suckers around it. It was probably always kept clear, and early on pruned to have a clear stem eight feet long. This is extremely impressive, as the tree is 118/19½ft and that clean length is cylindric. Above it, the tree breaks into five great nearly vertical limbs. Another, by the lake, and not among the elite, is 88/16ft at three feet. The two in Abbotsbury Garden are a contrasting pair, one tall on a medium-sized trunk, the other more squat with a great stem supporting a broad dome. The tall one is in the woodland valley and is 115/13½ft and the other, not far from the entrance, is 88/19ft.

At Lacock Abbey in Wiltshire, a fully developed thicket has, deep inside, the trunk of a tree of 85/20ft. But the girth is exaggerated by sprouts and an incipient fork, and the tree spoiled by all the outer works. In Bute Park, Cardiff, a branchy tree by the River Taff is 70/12½ft. Tregothnan in Cornwall has one with a good trunk, 80/10½ft and a low-branched tree by the lake in Kew is 50/10ft. In Hyde Park, London, a very public tree by Rotten Row near the Dell is rather squat with a short, three-foot clear trunk and is 70/13½ft at three feet, and another to the north, by the Carriage Drive, is 56/8½ft.

In the University Botanic Garden at Cambridge, a triangle of streamside between paths, grows a confusing open cluster of stems up to ten feet round holding aloft an 85ft crown, and by the Backs near the gate into Clare College a big tree is over 70/19ft at two feet on the stem, which forks at six feet.

Caucasian Wingnut (*Pterocarya fraxinifolia*): Melbury Park, Dorset

In Scotland, one among three at the top of Happy Valley, Culzean Castle, Ayrshire, is 60/9ft and one in the Royal Botanic Garden is 60/10ft. In Ireland a tree planted in 1930 in Box Avenue at Birr Castle, County Offaly is 62/11ft at three feet, and one below the Pepperpot at Powerscourt, County Wicklow, is 85/11½ft.

One planted at Christ's College, Cambridge, in 1971 was already 40/5ft in 1990, and one at Rosemoor Gardens, Devon, planted in 1975 was 30/3½ft by 1989.

HYBRID WINGNUT

Pterocarya x *rehderiana*

In 1879, the Arnold Arboretum near Boston, Massachusetts, received seed picked from a Chinese Wingnut, *Pterocarya stenoptera* growing in Lavalee's Nursery at Segrez in France, beside Caucasian Wingnuts. Two of the plants were hybrids between these species. When I saw them in 1975 the bigger was 85/10ft. The hybrid was not introduced to Britain until 1908, and I knew a few trees here already bigger than that. About 1920 several trees were raised at Borde Hill, Sussex, from two Chinese Wingnuts in the South Park near a Caucasian Wingnut, and these are the same hybrid, of independent origin.

The hybrid is a good mixture of its parents and exhibits hybrid vigour, which, in view of the rampant vigour of the Caucasian tree, seems unnecessary but adds to the interest. It inherits, luckily, the single stem habit of the Chinese and does not grow multiple trunks, but it does have the excessive devotion to root-suckers which is much greater in the Caucasian than in the Chinese. The fruit have a membrane nicely half way between the broad, circular shape of the Caucasian and the narrow oval of the Chinese and is broadly oval. The rhaches or central stalks of the compound leaves are a compromise between the smoothly rounded stalk of the Caucasian and the broad, leafy and toothed flanges or wings of the Chinese. It is round except for a narrow open groove without flanges, on the upper side.

The Hybrid Wingnut is among the most vigorous things on roots, in temperate regions. It so impressed me with its vigour that, with its suckering ability as well, I recommended it for trial with various poplars and willows for coppice production of cellulose, in plots scattered over Britain. With fine timing, the first two years after planting the trial, there were savage spring frosts and my wonder tree lost ground to the others from the start. So far, the only report of any success is that it was the most productive species on one of the Outer Hebrides. Not really all that I had hoped for.

One of the examples that fired my enthusiasm for the tree is the tree near the Main Gates at Kew. It was planted in 1953, in the poor terrace-gravel and when 14 years old it was 42/5ft. This growth rate took it to 60/6½ft as it came of age in 1974, and to 80/9ft now it is 36 years old. This pleases me mightily, because it has made this great growth with the aid of all that acid rain which misguided zealots insist is killing our trees. The Chestnutleaf Oak 300ft away was planted in the same year and is even bigger, now 68/10ft, so both trees seem to welcome the rain at Kew however acid it may be. Another of my yardstick trees is by Circular Drive in Westonbirt Arboretum. When I first adopted it, in 1966, it was 36/3½ft. Eleven years later it was 60/7ft and now it is 70/9½ft. It was raised from a sucker of the big tree at Pool Gate, at an unknown date. The figures show that this was very close indeed to 1950.

I planted a cutting in July 1980 which had been raised that year from the above Westonbirt tree and in 1981 it grew four feet, and the next year it added seven and a half feet. When eleven years old it was 36/3½ft. The only known original trees from the 1908 import in Kew were four blown down in 1987, the biggest then 80/12½ft, and the two in the collection near the Lion Gate are today 75/7½ft and 65/6ft. But the Pool Gate tree at Westonbirt, the grandfather of my own tree, is bigger, and is very likely another original. It is now 80/13½ft and is cleared of its infestation by suckers every few years.

Another tree whose progress I watch closely is at Birr Castle. It was planted in 1932 in Box Avenue and it has the finest clear trunk of any, about 15ft without a twig. I first saw it in 1966 when, 34 years old, it was 70/8½ft. By 1980 it was 72/10½ft and last seen in 1989 it was 80/11½ft, slowing down somewhat. Of nine trees of independent origin at Borde Hill, several were blown down in 1987 when about 65 years old and to 80/10ft, but the biggest, by the haha of the garden, was still there in 1989 when it was 65/12ft. Another big one survived at Wakehurst Place, also in Sussex, in the front

Hybrid
Wingnut
(*Pterocarya* x
rehderiana):
Borde Hill,
Sussex

paddock, around which nearly everything was flattened. In 1990 it was 75/12ft with a trunk cleaned by cattle to about eight feet.

One in the Royal Botanic Garden at Edinburgh was planted in 1928 and is now only 50/8ft. An undated tree in the National Botanic Garden, Glasnevin, near Dublin was 80/10ft in 1987.

ALGERIAN OAK

Quercus canariensis

This tree of great distinction seems to have had a fittingly royal start in cultivation in Britain when King Louis Philippe sent acorns from Algeria to Queen Victoria in 1844 or 1845. Its names have had a less happy history. It was known as *Quercus mirbeckii* for nearly 100 years, and hence as Mirbeck's Oak, until it was found that Willdenow's name, *Q. canariensis*, had priority. I cannot find out who Mr Mirbeck was, but he has every reason to feel aggrieved, because this old name is misleading since the tree is not native in the Canary Islands. The common name is now Algerian Oak, perhaps to put that straight, but that leaves Mr Mirbeck out in the cold altogether.

The tree has a characterful bark, nearly black, deeply fissured into loose square plates. Most handily, this is I find, a reliable indicator of the purity of the origin of the specimen. This oak is so attractive and healthy that owners often yield to the temptation of picking some of the acorns and sowing them. But the pollen from a Common Oak has usually fertilised them and the progeny is a mixture of hybrids.

Many will have sub-Canary foliage or form or both, and these have paler and smoother bark. Only those with the authentic Canary Oak bark have the unadulterated foliage and form of that tree. At Tockington Manor in Avon, the two old trees of the true species are readily distinguished from the six smaller trees, which are hybrid progeny, by their bark. There was a plot at Bedgebury Pinetum evidently raised from home-collected acorns and of scores of trees, only the three best and biggest had the dark, deeply crackled bark and were pure bred; the rest were hybrids with Common Oak.

The merits of the tree begin with the sturdy, rapid and healthy growth of a straight, evenly tapered stem bearing a neatly ovoid-conic crown with upper branches rising round the apical centre shoot. The foliage is a deluxe version of that of the best Sessile Oak, bigger and more substantial, unfolding coated, like the stout shoot, in a thick, soft down of orange which is soon shed to leave shining dark green. In autumn a proportion of the leaves turns yellow and the majority remain dark shining green until early spring. The exemplary shape is maintained until the tree is at least 80ft tall. The oldest trees we have, now nearly 120 years old, have not yet lost shape.

It grows equally well on a range of soils and as far north as Cumbria and Edinburgh. Since the northernmost trees are as good as most, it must be assumed that it would succeed well to the north in Scotland and it is strange that none seems to have been planted there.

The Algerian Oak is mainly a tree of the Atlas Mountains from Morocco to Tunisia, but there is a small outlier in the Algarve, southern Portugal. It may also grow in Spain near Gibraltar as a tree received at the Horticultural Society gardens in Chiswick in 1835 and seen by John Loudon came from there. The chief forests stand at 5–7000ft, so the tree should be hardy as it flushes late in spring here. It has not yet achieved any real popularity and many big gardens which should know better are still lacking a specimen. If native source acorns are unobtainable, grafts on Common Oak rootstocks will be necessary as home seed is so unreliable, and the grafts probably, as in Hungarian Oak, grow into specimens as fine as any.

A tree planted on the green in Ardingly, Sussex, in 1952 was 50/6ft in 1991 and one of about the same age at Canford School in Dorset, which was 33/3ft in 1967, had grown to 60/6½ft in 1988. At Forde Abbey near Chard, one planted in 1960 was 62/5½ft in 1988.

No original tree is known, but a very good case can be made for attributing the great pair at Ham House near Worthing to that origin. They were the biggest known in 1907 and still held that position when I last saw them in 1983 and they were 90/15ft and 85/14ft. Tucked down in a little dell near the mansion they had a good chance to have been missed by the great gale. Other than those, the oldest is an 1864 tree at Kew near the Isleworth Gate, a fine specimen, 88/12ft in 1987. At Westonbirt, the main oak collection is each side of Broad Drive in Silk Wood with, originally, Asiatic and European oaks on the west and American on the east. This was set out in 1876 and the two trees prominently marking the collection at the ride-side on the west are a Caucasian Oak and the very similar Algerian Oak. The Algerian is predictably a remarkably shapely tree despite its age, and it is now 102/9½ft.

Another splendid mature old tree is the best of several in Melbury Park in Dorset. Henry measured it in 1909 when it was 40/4ft, but he did not know its date. In 1989 it was 98/13ft, in the Pleasure Garden. He also measured one at Tregothnan in Cornwall in 1908 which was 60/6½ft and this, above the little pool, was 88/10½ft in 1989.

Two big trees at Tortworth will almost certainly have been planted within a year or two of the 1876 tree at Westonbirt, for neither Lord Ducie nor William Holford could bear to be behind his rival. The two at Tortworth were 75/10½ft and 70/8½ft in 1973. The Cavendish family at Holker in Cumbria were probably also among the first to have the tree and the one in their garden is among the finest, 72/12½ft in 1983. The two mentioned at Tockington Manor as the true species, were 72/10½ft and 72/11ft in 1983 when the best of the hybrids there was 72/9ft.

A tree in the 1880 oak planting in Alexandra Park, St Leonards, is now 88/11½ft. At Tregrehan the intolerably dreary, long Yew Walk of Irish Yews has a bright spot at the western end where it has a group of rare oaks. The Algerian Oak there is a splendid tree, 102/10ft. At Smeaton House, East Lothian there is one 72/10½ft and in the National Botanic Gardens at Glasnevin, Dublin, the tree in the Oak collection is 72/9½ft. A striking pair in Home Wood at Exbury Gardens in Hampshire is 62/5½ft, young trees growing fast.

CHESTNUTLEAF OAK

Quercus castaneifolia

The Chestnutleaf Oak is native to a restricted area on the souther flanks of the Caucasus Mountains, in Talysch Province and to a small area to the east in the Elburz Mountains. Until recently, it was thought also to have a distant outlier in North Africa, where a similar, if rather less exalted group of Tertiary flora grows in Algeria along a strip between the Atlas Mountains and the Mediterranean, just into Tunisia. The form of Chestnutleaf Oak there was distinguished as var. *incana*, but this is now regarded as a separate species, *Quercus afares*. In the Caucasus, the Chestnutleaf Oak was noted by Henry as growing a short, stout bole bearing a wide spreading crown on long, level branches. It was introduced to Kew in 1843 and the single tree raised from that seed and planted in 1846 on the Seven Sisters Lawn is a most remarkable tree and the biggest of any sort in Kew. It is almost certainly the biggest and finest specimen in the world. It was the biggest in Europe when it was first measured in 1909, and has never had a rival in Britain. It has luxuriant foliage, its leaves in most years to eight inches long and nearly twice the size of many

Chestnutleaf Oak (*Quercus castaneifolia*): Royal Botanic Gardens, Kew, Surrey

elsewhere. The vigour of growth in height and girth of the best specimens is unequalled among the oaks and matched by few trees of any sort.

This species has not been seen to suffer any disease, nor any damage from frost. It thrives at least as far north as southern Scotland, but it has been so rarely planted that this should not be taken as its potential northern limit. The most rapid growth is recorded in both the relatively warm and dry London area and in the cool, moist southeast of Ireland.

The doyen of the species, the original tree at Kew, was already 60/9½ft when planted for 63 years and 85/17ft when out 110 years. After 147 years it was 110/22½ft. It has a single trunk for 23ft before dividing into three limbs, and one large limb below that from ten feet up. A large branch removed at five to seven feet is now a rapidly occluding scar. The only other old tree known with an early measurement is in Beauport Park near Hastings, which Henry found in 1905, branching widely and 40/3ft 3in. Deep in old woodland, it is now 82/15½ft so has made excellent growth. One in Alexandra Park, Hastings, planted in 1888 is only 80/9½ft but is of a smaller foliaged, less vigorous form than many, like the tree at Batsford Park, Gloucestershire, 50/11ft. The Empire Oaks were planted in Windsor Great Park in 1937 in very poor Bagshot Sand. The best of the Chestnutleaf trees was 75/6½ft when 41 years old.

In the National Botanic Gardens at Glasnevin outside Dublin, a tree received from Kew in 1932 is 70/9ft and an undated tree at Castle Milk, Lockerbie, Dumfries, was 56/6ft in 1984, neither being evident grafts. Two more of independent and unknown origin have shown remarkable growth. One in Mount Usher Garden at Ashford in County Wicklow, close to the river, tucked in a hollow near a bridge was only 26/3ft in 1966. It has the luxuriant foliage of the old tree at Kew, and by 1989 it was 56/9ft. Its size in 1966 suggests a planting in about 1956, and the six feet increase in girth in 23 years is a mean growth of over three inches a year. The other is on the Museum Lawn at Kew. The origin is not known but it was planted in 1953. It has shown the most extraordinary growth for the poor terrace-gravels there, and one having spent its first dozen or so years in the levels of pollution then found at Kew. When four years old it was 16/1ft. When 17 years, it was 36/4ft, and at 40 years old it was 72/10½ft. It has low whorls of strong, straight branches, six below five feet, and five at six feet up. The girth increment over the last 23 years has been five and a half feet.

A specimen with commemorative plaque off Mitchell Drive in Westobirt was planted six feet tall in 1968. Despite this set-back it was, 24 years later, 65/4½ft and promised well.

TURKEY OAK

Quercus cerris

The Turkey Oak appears fully at home here, naturalised across southern England, especially in parts of Sussex and Devon, with seedlings springing up abundantly around big trees in hedges and at woodland edges. There are fine specimens through the Midlands and around the Highlands to the coastal plain north of Inverness. But it was 1735 when William Lucombe obtained and grew in the Exeter nursery the first in Britain.

This oak also masquerades as a fine timber-tree, with its rapid growth and, so often, a long, straight stem with little taper. In fact it is of no value for timber since even if the trunk avoids being 'shaken', fracturing annularly or lengthwise, on being felled, it becomes so on drying. The great value of the tree is in beautifying the countryside with trees of great stature, and giving shelter. It is of particular value for shelter in that its rapid growth is little retarded on poor soils, on chalk or in exposure to sea winds. Its resistance to cold, easterly winds is remarkable when its native area is south of the Cevennes, from Spain to Asia Minor.

The best specimens are trees of great presence and majesty, fine adornments to parks and gardens. Good trees grow in city parks being resistant to city air, as is shown by its frequency, in Central Park, New York, and many good trees in city parks in Britain. In autumn, the leaves turn briefly yellow, then a rather pinkish

Turkey Oak (*Quercus cerris*):
Knightshayes Court, Devon

brown before ending a good russet. On young trees the leaves in a zone, the 'juvenile cone', up to about ten feet from the ground remain attached and pale brown until the end of the year.

The finest specimen, and the tallest, also with the biggest clean trunk, is in the Park at Knightshayes Court, Tiverton, Devon, between the drive and the South Garden. A beautifully proportioned tree, and therefore much bigger than it looks from a distance, this is 142ft tall and 26ft round the trunk at five feet. It has its lowest branch, a twin one, arising at ten feet from the ground and a fairly regular great dome of a crown. It was 120/22ft 4in in 1959 so it is still growing fast.

A similar tree is in Bulstrode Park, Buckinghamshire and was 135/22ft in 1983, an impressive sight, dominating the wooded end of the garden. A more squat tree with big branches in Phear Park, Exmouth, Devon, near two of the biggest Lucombe Oaks in the country, is 80/19ft. A very fine specimen in Ugbrooke Park, Devon, also not far from one of the biggest Lucombe Oaks, was 100/20ft 6in in 1978. A tall, shapely tree at Trevorick near Falmouth in Cornwall, is 115/13ft. One planted in 1884 at Merthyr Mawr, Glamorgan, was 98/14ft 3in when 96 years old and a good tree. There is a splendid tree by the old nursery at Kingston Lacey in Dorset with a good, long bole. It was 100/15ft 6in in 1983.

In northern Scotland, there are four quite big trees in the Dell at Brahan House, Muir of Ord, Easter Ross, the best one 108/12ft 6in, but with little to choose among them, and there are good trees along the old A9 near Beauly. At Tulloch Castle, Easter Ross, one 92/9ft has a good bole for 40ft. Not so far north, at Gray House, near Dundee, Angus, is a good tree 85/15ft and at nearby Megginch Castle, Perthshire, one in the Park is 92/15ft and at Errol, also nearby, one is 105/14ft.

SCARLET OAK

Quercus coccinea

The Scarlet Oak is well named as it almost invariably displays in autumn an entire crown of foliage of that colour, more uniformly and more brightly than any other oak, or any large tree that we can grow. In the quest for better sales, the Red Oak is sometimes seen labelled 'Scarlet Oak' in the nursery. They are very different, for the Scarlet Oak has leaves glossy green above and below, deeply lobed, and the Red Oak has leaves with dull, matt green upper surfaces and matt slightly greyed glaucous green below, with much shallower lobes, and usually more varied in size with many much bigger.

The Scarlet Oak resembles the Pin Oak in foliage, although lacking the tufts of hair in the angles of the veins, but differs from that and the Red Oak in the shape of the tree. The trunk is rarely quite straight, tending to some sinuosity, and it is never smooth. It has sporadic blisters and little sprouts. Its branching has nothing in common with the dense regularity of the Pin Oak, or the radiating umbrella of the Red Oak, but is highly irregular, with few, widely spaced big branches snaking out a little above level making an open, shapeless crown with age. In Britain, with few species of the red oak group grown, the combination of crown and foliage readily identifies the Scarlet Oak, but in the United States with many other similar species and hybrids, some trees give nothing away. At an Oak Symposium in Pennsylvania, I was among some thirty botanists standing around under a magnificent tree, quite unable to agree what to call it.

The Scarlet Oak is native to the southwestern corner of Maine, along the Appalachians to Georgia, Tennessee and Missouri. It is not very long-lived and few are bigger than one 100/16ft at Haverford College near Philadelphia. It was first collected by John Banister in 'The Carolinas' and sent to Bishop Henry Compton at Fulham Palace in 1691. It is more adapted to cool summers than is the Pin Oak and there are several quite big specimens from the north of England into Scotland as far as Morayshire, and in Ireland. It flushes rather late and the leaves emerge pale yellow. It has an interesting habit, not found in the other red oaks but normal in the

Scarlet Oak (*Quercus coccinea*):
Bagshot Road, Guildford, Surrey

Common and Turkey Oaks, of retaining much of its lower foliage, brown on the tree until well into the New Year. A number of tall trees in Sheffield Park, Sussex, succumbed rapidly to an unusual fungal disease, just before the gale of 1987. Losses in gales have been singularly few.

The best specimen is well to the north, at Bishopsthorpe, the York residence of the Archbishop of York. It has an impressive trunk, long and straight for this species, and is 85/10½ft. Another almost as good is at Bramshott Hall, near the A3 at Liphook in Hampshire, which is 82/10½ft. One as big in girth, but shorter is on the edge of the Eucalyptus Grove at Mount Usher Garden in County Wicklow, 72/10½ft. A front garden tree in Fleet, Hampshire, in Knowle Road off the High Street, is a splendid tree, 80/10ft. One on Flora's Lawn in Syon Park, Brentford, is a little battered but 70/9½ft. In the grounds of Westonbirt School, Gloucestershire, a tree is 66/9½ft. At Killerton, Devon, a tree on the bank between the ex-stables, now a shop, and the entrance, a typically shaped tree with sparsely held big branches and sinuous trunk is 85/9ft. A tall survivor of the gales at Wakehurst Place, in the main pinetum, is 88/8ft. At the extreme north of England a very good tree at Etal Manor near Berwick-on-Tweed is 66/7ft with 20ft of clear, straight trunk. Well across the border, near Dunblane, Perthshire, a tree in a field below the house at Kippendavie is 88/8ft.

In about 1900, Anthony Waterer at the Knaphill Nursery near Woking, Surrey, selected the seedling 'Splendens'. It was marketed as showing superior autumn colour, but this is hardly necessary. The value of the tree lies more in its extra vigorous growth and big foliage. The seven inch, highly glossed leaves are also distinguished by small tufts of pale hairs in the angles of the main veins. The early stock graft of the original is by the gate into the nursery and is 80/9ft. Young trees are now frequent, and known in winter being grafted at base, and older trees are in many parks and gardens. Cannizaro Park, Wimbledon, has several to 90/7½ft; Stratford Park, Stroud, Gloucestershire, has one 85/8ft, and Alexandra Park, St Leonards, Sussex, has one 56/9ft. One planted in 1944 at Stratfield Saye was 60/6ft by 1982.

HUNGARIAN OAK

Quercus frainetto

The Hungarian Oak has the hallmark of top quality in every respect. From flushing out crimson on young trees, the leaves are as big as in any oak and more numerously and deeply lobed by far than any other. They are held well spaced, those on the top of the crown display their fretted edges against the sky giving a unique pattern. In autumn most of the trees turn from yellow to russet, and some maintain old gold and orange for many days. The trunk may not always be long, but few broad-leaf trees of any sort have one so positively cylindric and smoothly rounded. Nor have they a crown so regularly domed to a great size and usually of such straight branches radiating like the spokes of a half-opened umbrella.

The stature and rate of growth are in accord with this splendid form. The growth of young trees, in height and girth is rarely surpassed by any oak, and although no tree can yet be termed mature, many are already well over 100/10ft, and these are still growing rapidly. Charles Lawson, the Edinburgh nurseryman who acquired the first bulk seedlot of Lawson Cypress, introduced the Hungarian Oak in about 1835. He seems to have obtained grafting material from an unknown source within the native range of the tree in mid-Italy or in the Balkans, for all his known original trees are grafted at base on Common Oak. Wherein he was prescient to a degree. All the best trees are grafts like this and the few suppliers have, until recently used the same method. Acorns give varying and often inferior results. Home collected, they tend to yield only Turkey Oaks. Even a pocketful I carefully picked up beneath the downwind tree of the group of six in the Empire Oaks in Windsor Great Park produced only one out of 20 seedlings that looked to be anything but Turkey Oak. But the grafts are making fine, typical trees everywhere. One snapped off at base, with a clean break across the union. This was one of the older of the two pairs in the Pagoda Vista at Kew Gardens, which went quietly over on the traditional calm, windless day for these things to happen. A gardener told me that they were working nearby in 1986 when they saw it keel over. It dated from about 1870 and was 75/12½ft. Only three big trees have been recorded as blown in the 1987 and 1990 gales, all in some exposure in Sussex and Surrey.

The biggest trees are fairly well spread in England and in southern Scotland, particularly around Edinburgh, but few are in the far west, one in Wales and only two in Ireland. There is thus a marked bias towards the eastern areas. Warm summers may be more important to Hungarian Oak than they are to the equally southern Turkey Oak in which many of the biggest are towards the west.

The champion specimen stands in the open by the trout pool below Buxted Park Hotel in Sussex, visible from the terrace a long way above as a monumentally shapely big tree. It has no early record at all and was found only in 1991, going straight to the top of the table by a wide margin. It was 100/18ft, grafted at base and most likely a Lawson original, with two fairly minor spreading branches at six feet up and the trunk twelve feet high before dividing into four massive upright limbs. The tree it replaces was 82/14½ft dividing at 15ft into eight main limbs, and grafted at base, on an estate near Exeter which wishes to remain unknown. So the new champion is doubly welcome. Two more of similar size had been taken as Lawson originals and are grafted at base, but from early figures it looks as if they have grown too fast to be so old. The fine tree by the front drive to Westonbirt School was 82/14½ft in 1989 and was 70/11ft in 1966 and 50/4½ft in 1927 suggesting a planting date around 1890. The tree near 'Flora' in Syon Park, Brentford, now 95/14½ft was 75/11½ft in 1967 and 56/4½ft in 1910 pointing to around 1880.

The cluster around Edinburgh includes a superb tree at Carberry Tower Musselburgh, 102/13½ft; one in an island in the road in the campus at Riccarton, 80/11ft, which was eight and a half feet round in 1967, and one in Dalmeny Park, a good tree 77/10½ft, while somewhat further away, a splendid tree in Camperdown Park outside Dundee is 108/11ft with a good bole.

At Kew, the survivor of the pair in the northern part of the Pagoda Vista is 100/12ft and the larger of the other pair, planted in 1893 is 92/12ft. Osterley Park, Hounslow, had nine big trees in 1982, five of which survive. Two of these in southeast woods are 95/12½ft and another 100/12ft, while one in the eastern prospect is 62/13½ft. Since in 1909 the two reported were 35ft tall without mention of girth, they had probably been planted only about 20 years by then. At Stratfield Saye House, the two best of the three in the Arboretum north of the House are 108/12½ft and 105/12ft and growing fast as they were eight and a half and eight feet round in 1955. The larger of two at Avenue House, Barnet, is 80/12½ft. By the northern entry to Wakehurst Place, a typical graft with an eight-foot bole is 85/12½ft. The lone big tree in Wales is at Dyffryn Park, 66/11½ft.

Some younger trees of known date, setting out to become this sort of size as soon as possible, will be of interest for noting their progress. One that is already big, was planted as recently as 1929 at Anglesea Abbey, near Cambridge. By 1973 it was 62/8½ft and in 1990 it was 85/11½ft and a splendid specimen. The six Empire Oaks Hungarians were planted in 1937 on poor acid sand. They have been outgrown by the Pin Oaks which are more suited to the site, but are a fairly uniform 60/6ft in 1978 with the biggest, 'Nyasaland', 70/6ft. A shapely, upright tree at the Hillier Arboretum at the top of

Hungarian Oak (*Quercus frainetto*): Buxted Park Hotel, Sussex

the bank above the pool dates from 1954 and is 50/5ft. At Wisley, one planted by the Trial Grounds in 1956 is 56/6ft. At Harlow Carr, in Yorkshire, one planted in 1959 has big low branches and has to be measured at three feet but 52/6½ft in that time is good progress. One in the sandy soil at the Englefield Green London University Botanic Garden planted in 1963 had grown to over 55/4½ft when it was 26 years old.

LUCOMBE OAK

Quercus Lucombeana

William Lucombe was joint founder of the nursery, Lucombe and Pince, in Exeter in 1720. It was this nursery that introduced the Turkey Oak in 1735 and sowed the first acorns it yielded in Britain, in 1762. Among the seedlings, Lucombe noticed one which made extra vigorous growth and retained its leaves green into the winter. He planted it in the nursery and began at once to make from it as many grafts as he could, using the Turkey Oak seedlings as rootstock. He recognised that this was a hybrid with its other parent a Cork Oak that was nearby in the nursery. When it was seven years old, this tree was 21/1ft 8in and when it was 20 years old it was three feet round. So Lucombe cut it down. He was of 'advanced years' and wanted to be buried in a coffin made from his oak.

Whatever little coffin boards a 20 year tree could yield must have been entirely of sapwood, and did not last long, whereas old nurserymen go on nearly for ever and Lucombe was still flourishing when the planks, stored beneath his bed, became useless. So, at some unrecorded date, he had another Lucombe Oak felled, planked and put under his bed until, at the age of 102, he was buried in them. This other tree must have been one of the first grafts but in 1838, Pince's grandson referred to it as 'older and bigger' than the original tree. By then there was much confusion between the genuine original and the numerous grafts of it. Pince furnished Loudon with an engraving of 'the original tree' when 27 years old and 60/4½ft. The original tree was cut down in 1782, so this, and all later references to 'the original' tree are really early grafts. Since no other clone was known until the 1792 seedlings were raised, all mentions refer to grafts of the 1762 tree, and Pince's 'older and bigger' tree was older only in the sense that when cut it was more than 20 years old and more than three feet round.

There is no doubt that the name adopted by Rehder and others, '*Quercus* x *hispanica* var. *lucombeana*', cannot stand, and the range given by Rehder as the Balkans to the south of France, without mention of Spain, is equally bogus. How this absurd mix-up came to be accepted by reputable botanists is hard to see.

Elwes in a footnote in Elwes and Henry wrote that Lamarck applied the name 'not to a Spanish Oak but to three trees cultivated at the Trianon, which were specimens of the Lucombe, Fulham and Turner's Oak. The first of these was erroneously supposed to grow wild in the neighbourhood of Gibraltar'. The name is therefore completely illegitimate, and no type specimen existed or could exist. The name 'Quercus x lucombeana Sweet (Hort. Brit. 370 1827)' must replace it. The original cross should be distinguished from later seedlings, as the cultivar 'William Lucombe', and the 1790 and 1830 seedlings described by Loudon as further cultivars.

Henry was concerned that none of the forms of Lucombe Oak had anything like the vigour reported for the original seedling. This is explained in that all the later seedlings were plainly back-crosses to the slow-growing Cork Oak, which fact was oddly missed by Henry and by all subsequent writers. The original cross was the only one that could exhibit true heterosis.

Observations in Exeter add some enigmatic features. At County Hall, an exceptionally fine tree near the Hall is 80/15ft with non-corky, grey, shallowly ridged bark. It would pass as a good 'William Lucombe' except for three odd features. It shows no sign of being a graft; it has strikingly regular triangular or ovate lobes, six a side on two-inch leaves and seven to nine a side on dominant six- to seven-inch leaves. It has rampant growth of seedlings round its perimeter, such that maintenance of access and lawn require continual removal of swathes of them.

Below this tree a line of three corky-barked dark-crowned broad trees are plainly grafts and pass for the common backcross, but the biggest of them, 80/13ft 8in, has six-inch leaves, bright green beneath with irregular, shallow lobes including some fiddle-shaped with three to five lobes each side. This appears to be an unknown clone.

This original clone is common and prominent in and around Exeter, notably in November and December when big domed crowns hold all their exterior leaves and most of the interior, dark olive green. By January they are still very leafy but the outside is turning dark coppery brown. The leaves are highly variable but there are always many bigger than on the more evergreen clones common over the rest of the country. These original graft leaves are up to four and a half inches long, broadly oblong-ovate with a broadly rounded base, but in the dense sprays on older wood there are some slender, lanceolate-acute, cuneate leaves three inches by one inch, and some long-triangular leaves and all shapes between. The big old original clone grafts have very distinctive crowns. Broader than they are tall, they have a bole of eight to ten feet, then one huge nearly vertical limb with level branches and the main stem continues vertically and central, bearing numerous stout and level branches, the lower ones drooped towards their ends. All branches have a swollen, conic origin.

In 1792, the younger Lucombe sowed acorns from an early graft and raised three seedlings which he selected and from which he made numerous grafts on Turkey Oak rootstock. Loudon named these varieties *suberosa, crispa* and *incisa*. In 1830 two more were raised, *heterophylla* and *dentata*. The 1792 trees have been regarded as second generation hybrids, but they cannot be true F_2 since there was at the time only the single clone. They can only be self-pollinated seedlings or backcrosses to Turkey or Cork Oaks. Oaks are not known to be self-fertile, whereas Lucombe's nursery was growing Turkey and Cork Oaks which had interpollinated, so the backcross is much more likely. The progenies themselves do not decide the issue. 'Suberosa' is a very good candidate for a backcross to Cork Oak, and 'Crispa', if it is the tree I think it is, nearest to but not identical with Loudon's description, is also towards Cork Oak. 'Heterophylla', very rare, is upright in branching and has fiddle-shaped leaves and could be a backcross but are scarcely separable from 'Crispa'.

The Lucombe Oak most seen outside east Devon is one I will call 'Crispa'. It is certainly not the original clone which is present but scarce across England. 'Crispa' is frequent in city parks and in large gardens, especially around London. It is evergreen through all but the hardest winters, looking from a distance like a Holm Oak, and has a bark corky in places, dark and pale grey but is best recognised by its small, dark green leaves, barely three inches long with very small lobes, and grey-white beneath.

Elwes saw the original 'Suberosa' at Lucombe's in 1902 before it was cut down, and considered the corky-barked tree by the Chapel at Killerton to be of that clone, and the only example that he found. That tree is highly distinctive less from its pale grey, not very deeply fissured bark than for its crown and foliage. It has a clean bole to ten feet where it breaks into several big branches, curving out from level to upswept, making a broad, short crown with no central axis. The foliage is dense and blackish, glossy dark green above and pale grey beneath, each leaf only at most three inches by one and a half on a white one inch petiole. The tree has grown slowly, since from an assumed 1793 planting it was only 60/8ft in 1908 and is now not quite 80/11ft.

After admiring this tree recently, I discovered two more. One beside the house at Cowley Place, near Exeter is about 60/9ft and stands out with its pale grey column of trunk holding a dome of blackish small foliage branching out ten feet up. The black foliage accentuates the pale bark and makes the trunk look like a stone pillar. The other is a somewhat gale-shattered big tree 65/16ft by the drive to Bicton College. But it is not too broken to show the unmistakeable pale-barked column ten feet long holding up a spreading crown of broadly upcurved branches laden with little black leaves. These have a high-gloss upper side and blue-grey underside and are less than two inches long.

The biggest trees are all of the big-leafed original clone. The two biggest of these are in Phear Park, Withycombe, Exmouth, and are slightly atypical in having been pollarded, it seems. Neither has the single big upswept limb but both break at six feet into five spreading limbs of great size. They are enormous trees, 82/25½ft and 88/24½ft. Two are known to have been planted by Lucombe's nursery, one in 1765 at Carclew near Falmouth, where it stands today by a gate into the garden, magnificent and 115/19½ft. The other, planted in 1770 at Castlehill, Devon, is a broader tree 98/21½ft. At

Lucombe Oak (*Quercus Lucombeana*): Killerton, Devon

Killerton, a tree in the garden has been taken to be a 1765 planting, because its label says 'Exeter Oak, raised in 1765' but it is now only 85/15½ft and I do not think this refers to its date of planting. A very typical original clone tree in the Park below, is however 92/18½ft and might be of that date. By the Chapel, next to the 'Suberosa', there is an original type, presumably of the same date as the corky tree, 1793, and that is now 102/17ft. At Ugbrooke Park two of the big Lucombes are among the first original grafts planted and in 1978 they were 85/19½ft and 92/17ft. A superb old early graft stands in the grounds of Cowley Place on the A377 a few miles out of Exeter, well visible from that road just after the bridge over the Exe. It is growing well, as it was 19ft round in 1967 and is now 88/21½ft. There are two at Bicton, Devon. The bigger is a very typical specimen off the drive towards the College and was 95/18ft in 1967 and is now 108/21ft. The other is the better known tree in the Rock Garden which delays putting out its one big upright limb until it has a trunk 20ft long, possibly the result of early pruning. It appears to be a younger tree and is now 111/15ft.

Similar specimens more remote from Exeter include the hugely spreading tree at Red Oaks in Henfield near Brighton, which is 70/23½ft measured among the branches, and the tree at Kew, now 80/18ft. This is on the borders of the area of the old Botanic Garden started in 1761, wherein are the first Ginkgo and Pagoda-tree. There is no record of the origin or date of the tree but one can speculate that Lucombe sent a first graft of his tree to be put in the collection, in or before 1765. Thomas Rivers may have been an early recipient, or a customer, for the tree which was in the old Sawbridgeworth Nursery and is now in an island cut off by road re-alignment is a fine, typical original, 70/18ft. More remote is the great spreading tree at Trinity Manor on Guernsey which was 65/22½ft at three feet in 1976.

Some big trees of unchecked clone are one at Wilton, dated 1817 and 92/18ft in 1985; the one in Dartington garden, 105/16ft in 1985; a superb, upright tall tree in Sunnyside Park, Iron Bridge, 111/16ft; another tall tree at Peper Harow, Surrey, now 118/14½ft and two in Scotland. A very fine tree at Innes in Morayshire is 82/13ft and one at Kilmaron Castle in Fifeshire is 88/11ft.

CAUCASUS OAK

Quercus macranthera

A tree of this origin can hardly fail to be of high class. It grows on the southern flanks of the Caucasus Mountains and along the Caspian shores of the Elburz Mountains in northern Iran, the home of the remarkable relict Tertiary flora with so many fine species.

The Caucasus Oak has one feature very unusual in this flora. It has thick, brown pubescence on its shoots and leaf-stalks, with a lighter covering on the underside of the leaf, most visible on the midrib. Otherwise its foliage is very like that of the Algerian Oak but the leaves are more deeply lobed and tend towards those of the Hungarian Oak (a tree which really ought to be a Caucasian. Perhaps it did originate there but moved away to the west). The bark is purplish grey, smooth in patches between dark, flaky sided fissures, and flaking coarsely with age.

It seems that the introduction was by Sir William Holford who had two trees in about 1874. He planted one by what he called Straight Drive in the Arboretum at Westonbirt, re-named in 1956 by the Forestry Commission, Mitchell Drive (after John Mitchell who was curator from about 1900 to 1956). The other he planted prominently in front of a bay of the Eurasian oaks in the collection by Broad Drive in Silk Wood, in 1878. It is a tribute to Sir William's botanical observation and foresight that, although he cannot at that time have seen more than a seedling, he paired this tree with an Algerian Oak. They make a well-balanced pair of very handsomely foliaged, similar trees. The next trees to be planted were sent to Kew in 1895. Until the bold, healthy foliage attracted the recent planters of oak-collections and gardens, few were planted and although it is very hardy, and thrives in Edinburgh, nearly all the established trees are in the southern half of England.

The 1875 tree by the Mitchell Drive is 102/8½ft and the tallest yet found. It is somewhat hemmed in by other trees, but this must not be taken to be the reason for its superior height. Foresters talk about trees being 'drawn up' but research has shown that this is based on the optical illusion that a narrow tree looks taller than a broad one of the same height. Although the growth energy of a crowded tree is more concentrated on the upward growth of the central stem, the amount available is much less than in a tree with a fuller crown, and the upward growth of both is much the same. The 1878 tree in Silk Wood is 85/9ft. The 1895 tree at Kew on Sundial Lawn, beside a path and has splendid big foliage and a broad crown. It escaped gale damage and is now 80/10ft.

The next biggest is in Sheffield Park, Sussex, across the bottom lake in Queen's Wood and is now 75/9ft and a fine tree. The biggest of three in the Royal Botanic Gardens, Edinburgh, are 72/7ft and 75/8ft. An undated tree in Hidcote Garden, Gloucestershire, is 66/7ft and one in the Jephson Gardens in Leamington Spa is 60/6½ft. A tree in the open in the Park by the Lake at Birr Castle, County Offaly, is 60/4½ft. In the Empire Oaks in Windsor Great Park, a tree planted in 1937 was 52/4ft in 1977. In the oak collection at Thorp Perrow, Yorkshire, the tree is 64/4ft. At Wisley in Surrey, a tree planted in 1956 in the Portsmouth Road border is 38/4ft. At Eastnor Castle, Herefordshire, a tree on the slope near the gazebo is 60/5½ft.

PIN OAK

Quercus palustris

This tree combines great elegance with rapid growth when well suited to its site. It is one of the red oaks from eastern North America and although it thrives on a range of soils, from acid sands to heavy clays, it is not adaptable to a climate with cool summers. This is clearly shown by the occurrence of large specimens tailing off sharply north and west of the Thames Valley. Even in the English Midlands there is none of any consequence and north of the small trees in Tatton Park and Ness Botanic Garden in Cheshire there is only a 40ft tree in Edinburgh. In 1974 there was one at Kilruddery Park in County Wicklow, then 61 years old, and 56/7ft at three feet, but it was not found in 1990, and the only other in Ireland is at Abbeyleix, County Leix, 70/6ft.

The Pin Oak acquired its common name from the rigid, slender and straight minor shoots which grow at right angles from the small branches which spray out in a downward, then outward curved, flared skirt, from some eight feet up the bole. These lower branches make a densely twigged lower crown; above them is a zone of level branches, and above that the numerous small branches curve upwards increasingly with their height of origin until making an upswept spire to a single long tip. The skirt, or clear signs of it, are retained by even the oldest trees. Inside, there is a straight almost, cylindric trunk with smooth, dark shiny brown bark. Street trees are pruned to the base of the full skirt to give them a good clean start, and park trees prune themselves, more slowly, by the dense foliage of the skirt shading out the small branches below. The result is a splendidly shapely and distinctive tree, which with its pretty foliage, autumn colours and rapid growth make the tree a frequent choice in cities in warm regions.

The Pin Oak is native from the Hudson Valley and a few areas to the east and north, west and south of the Great Lakes to well across the Mississippi. It is planted today north to Toronto and Montreal and west into Idaho and Nebraska as well as in the western states of Washington and Oregon and in Vancouver. It is the most frequent tree in Central Park, New York. It was brought to England in 1800 by John Fraser.

In this country, growing many fewer species of red oaks than the United States, and not confused by their numerous hybrids, we can easily identify the Pin Oak by its foliage as well as by its crown shape. Like the Scarlet Oak, it has glossy leaves with three big lobes widely separated by deep, rounded sinuses, but, unlike Scarlet

Oak, the underside of the leaf shows prominent pale brown tufts in the angles of the main veins. In the autumn, the colour starts when the tips of branches have yellow, then orange leaves and when these turn scarlet, the main body of the crown foliage is still fresh green. Too often the leaves have been shed before they can all colour.

With all its big specimens in the areas swept by the gales of 1987 and 1990, it is a pleasant surprise that so few have been known to have blown down. My favourite tree on an open lawn at Kew just south of the Palm House, and 85/8½ft in 1963, was unscathed and is now the tallest and one of the three biggest in girth known. It is 102/10½ft. The three at Syon Park across the river also survive. The best, on Flora's Lawn, is 98/9ft and a very sturdy one by the tennis court in the Duke's Garden is 70/9½ft. Two over 100ft tall by the Terrace at Nymans, Sussex, were lost, and one of two in a field behind Claremont House at Esher, Surrey, which were 70/10½ft and 75/9ft in 1986. A superb tree at Godinton Park, Ashford, Kent, 70/10½ft in 1983 was obviously at risk but may still be there. Two others that were in great peril escaped possibly by being in a slight dell behind the police station in Hyde Park, London. The

Pin Oak (*Quercus palustris*):
Royal Botanic Gardens, Kew,
Surrey

larger is among the very finest specimens and is growing well. It was 70/8½ft in 1967, and is now 85/10½ft while the smaller one is 95/8½ft.

Some younger, dated trees have made good but not exceptional growth. In the Empire Oaks group in Windsor Great Park, on what appears to be dry sandy soil planted in 1937, five Pin Oaks have outgrown even the Hungarian Oaks and when 41 years old one was 70/6½ft. The grove of the same date above the Totem Pole were up to 70ft tall and five and a half feet round also in 41 years. A tree in the lower part of Central Park in Bournemouth, planted in 1943, was 82/6ft in 1985.

SESSILE OAK

Quercus petraea

The Sessile or Durmast Oak was a fairly early post-Ice Ages arrival, well in advance of the other native oak. Some academic foresters half humorously began suggesting around 1955 that only the Sessile was truly native and that the Common Oak was an early introduction. The argument rested largely on the distribution today when the English Oak is very predominant in the southeast and east of England and Scotland and the Sessile is the oak of the hills of the west and north and in Ireland. Hence it can be held that the English Oak is in the lands settled first and replaced the native Sessile, leaving that confined, like the earlier human settlers, to Wales and the western hills.

However, the same pattern would arise, and more closely in detail, if the Common Oak spread here naturally from the land-bridge in the southeast. The pollens of the two cannot be separated in the peats providing the pollen records. The Sessile Oak is very much the oak of the wooded hills of Wales, Cumbria and Scotland and of much of Ireland. There are some anomalous populations in England. There are small areas in parts of the High Weald in Surrey and Sussex; there is the Sessile of Enfield Chase for many miles of the right bank of the River Lee in Hertfordshire and Middlesex, and there is the strange case of mid-Dartmoor where the Sessile of the lower hills is replaced at height by Common Oak, as at Wistman's Wood.

The Sessile Oak tends to occur on lighter, more rapidly draining soils than the clays favoured by the Common Oak, but has an equal, or probably greater, need of moisture, so it flourishes best in the high humidities and rainfalls of the western and northern hills, and of Ireland generally. Several features of this oak combine to give its woods a very different ecology from that of Common Oak woods. It spreads its leaves, which are generally much larger, evenly over its shoots, not clustered in separated bunches as in the other oak, so it casts a more even and definite shade. It tends to grow a straight trunk holding straight, variably upraised branches and therefore the trees in a wood can stand quite close together. The woods tend to exclude other tree species and tall shrubs because of space as well as low light levels, and the undergrowth is grasses, moss, ferns, and herbs. With the upswept branches holding the lower crown well clear, there is fly-catching space. Sessile oakwoods are the prime habitat for wood-warblers, redstarts and pied flycatchers. In fact the distribution of pied flycatchers is tied closely to the occurrence of Sessile Oak from small areas on the eastern flanks of Exmoor and Dartmoor, to the Sma' Glen in mid-Perthshire.

The foliage is so superior to that of the Common Oak that it can be noticed from a moving car. The salient feature is that each leaf tapers, with lobes decreasing in size, to an acute tip, and the bases taper to one inch stalks which are prominent and yellow. Many trees have bigger leaves, much more substantial, largely free of galls and of parts eaten away by insects, and shiny and healthy. In the years of plague of Oakleaf roller moth, *Tortrix viridana*, the Sessile Oaks can stand out, little defoliated. There are many trees which are intermediate with Common Oak in several features, notably in having stalked acorns and short leaf-stalks or slight auricles at the base of the blade. These are usually regarded as basically Sessile and conform with that in their branching. Often in Sussex woods particularly they can be distinguished from a distance by their superior height, form and healthy foliage.

The Common Oak was the preferred timber tree largely because its natural sinuous branching provided crooks for shipbuilding before steam-bending, and it may also be marginally harder and more dense than Sessile timber, because it seldom grows as fast. Plantations were made of Common Oak in some Sessile Oak areas. This became apparent in the Forest of Dean, when Dr Bruce Campbell put up bird boxes in a Common Oak plantation to study the breeding of titmice. Many of the boxes were occupied by pied flycatchers, which had not been noted as breeding there before, but proceeded to build a flourishing population in his boxes. As a managed plantation, this had the clear flycatching zone normal in Sessile oakwoods, but young trees do not provide sites for hole-nesting birds.

Three specimens have claims to be given pride of place in the list of specimens, one for the biggest trunk and presumed greatest age, the second as once the tallest oak of any kind and with the longest clean stem, and the third as a superb specimen of remarkable growth recorded over 120 years. The biggest is The Giant at Powis Castle, a few hundred yards across the approach road from the east. This is a very hollow pollard with about a dozen stems rising steeply from around ten feet to over 70ft and the trunk, which was 29½ft round in 1904 is now 36ft round. The crown is in vigorous health although these figures give a probable age of some 450 years.

The tallest tree was at Whitfield House in Herefordshire and it was the tallest known when it was 130/12ft in 1906. It had been damaged by lightning but had a good top still growing until it was 144/16ft. It had a superbly near-cylindric stem for 62ft, but died back and fell in 1992. At Easthampton Farm, Shobdon, Herefordshire, the tree across the road in a field was 20½ft round in 1870. By 1959 the tree was 90/29ft with a grand domed crown springing from about eight feet. Today the tree

Sessile Oak (*Quercus petraea*): Cowdray Park, Sussex

is 82/33ft. The increase of 150in in 120 years when already 20ft round, well beyond the vigour of youth, implies that it was then only about 170 years old and will today be less than 300 years.

A beautiful tree in a field beside Swanwith Lane, Mickleham, near Dorking, well in Common Oak territory, has a regular hugely domed crown of straight, radiating branches, the lowest ones at ten feet up being quite level. It is 120/21ft and has added 16in in ten years. Nearby a Common Oak probably of the same planting is a poor tree 18ft round. In Cowdray Park, Sussex, towards the polo ground from a loop off the A272 there are three big Sessile Oaks. The best, with a superb bole for ten feet has been damaged recently by lightning and is 92/25ft. The much less perfectly boled one 300ft away is 105/25ft. The former was 14ft 4in round in 1819, so growth has not been very rapid. At Leonardslee in Sussex, a tree on the terrace below the house is a shapely 108/13½ft with a clear, quality trunk of 23ft. In Windsor Great Park, near the Mezel Depot, a magnificent tree is 125/20½ft and is as tall as any.

At Kenwood, Highgate, a fine tree is 85/17½ft and in the park as a whole, the Sessile Oaks stand out from the others by their quality and handsome foliage.

In Woburn Park several big Sessiles stand near the old willow collection. They have broad, low crowns but splendid foliage and in 1977 the biggest was 80/22ft. Several estates in Herefordshire, Shropshire and Powys grow good specimens in parkland. At Croft Castle, Herefordshire, one by the drive is 115/24½ft and one in a field nearby is 105/26ft while a short-boled one in the Home Park is 65/28ft at three feet. Oakley Park, Ludlow, has more. One above the entrance drive was 88/23½ft in 1978 and one beyond the pinetum was 85/23½ft in 1971 with a crown spread of 102ft. In the garden at Hawkstone Park, a beautiful tree is 100/19ft with a clear trunk for 20ft. Nettlecombe Estate in Somerset is similarly adorned. The biggest is among several on the rise above the House and is 120/24½ft.

In Yorkshire there are few, but the one in the orchard at Newby Hall would be a good tree in any company and is 98/26½ft. Scotland has great numbers of fine specimens, although that is hardly descriptive of the old Capon Oak just south of Jedburgh by the A68. It has its plaque and is a recognised stop for touring coaches but is really rather a wreck, 60/26½ft. In Roxelle Park, Ayr, a very shapely specimen in a field is 85/18ft with a regular dome. At Drumlanrig Castle, Dumfries, a tree on the flat towards the Castle was noted as a good tree in 1904 when it was 16ft round. It is now 105/21½ft and has a bole 23ft long. At Gray House, Dundee, near the drive, a fine specimen is 102/24ft. In Glenlee Park, Newton Stewart, one in a field east of the House is 85/20½ft and in Munches, near Dalbeattie, two good trees are 105/16½ft and 120/19½ft. In the far north, the remarkable planting is the 25 trees along the rim of the Findhorn Gorge at the Meads of Saint John on Darnaway Estate. The first is much the biggest, 50/32ft; the twenty-first is 80/25½ft but only three others are over 20ft and none of the trees has a good trunk. At Conon House, Easter Ross, a splendid tree outside the wall-garden is 121/17½ft with a good bole.

In Ireland the most notable seen are one at Avondale, County Wicklow, by the road past the car park, 95/17ft with a superb bole 23ft long, and one in Emo Park, Leix, by Mad Marjorie's Walk, 120/18ft with no less than 40ft clear.

COMMON OAK

Quercus robur

When Linnaeus used 'robur' as the epithet to distinguish this species of oak, he was probably indulging his liking for mild plays on words. It combines two concepts, the strength of the timber and the rugged robustitude of the plant. There is no need to extol the value of the timber. The robust growth is less celebrated. The foliage feeds a huge array of insects and supports numerous galls of others which spend part of their lives in galls on the roots. The caterpillars of the Oakleaf Roller Moth,

311

Tortrix viridans, can strip whole trees bare; chafers and other beetles may eat a big proportion of each leaf, but a stripped tree leafs out again, and despite supporting directly and indirectly almost all the animal life in the woodland, the oaks go on with undiminished vigour for a very long time. Furthermore, they are more resistant than all but a few trees to honey-fungus, *Armillaria mellea*.

The property of exceptional longevity invariably attached to the oak is, however, less deserved. It is long-lived in comparison with poplars, willows, ash or beech, but is probably no more so than the Sweet Chestnut, Broadleaf, Small-leaf and Common Limes and the Sycamore, and is certainly far surpassed by the Yew. The story of great longevity is required to support many of the reputed historic associations and very few are credible. Too many rely on its supposed very slow growth. In fact, this oak grows relatively fast for much of its life, and few of the trees in question are anything like big enough to confirm their histories.

Many parks, gardens and village greens have oaks with plaques showing the date of their ceremonial planting. They are all fully in the open, with full, natural crowns, and the measurements of over a hundred of these give a unique insight into the rates of growth of such trees over their first 110 years. Plotting the girths against the age shows very few trees far from the mean growth over that period, of one and a quarter inches a year. So an average full-crowned oak nine feet round will be 100 years old. Remeasurement of hundreds of larger oaks over shorter periods show that until they are 18–20ft round their annual increase slows to one inch a year and then, as the crown begins to die back, to well below this. Bearing in mind the more rapid early growth, it will be seen that the mean annual increase over most of the life of the tree is remarkably close to one inch a year.

Pollarding of oaks was a common practice, to harvest the smallwood by cutting it at eight feet up when the tree was about 20 years old, and ensuring that the regrowth is out of the reach of grazing deer. A pollard thus suffers an initial loss of crown and thus of growth in girth, but within a few years it starts to gain from having a multiple crown and much more foliage volume than a 'maiden' or uncut tree. Further, a maiden loses the ability to grow sprouts of any size from its upper stem and depends on its one or very few original stems, vulnerable to breakage. A pollard can grow new shoots and a new crown at any time until very old age, even when the original trunk has long been very hollow. It can outgrow and outlive any maiden tree. The biggest and oldest oaks are therefore all pollards.

The second biggest oak, and in some ways the finest of them all, 'Majesty' in Fredville Park, Kent, looks as if it may be a maiden tree, but it could be a pollard in which a central stem became dominant. It has a smooth and apparently sound trunk over 38ft round, with two fairly big, level branches at six feet up then continues as a massive bole to about ten feet where many branches spring. It has grown at only a little less than one inch a year since 1906 and cannot be much older than 450 years.

The only oak bigger, with a nearly complete trunk, is at Bowthorp, near Bourne in Lincolnshire, now 39½ft round. It came to light only in 1990 on the back of an engraving bought by Mr Arbon of Lincoln, that this had a known history before it was found by the Hon. Maynard Greville in 1950. This quotes an account written by Howell in 1805, which states that a drawing was made of it by Nattes in 1804 and that Howell wrote 'No tradition is to be found respecting it, having ever since the memory of the older inhabitants or their ancestors, been in the same state of decay. The inside of the body is hollow and the upper is used as a pigeon-house. Floored by George Pauncefoot in 1768 with benches placed round and a door of entrance frequently twenty persons have dined in it with ease. The trunk according to Armstrong is 37ft in circumference'. That was almost 200 years ago. This must be now some 800 years old at least, and probably nearer to 1000.

However, none of the trees with reputed histories taking them back to Elizabeth I, to say nothing of 'Thousand-Year-Old Trees', is of this size and appearance. Furthermore, of 17 trees reliably dated as 120 to 200 years old, the majority have grown at above 0.8 inches a year and few below 0.7 inches and none at all at less than half an inch. It can therefore be said that no normal, healthy oak grows so slowly that if it attains 400 years it could be only 17ft round, and in fact, a good healthy tree likely to live that long would already be that size when it was 200. The only open question is how much and for how long an oak over 25ft round can decrease in vigour, and so how much older than, say, 250 years it can be. But it seems that to be 1000 years old, it should be around 40ft round, and no oak is so big.

Another generally held belief is that oaks have a large, deep-going taproot. This is true for three or four years, at least. The jay-sown plants arising in flowerbeds have to be dug up or pulled out in their first three years, and as one-year plants with slender three-inch shoots already have a taproot to three feet long. However, it soon loses dominance as lateral roots grow faster and develop sinker-roots, and these look after the stability of the tree and its water-supply from the water-table. The original taproot may rot away, and is not discernible in developed root-plates. In the gale of October 1987, great numbers of mature oaks on Wealden clays were blown down in Sussex, and it was soon seen that the taproot story was a myth.

Although Common Oak grows mainly in the low rainfall regions of the east, no tree is seen to suffer even in the longest, most severe droughts. This is a part of the highly robust nature of the tree, and is not entirely owed to their usual position in deep, retentive clays, because it applies equally to the scrub oak on sandy, drying heaths.

It is commonly assumed that mistletoe often grows on this oak, but this is so far from the case that even John Loudon with his extensive network of correspondents knew in 1837 only of two trees. Both were in Herefordshire near Ledbury. In 1905, H.J. Elwes could list only 21 more reports. The best bunch he saw was near Bredwardine, also in Herefordshire, and so were six of the remainder with another six in adjoining counties. Three were in Surrey, two in Norfolk and the furthest north was in Anglesey. The Proceedings of the Woolhope Club in Herefordshire noted many more in that county. It is relevant here, more to inability of humans to see what is before them in general than only in this context, that Christmas card artists, like most of their customers, see the berries of mistletoe as borne between the leaves, yet a glance will show that they never are. They are always borne in the angle of the two shoots beneath. Another fallacy, this time returning to oaks, is that there are 'Domesday Trees' which feature in that compilation. It has been pointed out by both Miles Hadfield and Dr Oliver Rackham, who have studied the book, that no single tree of any sort is anywhere mentioned. It dealt only with whole woods.

Woodland of Common Oak differs from that of Sessile Oak in several ways. For one, it is rarely pure oak over and beyond very limited areas as the old trees have long, level, twisting branches and when they fall, a large area is available in which pioneers like birches and sallow can dominate for a while and be replaced by ash, thorn and hornbeam along with more oak. Secondly, this oak scatters its foliage in bunches, allowing through enough light for some of these species to continue and make a mixed woodland. A layer of tall shrubs grows up and the herb layer is patchy. There is little space for flycatching, so there are no pied flycatchers and few wood warblers.

Outstanding specimens worthy of individual mention fall into three classes. There are the giants with huge boles, mainly pollards and mainly hollow; there are the few very big stems which are not pollards and are tall, and there are those of less size but with long, clean, impressive stems.

The biggest complete trunks, with no open cavity and appearing from the outside to be fully sound, are the Majesty Oak at Fredville Park, Kent, 62/38ft, already mentioned, and two which achieve this only by being solid burr all round. 'Billy Wilkins' in the Park at Melbury in Dorset is really only a hulk, 39½ft round the nearly smoothly circular coalesced burrs, while the tree at Lydham Hall in Shropshire is a better tree, 60/38½ft and about equally smooth. The rest of the biggest trunks are variously incomplete. The biggest is the Bowthorpe Oak near Bourne in Lincolnshire, mentioned above. The Pontfadog Oak at a farm above Chirk in Clwyd, is just open basketwork, 37ft round. A much superior tree at New Bells Farm, Haughley, Suffolk is 50/37ft and has added 19in since 1952.

The most famous surviving oak is probably the Major Oak in Sherwood Forest near Ollerton in Nottinghamshire. It is nowhere near the biggest, nor can it be the oldest, but one is assured by locals that it is both. It is a pollard at eight feet with one great branch leaning out and leaving only five feet of bole. The central branch of the outer four is vertical and that accounts for the tree having sometimes been said to be a maiden, but the others are grossly thick too, and arise from an ugly swelling above a poorly shaped bole with a narrow opening five feet tall. This has been made hideous by being lined with a thick layer of gangrenous green polystyrene in a wholly misguided effort to show the public that care has been taken to prevent a recurrence of the fire which raged for most of one night inside the trunk. In fact, of course, the fire usefully removed all the inflammable decay and left it lined with deeply charred wood, which is all the fire-proofing it could need. No true Briton ever dares to stand up to a misinformed and ignorant public campaign and say 'No. We will do no such absurd and unnecessary thing'. This would isolate it from its natural habitat and make it like a museum exhibit in a glass case. Far better that the tree should die in its own way and time, with some dignity.

Although ugly in some details, the tree has a grandeur, and has long had ten-foot posts supporting some of the widest spreading branches. It is 52/34ft. From early measurements, including 30½ft in 1906, its age can be estimated fairly closely as around 480 years.

The Hazelgrove Oak at King's School, Sparkford, Somerset is a fine old tree. It is 82/34½ft with a full crown of wide- spreading branches. One rests on the ground, but they all originate from some eight feet up, so it has a clear bole of that length, and

Common Oak (*Quercus robur*): Holme Lacey, Herefordshire

315

although far from smooth and rather deeply waisted at around five feet, it is splendid for its size.

A smoothly rounded complete bole, but a short one, is possessed by the good oak in front of Neatham House, near Alton, Hampshire, which is 50/29½ft. At Gathmyl House towards Newtown, Powys, the giant oak is of a different form. It is 60/33ft but has to be taped at four feet as it has many long, level, low branches arising at around this point. Rather similar, but spreading extraordinarily, is the Sun Oak beside the St Leonards road east of Horsham, Sussex. It deserves some fame but seems to be almost unknown even in that area. It is 72/27½ft at a little below five feet, where branches extend level at the base of an enormous domed crown and stretch for about 60ft each side. The name 'Sun Oak' comes from the Sun Inn partly enveloped by the crown, but now a private house, 'Sun House'.

The most perfect of these pollards, in bole and crown, is across a field from the drive to Gargunnock House, west of Stirling. This is 100/21ft with a regular dome of radiating straight branches on a ten foot long, smoothly cylindrical bole. Excluded from the roll-call of superior specimens is one which could be claimed as the biggest of them all, and once certainly was. This is the Marton Oak in a farmyard in Cheshire. A tight tape around it gives a reading of 46½ft, but this is encompassing two big fragments with eight feet of air between them.

Trees of the second kind, big maidens with long trunks, may include 'Majesty' already mentioned. A famous tree that certainly qualifies is the Panshanger Oak in Hertfordshire, now 65/24ft 3in with a stout solid bole for about 45ft. It has been measured frequently since 1804 when Arthur Young found it to be 17ft round. J.G.Strutt, who measured trees at three feet up in 1830, made it 19ft 2in and H.J. Elwes made it 21ft 4in at five feet in 1905. The Crimea Oak at Althorpe, North-amptonshire is very similar, 72/23ft with only twiggy little shoots on the bole for 20ft. It was 90/19½ft in 1906. The Radley Oak at Radley School, Berkshire, 82/29ft, has a fine clean bole for over ten feet but evidently once forked there then lost one half, long ago. The other stem now stands erect and central. In Bressingham Garden, Norfolk, a superb oak is 102/18ft with a clear, cylindric bole for 15ft. A fine tall tree stands on the bank above the River Skelt between Fountains Abbey and the Studley Royal Water Garden. This is 132/12½ft. Another very tall, fine oak is at Walcombe, by Wells in Somerset, 124/12½ft. A lightly branched tree in the valley at Abbotsbury, Dorset, is 115/16ft with a good trunk. A remarkable oak in the Park at Tullynally, County Westmeath is 124/15ft with a clear trunk for 36ft.

Two trees have even longer clear stems. The longer is at Castle Howard, Yorkshire, by Temple Rush, 102/10ft without a branch for 65ft. The other at Mote Park, Maidstone, Kent, is 82/15ft with 60ft clear.

CYPRESS OAK

Quercus robur 'Fastigiata'

Fastigiate plants of Common Oak have been found in forests from Spain to southern France and Italy, but the parent of the first clone to be distributed in Britain was a wild tree near Frankfurt-am-Main. It had been known long before 1783 when grafts were grown in German parks and nurseries. The trees in Britain of known German origin are compact, very fastigiate, columnar with a slender conic top and all the grafted trees are similar. In North America the common clone is leafier with bigger, longer leaves.

In most trees propagated by grafts, the character for which it was selected, the fastigiate shape, golden foliage or large flowers, are single-gene characters, and recessive. That means that the offspring need to inherit the feature from both parents if they are to show it themselves. The flowers on the selected form can, however, be pollinated only by the males on ordinary trees around, and so it is rare for the feature to breed true. Which is why propagation by grafting is needed. This is a good thing in that the fully developed variant is preserved and not merged with the wild form through a range of intermediates. Occasionally these could be an interesting mix, and the Cypress Oak acorns do give such progeny. So, while the

Cypress Oak (*Quercus robur* 'Fastigiata'): the first tree of this kind in Britain was from Germany

best form, true Cypress Oaks, are grafts, there are gardens growing a range of variants from trees nearly as formal and fastigiate as the grafts, to broad but erect and to upswept goblet shaped. Hardwicke Park near Bury St Edmunds has a group of big trees of these various forms.

Fortunately the Cypress Oak has been taken up recently by architects and is being planted more than it was. It may be that they want the spire shape but fight shy of the Lombardy Poplar near buildings, and the Letraset symbol for that tree is always at hand to stand in for the oak.

A tree of known German origin was planted in 1875 in the garden by Woburn Abbey. In 1982 it was 85/8½ft. Three trees from Potsdam were planted on the lawn at Bagshot Park in 1908, all very neat and shapely. By 1982 two of these were 95/9ft and 77/8ft. The big tree at Whiteknights near Reading, admired by Henry in 1908 when it was 82/8ft, had died back by 1971 when it was 11ft round. He also noted and photographed a beautiful tree at Melbury Park, Dorset when it was 65/3½ft and this tree is now 85/9ft and still as well-shaped. At the top of the Valley Garden there is another, 82/7ft and one on the dam below it is 88/6ft. The tree that Elwes noted at Hardwick Park, 61/5ft in 1908, is presumably the most slender of those there in 1974 when it was 75/11½ft and one of the seedlings, with an ovoid, upright crown, was 70/10ft. Two seedlings which Elwes raised and planted in his garden at Colesbourne, in the Ring Meadow, in 1902 are good fastigiate trees, 80/7½ft and 70/4ft in 1984

A broad-crowned tree in what was Rivers' Nursery, and is now an island in the straightened road near Sawbridgeworth, was 88/11ft in 1984. Two trees stand on the lawn behind Cliveden House, one of them of the classic shape and now 75/8½ft, and the other with a more branchy, broader lower crown, 82/10½ft, while a presumed seedling near the Blenheim Pavilion is a broad, but erect tree, 82/7½ft. An exemplary classic specimen beside the pool near Seven Acres Lawn at Wisley, is prominent to those walking to the Restaurant, and is growing well. It was 50/3½ft in 1964 and 82/6½ft by 1988. A less shapely tree survived at Wakehurst Place in a shrubbery beside the Mansion when most of its neighbours were blown down in 1987 and is now 95/9½ft. A very fine, slender tree in the remains of the garden at Rood Aston in Wiltshire was 68/7 in 1981. At Kew, the graft in the Oak Collection is now 72/6½ft and an obscure variant labelled 'Grangei' with stronger branching is 75/7½ft.

A typical graft in the Old Garden at Cardine House in Perthshire is 80/7½ft and a superbly shaped tree in Kingsway Gardens, Chandler's Ford, Hampshire was 72/8ft in 1983, measured at three feet because of the congestion of branches at five feet. Two more big and spreading trees, presumed seedlings, are one at Orchardleigh near Frome in Somerset, now 85/9ft and one at Avenue House, Barnet, 72/8ft in 1983.

RED OAK

Quercus rubra

This is the type member of a group of about 20 'red' oaks which is confined to North America. They intercross to some extent and 50 hybrids among them are accepted as wild, but none crosses with any oak in the other groups. The red oaks share three general features; a largely smooth bark; acorns needing two years to swell and ripen, and a bristle tip to any lobe or tooth. Where the leaves are smooth ellipses without a lobe or a tooth, as in the Willow and Shingle oaks, the apex of the leaf bears a bristle.

The Red Oak ranges from Nova Scotia to Minnesota in the north, to Arkansas, Louisiana and Georgia in the south. With such a vast range, it will have been seen by all the early travellers and collectors, but somehow it eluded John Banister and any others who sent trees to Bishop Compton before 1700, or it failed to survive the journey, and is not recorded as being grown at Fulham Palace. It is said to have been introduced in 1724 which fits well with the time that Peter Collinson of Mill Hill was receiving quantities of Appalachian trees from John Bartram. It does not live long enough, in cultivation or in the wild, for any trees of that age to be alive today.

The Red Oak grows rapidly when young and maintains a steady increase in size until senile. The first shoot from an acorn has been known to be five feet long, and a forestry planting on a Welsh hillside was making annual shoots of seven feet in its second year. This is a good example of how the use of small plants, one to two years old, gains time. For such plants are universal in forestry and here, notch planted at many hundreds a day and given no further attention beyond a summer weeding, on a rough hillside, they made this growth. Too many gardeners still think that they steal a march on time by spending huge sums on absurdly tall plants which after an elaborate planting and needing a stake in the rich soil of a sheltered garden, well cultivated around for years, struggle to grow more than a few inches for several years and never make their proper growth.

Although the range of the species includes such places as Prince Edward Island and part of Quebec, with very cold winters and cool summers, the early introductions will have been from somewhere between Pennsylvania and North Carolina, and probably the later ones also, areas with hot, long summers. It might have been expected that the Red Oak would be like the generality of trees from that part, like the hickories, Tulip-tree and Sweetgum, and have grown best in the warmer southeast, and progressively less well northwards and possibly failing in the far north. But the Red Oak is tough and highly adaptable, and grows vigorously well north of Inverness. In fact, more of the scarce forms with outsize foliage are seen in Scotland than in the south.

Red Oak (*Quercus rubra*):
Cassiobury Park, Watford,
Hertfordshire

The great majority of big trees have stout but very short boles, dividing into many limbs within six or seven feet of the ground, and many have very big branches below that. A long trunk is a rarity and none is noteworthy. Some trees grow strong sprouts around their base and these bear leaves to over eight inches long, very shallowly lobed. Presumably they could grow into large, competing stems but this has not been seen, nor has mature coppice growth, although the stumps of felled trees can sprout strongly.

It is odd that no standing tree is known with a date before 1874 although several must be much older than that. One at Westonbirt can with some assurance be attributed to an 1856 planting because it is in Down Cover, which was planted in that year and by the gate into it from the 1829 planting. This tree is 100/13ft and has looked to have shot its bolt a few times but has been reprieved and then recovered adequately. The 1874 tree is in the Kew oak collection, by the Thames, and is 80/11½ft, but there are several bigger at Kew and probably older. The biggest currently is in the Pagoda Vista, probably dating from 1856 and is 98/15ft. A fine tree by the Japanese Gate is 88/13½ft and the tallest is a younger tree off Holly Walk, 111/12ft. Another good one near Palm House Pond is 88/13ft.

Until 1976 there was one eminently outstanding tree, in Cassiobury Park, Watford. It was then 92/20½ft with a massive, clean bole for 20ft. It shed a big branch in that year, and as it was in an area much used for games and picnics, it was an unacceptable danger. Since then none of this quality has been known, and only one of that size. In a private garden backing on to Pains Hill Park at Cobham, Surrey, this majestic tree, 75/21ft, has several low branches spreading far and reaching the ground, but a huge trunk persists through numerous more branches, and this was badly split in 1992.

A tree much advanced in senility some years ago may survive a long time yet at The Gliffaes Hotel near Crickhowell in Powys, where it was 65/16ft. A slightly less geriatric tree at The Whittern in Herefordshire is 80/15ft. The only other Red Oak of this size is in Scotland at Gray House near Dundee, 72/15ft. The trees in the north and in high rainfall areas of Wales and the west seem generally to have more luxuriant foliage with bigger leaves than in warmer, drier regions. Others not far away are one at Moncrieffe House, 88/13 and at Snaigow in Perthshire, 75/12½ft. In much less humid country, a tree in the woods at Revesby Abbey, Lincolnshire, is 80/14½ft.

The early rapid growth usually achieved is exemplified by an undated tree in Silk Wood, Westonbirt, which was 42/3ft in 1965 and 26 years later was 75/6ft. One I raised from an acorn picked up beneath a group near the Black Nest Gate into Windsor Great Park, which took my fancy from their shape and bright orange autumn foliage, was 25 years later 55/4ft. The Coronation tree on Tilford Green in Surrey was 42/6ft when 38 years old.

CORK OAK

Quercus suber

It seems to be expected of everyone to gaze in admiration at any Cork Oak however stunted or misshapen it be. The aspects supposed to inspire unbridled marvelling are, first, that it grows so far to the north, wherever the garden be, and second that this is actually the tree which yields the cork of commerce.

I must be a major disappointment to many owners of these jewels of the arboricultural scene. Their survival at any northern latitude has not impressed me since I saw my first big specimen, just felled at Gordon Castle, Fochabers, Morayshire. It is possible to be a mile or so further north on the Buchan Peninsula, and a few more on the western side of the Firth, but before long, John O'Groats looms. As to the source of cork, that is a matter of very little interest. I do not even think any better of the Bat Willow as a tree because of its product, although that really is an essential part of civilisation as we know it.

To exacerbate the problem of trying to be as polite about it as possible, the tree is usually a miniscule, shrubby object without any charm, not worth measuring and rarely with a trunk for five feet anyway. The one part of it which is not dreary and ordinary, apart from the peculiar, gross, thick bark, is the underside of the leaf. That is a surprisingly bright blue-white, which ought to be a relief from the blackish green of the upper side, but shows little in the dense mass of foliage held on a tangle of slender shoots.

The tree starts life, on planting out, as it means to go on – as a bushy little plant with excruciatingly slow growth. Soils and exposure make little difference, because any falling away of growth is barely noticeable. For any purpose that might call for a Cork Oak, such as winter greenery, shelter or screen on poor soils, there are several other trees superior in every way. Even the unappealing Holm Oak is much faster, taller-growing, tougher and looks quite bright for a week in June when it flowers.

In view of the disparagements above, it may be unexpected that there are any specimens accepted as fine, noteworthy trees, but there are three well qualified. Two are within a few miles of Tor Point, Cornwall, on different estates. One is in Mount Edgcumbe Country Park, and is a graft at six inches, now 65/17½ft and quite a shapely tree. The other is at Antony House, 72/15½ft with a stem of eight feet breaking into several big upraised limbs. The best, however, is at Standish House at Stroud, Gloucestershire, 70/18½ft, with big branches at four and six feet.

After these there is a gap in quality as well as in size. The next biggest was, in 1987, 65/13½ft at Killerton, Devon, but one on the same lines as the two best was at Linton Park near Maidstone in Kent. It was planted in 1778 and had a splendid cylindrical stem for ten feet. It was 50/10ft in 1965 and was blown down a few years later. Others not seen for 20–30 years, and which must be regarded as at some risk of not being there now, are a notably fine tree at Sharpham House, Totnes, Devon,

Cork Oak (*Quercus suber*):
a mature tree with some
branches removed

56/14½ft with a six-foot bole from which big limbs spread, in 1965, and one 46/14ft in 1970 at Powderham Castle, Devon. A good tree planted in 1830 by the church at Sidbury Village in Devon was 55/10½ft in 1959. A fine specimen at Sherborne Castle in 1963 was 67/11ft. Two at Haldon House near Exeter were in good order in 1973, one 62/11ft with a ten feet bole, and the other 64/11ft with five feet of clear bole.

Recently measured trees more likely to be present now include a good tall one in the garden at Tregrehan, 72/10½ft and one at Tregothnan, 52/10ft, both in Cornwall.

TURNER'S OAK

Quercus x *turneri* (plate 7)

Turner's Oak is a modest little tree but a quietly attractive and interesting one. There is only one hybrid oak that is, at least locally, prominent or common and that is the Lucombe Oak, and Turner's is the only other that is less than genuinely rare. It is not very frequent, but is seen in some London parks and in parks and large gardens in small numbers in all parts.

This tree is a cross between the Common Oak and the Holm Oak, and it seems inexplicable that while those trees are everywhere growing within easy pollen range of each other, this hybrid has been found only once, in about 1780 in Spencer Turner's nursery in Essex. Elwes suggests that this arose in Lucombe's Nursery in Exeter and this Essex tree is a graft. All the specimens are grafts deriving from that tree. It is worth diverting here to note that the Sessile Oak has also crossed with the Holm Oak, and only once, and that hybrid, *Quercus* x *audleyensis* is so rare that only the Audley End tree, beside the House in Essex, was known until I found a graft from it growing in Christchurch Park, Ipswich, in 1991 when it was 46/9½ft. The presumed original at Audley End is of unknown origin or date but was 85/11ft in 1903 and 75/14ft in 1985.

Turner's Oak should be a gloomy tree as it has dark, nearly evergreen foliage and dull, dark grey bark. It grows slowly, and is usually broad in the crown and branchy. It is, however, a tree of character and always a welcome sight with its broad dome of substantial foliage, dark but a pleasing green through the winter, greatly enhanced by each leaf tapering to a narrow base. Cuneate leaves like this are typical of American oaks and very rare in others, so in this very European and evergreen oak they are unexpected. The tapered base gives a lightness in foliage that without it would be heavy and dull. Particularly in winter, this handsome greenery is a great asset to a garden or to woodland.

Some trees have leaves uniformly cuneate and unlobed in the basal half, and have been distinguished as var. *pseudoturneri*, and longer and narrower than the leaves of the typical form, but there are intermediate forms and Henry suspected that they are all grafts from the original tree, raised from different shoots. The distinction is not often made now. Thomas Rivers had one of the first trees in his Sawbridgeworth Nursery and that is a good *pseudoturneri* and is the origin of many of the trees of this kind. Loudon wrote that this tree dates from about 1798. The Kew tree is of this form too, and is at least as old, and probably a little older.

This Kew tree is the doyen of all the Turner's Oaks today and is near the Ginkgo, in the original 1761 botanic garden. It is hugely branched from near ground level. Taped among the branches as nearly at five feet as possible, it is now 72/17ft. Elwes in 1907 is not precise about which tree at Kew, of several he mentions, was the one he measured, but it was only 37/5ft so either this was one of those in Syon Vista, where today the biggest is 60/10ft, or he was putting the tape round high up the old tree. If so it is curious that he says no more about what even then must have been the biggest and grandest of all. It looks as if he did not see it. The Rivers tree he found to be about 50/5ft in 1908. In 1984 it was a splendid specimen, down near some old buildings near the road, 62/12½ft.

The tallest is at Eastnor Castle, Herefordshire, by the drive towards the moat, a broad-crowned tree, 87/12ft in 1984, and one about the same height is at Tullynally Castle in County Westmeath, but smaller, 85/7½ft. By the drive to Bicton College in Devon, a tree with a clean bole for eight feet is 70/11½ft. At Osterley Park, Hounslow, the bigger of two on the lawn in 1991 is 56/11½ft.

ROBINIA

Robinia pseudoacacia

A few trees which do not earn a place in this work by the size or beauty of even their best specimens, may be allowed an entry on the strength of their part in horticulture and their long history here. The Robinia is a case in point.

To the non-gardening, non-botanical public, this is the 'acacia', but while that is the right family, the Pea Family, Leguminosae, it is in the wrong part of it. The acacias are thorny, like the Robinia and have much-divided leaves, but they have small flowers like powder-puffs and the Robinia has true pea flowers hanging in big heads like those of Wisteria. Linnaeus recognised the dominance of the common error in 1753 when he named the tree *pseudoacacia*. I have used here the name 'Robinia' because it is not only euphonious but commemorates the family most involved in introducing the tree to Europe. The Americans however know their tree as the Black Locust, or at least as the Locust-tree.

Augustine Henry states that Jean Robin, gardener to Henry IV of France, received the first seed in 1601. Apparently nothing came of it for he says that the first known tree planted in France was planted in 1636 by Vespasien Robin, seven years after the death of Jean, his father. John Tradescant the Younger introduced it to England some years before 1640, if the usually reliable John Parkinson is to be

Robinia (*Robinia pseudoacacia*):
known in America as the Black
Locust

believed, as he wrote in 1640 that those trees had grown to 'an exceeding height'. It does grow fast, and 'an exceeding height' for a tree never grown before need not be above perhaps 20ft, which they might have achieved in five or six years.

I am sorry for William Cobbett because he raised and sold a few million trees on the correct observation that they would easily outgrow oak on great stretches of heathland and other poor wasteland and yield timber as strong as oak and much more durable in the soil. He should have had the answer to large-scale production in these areas, of timber for farm buildings, fencing and fuel. But somehow, the project never properly took off, and it died with him.

Robinia is at home in hot, dry and paved-over soils because it has a wide ranging root-system with nodules to accommodate nitrogen-fixing bacteria and is independent of an external supply. Thus it is exceptionally valuable for planting on slag and spoil-heaps, even those 'byngs' which are hot underground, as well as in city streets. A long planting by the arterial Chertsey Road, A316 near Twickenham was planted, I am told, at the recommendation of a bee-keeping councillor or his wife, as the flowers are favoured by bees and yield good honey.

Good flowering is very dependent on a continuously hot spring, and early summer, so it is unreliable. As a park tree, Robinia makes too poor and shapeless specimens to be considered. As a plantation it causes problems because every tree cut to the ground as a thinning re-grows spine-clad sprouts five feet tall, and the thin canopy of the main crop fails to suppress them. Perhaps this is what sabotaged the works of Cobbett's customers. So, outside city centres and away from old coalfields, there is little use for the Robinia.

It is very little better in its own country. The wild range is in the Allegheny Mountains from Pennsylvania to Georgia and on lower hills west of the Mississippi Valley, but now it is in every state and only a little less of a national menace than the Tree of Heaven. The best trees were in the valleys in the great Smoky Mountains in Tennessee which were famed for their 'shipmast locust'. There can be little left because even in Cade's Cove and by Locust trail, there was only one tree I would look at twice even in England, and that was only 120/8ft. The rest were the sort of arboreal wreckage that should be good for birds. Oddly, though, there is an immediately distinguishable superior form on Long Island, beyond the natural range. Particularly common along the roads threading the little properties inland from the ocean shore through towns like the Quoges, it has a straight pole of a trunk and high, small level branches. Elmer Little equates this with ship-mast locust and calls it the cultivar 'Rectissima' which is not mentioned in European works, nor is it apparently grown here.

The Robinia must be a short-lived tree here. Elwes and Henry seem to have liked the tree, although they were gentlemen of some discernment on other subjects, for they listed 30 specimens. So far as can be found only three remained for Maynard Greville to find after 1950, and there is some doubt about one of those. Greville went on to add 32 of his own selection, and only three of these have been found after 1980. The doubtful Elwes and Henry tree is the old hulk in Kew. This is in the first acres, where the Ginkgo and Pagoda tree were planted in 1761 and is co-eval with them. The hulk still there has no date on its label, but I think it had one in 1964 when I measured the tree, as less than 40/15ft. But Elwes and Henry had their 1762 tree at Kew 60/17½ft in 1904. They made the very rare mistake, and it seems most unlikely that there were two similar trees at the time, so we can assume that their tape was at a low level, or that there were then snaggy branches to circumnavigate, for today the tree is just approaching 17ft.

In Hampton Park near Seale in Surrey, a tree in 1984 was 85/22ft but this is a forking stem. A tree at The Old Rectory, Sudborough, Suffolk, in 1987 was 56/17½ft and is not forking, but it does bear big low branches. At Easton Grey in Gloucestershire, one is 52/14½ft and in the depths of Taymouth Castle Garden at Kenmore in Perthshire a broken stem is 12ft round. In the Pagoda Vista, south end at Kew, a tree with a respectable bole is now 65/13½ft and may be the one that I had as 56/10ft in 1956, growing unexpectedly fast. The one good stem I recall was in the pinetum at Bayfordbury in Hertfordshire in 1973 which was 92/10½ft and a clear stem for 26ft. Many young dated trees have grown moderately fast but none is worth a mention, beyond the 1961 tree at Churchill College near Bristol which is 62/5½ft now that it is 30 years old.

GOLDEN WEEPING WILLOW

Salix 'Chrysocoma'

This tree has been through the mill so thoroughly with regard to its status, English and botanical names, that it is included here less for its modest big, short-lived specimens than for the excuse to air the work which has sorted it out recently. This has been done by Desmond Clarke, who wrote the revised Bean's *Trees and Shrubs Hardy in the British Isles*, in the main text and in the Supplement, and by the Czech Professor Chlemar in the 1983 Yearbook of the International Dendrology Society. The intricacies and niceties of botanical nomenclature have only a marginal place here so this will be a brief summary.

First, the tree was called the 'Babylon Willow', *Salix babylonica*, as it still is in some catalogues. There is no willow native to the region of Babylon. The tree reputedly bedecked by harps is a poplar, *Populus euphratica*. The Weeping Willow referred to is a clone selected in China from the Pekin Willow, *Salix matsudana*, and carried along the ancient silk-trade routes to the Levant. After hundreds of years cultivated there, the common clone, a female tree, was one that is tender in colder climates, and this was introduced to England from Aleppo in 1730 by a Turkey Merchant, Mr Vernon, as reported by Peter Collinson. It has not proved hardy and none of this origin is known today. It was this form which was planted at Napoleon's tomb on St Helena in 1821. Cuttings from those trees soon became fashionable in English gardens and one was grown at Kew in 1825, brought by Thomas Fraser, and died in a drought in 1867. The tree is the common weeping willow in the eastern United States as far north as somewhere between Washington DC and Philadelphia, where it overlaps with and is then replaced northwards to Quebec by the Golden Weeping Willow.

Then the Golden Weeping Willow was recognised as a different tree from the Babylon Willow and appeared under several names like *S. vitellina* 'Pendula' and *S. babylonica* 'Ramulis Aureis', until it was accepted as *S. alba* 'Tristis'. We should have seen that this was a grave error, but it was not until 1983 that Professor Chlemar opened our eyes to the fact. For one thing, the name made the tree merely a weeping cultivar of White Willow, but it had long been thought to have been a hybrid with the Babylon Willow, partly because the flowers are male and female, often mixed on the same catkin. It is not therefore just a cultivar of White Willow. But there is a true *S. alba* 'Tristis', a fairly common tree, which we had quite failed to notice was a very distinct tree. It is a rangey, tall tree with sparse upcurved branches making an open crown, but with similar weeping outer shoots and these are unlike the true hybrid Golden form in being thinner foliaged, frequently infected by fungal disease and, most noticeable, being shed after the first frost. The Golden Weeping Willow shows hybrid vigour and its more luxuriant foliage persists on the tree, green until late autumn. Its hybrid origin was first recognised by Dode in 1908 when he named the tree *Salix* x *chrysocoma*. The group of *alba* x *babylonica* hybrids is, strictly, *S. x sepulchralis*, but it is preferable to treat this form as one does the Japanese cherries of complex or unknown origin, and fine it down to the cultivar name alone.

It became common in the trade after about 1880 and is now much the commonest weeping tree in England as far north as mid-Yorkshire, but none has been noted southwest of Somerset nor west of Hereford and Shropshire. The big concentrations are in and around London along the Thames and in Cambridge, and lesser groups in Essex and Gloucestershire around Cheltenham. There is a seven year old tree in Easter Ross at Fairlie House growing quite fast, almost the only tree in Scotland. It is a frequent sight dominating tiny front gardens in Hampstead and a highly ill-advised choice as the roots will choke drains, dry out the garden and, on London Clay, threaten the footings of buildings.

The noteworthy specimens are few and probably fleeting so the selection is limited. The biggest by far are two towards the house of West Kingsclere Farm in Berkshire. These can be admired over a cup of coffee in the Little Chef on the A339, across the field opposite in their brilliant yellow-green unfolding foliage in late March. They were 60/18ft and 60/15½ft in 1989. A good tree in Newby Hall garden in Yorkshire is 50/12ft and a tall one in the University Botanic Garden in Oxford, is 72/12½ft. Early growth is often very vigorous indeed. On Surrey University Campus, Guildford, it has taken 23 years to reach 36/6½ft; at Scotsdale Nursery, Cambridge, it is 50/6ft in 25 years; in Hester Park, Cheltenham, it is 52/7½ft in 34 years.

Golden Weeping Willow (*Salix* 'Chrysocoma'): Syon House, Isleworth

AMERICAN BASSWOOD

Tilia americana

In North America they will have no truck with using the ancient name of a citrus fruit, the lime, to designate any species of *Tilia*. Even the respectable name, 'linden' which is the basis of most names in Europe for the genus, and is familiar in America, is replaced in official checklists by the name 'basswood' for every species, derived from the Indian use of the inner bark, or bass, for ropes and string. Several species are also known as 'bee-tree', for obvious reasons, and although more generally applied to the White Basswood, use of the name has spread to include the American Basswood, partly because botanists often unite these trees, despite the silvered underside of the leaf being a prominent feature of the White Basswood in the Alleghenies.

The natural range of the basswoods is confined to the eastern side of the subcontinent and none reached as far west as the foothills of the Rockies because an inland sea blocked their migration west after the Ice Ages, as it did the spread of the elms. The range of the American Basswood shows clearly the eastern margins of that sea, running almost due south from the Canadian border in Manitoba, along the eastern margins of North Dakota, South Dakota, Nebraska and Kansas to Oklahoma.

John Bartram sent seed of the American Basswood in 1752 to Philip Miller at Chelsea, and Peter Collinson at Mill Hill will have had some as he and Miller were sharing the Bartram imports and distributing them. It did not make much impact, and may have been short-lived. Henry in 1913 knew of only three specimens, all young. It is still very scarce, but not as rare as I had come to believe. By 1974 I knew very few specimens and they were far from inspiring. The biggest were near the Flagstaff at Kew and in Willesley Drive in Westonbirt. They were notable only for their unthrifty growth, curiously moth-eaten bark and outsize, floppy very dull leaves. The small tree by the Totem Pole in Windsor Great Park was notable for the densely set rings on its bark, from the base to near the tip, from sap-sucking by great spotted woodpeckers, a phenomenon beginning to be noted before 1980. It was otherwise just a small, rather scruffy specimen with small leaves. Then two unremarkable small limes outside a school in a road in Farnham, Surrey, were found on closer inspection to be the American species, as were two more by a farm gate at Kingsley not far away.

Then I recognised a tree 75/8ft and slightly woodpeckered at Grayswood Hill near Haslemere in Surrey, and a handsomely foliaged tree 60/4ft in the lime group at Winkworth Arboretum, also in Surrey, both in 1976, (and both blown down in 1987). Then I spent much more time in America and found that in streets I was recognising the tree easily not by big leaves or poor shape but by normal-sized leaves with an upper surface of rich, shiny green, prominently marked with yellow

American Basswood
(*Tilia americana*):
Lion Green,
Haslemere, Surrey

veins, parallel and straight, and very shapely, conic pointed crowns. Back in Britain, I saw one exactly of this form in a typical American city position near the Shell Building on the South Bank. Next, I saw that the line of limes on Lion Green in Haslemere was American, not the Broadleaf. Now I had the key to why this tree had seemed so rare.

There was an avenue to a church in Farnham (until 1987) and a superb young tree, planted in 1950 in a garden in the Lower Froyle and 52/5ft in 1988 and it was six feet round in 1993. It began to look as if American Basswoods were frequent around Farnham and that they could be so around Britain. But they are not. There are young trees in some parks and gardens, but the big finds are limited to a good avenue in Calderstone Park, Merseyside; two more trees in Surrey, one at Kew in the Pagoda Vista, 72/9ft in 1989, and one by the Seven Acres Lawn at Wisley, 88/6ft in 1989. One at The Bowes Museum at Barnard Castle, County Durham, 75/8ft in 1990. The biggest, a tree grafted at five feet in Alexandra Park, St Leonards, Hastings, was 75/10ft in 1991.

SMALL-LEAF LIME

Tilia cordata (plate 8)

As a young tree, the Small-leaf Lime is neat and shapely, its ovoid-conic crown of numerous light branches topped by a spire surrounded by nearly vertical uppermost shoots. It can be as formal as a Pyramidal Hornbeam, although more open. It is unfortunate that it has not passed this on to its hybrid, the Common Lime. Odd, too, for the other parent of that hybrid is the Broadleaf Lime which radiates a regular dome, increasingly shapely as it matures, but the Common Lime shows nothing of this inheritance and always has an irregular crown of awkwardly placed big branches. The deplorable suckering that disfigure it round the base and from ugly burrs on the trunk, however, must be blamed squarely on the Small-leaf Lime, for the Broadleaf shows nothing of this sort. The Small-leaf usually escapes it until well into maturity, but thereafter the tree is progressively sabotaged by these aberrations from respectable growth.

The Small-leaf Lime has highly attractive foliage, free from the limp imprecise shapes of that of the Common Lime. Each leaf is small, firm, almost hard, heart-shaped at base and abruptly tipped but so nearly round that in the mass they look circular and dainty. The underside is a contrast to the rich dark green above, being a soft bluish pale glaucous green, embellished by pale orange tufts in the angles of the veins. A few origins yield trees with more oval-lanceolate leaves. The shoots are short-jointed and thin and the spray can be identified as this lime, in winter, by these and the dense systems they make. However, as Dr Pigott at Cambridge Botanic Garden has been discovering, there are clones in the Common Lime complex which tend strongly towards this foliage.

To sort these out, it is sufficient to return in June when the Small-leaf is in flower. It flowers later than, although it may overlap with, the Common, but its flowering is very different. At this time, Small-leaf Limes can easily be identified from a passing car among miles of the other two. The others have big, pale whitish yellow flowers hanging beneath a big pale bract which itself is below the leaves, in a row. The Small-leaf has smaller, usually more numerous (up to ten) flowers, bright yellow, standing out sideways or standing up from small green bracts which themselves spread at all angles among the foliage or stand above it. So this lime sparkles with gold stars in random bunches.

The Small-leaf lime is a native tree which probably arrived here well after the early species like Wych Elm and Aspen but before the Beech and Hornbeam. Perhaps well after the Sessile Oak but at about the time of the Common Oak. Dr Oliver Rackham, also at Cambridge, has shown that this lime was the dominant tree over much of England before the Common Oak and was important in the production of small-wood and bass. But by Saxon times it had been exterminated in areas like Epping Forest, and this was more from the seedlings being nutritious grazing for their cattle than from over exploitation, and once the fallow deer and rabbits from the Norman invaders spread, the tree could not recolonise. It will coppice easily, so it can be worked on a sustained basis, as it has been in areas like the Forest of Wyre. It can also layer its bottom branches and individual trees can reach far, long after the main stem has decayed away. Dr Rackham considered the great spreading bush by the Broad Drive in Westonbirt to be around 1000 years old.

Stands considered to be wild, or derived from the wild population through generations of natural or aided regeneration, are known around Bristol, Worcester,

Hereford, Northamptonshire and Lincolnshire, and the tree is thought to have ranged north into Yorkshire and Cumbria. It is scarce today, north of those counties, as a planted tree in a few parks and gardens and is seen north of Perthshire, Angus and Argyll. Nor does it occur at all frequently westward into Wales or Ireland.

It is sometimes suggested, that with its small foliage, this tree would not grow as fast or achieve such sizes as the Broadleaf and Common Limes. As a young tree the Small-leaf is the fastest of the three, and in the fullness of time it will nearly always make a bigger tree than the Broadleaf. The best growth found was that of an unfortunate group of trees planted in 1956 at Juniper Hall, near Dorking. Two were planted by the little stream, and they are in good shape, 60/4½ft when 31 years old, but a splendid group of four on the lawn were unknowingly planted on a shallowly buried Roman road. This restricted their rootrun and made them vulnerable to the 1987 gale which blew all four down. One of those was then 60/5, the fastest growth recorded for the species. No other specimen measured has exceeded one inch a year significantly.

As a native tree, specimens will exist up to the limit of the age span, and inevitably the oldest and biggest will be hulks or will have fragmented stems, the measurements of these misleading or of little interest. One noted by the Scottish arboriculturist, John Grigor, in 1841, is worth a mention as he gives its date as 1649 and its girth as 24ft 7in at ground level, at Sprowston Hall, Norwich. Mr P.H.B. Gardner found in 1965 one at Algakirk, Lincolnshire, 21ft 10in round at three feet. The biggest more recent measurement is of one of many fine big specimens at Oakley Park, Ludlow. By the drive, this was 105/19ft in 1978. Another in the Arboretum was 115/16ft. In a long broad avenue along a road at Turville Heath, above Henley, Oxfordshire, much the biggest in 1983 was 83/18½ft with a clear trunk for six feet. At Forde Abbey near Chard, a rather rough tree is 80/17ft. Lydney Park, Forest of Dean, has one in the Deer Park 70/15½ft. There are several tall specimens in Wrest Park, Bedfordshire, all liberally adorned with huge bunches of mistletoe and a shorter but bigger one on the lawn 82/14ft in 1977. One of several tall trees at Tottenham House, Savernake, in 1984 was 132/12ft.

In the garden of the museum in York, a tree planted in 1827 was 88/15ft in 1989. A fine tall tree was 115/13ft in a roadside car park at West Wycombe Park in 1980, but it was very exposed and looked vulnerable to gales. In Scotland, a tree at Auchterarder House, Perthshire, in 1977 was 111/11½ft; one at Blairhoyle in the same county is 85/11ft and one by the River Tay, on the North Inch in Perth near the A9 bridge, is 60/10ft.

CRIMEAN LIME

Tilia euchlora

High gloss foliage is a strong point in the favour of any tree and will permit many failings to be overlooked. It was one of the two important features for which the Crimean Lime was chosen for many town planting schemes after about 1930. There had long been a pressing need to find a replacement for the Common Lime as the ubiquitous roadside tree in towns and in city parks. The Common Lime is usually so densely colonised by aphids which rain down a constant mist of honeydew, that its leaves take on a spurious and sticky gloss and the cellulose spray finish of the cars was corroded.

Naturally for a clean, healthy, vigorous tree one turns to the Caucasus region. There are several limes there but three of them are big trees and exceedingly rare and only the Crimean Lime was to hand, in the nurseries. It is, arguably, a Caucasian species with a small outlier in the Crimea, from where we had seed in about 1866. It has other merits to add to its normal freedom from aphids, its moderate size and splendid foliage. It is easily grown with a straight, smoothly cylindric stem six feet or more long, clad in smooth gun-metal grey bark freckled brown. It has large yellow flowers later than other limes and often showy in August, and its leaves turn bright gold in autumn.

It has a few demerits. Formerly, some trees were raised from grafts, with the union five feet up, and the rootstock has usually sprouted copiously around the base. The mature crown is increasingly mushroom shaped, with a dome of downcurving

Crimean Lime (*Tilia euchlora*): Hyde Park, London

branches that becomes dense and untidy. After about 1970, the trees in Salisbury Cathedral Close began to suffer from a canker killing some upper branches, but this seems not to be a problem elsewhere at present. Bee-keepers dislike the tree, and give it a reputation for killing their bees. At least one entomologist has queried this and says that it is bumble-bees rather than hive-bees which become addicted to the nectar, and, in any case, the casualties are on nothing like the scale of those seen carpeting the ground beneath a flowering sycamore, and bee-keepers do not seem to object to sycamores.

The distribution of plantings is mainly southern with few trees in Scotland and only one of those noted north of Edinburgh, at Doune House, Dunblane, Perthshire, although there are several in the Border counties. It is scarce in Ireland and in Wales, although there are some recent plantings. Letchworth, Cambridge and Cardiff have notable older street avenues. In these lines, the winter feature of bright yellow-green shoots shows up well. The word 'euchlora' means something like 'well-greened' and this is seen to be apt in winter for the outer twigs on an avenue.

The biggest Crimean Lime is one surviving in an informal avenue in the west prospect at Osterley Park, Hounslow, where there are others in the east prospect and a line beside a farm road. This big tree is 66/9ft. The next biggest is one in the lime collection at Kew. This was planted in 1872 and is now 62/8½ft, near another of the same date, 56/7½ft. In the extension of the collection along the walk by the eastern wall of Kew, one planted in 1871 is 62/6ft while one in the beds behind the Palm House dates from 1873 and is 50/7ft. A pair on Pagoda Vista, planted in 1903 or soon after (the dates on the labels at Kew are actually the year of acquisition), are 50/7ft and 46/6ft. By the Willesley Drive in Westonbirt, and almost certain to date from 1876, a tree with typical good stem but bushy mushroom crown, is 70/6ft. Another very typical tree is north of the Lake in Syon Park, Brentford, and is 65/6½ft. The biggest in a short avenue at Antony House, Cornwall, is 60/6ft.

Among the younger plantings, the best tree in Burton way in Letchworth is 50/6ft and in Broadways, planted in 1923, also in Letchworth, one is 56/5ft. One in Abbey Park, Leicester, is 50/6ft, and a tree in the Royal Botanic Garden in Edinburgh is 46/5ft. In Maindy Road, Cardiff there are trees to 52/5ft and in Queen's Road along the Backs in Cambridge, to 60/4ft.

COMMON LIME

Tilia x *europaea*

The Common Lime is an unfortunate and ill-favoured tree and has suffered much ill-use. It is a natural hybrid between two species of considerable distinction, and has inherited only bad features from each. The Small-leaf Lime, one parent, has very pretty, small foliage and bright yellow flowers in neat bunches held upright or to either side. The Broadleaf Lime, the other parent, has a gloriously regular crown, a dome of radiating branches; a clean trunk without sprouts or suckers, and big, pale yellow-green, prominent bracts above a few big pale yellow flowers, and well-arranged, often handsome foliage.

The hybrid has coarse foliage poorly arranged, on a scrawny tall crown with vertical stems to an untidy top, and awkwardly set lower branches making abrupt turns to the vertical or spreading to great distances and sometimes rooting far out. Its trunk is often beset with huge unsightly burrs growing dense bunches of sprouts; its base usually infested by strong suckers in great numbers, and its pale flowers droop from dull greenish yellow bracts. It nourishes more aphids to the square inch than any other tree and the honeydew that rains down makes the leaves shiny and sticky then black with sooty-mould.

With all these failings, this tree is the worst possible one for planting in streets, squares and odd urban corners and high in any list of those to avoid in avenue plantings, has long been the favourite one for all these usages. The results include shaded upper windows, severe pruning or lopping; broken and lifting pavings; corroded cellulose surfaces on cars parked beneath and avenues abandoned to the park cattle and new lime-free ones planted.

However there are a few mitigating features. This tree is almost invariably the tallest broad-leaf tree in the district. It flowers as copiously as most limes and is equally strongly and sweetly scented. Being an almost sterile hybrid very rarely yielding seedlings, it has been propagated from layers or cuttings from stools, and there are several clones. One is thought to be the origin of the worst offenders for bases surrounded by strong sprouts; another for massive, sprouting burrs on the trunk, but one is relatively or quite clean, and one has foliage well towards that of the Small-leaf Lime. Also, the most unsightly outgrowths are in many places, including London parks, the site chosen for nesting by spotted flycatchers. This elegant bird is attracted to Common Limes in paddocks and field hedges, regardless of burrs, because cattle and horses find the young foliage much to their taste and browse the low branches within reach clear of small shoots. That leaves the bigger shoots and branches as perches with good views for flycatching. Further, the animals drop dung when in the shade of the tree and numbers of dung-flies gather.

A few trees in most localities will turn a respectable, if rather brief yellow in autumn and some will go on to shades of orange, but the poverty of autumn display is as bad or worse in all limes other than the Crimean and the Silver Pendent. Many trees grow leaves much bigger than those of the Broadleaf Lime, particularly on their basal sprouts. These are easily distinguished because they lack entirely the close, soft hairs on the shoots and petioles, and the soft down on the veins on the upper surface.

Common Lime is the most mistletoe-infested of all big trees and this is prominently visible as in the area from Windsor to Egham, Epsom, Runneymede and Staines. Near Virginia Waters in Windsor Great Park, is an 80ft tree which, when

Common Lime (*Tilia* x *europaea*):
Charlton Park, Northamptonshire

I took a now treasured slide of it 20 years ago, was nearly all mistletoe, the lime's own foliage limited to a few straggling shoots beyond, but alas, when last seen this lime was reasserting its rights to its crown.

Despite being among the tallest trees in any area, Common Limes are normally remarkably windfirm, and even in the gales of 1987 and 1990, many exposed trees remained. In London parks, however, lines of trees of moderate size were laid low, and this seems to arise from their root-run on one side being under tarmac or paving. They are quite good at holding on to their branches. It is difficult to assess the likely life-span as so few big trees are of known date; the origin of the tree is conjectural, and growth in girth becomes very slow.

There are three possible origins of our Common limes. It will have arisen in Europe where both parent species are common, and a very long time ago, since some, but a minority, of the locally renowned 'GrandsTilleuils' across the Continent are the hybrid. It may then have migrated post-Ice Ages along with the parents into southern England and so qualify as a native. This is to some degree unlikely since it so rarely yields fertile seed. It could have arisen spontaneously here where the parent species grow within bee-flight, or it could have been introduced. It will not arise often, as the Broadleaf Lime is much the earliest lime into flower and the Small-leaf is late, seldom seen to overlap it. It has often been assumed, therefore, that it was introduced, and the favoured period is that of Charles II. The oldest reputed planting date is 1600–1620 for an avenue at Hawstead in Suffolk. The next is 1660 for an avenue at Ashridge Park, Hertfordshire. A fine, wide avenue with a few contemporary Sycamores at Huntington Castle in County Carlow dates from 1680 with dozens of trees, about half of which are badly suppressed with poor slender crowns, but the rest are stately trees. The sizes show the difficulty in ageing limes by their girths. The biggest is a lightly suckered tree with sharp taper for the basal five feet and best measured at six feet where it is 18ft round, and it is 111ft tall. The next biggest is 121/12½ft. Remeasures of the few clean boles in general show very slow increases, but several dated young trees show that early growth is reasonably rapid. At Park End in the Forest of Dean, roadside trees planted in 1902 include one 95/8½ft. A 1903 tree at Haddo House, Aberdeenshire was 66/6½ft when 77 years old. The single example of really rapid growth is a 1910 tree at Tullynally Castle, County Westmeath which is 88/14½ft. In the 1936 avenue to the Beale Arboretum in Hertfordshire, the best tree of 72/6ft, and one planted in 1958 at Brocas Farm, Bentley, Hampshire, and now 50/4½ft, are more of the expected best growth.

Ignoring the sprouty-based trees up to some 30ft round, there were two contenders for top position: the best, all-round a clean and remarkable tree at Gatton Park School, Reigate, Surrey, was blown down in October 1987. When I saw it in 1979 it was 143/16½ft. This tree was passed by Elwes or Henry in 1904 as a Broadleaf Lime, then 132/12½ft. The other is at East Carlton Park in Northamptonshire, a pollard with a smoothly but deeply fluted bole, completely clean to about eight feet and 95/22ft. At Ranston House, Dorset, there were in 1978 two outstanding trees very much in the pattern of that at East Charlton Park, short but clean boled pollards, 98/20½ft and 98/20ft. A tree at Drayton Park, Northamptonshire, with its top damaged by lightning is still tall and has a good trunk. This tree is 132/21ft. Sprouty but properly measurable, a big tree near the trout-pool at Buxted Park Hotel, Sussex, is 82/21ft. Clean, short-boled pollards at Broombarns, Perthshire towards Dundee, are 85/20½ft and 105/19ft. Nearby Kinnaird Castle has a sprouty tree 115/23ft. At Drummuir Castle, Banffshire a pollard with five feet clean bole is 111/19½ft.

Trees qualifying for mention by their height and good shape are: two at Bicton, Devon, beyond the Italian Garden on a wooded bank, splendid trees, 135/15½ft and 124/13½ft; at Scotney Castle, Kent, a survivor of the gales, prominent in a small glade down to the stream, has a very fluted but fine trunk and is now 132/18ft. At Scone Palace, Perth, near the car park, an excellent tree is 132/13ft. At Croft Castle, Hereford, one of this kind is 135/19ft, not far from one of the few limes with layered branches, 105/14ft. Bowood in Wiltshire has two quality trees, 138/14ft and 130/13ft. Another at Newby House in Yorkshire is 135/13ft and one at Lennoxlove, Midlothian is 132/13½ft, and below the drive at Castle Leod, Easter Ross, one is 135/15½ft. In front of the car park at Belton House, Grantham, is a group of limes, much the best of which is 130/13½ft. The longest trunk noted is at Beaufort Castle, Inverness, where a tree 102/12ft has one 30ft long.

In Walcombe, a garden in a wooded combe outside Wells, another Common lime classed as Broadleaf Lime in 1912, when it was 100/14ft, is 100/16½ft and has a great branch leaving the bole, quite level, at six feet, extending, slightly drooping, for some 65ft. One tree just escaping the ban on those with trunks swollen by swarms of sprouts, is at Stanway House, Gloucestershire, at the side of the prospect up to the great Cedar of Lebanon, as this can more or less be measured among the sprouts, and is 118/31ft at two to three feet. Knebworth House in Hertfordshire has two classically awful trees, bursting into enormous twiggy bosses and should have no place here, but their boles, however fluted, are quite clean for ten feet and one of them is 72/17ft.

SILVER PENDENT LIME

Tilia 'Petiolaris'

No wild population of Silver Pendent Lime has been found. The origin of the tree is therefore a matter of speculation. It has the air of coming from the Black Sea and Caucasus region and this is in accord with it being evidently most closely related to the Silver Lime of that area. It differs markedly in form and foliage from Silver Lime, but little or not at all in its flowering, and must be presumed to be derived from a single highly variant individual and so it is now treated as a cultivar, but not assigned to any species as it might be a Silver Lime hybrid with one of the four other limes in the region. It cannot be given the full species name *Tilia petiolaris* under which it was long known.

As with the other clonal trees, there can be no source of seed, even where a close group yields some, because these must be self-pollinated and either sterile or producing selfs which will most likely be atypical, dwarf or misshapen. It was introduced a little before 1842, presumably from Europe or the Black Sea region, and as scions to be grafted. The oldest with recorded dates are at Kew planted in 1872, but most of the big trees mentioned below will be older than that, as they are all very much bigger. All are grafts at six, or sometimes at eight feet up on a rootstock normally of Broadleaf Lime but occasionally on Common Lime. The Broadleaf is supposed not to sucker and sprout, unlike the Common which does both, but as a rootstock the Broadleaf not infrequently does so too. The union is always obvious as the more vigorous scion of Silver Pendent divides at once into three vertical stems, with smoother bark, and often makes a big swelling at that point.

Growth is rapid at all ages seen so far, and exceeds the Silver Lime in height and about equals it in girth, making it the fastest of all the limes. Its three vertical stems are somewhat sinuous and make the crown a high narrow dome from which the outer shoots hang for 10–15ft or more, part of which twists to display the silver underside of the leaves. In late autumn the leaves turn the brightest lemon yellow of any lime and may stay on to be bronzed to old gold. Growth is little affected by city conditions and good trees are in city parks, as are many Silver Limes. Hot summers are appreciated, to judge from growth in Pennsylvania where trees to 115/18ft are at Swarthmore College. Big trees in the British Isles show this to a minor degree, the majority being in the south Midlands or the east, and none has been found in Ireland. However, there is one each in Cornwall, South Wales, Cumbria and Central Perthshire.

After the loss in the 1987 gale of the remarkable tree, 105/15½ft, on the golf-course in Beauport Park, Sussex, the mantle of top tree falls on one at Egrove House in the campus of Templeton College near Oxford. This has a crown broader than typical and is 105/13½ft. A mile to the west is another great tree, beside the approach to Magdalen Bridge. This is 92/12½ft and, being grafted unusually low, at four feet, the girth is that of the Petiolaris not of the rootstock. A similar, superb tree in Bath Botanic Garden is grafted at three feet, which may add a little to its girth at five feet as again this is measuring the more vigorous scion and not the rootstock. An imposing tree, this is 111/13ft. In 1962 it was 100/11ft. An equally eminent tree is at Green Park, a former Rothschild mansion in Buckinghamshire, is a very shapely tree and the tallest yet found, 121/11½ft.

In the private garden at Wilton House a good tree is 95/12½ft and two much the same size are at Killinchassie over 400 miles to the north on that south-facing slope to the River Tay below Aberfeldy which grows outsize trees of several kinds. It has some

Silver Pendent Lime (*Tilia* 'Petiolaris'): Hyde Park, London

of the biggest walnuts, Sitka Spruces and Giant Sequoias in Britain within a few miles. The Silver Pendent Limes are 92/12½ft and 105/12ft. Trees of similar sizes in the west are two at Tal-y-Garn, Glamorgan, 82/12ft and 108/9½ft; one at Wray Castle, Cumbria, 70/11½ft, and one at the edge of the upper garden at Penjerrick near Falmouth, 105/11½ft. A fine, narrow-crowned tree in the north arboretum at Stratfield Saye House on the Hampshire-Berkshire border is 111/11ft. In Midlothian, at Morton House, there is one 88/11½ft and south, in Lincolnshire at Revesby Abbey, a good pair are 105/11ft and 105/10½ft in the woods. Near the house at Anglesea Abbey, Cambridge a shapely tree is 111/8½ft, and at Campden House in Gloucestershire one is 82/11ft.

Two trees measured in 1912 have not made any great growth since. One in Gunnersbury Park, London was then 56/6ft and was 98/10ft in 1987 and the other at Bargaly in Ayrshire grew from 41/4ft 8in to 75/9ft in 1985, both well below one inch a year. But several young trees have added between two and three inches a year, like one at Bowood, 35/5½ft when 21 years planted, and one at Writtle College, Essex 40/3ft 3in at 18 years from a 1963 planting.

BROADLEAF LIME

Tilia platyphyllos

The Broadleaf Lime can be absolved of any blame for the defects in the hybrid Common Lime, because in the offending features it is either exemplary or rarely transgresses. Its crown becomes irregular in its big branching only after a long spell reaching maturity with a shapely, regular dome, and the stem and branches are completely clear of sprouts. Only a few have been found with a basal ring of sprouts and this is so rare that the species has always been chosen for the rootstock of grafts of Silver Pendent Lime and other forms which have to be grafted. It is unfortunate that this tree as a rootstock will often break out with basal sprouts. The general superiority of the species to the Common Lime is well shown in the long avenue into Clumber Park in Nottinghamshire where the one outstanding specimen about half way along is the solitary Broadleaf among the otherwise uniformly Common Lime planting.

The terms 'broad-leaf' and its alternative 'bigleaf' are comparisons with the Small-leaf Lime and not with the Common Lime in which the leaves are much the same size, and, on sprouts, often much bigger and broader. A better distinction is the softly hairy young shoot, leaf-stalk and both surfaces of the leaf. There is a not infrequent form of Broadleaf with leaves little bigger than those of the Small-leaf Lime, and this has densely hairy shoots and leaf-stalks. A useful feature that identifies this lime among others late in the year is that when the leaves have been shed, the fruit and their bracts remain brown at the tips of branches over the outer

Broadleaf Lime (*Tilia platyphyllos*): Trentham Park, Staffordshire

crown well into the new year. In flower, it is distinguishable by the large, pale, whitish-green bracts each bearing only three to five large, pale yellow flowers.

Although there is some doubt as to its status as a native beyond a limited area, it is usually accepted as indigenous to the limestone cliffs of the Wye gorge above Chepstow and on base rich soils in the adjoining counties through Breconshire to Shropshire but mainly planted beyond that. There are big trees in parkland and gardens in Scotland, through Perthshire, Aberdeenshire and Morayshire to Easter Ross, but only as individuals here and there. Like the other limes, it needs fertile, base-rich deep and well-drained soil, the ideal soil for most trees, and it does not grow or is not grown on anything else, so struggling, unhappy trees are not seen.

The smooth bark of immature trees is sometimes seen closely ringed by the little pits made by great spotted woodpeckers. They have yet to be seen making these rings, but there are no other suspects. Sapsuckers do this in North America, and they are a group of woodpeckers. The sapsucking rings in Britain are very much neater and smaller than those, but can only be made by a woodpecker. They are found beyond the more limited range of the lesser spotted, which is not found in the north of England, and the green woodpecker, which is now in Perthshire but not in the north of Scotland. The habit was either unnoticed or had not been adopted before 1970 but is widespread now. Among other native trees attacked is the Common Oak when young and with smooth, shiny bark, but also the thick, rough barked Box which needs bigger, more open holes like those made by sapsuckers. The most favoured trees, however, are exotics like the scarce American Lime, the Red Oak, the Rauli, the Berlin Poplar and, most of all, the hybrid Nymans Eucryphia.

Young, dated trees have grown at moderate rates not much above one inch in girth a year, and it is interesting that the only one noted to have added two inches a year is as far north as Bracla, in Morayshire. It was planted in 1964 and by 1989 it was 33/4½ft. One of the few dated Red-twigged cultivar, 'Rubra', is even more vigorous down in Dorset. Planted at Milton Abbas in 1954, it was 42/6ft by 1982.

The biggest trunk recorded this century was at Ancrum in Roxburghshire, 26ft round at six feet up in 1909, and none of that size is known today. The doyen now is clearly the remarkable tree at Pitchford Hall in Shropshire. It holds a house in its spring of three limbs six feet up, and this is no Wendy House but a Gothic tea-house recently restored and re-decorated, with glazed windows, plank floor and space for a table and about six chairs. The trunk holding it up is 24½ft round at its narrowest, between root-swell and the swell of the branches, and that is at the standard five feet. The house is said to have been there by the year 1600 so the tree must be a good one hundred years older, for its branches to hold a structure of this size and weight securely. The second biggest is on the neighbouring estate of Longnor Hall, a fine tall tree 98/20ft, with a straight axis that precludes decoration with housing. It must say something about the climate and fertility of the soil, that Longnor also grows the two biggest native Black Poplars in Britain.

At Killinchassie, on that long brae so notable for big trees, above the Tay below Aberfeldy, a specimen is 70/19ft measured at three feet. The next two biggest boles are also in this region, one at Taymouth Castle, Kenmore, in the old Park, now a golf-course, 82/15ft, and the other at Kinnaird Castle, just over the border in Angus, 102/15ft. Further north at Haddo House, Aberdeenshire, a big tree can be measured only at two feet and is 65/17ft. A tree at Croft Castle, Hereford, in the Home Park, is 98/15½ft, and one at Flitwick Manor, Bedfordshire, is 98/15ft. The tree mentioned earlier, at Clumber Park in the Avenue, which was planted in about 1840 was 108/12½ft in 1979. A fine, shapely tree among the mixed group of hardwoods by the Costume Museum at Castle Howard in Yorkshire is 85/19ft.

The cultivar 'Rubra', Red-twigged Lime was found in France in 1755 and there are a few old trees of considerable size. The biggest was at West Dean House near Chichester, in 1985, when it was 105/19ft but it may well not have survived the gales. A good specimen is by the drive to Bicton College in Devon and was 88/15ft in 1993, having added three feet to its girth since 1967. In the grounds of Dalmahoy Club in Perthshire there is one 80/13½ft, and one at Anglesea Abbey, Cambridge, is 85/12½ft.

Several lime species from eastern Asia have markedly lobed leaves and the Broadleaf Lime has two cultivars of this kind. One has leaves shallowly three-lobed and is rare. It arose in 1875 and is 'Vitifolia' with one big tree, 75/10ft in Alexandra Park, St Leonards, Sussex. The other takes the feature to the extreme and is the Cutleaf or Fernleaf Lime and a very different sort of tree. Found in 1835, it has reduced its leaves almost to threads, and with such reduced working area, it grows very slowly. But this may also be because it devotes such an extraordinary amount of its substance to flowering. The big whitish bracts and big cream flowers hang in dense rows beneath the scant foliage so that there is little other than bract and flower to be seen, and from a short distance the tree is a mass of flowers like a hawthorn. It attracts all the bees for miles around. Most of the older trees are 50/4 and the few notably bigger are all in the north. At Fasque House, Kincardineshire, it is 62/8ft; at Belladrum, Inverness, 60/7ft; at Drumkilbo, Perthshire, 85/7ft, and at Beaufront Castle, Hexham, it is 70/6½ft.

SILVER LIME

Tilia tomentosa

This tree is of sturdy, smooth and vigorous growth at all stages in its life. Its shoots are thicker than those of any other lime and its stout branches have smooth, pale grey bark. The trunk may be short, but it is straight and rapidly adds to its diameter with bark only lightly ridged at the biggest sizes. It is usually an extraordinarily shapely tree and its raised radiating branches divide at short intervals to build a crown which is a regular ovoid with a curiously formal, smooth outline.

The Silver Lime is native from Hungary and the Balkans to northern Asia Minor and has the features of a Caucasian tree, perhaps having spread from there but no longer a native in those mountains. It was introduced in 1767 but none is known of earlier planting than 1870. It is apparently not very long-lived as none of the seven trees noted by Elwes and Henry up to 1909 survives today and despite the big branchy crowns, very few were blown down in recent gales. Nor do most of the biggest and oldest show signs of decay today. Henry considered the trees in cultivation to be nearly all distinguishable as *Tilia argentea* a form he thought might be a sport, but of unknown origin, since the trees he saw in the wild had thin leaves, greyish on the underside and slender petioles. The trees we know have quite substantial, hard leaves, very white beneath, and stout short petioles.

The species is reasonably frequent in the south of England, but scarce in the north and in Scotland and very rare in Ireland. I have seen none further north than Darnaway in Morayshire, and only three in Perthshire but several south of the Clyde. It is very resistant to fairly polluted city air, which merit has been long recognised in eastern North America where some city parks have huge trees. It has been more recently appreciated in London, where there are many notably in the area of Regent's Park and Kensington Gardens.

John White, dendrologist at Westonbirt, has noted the biggest tree at Buckland House, Brecon, 92/19ft in 1988. My top tree is in a grassy bay beside the church at Tortworth in Gloucestershire. It is the other side of the church from the famous old Sweet Chestnut, and tree-measurers and writers must have trouped past it unseeing for a hundred years because there is no record of it before I measured it in 1964. It

Silver Lime (*Tilia tormentosa*): Tortworth, Gloucestershire

was then 90/13ft and subsequent growth suggests that it was in Henry's day considerably bigger than at least two of the specimens he noted. It is now 115/15ft and has a branch spread of 105ft. The trunk forks at eight feet and the effect of this would add some inches to the girth at five feet, so it was measured at four feet up. It fills the bay and is prominent from the path to the church porch, so it is a mystery how it escaped notice for so long. At Tottenham House in Savernake Forest, an old tree was broken back to 52/13ft in 1984. In the lime collection at Kew, a tree planted in 1872 is now 92/10½ft and a finer tree in the extension of the collection along the East Walk, planted in 1871 is 112/9½ft. At Emmanuel College in Cambridge, there is a splendid tree 105/12½ft. Worth Park Avenue in Crawley, Sussex, had 11 big trees along one side before the gales, ranging to 95/10ft. The best at Westonbirt is in The Downs and was 95/11½ft in 1988. At Osterley Park, Hounslow there was one 80/11½ft in 1991. Waterlow Park in Highgate had one 90/10ft in 1982.

SMOOTH-LEAFED ELM

Ulmus carpinifolia

The Smooth-leafed Elm is accepted by most authors as being the native English population of the continental Field Elm, almost confined to East Anglia. It hybridised freely with the Wych Elm and is in any case highly variable so the crowns and size of leaf show great variation, often along the same hedgerow. There were a few magnificent specimens of what I consider to be the typical form, of two distinct crown shapes. One was a massive dome on a short straight stem, bearing very slender, somewhat curled, hanging shoots with small narrow leaves. One at Dane End village in Hertfordshire was 85/20ft in 1968, and one, surely a planted tree, on the bank of the A433 at Trewsbury by a railway bridge, and was 78/21ft with a clear trunk for eight feet.

The other form had a longer bole and this would persist for 50 or 60ft or more into an open crown with a few big ascending branches, making a high open crown rather less pendulous on its outside. I saw the classic specimen in a field by the road at Chicheley in Bedfordshire in 1983 when very few were left. It was magnificent, 124/20ft and showed only a twig or two of discoloured foliage showing that the disease might have found it recently. Alas, within three years the tree was down. Another similar but smaller was 120/14ft on Jesus Green in Cambridge in 1982, and seemingly healthy, but like all the other elms on the Green it had to go by 1989. Then there was the very tall one in a small group of other elms on the North Inch in Perth. In 1987 it was 135/11½ft but badly infected and soon had to be removed.

Big old trees and hulks were frequent before 1955 in Essex, especially in villages with 'Great' attached to their names. Great Waltham had two, one of them 90/24ft and Great Parndon had one 23ft round in 1952 and in 1949 the Great Saling Elm was 110/22ft. Its stump is still there. A hulk at St Osyth Priory was 50/22½ft in 1984, and may survive. There was a fine tall tree in Kensington Gardens, London, 118/11ft in 1967.

In 1993, the known survivors are, as in the Cornish Elm, in Scotland, with one exception. The village of Abbotts Ripton in Cambridgeshire was, in 1993, still lined with a mile of trees to 80/10ft. In Scotland, in Dovecote Road, Corstorphine, Edinburgh, one possibly already infected was 72/12ft in 1990. At Kippenross, Dunblane, a not very typical tree in the park was 70/16ft in 1987. In 1991, a young tree in the Royal Botanic Garden, Edinburgh was 41/3ft, but much further north a surprising tree at Innes House near Fochabers in Morayshire is 102/11ft.

The English name, Smooth-leafed Elm, brings out one important feature that distinguishes not only this elm itself, but its hybrids as well, from the other two elms common within and around its range, the Wych and English Elms. These have densely hairy shoots and harshly hairy upper leaf-surfaces where the shoots of the Smooth-leaf are soon shiny and smooth and the upper side of the leaf is positively

Smooth-leafed Elm
(*Ulmus carpinifolia*): the
native English population
of the continental Field
Elm

leather-smooth. This shows up the dozen or so straight, parallel veins that make the leaf so attractive, together with its neat, small toothing.

It also brings up the inevitable subject of the botanical names for the tree, which are many. As the Continental Field Elm, this species went for a period under the ambiguous name *U. campestris*, sharing it with the English Elm. Luckily, its shiny leaf had earlier caused it to be called *U. nitens* ('shining') and this was used in place of *campestris* until a re-sorting of elm names brought back the much earlier *carpinifolia* used here. This refers to the prominent pattern of straight veins, recalling that of the hornbeam leaf and is an adjective used by botanists in other genera, in *Acer carpinifolium* for example.

WHEATLEY ELM

Ulmus carpinifolia var. *sarniensis*

This elm has, naturally, had troubles with its names, common and botanical. It is the elm of the Channel Islands, and is often referred to as the Jersey Elm or sometimes the Guernsey Elm. To the local authorities who used to plant it so extensively, it was the 'Cornish Elm', an error of identification that was almost hallowed by long usage. It is unclear why we now call it the Wheatley Elm, but it is an unambiguous and euphonious name and long may it stay. It seems to have been bestowed first by the Metz nurseryman Leon Simon-Louis who published it in his catalogue for 1869. Perhaps he had received his first plants from a nursery of that name either in the Channel Islands or in England, for it had been grown in England since about 1815.

Botanically, this tree has been the rounds of the Smoothleaf Elm complex of names, specified as 'wheatleyi' or 'sarniensis' and then settled with the name used above, but Dr Melville considers it with the Cornish Elm as a form of the Goodyer Elm and prefers to call it *U. angustifolia* var. *sarniensis*.

This was an ideal tree for avenues as it is exceedingly uniform in its regular conic shape and bears multitudes of small, rising branches and, until fully mature, no heavy ones liable to drop on the passage between the lines. It was used for formal plantings like the approaches to memorials and lining streets and in less formal, more rural, roads to villages, as well as some very large avenues in parks and big gardens. Individual trees made monumental, shapely specimens in parkland, and it grows rapidly. It flushes late in the season, and like the Cornish Elm, holds out against Elm disease in areas with an English Elm background until all those have died, and to some extent in the north, but once infected it succumbs quickly. In cultivation, it does not spread by suckering, unlike in the hedges of Jersey, so where trees have gone there is no regrowth and it has become rare in southern England.

Wheatley Elm (*Ulmus carpinifolia* var. *sariensis*): Cranborne House, Dorset

347

Among the most notable plantings that are no more, was the biggest specimen of them all, at Avington Park, near Winchester, which was 105/19ft in 1977 and died soon after. One outside Cowdray Old Castle at Midhurst, Sussex, was 116/16ft in 1965 and had been noted in 1906 as 113/13ft. One at Bagshot Park was 100/15½ft in 1973 and 98/11½ft in 1907. A tall one across the A30 from the gates of Wilton House was 122/12½ft in 1972; one at Jordans, Ardingly, Sussex was 110/15½ft in 1973 and one in the Stowe Avenue was 100/14½ft while a fine avenue behind Cranborne House, planted in 1875 was around 100/10ft in 1970. Some towns, like Cuckfield in Sussex, had good trees in numbers, and Southampton had big trees at the Civic Centre and on the Common.

Today, the South Sussex Enclave, notably from Seaford to Eastbourne, is liberally supplied with trees in streets and parks. The avenue of big trees, 26 in number in 1983 and now a few less, in Preston Park, Brighton by the London Road has trees to 102/12ft. There is a single slim 50ft tree by the A287 at Beacon Hill, Surrey, but all the others are in the north. At Dean Castle Park, Ayr, one was 85/7ft in 1988. Edinburgh has roads lined with Wheatleys still, notably by the Prince's Street gardens where the biggest in 1991 was 85/7ft, and one in the Royal Botanic Garden, planted in 1904 is 85/8ft. On Guernsey, the biggest seen in 1986 was 70/12ft in Suamarez Park.

Young trees are quite similar to young Cornish Elms but more evenly and densely branched and their bark is less strongly vertically ridged but like the English Elm, breaking into small blocks. The leaves are broader, much darker and plane, not cupped.

CORNISH ELM

Ulmus carpinifolia var. *cornubiensis*

The loss from disease of nearly all Cornish Elms has cruelly deprived us of one of the joys of life. After some days in Cornish gardens and countryside with this most distinctive elm on all sides, I would drive back to Surrey and once east of Ivybridge I sought and noted those little patches and single trees that passed with decreasing frequency as the journey proceeded east of Exeter. There were one or two trees near Rockbeare, and near Lyme Regis, several fields surrounded by Cornish Elms. There was a solitary tree in Winterbourne Stoke, and, at Devizes, there was the line of splendid trees by the canal. Then in the last few miles, heading out of Crondall on the road to Farnham, a grand Cornishman stood proud on the horizon.

In Cornwall itself, a prominent group lined a curve in the A30 near Lanivet and lines, clumps and thickets crowned the innumerable whalebacks visible from the switchback road from the Tamar Bridge to Liskeard. Estates like Trelissick and Caerhays were sheltered by them. One in the park at Trelissick was 102/15½ft as late as 1979. A line at Knightshayes, Tiverton, planted in 1864 had trees to 110/16 in 1970. The biggest of four at Woburn Abbey, Bedfordshire, was 118/16ft in 1970. The most celebrated planting was the Waterloo Elms planted round Salisbury Cathedral in 1815 with eight trees, the tallest two 118ft and the biggest 13ft round in 1967. Northwest London was a good area for them, from Regent's Park near the Zoo and nearby squares, inward to Kensington Gardens. There were four, to 95ft in Halliford Park, Sunbury and Walsingham Abbey in Norfolk was surrounded by them, to 95/14ft in 1969. Firle Place, east of Lewes, earlier within the Brighton protected area, had many big English and Cornish elms in 1981 but by 1986 only one Cornishman 98/15ft was still there.

Survival of the few further north is better, and living trees today outside the Brighton-Eastbourne enclave, are in Scotland. Within the enclave there are many quite small street trees and a few big trees. In Preston Park, Brighton, one is 98/10½ft. At Alfriston Church a fine tree was 88/10ft in 1989 and at Berwick House nearby, of three there in 1989 one was 82/10ft in 1991. In Scotland, a group of young trees in Roxelle Park in Ayr was healthy, to 50/4ft in 1989. In the woodland garden at Tyninghame, East Lothian, one was 85/10½ft in 1984, but the best was much further north. It stood by itself on the edge of a small front garden bordering the A96 a mile east of Elgin in Morayshire. It was 85/13ft in 1980 but was felled in full health in 1993.

The Cornish Elm comes into leaf long after other elms and this is one reason why it lasted longer than most others. When the beetle carrying the disease emerges it needs new elm shoots for its maturation feeding. While there were English Elms around, their new shoots expanded and attracted all the beetles. Only when these elms had all died, did the beetle have to move on to Wheatley and Cornish Elms. In Scotland there are only Wych Elms generally and they resist the northward spread of the disease quite well for a while, aided by the cool climate allowing only one or two generations of beetle a year, in the place of up to six in southern England.

At its full extent, the semi-natural range of the Cornish Elm was from all of Cornwall east to the A386 in west Devon, on to the western slopes of Dartmoor and round to the Hams region in the south to around Ivybridge. Several populations in wooded valleys just west of Exeter looked as natural as any, but east of Exeter the trees are in obviously planted groups or are solitary. (More details of this, and the overlap with English Elm, are given under that species.) In Ireland it was Cornish Elm all the way from Waterford up the Lee Valley to east Cork and to Limerick and there were some very big trees. One at Gurteen le Poer, County Waterford, was 114/17ft in 1968 and one at Castletownroche, County Cork, was 98/13½ft in 1965, but I have seen none during visits to the area since 1985.

The mature Cornish Elm has an unmistakeable appearance. Some books describe the crown as upright and narrow, probably unaware that beyond youth, this describes only the Wheatley Elm. Most Wheatley Elms were called 'Cornish Elm', anyway. The two are very different in bark and foliage, and increasingly with age, in crown. The true Cornishman fans out towards the top with moderately big branches which arch from their strongly raised bases to make domes, always plainly 'Cornish' by having dense foliage closely along the branch and much daylight between adjacent ones; alternate curved stripes of foliage and sky, like no other tree. The bark is grey with dark fissures dividing it into long, parallel ridges. The neat, pretty foliage is several shades brighter green than other elms, glossy, leathery, nicely toothed and slightly boat-shaped or cupped. The leaf is much narrower than that of the English or of the closely related Wheatley Elm.

The origin of the tree appears to be Brittany but there are different views on how it came to England and Ireland. The presence in Ireland does suggest that this was one of the plants from the post Ice Ages refugium, like the Strawberry-tree, and that the populations in Brittany, Ireland and Cornwall could then be the last footholds of the tree as the refuge eroded away. But it may be that an early tribe brought it from Brittany to plant in its limited lands in the British Isles. Crossing the A386 seems to have been more hazardous then than it is today, but the tribe advanced round the south of Dartmoor.

As a member of the Smoothleaf Elm complex, the Cornish Elm has inevitably been shuffled among many combinations of botanical names. There is enough about these already in other elms, so it only needs to be said that for most of its time the Cornish Elm was known as *Ulmus stricta* and is now well-placed with the Wheatley Elm as a variety of the Smoothleaf *U. carpinifolia*.

HUNTINGDON ELM

Ulmus x *hollandica* 'Vegeta'

The Huntingdon Elm stands out among other elms by its symmetrical and archi-tectural crown, a regular dome on branches of near perfect straightness for many yards from their bunched origin eight or ten feet up on a very straight, sturdy trunk, highly pleasing throughout the year. In March it is also prominent as the elm with the most numerous, biggest and brightest red flowers. This superiority continues when the foliage unfolds, as it has the biggest leaves, well displayed on yellow-pink stalks longer than those of other elms. It is again evident in the great vigour of growth, the feature for which the name 'vegeta', meaning just that, was awarded. Many were very big trees and one was the biggest tree known in Britain at the turn of the century. This was at Magdalen College in Oxford, and was 143/28ft 3in in 1911 when it was blown down.

It is also unusual among European elms in the relative simplicity of its nomen-clature and the precision of the knowledge of its origin. The English name refers to the nurseries of its origin, in Huntingdon, where the nurserymen Ingram and Wood took the seed they had picked in nearby Hinchinbrook Park in 1760. The only other name, seldom used and not explained, is 'Chichester Elm'. The actual parent trees

Huntingdon Elm (*Ulmus x hollandica* 'Vegeta'): Letchworth, Hertfordshire

cannot be ascertained as there were many big elms in the Park, and the Huntingdon Elm is a hybrid between a Smoothleaf and a Wych Elm.

This origin explains the hybrid vigour shown in most of the features of merit. Unlike so many hybrid elms, the parentage has never been questioned and the vernacular name has persisted with only a few short-lived attempts to replace it. The group name for the many hybrids of this origin has, of course, been a botanical plaything. Melville saw Plot's Elm involved in its parentage, making it a triple hybrid, and there were some half a dozen names in use before Miller's '*hollandica*' was adopted as the group name for all the Dutch elms and 'Vegeta' was placed among them.

The Huntingdon Elm was for many years fairly resistant to Elm disease, and the Dutch bred some lines improving this, with clones like 'Bea Schwarz', 'Commelin' and 'Groeneveldt'. These were successful until the virulent strain of the disease, arriving from Canada around 1965, spread widely after 1970, when they began to succumb. About that time the disease began killing many lines and avenues that had weathered the storm so far. The avenue to Knockdown House near Westonbirt was a great loss. Planted in 1843, the trees were typically uniform in shape and up to 110/14ft. Northwards on the same road, the A433 to the north of Tetbury, a few miles of widely spaced trees each side went down to the beetle breeding in the trunks of healthy trees, which was against the rules. Many outposts of trees soldiered on well into the eighties, like a fine specimen in Horsham, Sussex, near the station and smaller trees on the green at Haywards Heath. Cambridge City held on to numerous grand trees on Jesus Green, Parson's Piece and on The Backs until all went in about 1985. There were 13 big trees on Jesus Green in 1982, to 80/15½ft. In 1990 there were still three in Queen's College, the best 130/12½ft but the prognosis is not good. A great line of three at Howlett's Park Zoo in Kent was healthy, to 132/12½ft in 1983, but the gales since may well have been fatal, if the disease has not been.

Known trees in 1990 were numerous street and park trees in the Brighton enclave and a treasured survivor off Willesley Drive in Westonbirt which, in 1991, was 98/12ft.

WYCH ELM

Ulmus glabra

The Wych Elm is the only undisputed native elm in Britain. The Smooth-leafed Elm is accepted by many as a native and the Cornish Elm by some, particularly its Irish population, and the English elm by a few, but no one can question the claim of the Wych Elm as a native. Its distribution fairly clinches the matter, as it is found high in the Craven Limestones, far up becks and cloughs in Cumbria and still more often along burns far into the Highlands in the far north, in places remote from any likelihood of their being planted. And everywhere it seeds itself abundantly every year.

The Wych Elm is supposed to be completely non-suckering and so the best species for rootstocks of grafts. There was a possible exception in a roadside line of trees at Quendon in Essex, which suckered freely, but they may have been a hybrid with a tinge of Smooth-leafed Elm in them, and were taken to be a clone, given the name 'Quendonensis'. A few of the biggest old trees have a spread considerably greater than their height, and some of these in England had lowest branches resting on the ground yards from the trunk.

The quite large and pale red flowers open in February or March and by April, before the leaves unfold, the numerous big bunches of fruit are bright yellowish pale green so from a distance the tree could be thought to be a handsome flowering tree. The fruit ripens brown among fully opened leaves in June and is then shed.

Old records of big trees in England include one at Cassiobury Park, Watford, 100/26½ft in 1904 and one 25ft round at Monks' Eleigh, Cambridgeshire in 1949.

Wych Elm (*Ulmus glabra*): Brahan, Easter Ross

More recently and doubtfully still there, one at Dyrham Park, Gloucestershire in 1976 was 90/22ft and a superbly shapely tree in Hinchingbrook Park in 1974 was 77/19ft and if it was not big enough to have been a parent of the Huntingdon Elm raised from there 214 years before, was most probably related to that tree.

The big trees seen to be present and healthy in 1992 were nearly all in Scotland. In England, the Brighton area has many trees but none of great size. Devon had a huge tree, 86/19½ft, at Lindridge Park near Newton Abbott in 1989. Wansfell at Ambleside, Cumbria, had one 95/15ft in 1987, and Hutton-in-the-Forest grew one 130/9½ft in 1985.

Beside the Museum of Costume at Castle Howard in Yorkshire, a fine tree was 135/12½ft in 1985. If, or when, these have died, we have to go further north, well into Scotland to see such big trees.

In the cool summers of the north, the disease has spread slowly and is sporadic in small areas and currently is not noticeable in the far north. This is fortunate as the parks and squares in and around cities like Edinburgh, Glasgow and Dundee, rely heavily on Wych Elm for their greenery. It also allows a small measure of confidence that the specimens cited, measured when healthy up to five or six years ago, will be there for some years yet.

This is most doubtful in the little group of superb trees below the drive at Rossie Priory, near Dundee, for I am told that one has gone. In 1985 one was 138/15ft and another 135/13½ft. The oldest dated tree, reputed to have been planted about 1600, is at Pollok Park, Glasgow, and was 70/15½ft in 1986. One in the Royal Botanic Garden in Edinburgh was 82/14½ft in 1991. The best specimen is at Ballindean north of Dundee and was 115/21½ft in 1987 and is outstanding. Nearby, at Kinnaird Castle, Angus, one was 92/17ft in 1986 and another at Kinordy Castle was 105/13½ft in 1990. By the Estate Office at Drummuir, Banff, a fine specimen was 102/17ft in 1985.

Further north again, a notable specimen is on the island of Mull, at Torosay Castle, and was 90/16ft in 1988. Over to the east, is a tree at Dalvey in Morayshire, which was 105/17ft in 1989, and a rather burred stem at Fairburn Castle, Easter Ross, was 70/19ft in 1987. Nearby, at Brahan House, two in the field below the arboretum were over 20ft round, and much the better was 85/22½ft in 1989, the biggest bole at present known. North again but still in Easter Ross, an excellent old tree near the 1550 Sweet Chestnut at Castle Leod, was 85/19ft in 1985.

ENGLISH ELM

Ulmus procera (plate 8)

The English Elm is involved in the remarkable confusion of names and origins that bedevil the elms of Europe. Its English name is now generally thought to be a misnomer as few now believe the tree to be a native of England, but the tree's origin is rather mysterious. It cannot be found wild anywhere. Early botanists scoured the coasts from Ushant to Denmark in the hope of finding the relict populations from which it spread to Britain, but there are none. Old English Elms in many royal parks in Spain were at one time thought to have been a source for its introduction to England, but now it is known that King Philip III had these parks planted in 1575 and there seem to have been no wild populations there. The view that it is native to England has to overcome two objections. First that it is unacceptable to botanists that in the six thousand years that was all that was available for immigration, a species could move across entirely without leaving any trees on the mainland, an unlikely bulk movement of an entire population. Secondly, the tree very rarely produces viable seed, but spreads by the much slower method of root-suckers. It has been suggested that the failure of the seed is due to the frosts of February killing the flowers, and that this points to a southerly origin, perhaps Spain, and that there is no reliable record of the trees in Spain having been imported from England, so maybe it was the other way round.

The usual view now is that this elm was brought by pre-Iron Age tribes from some local variant of the elm in southern France, and was first planted in the Vale of Berkeley. The more precise origin is unresolved, for Dr Richter of Cambridge and Dr Melville of Kew, who made extensive studies of elms, disagree as to whether the closest form to English Elm can now be found in the Savoy region or in the Pyrenees.

A measure of the confusion of naming is shown by the difficulty in identifying in today's terms most of the numerous elms described in such detail by John Loudon in 1837. Despite drawings of leaves, some of these cannot be matched with any today. This is partly because, as Richter showed, there is across East Anglia and the Midlands a complex of hybrids involving the Smooth-leafed elm. He used statistical analyses of the ratios of length, breadth and other features of the leaves and distinguished clones from which he deduced tribal boundaries in Cambridge-shire, Hertfordshire and Essex, the region of the greatest variety of forms. He and Melville assigned many elms to hybrids among varieties, and to triple hybrids. It is all extremely complex. For broader identification, I found when working on elms for the twenty years or so before they largely disappeared, that prominent differences in the bark and the form of the crown sorted the normal forms and many variants quite well. Had Loudon described these adequately, or at all, his work would be less opaque than it is.

The tangle of botanical names is so convoluted it is beyond any brief summary, and is more concerned with the Smoothleaf Elm complex than with the English, so here it need only be said that English Elm became caught up in it by the use for nearly 200 years of the botanical name *Ulmus campestris* by Linnaeus in 1754, for the only European elm he distinguished. His herbarium contained only Wych Elm but he refers to other authors who were writing about both the English and the Smoothleaf Elm, so his epithet cannot be safely assigned to any of them. It is a *nomen ambiguum* and had to be replaced by *Ulmus procera* given to the tree by Richard Salisbury, but by the time that was resurrected the English elm had long shared the name *campestris* with the Smoothleaf or European Field Elm. The wide differences between the two had been made little of and English Elm was seen, in some quarters, as a local extension of the Smoothleaf, the native form.

The distribution of English elm was interesting, and mapping its boundaries and overlaps with the Cornish Elm gave me many pleasant hours on country roads. South of Dartmoor from near Ivybridge to Horrabridge, the two cohabited, but northwards, the A386 was a good boundary from Okehampton to Barnstaple with only one marked incursion of Cornishmen making a small tongue on its eastern side and only a few individual English on its west, one in Cornwall, near Bude. Small Cornish Elm outliers in valleys west of Exeter looked semi-natural, while others further east around Lyme Regis, lining hedgerows, were plainly planted as were those at Croome in Worcestershire, and on the Ailesbury land in Savernake Forest and at Walsingham, Norfolk.

The English Elm swept along the Oolitic limestones and clay vales, dominating the landscape of the Cotswolds, Vale of Aylesbury, the Sussex coastal plain, north and east to the Vale of York, and west to the Usk valley and the Cheshire plain.

Oddly, however, I found that east of Canterbury it gave way to Smooth-leafed Elm. This was presumably the territory of a different tribe, but I have seen no mention of this very evident change in the tree-scape.

English Elm coped well with sooty air despite its hairy foliage, which unlike those of catalpas, planes, Black locust and other trees growing well in cities, will not wash clean so easily in the rain. There were large trees, like one at Fulham Palace 28ft round in 1910, and another in Carshalton Park, a tall hollow stump by 1973, and the Royal Parks were well scattered with trees around 90/10ft. A tree 150/20ft was at Forthampton in Gloucestershire in 1895 and one at Ombersley Court, Worcestershire was 130/23½ft in 1907. A truncated bole at East Bergholt, Suffolk, was 31ft round in 1942, and later similar survivors were 24½ft at Tichborne, Hampshire, and 25½ft at Aylesford Church in Kent, 1965.

The South Sussex enclave has hundreds of trees of moderate size around Brighton and Eastbourne and some 15-16ft round at Mouslecombe and 20ft hulks in Preston Park. Longbridge near Alfriston has two tall slender trees, 111/8ft and 98/8ft. In the north, some isolated specimens survive. One in the graveyard at Howick in Northumberland is 105/13½ft and, in the same county, two of an unrecorded clone not seen anywhere else are at Belsay Castle, both dated as 1835 planting, 105/16½ft and 105/14½ft.

All over England, former roadside clumps, lines and thickets have re-sprouted vigorously and many are 40ft tall. Some of them are currently free of attack by the elm-bark beetle and in areas cleared of dead elms these may well provide big trees again.

CAUCASIAN ZELKOVA

Zelkova carpinifolia

This tree has one extraordinary and inexplicable eccentricity. In its native woods in the Caucasus and Elburz Mountains, it is, by all accounts, of normal shape with a good, long, single bole. In cultivation in Great Britain, all but two of the bigger, older trees are of anything but normal shape. They are all like giant whitewash brushes, or erect bushes on short stems. The broad base of buttressed roots gathers itself into a deeply fluted bole which has a waist at one to three feet up. It then expands into a sort of capital from which spring vertical dividing branches so that at ten feet up there may be about 200 stems, the outer ones spraying out somewhat then arching at a fair height, so the whole crown in the upper parts is like a fountain. The wood is not durable, and often many of the interior stems, dying from being shaded out, are rotted and provide homes for woodpeckers.

It has been suggested that all these trees are one clone, propagated from the original trees which happened to be cuttings from one such oddly shaped individual.

Caucasian Zelkova (*Zelkova carpinifolia*): Worlingham, Suffolk

It is true that the medium sized trees at botanic gardens like Edinburgh and Glasnevin very probably derive from one or other of the three original trees at Kew, but there were, until the gales of 1987 and 1990, five trees believed to be from the original 1760 import, the other two being across the river, in Syon Park. They were all of this extreme shape. If they were from seed, as is most likely, it would be next to impossible that all five would inherit a peculiarity which must be genetically recessive. It therefore seems that the strange shape is a response to the new environment. But that fails to account for the two (out of 77 large trees recorded) which are perfectly normal in shape, and indeed have fine, long stems.

One of the very big Zelkovas also features in the impossible tales in this book. The biggest Zelkova of the sixteen outstanding specimens listed in 1908 was one at Holme Lacey outside Hereford. It was then 95/19ft at three feet and was in the sunken rose garden. In 1962 I made it 92/24ft at three feet, and admired it in its rose garden. In 1976 I returned to see how much it had grown. I had measured all the other trees of good size in the garden before it dawned on me that I had missed the Zelkova. I went to the rose garden again and it was a perfectly ordinary rose garden with a symmetrical pattern of beds. And no Zelkova. At this point a gardener came over and we talked about the trees. I said what a pity it was that the finest Zelkova in Britain had gone. 'What was that?' he asked. 'An enormous tree rather like a beech. You must be glad to lose its shade, though'. 'Never seen one,' he said. 'It was there in 1962. Presumably before you came'. 'I have been here forty years. Never been one there'. The stump will have been over nine feet across and a vast excavation will have been needed. There was no sign of disturbance. It could not possibly have been dug out without the gardener knowing.

A splendid specimen has been left half a plot to itself in a housing estate at Worlingham in Suffolk near Bungay. It is in Worlingham Park Drive and is 88/23ft at three feet. It is a classic big bush-on-a-leg. A very similar one was in a garden of what was Redhouse Park, Ipswich, Suffolk, and was 92ft tall and 21ft 6in round at four feet, but was blown down in 1987. At Pitt House by the old A38 at Chudleigh Knighton, the most prominent of a scattered line of four was killed by salt spray in a gale, but two others are now almost as big, 111/19ft and 72/16ft while a third is a little bigger, 111/20ft 6in. Three more big ones are spaced along the several hundred yards of Zelkova suckers which form the roadside hedge. At nearby Knowle, Ashburton, three, perhaps of the same origin as the Pitt House trees, at the edge of a wood, 115/15½ft in 1986, were blown down in 1990.

Of the five believed to be 1760 originals, the one at the Herbarium entrance on the Green at Kew, was blown down in October 1987 and the one on the lawn by the Main Gate went in January 1990. A third behind the Herbarium was 72/13ft in 1981 and went also. One of the two Syon trees was blown down in 1987; the other is 106/19ft 5in. The better of two at Bicton in Devon, near the House, was blown down in January 1990, leaving the one in Hermitage Walk 95/15ft at one foot. Halliford Park in Sunbury, Middlesex, has a unique collection of 22 Zelkovas of four main ages. The oldest include one 102/15ft, then there are nine around 80/10ft, four around 65/6ft and six much younger.

Christchurch Meadow, Oxford, has two, somewhat crowded, with the larger 80/14ft 6in at three feet. Dulwich is well supplied, with two by the College playing fields 70/12ft; two in College Road and two more, quite small, in Dulwich Park. At Kenwood House, Highgate, London, a typical old one has lost its shape and is in poor repair but is 75/20ft at three feet. A fine, tall tree is at Capel Manor, Edmonton, 105/15ft, and well placed.

KEAKI

Zelkova serrata

It cannot help the Keaki to have no common name except this Japanese vernacular one, which remains unknown, like the tree itself, beyond a narrow circle of gardeners. It is such an amenable and highly attractive tree with so many potential uses that it should be better known and more planted. It is fully hardy in the University Botanic Garden in Aberdeen, so it should flourish anywhere, but it has not been planted at all widely. The only other northerly trees noted are several in the Royal Botanic Garden in Edinburgh; one in Harlow Carr and three in Thorp Perrow in Yorkshire, with one in the west in the Granada Arboretum in Cheshire. There is a slight gathering of specimens from Kensington Gardens and nearby squares into N10, but otherwise they are scattered across southern England and Ireland in some of the expected big gardens.

The Keaki grows across large areas of northern China, in Korea and Japan. It arrived in Britain in 1862 among many Japanese and Chinese plants that had been assembled in the Yokohama garden of the American Dr George Hall, including some collected by Robert Fortune. They were grown in Wardian cases and sent to Parsons of Flushing, Long Island, the first shipment of live plants from Asia to America. Some of the plants were sent on to Britain, including the Keaki. Its worth as a street and city tree was appreciated in the United States long before it was in Britain. The three biggest I have seen are street trees in Washington D.C., one on the corner of G and 6th Street, 70/13½ft, and one behind a church in Ardmore, Pennsylvania, 88/13ft. Younger trees are frequent in car-lots, including that at the Pentagon at Langley, and in malls, a use which has barely begun here.

The tree is of only moderate vigour but considerable charm. The bark is for many years smooth and, on a small scale, colourful, finely striped pink, green and brown. A few big branches usually arise fairly low on the trunk and may divide at below eight feet, and open out into an umbrella of fine, straight branches with long wands arching from their ends. In summer, these shoots bear long regularly placed rows of alternate leaves, flat on each side, each leaf slender ovate with a long-tapered tip and prettily toothed from the base. In autumn these turn yellow, amber, pink and pale red. Growth seems to be little affected by paved root-runs, city air or moderate exposure nor by pests or diseases.

An original tree from the 1862 import was growing at Lower Coombe Royal near Kingsbridge in Devon in 1977 when it was 56/9ft, but an extension to the house a few years later piled too much soil on its roots and it died. The finest specimen is at Kilmacurragh in County Wicklow, which was 40/3ft in 1904 and is now 60/10½ft with a clear bole of eight feet. It may well have been an original tree, but its date is not known. A very big tree by the Coach Path above the Lodge at Endsleigh in Devon is spoiled by its failure to sort out its stems. It is 72/10ft round a double stem

Keaki (*Zelkova serrata*): Lower Sherrif Farm, Sussex

with a third nine feet round, very close. A superb tree hangs over the road and house at Lower Sheriff Farm near Horsted Keynes in Sussex. Its broadly domed crown is held high on a 15ft clear stem. This was planted in 1890 by Colonel Stevenson Clarke and has grown faster than most, since it was 62/8ft in 1967 and 62/9½ft in 1984. One of several in Battersea Park, London, is 60/9½ft and the best of a uniform group by the Brentford Gate into Kew Gardens, all planted in 1917, is 60/7ft. A tree at Hergest Croft at Kington, Herefordshire, may date from 1897, and is 72/8ft. The best of three in the Royal Botanic Gardens, Edinburgh, is 56/7ft. One at Tilgate Park, Crawley, in the Dell is 62/8ft. Reasonably rapid growth has been made by a 1929 tree at Anglesea Abbey, Cambridge, now 50/6ft, and one in the University Botanic Garden in Cambridge is growing much faster. It was planted in 1960 and when it was 20 years old it was 23/3½ft and when 29 years old it was 33/5½ft.

PLACES TO VISIT

The Botanic Gardens are usually open every day. Westonbirt and Bedgebury and the London parks are always open. The National Trust gardens (**NT**) are often open all year or closed in winter, as are the Scottish gardens (**ST**). Gardens open under the National Gardens Scheme (**NGS** [**SGS** in Scotland]) are included only where they are open for several days each year and can be found in the current *Gardens of England and Wales*. The Countryside Parks (**CP**) may open only in the summer

England

AVON

Bath Botanic Garden (many rare species, including Ginkgo and Golden Catalpa). *Victoria Park*, Bath. *Henrietta Park*, Bath (Gingkos, double Horse-chestnut line). *Sydney Park*, Bath (superb beeches, Hybrid Catalpa).

BEDFORDSHIRE

Woburn Abbey, Pleasure Grounds (big Cornish Elms, Sessile Oaks, Golden Swamp Cypress, big Deodars).

BERKSHIRE

Windsor Great Park (large collection of rare conifers). *Savill Gardens* (good Metasequoia). *Valley Gardens.*

BUCKINGHAMSHIRE

Waddesdon House, Aylesbury **NT**. *Cliveden House*, Taplow **NT** (remarkable Butter-nut, fine Cypress Oaks). *Green Park*, Aston Clinton (outsize Cappadocian Maples; Weeping Beech and Silver Pendent Lime).

CAMBRIDGESHIRE

University Botanic Garden (notable Catalpas, and Metasequoias). *Clare College Garden* (fine Metasequoia, Swamp Cypress). *Anglesea Abbey.*

CHESHIRE

Granada Arboretum, Jodrell Bank. *Tatton Park*, Knutsford **NT**: many unusual specimens. *University of Liverpool Botanic Garden*, Ness, Wirral.

CORNWALL

Glendurgan, Mawan Smith, Falmouth **NT**. *Boconnoc* (Lostwithiel), *Penjerrick* (Falmouth) and *Carclew* (Mylor) (open for a few days in spring). *Tresco Abbey*, Isles of Scilly (an extraordinary collection of southern hemisphere trees).

CUMBRIA

Patterdale Hall, Ullswater (fine conifers and a remarkable Western White Pine). *Muncaster Castle*, Ravenglass (huge Southern Beeches and fine conifers). *Monk Coniston* (Holiday Fellowship) (outsize conifers).

DERBYSHIRE

Chatsworth House (a pinetum with notable specimens).

DEVON

Bicton, East Budleigh (selection of outstanding specimen conifers and Cypress Oaks).

Knightshayes Court, Tiverton **NGS** (largest Turkey Oak). *Killerton*, Silverton, Exeter **NT**. *Dartington Hall*, Totnes **NGS** (notable Lucombe Oak).

DORSET

Abbotsbury (many large and rare trees; Pterocarya). *Minterne*, Cerne Abbas **NGS** (many fine conifers, Davidias and Maples). *Forde Abbey*, Chard. *Kingston Lacey* **NT** (fine Lucombe Oak, Horse-chestnut). *Coy Lake area*, Bournemouth (huge Dawn Redwoods, many fine poplars and Cricket-bat Willows; possibly the only Golden Chinese privet in the country).

ESSEX

Hatfield Forest (some large and uncommon trees).

GLOUCESTERSHIRE

Westonbirt, near Tetbury (Aboretum) (100 acre landscaped planting of immense variety, plus (Silk Wood) 2km walk lined both sides all the way with rare trees and bays of collections). *Batsford Park*, Moreton-in-Marsh **NGS** (large and varied collection, some very big trees and a collection of rare oaks). *Stanway*, near Winchcombe **NGS**.

HAMPSHIRE

Rhinefield Terrace (public [gated] road from A35 to Brockenhurst). *Bolderwood Arboretum*. *Exbury*, near Beaulieu (many rare and big trees). *Hillier Arboretum* (Hampshire CC), Ampfield **NGS** (immense collection of young trees, verging on the completely comprehensive.)

HEREFORDSHIRE

Hergest Croft, Kington **NGS** (huge collection, especially of conifers, Maples and Oaks, many very rare). *Queenswood*, Hope under Dinmore, on hill by A49 (new planting, many unusual trees). *Whitfield*, Wormbridge **NGS** (some very big trees, notably Gingko, redwood grove and cedars). *Eastnor Castle*, Ledbury **NGS** (vast collection of mostly huge conifers, some Maples and Oaks. Notable Santa Lucia Firs, Deodars, original Blue Atlas Cedar).

HERTFORDSHIRE

Cassiobury Park, Watford.

KENT (severe losses in gale of 16.07.87 and few trees left in some gardens)

The National Pinetum, Bedgebury, near Goudhurst (nearly comprehensive collection of hardy conifer species. Over 100 forest plots of different species, mostly conifers. Some rare oaks, maples and other hardwoods). *Scotney Castle*, Lamberhurst **NT** (some fine big conifers). *Sandling Castle*, near Hythe (some old and large conifers and an outstanding Alder).

LANCASHIRE

Wythenshawe Park, Manchester (fine Metasequoias, Western White Pine, Lucombe Oak).

LEICESTERSHIRE

University Botanic Garden, Leicester (fine Bristlecone Pines, birches, thorns, apples and a remarkable Medlarleaf sessile oak).

LINCOLNSHIRE

Brocklesby Park (many conifers and Turkish Hazel). *Lincoln Arboretum* (good park trees and Black Walnut). *Boultham Park*, Lincoln (giant Railway Poplar and good park trees).

LONDON

Hyde Park and Kensington Gardens (remarkable trees of rare oaks, Maples, Ash and many other species). *Regents Park* (may fine Cornish and Dutch Elms and other trees). *Syon House*, Brentford (famous big and rare oaks, Maples. Catapas, Zelkova and Swamp Cypresses). *Osterley Park*, Hounslow (some very fine and rare oaks). *Marble Hill*, Twickenham (public park) (notable huge Black Walnut, tallest Lombardy Poplar and Italian Alder). *Cannizaro Park*, Wimbledon (large collection of Maples, Oaks and remarkable Sassafrasses).

MERSEYSIDE

Calderstones Park, near Liverpool (a wide range of trees, Sorbus, limes, alders and some rare specimens).

MIDDLESEX

Capel Manor (tall Zelkova and a huge Purple Beech). *Forty Hall*, Enfield (cedars, pines).

NORTHUMBERLAND

Cragside, Rothbury **NT** (big planting around 1860 of conifers now immense).

NORFOLK

Lynford Arboretum, near Mundford (wide variety of groups of less usual conifers. Big old Crimean and Corsican Pines).

OXFORDSHIRE

Oxford Botanic Gardens (some old trees of rare species). *University Parks*, Oxford (many fine trees). *Blenheim Palace*, Woodstock **NGS** (notable Cedar of Lebanon, Sugar Maple and London Planes).

SHROPSHIRE

Lillieshall Sports Centre (many fine conifers and other trees).

SOMERSET

Nettlecombe, near Willaton (outstanding Himalayan Cypresses and many other trees).

STAFFORDSHIRE

Sandon Park Hall, near Stafford **NGS** (many good trees). *Trentham Park*, Stoke-on-Trent (gardens with many hardwoods and buckeyes. Pinetum with good, unusual conifers).

SUFFOLK

Abbey Gardens, Bury St Edmunds (notable Tree of Heaven, Buckeye and Père David's Maples).

SURREY

Royal Botanic Gardens, Kew (the largest specimens of numerous of the rarest species; unequalled collections of most genera, notably oaks, Celtises, limes, Zelkovas and Catalpas). *Royal Horticultural Society's Gardens*, Wisley, Ripley (very good pinetum with a wide range of other trees). *Claremont*, Esher **NT** (notably splendid Cedar of Lebanon, oldest Cunninghamia and a fine Sequoia and Bishop Pine). *Grayswood Hill*, Haslemere **NGS** (many fine trees of wide range and a notable Montezuma Pine). *Winkworth Arboretum*, south of Godalming **NT** (notable collection of Sorbus and Acer).

SUSSEX (severe losses in the gale of 16.10.87)

Hollycombe, near Liphook (but Sussex) (remarkably large specimens of rare trees; Black Birch, Chinese Wingnut and Chinese Cork Oak). *Wakehurst Place*, Ardingly (out-station of Kew RBG) (immense collection of conifers and broad-leafed trees and many fine specimens of extremely rare trees). *Borde Hill*, north of Haywards Heath **NGS** (huge park and six woods full of rare trees. A notable maple collection, and also a collection of oaks, pines and spruces). *Nymans*, Handcross **NT** (two pinetums, three gardens and a large wilderness filled with rare and some tender trees. Outstanding specimens of rare Nothofagus species). *Leonardslee*, Lower Beeding (open in May and October) (many fine conifers). *Sheffield Park*, Uckfield **NT** (wide variety of fine conifers and a unique planting of Nyssa. Notable Maritime and Montezuma Pines).

WILTSHIRE

Stourhead, near Mere **NT** (large collection of very big conifers and hardwoods. Largest Macedonian Pine). *Wilton House*, Wilton (many fine old trees). *Longleat*, near Warminster (many big conifers by the roads).

WORCESTERSHIRE

Spetchley Park, east of Worcester **NGS** (notable Metasequoia).

YORKSHIRE

Studley Royal and Fountains Abbey, near Ripon (notable Sweet Chestnut and oaks). *Thorp Perrow*, Bedale (extensive plantings of collections of genera with notable rare maples, oaks, limes, cherries, poplars and conifers). *Castle Howard* (many fine old hardwoods).

Wales

CLWYD

Vivod Forest Garden, above Vivod House, near Llangollen (young arboretum of many rare species).

GLAMORGAN

Roath Park and other public areas, Cardiff. *Cathays Park*, Cardiff (large plantings of cherries, birches, Gingkos and magnolias). *Singleton Abbey*, Swansea (public park) (large and varied park and garden trees, many rare). *Clyne Castle*, Swansea (public park) (many good trees).

GWYNEDD

Bodnant, Tal y Cefn, Conway **NT** (huge collection of conifers, magnolias and maples. Notable *Nothofagus obliqua*, Low's Fir, Lodgepole Pines and Grecian Fir). *Penrhyn Castle*, Bangor (very large old conifers along the drive and fine trees in the garden). *Portmeirion* (fine Hibas and Himalayan Fir).

POWYS

Gliffaes Country House Hotel (**NGS** daily in summer). *Powis Castle*, Welshpool (**NT** gardens) (the Park has big trees, but not all are visible to the public at present. The Gardens have Gingko, big Silver Firs and Sequoias, Davidia and *Populus lasiocarpa*).

Scotland

ABERDEEN

Balmoral Castle (fine avenue and small pinetum of well-grown conifers in variety). *Drum Castle*, Aberdeen **SNT** (some good conifers). *Fyvie Castle* **SNT** (Cappadocian Maples).

ANGUS

Camperdown Park, Dundee (wide variety of fine parkland trees, notably oaks and a pinetum of splendid specimens in variety). *House of Dun*, Montrose **SNT** (remarkable crescent of early Giant Sequoias and big old larches). *Glamis Castle* (policies of huge conifers and a big old pinetum).

ARGYLL

Strone, Cairndow **SGS** (tallest tree in Britain in a group of very big conifers). *Benmore*, Younger Botanic Garden (Royal Botanic Garden, Edinburgh) (large areas of huge conifers and new garden with comprehensive collection. Notable Western Hemlock, Wellingtonia avenue, *Abies amabilis* and *Picea jezoensis*). *Crarae Gardens and Forest Garden*, Furnace (wide collection of rare trees and plots of rare conifers).

AYRSHIRE

Culzean Castle, Girvan **ST** and **CP** (many fine conifers and other trees, especially in Happy Valley). *Glenapp*, Ballantrae **CP** (small group of big conifers in vally off main valley). *Kilkerrean*, Maybole **CP** (small pinetum above House. Notable Scots Pine and Noble Fir. Big Araucarias and Wellingtonias, and a big larch and silver firs in Lady's Glen). *Blairquhan*, Straiton (long woodland walk of fine specimen conifers in variety. An orchard pinetum of big, often rare trees).

BUTE

Brodick Castle, Arran **ST** (many trees and rare maples).

DUNBARTONSHIRE

Balloch Country Park (extensive and varied).

EDINBURGH

Royal Botanic Gardens (notable collections of birches, maple, limes and conifers. Notable trees of *Corylus clourna*, Tetracentron, *Quercus dentata, Fagus orientalis*).

EAST LOTHIAN

Smeaton House (wide range of notable conifers. A big Italian Maple). *Whittingehame*, near Haddington (many large conifers). *Carberry Tower*, Musselburgh (Church of Scotland) (very varied trees with magnificent Hungarian Oak). *Tyninghame* (very fine beech and conifers [notable Crimean Pine, Bosnian Pine] shelter varied plantings).

INVERNESS-SHIRE

Moniac Glen, near Beauly (Forestry Commission picnic site) (small area of very tall Douglas Firs). *Balmacaan*, Drumnadrochit immense Grand and Douglas Firs).

KINCARDINESHIRE

Inchmarlo, Banchory (very large conifers around recent garden of unusual hardwoods). *Crathes Castle*, Banchory (some big conifers).

NAIRNSHIRE

Cawdor Castle (huge conifers in the valley and pinetum).

PEEBLES-SHIRE

Dawyck, Stobo **SGS** (extensive collection of conifers, maples, and many rare trees. Original Dawyck Beech).

PERTHSHIRE

The Hermitage, Inver, Dunkeld **ST** (a few very big trees. one large Douglas Fir). *Blair Castle*, Blair Atholl (Diana's Grove full of tall conifers. An outstanding Japanese Larch. Outside are an early European Larch and and original hybrid larch. St Brides has immense *Abies procera* and *Abies magnifica* side by side). *Keir House*, Dunblane **SGS** (large number of big conifers and rare maples. Notable *Abies spectabilis*). *Doune House*, Dunblane (the valley near the Motor Museum) (well-spaced huge conifers, small maple and oak collection. Notable Western Hemlock, Wellingtonia. The largest Lawson and Nootka Cypresses in Scotland). *Scone Palace*, near Perth (the garden has original Douglas Fir; a huge pinetum in widely spaced lines planted 1860 among 1852 trees. Notable Jeffrey's Pine, Western Hemlock, Wellingtonia, four massive Sitka Spruces and Noble Firs).*Cluny Garden*, near Aberfeldy (very rapid growth of fairly recent trees in great variety around biggest Giant Sequoia).

ROXBURGH

Monteviot (pinetum of big conifers and variegated oak).

STIRLINGSHIRE

Culcreuch Castle, Fintry (outstanding large conifers in pinetum and by drive, with hardwoods on rear drive).

WIGTOWNSHIRE

Castle Kennedy and Lochinch (large scale early planting of wide range of conifers, also tender hardwoods. Avenues of unusual species. Notable Bishop Pine, line of Cordyline and Nothofagus spp.). *Logan Botanic Garden* (noted for tender evergreens, Cabbage-trees, Chusan palms and Eucyphias).

Northern Ireland

Castlewellan, Newcastle, County Down (Forestry Service) (an immense collection rich in rare and tender conifers and other trees, many of great size). *Rowallane*, Saintfield, County Down (many fine rare and tender trees and a notable *Nothofagus* collection). *Tullymore Park*, County Down (fine Monterey Pines, Blue-gums and other trees). *Gosford Castle*, Markethill, County Armagh (big conifers, record Himalayan Fir and a huge Noble Fir).

Republic of Ireland

Fota Gardens, County Cork (wide variety of old, huge, mostly dated and rare conifers). *Ashbourne House Hotel*, County Cork (best Ginkgo in Ireland). *Powerscourt*, County Wicklow (huge collection of mainly conifers many of which are well-grown, rare and big). *The John F. Kennedy Memorial Arboretum*, New Ross, County Wexford (rapidly expanding collection on a vast scale). *Glasnevin Botanic Garden*, Dublin (large collection with many fine and rare trees). *Birr Castle*, County Offaly (enormous and widespread general collection. Numerous extreme rarities).

INDEX